Transforming the Future

People are using the future to search for better ways to achieve sustainability, inclusiveness, prosperity, well-being and peace. In addition, the way the future is understood and used is changing in almost all domains, from social science to daily life.

This book presents the results of significant research undertaken by UNESCO with a number of partners to detect and define the theory and practice of anticipation around the world today. It uses the concept of 'Futures Literacy' as a tool to define the understanding of anticipatory systems and processes – also known as the Discipline of Anticipation. This innovative title explores:

- new topics such as Futures Literacy and the Discipline of Anticipation;
- the evidence collected from over 30 Futures Literacy Laboratories and presented in 14 full case studies;
- the need and opportunity for significant innovation in human decision-making systems.

This book will be of great interest to scholars, researchers, policy-makers and students, as well as activists working on sustainability issues and innovation, future studies and anticipation studies.

Riel Miller is Head of Futures Literacy at UNESCO, Paris, France.

Transforming the Future
Anticipation in the 21st Century

Edited by Riel Miller

First published 2018
by the United Nations Educational, Scientific and Cultural Organisation
(UNESCO), 7, place de Fontenoy, 75352 Paris 07 SP, France

and Routledge, 2 Park Square, Milton Park, Abingdon, Oxon OX14 4RN

and by Routledge
711 Third Avenue, New York, NY 10017

Routledge is an imprint of the Taylor & Francis Group, an informa business

© 2018 UNESCO

UNESCO ISBN 978-92-3-100268-7

This publication is available in Open Access under the Attribution-NonCommercial-NoDerivs 3.0 IGO (CC-BY-NC-ND 3.0 IGO) license (http://creativecommons.org/licenses/by-nc-nd/3.0/igo/). By using the content of this publication the users accept to be bound by the terms of use of the UNESCO Open Access Repository https://en.unesco.org/open-access/terms-use-ccbyncnd-en.

The designations employed and the presentation of material throughout this publication does not imply the expression of any opinion whatsoever on the part of UNESCO concerning the legal status of any country, territory, city or area or of its authorities, or concerning the delimitation of its frontiers or boundaries.

The ideas and opinions expressed in this publication are those of the authors; they are not necessarily those of UNESCO and do not commit the Organization.

Trademark notice: Product or corporate names may be trademarks or registered trademarks, and are used only for identification and explanation without intent to infringe.

British Library Cataloguing-in-Publication Data
A catalogue record for this book is available from the British Library

Library of Congress Cataloging-in-Publication Data
A catalog record has been requested for this book

ISBN: 978-1-138-48587-7 (hbk)
ISBN: 978-1-351-04800-2 (ebk)

Typeset in Times New Roman
by Swales & Willis Ltd, Exeter, Devon, UK

With special thanks to Innovation Norway for funding the availability of this publication in open source.

Contents

List of figures x
List of tables xi
List of contributors xii
Foreword xxi
AUDREY AZOULAY, DIRECTOR-GENERAL OF UNESCO
Acknowledgements xxii

Introduction: Futures Literacy: transforming the future 1
RIEL MILLER

PART I
Discovering anticipation in the 21st century: towards Futures Literacy? 13

1 Sensing and making-sense of Futures Literacy: towards a Futures Literacy Framework (FLF) 15
 RIEL MILLER

2 The Discipline of Anticipation: foundations for Futures Literacy 51
 RIEL MILLER, ROBERTO POLI AND PIERRE ROSSEL

3 Towards a formal framework for describing collective intelligence knowledge creation processes that 'use-the-future' 66
 ANDRÉE EHRESMANN, ILKKA TUOMI, RIEL MILLER, MATHIAS BÉJEAN AND JEAN-PAUL VANBREMEERSCH

viii Contents

PART II
Futures Literacy Laboratories: design principles and case studies 93

4   Futures Literacy Laboratories (FLL) in practice: an overview of key design and implementation issues 95
    RIEL MILLER

5   The Futures Literacy Laboratory-Novelty (FLL-N) case studies 110
    EDITED BY STEFAN BERGHEIM
    Case 1: Cultural heritage research and the future 110
    MARTIN RHISIART
    Case 2: The future of science in society 118
    CRISTIANO CAGNIN AND LYDIA GARRIDO LUZARDO
    Case 3: Using the future for local labor markets 131
    KACPER NOSARZEWSKI AND LYDIA GARRIDO LUZARDO
    Case 4: Using the future for innovation policy learning in Norway 139
    PER M. KOCH
    Case 5: Imagining the future of the transition from 'youth' to 'adult' in Sierra Leone 147
    KEWULAY KAMARA
    Case 6: Imagining the future of sports 154
    JEAN-JACQUES GOUGUET
    Case 7: All Africa Futures Forum: transforming Africa's futures 161
    GECI KARURI-SEBINA AND RIEL MILLER
    Case 8: Overcoming fragmentation in Ecuador: the Manabí Será *initiative* 168
    ORAZIO BELLETTINI CEDEÑO AND ADRIANA ARELLANO
    Case 9: Young citizens for a sustainable planet 177
    MATTHEW GIUSEPPE MARASCO, JENNIFER RUDKIN,
    GECI KARURI-SEBINA AND A CONCLUSION BY
    BAYO AKOMOLAFE
    Case 10: Future-proofing an entire nation: the case of Tanzania 187
    AIDAN EYAKUZE AND EDMUND MATOTAY
    Case 11: Africa Horizon 2035 195
    SANDRA COULIBALY LEROY, NGARKIDANÉ DJIDINGAR
    AND NICOLAS SIMARD

*Case 12: Rethinking non-formal education for
   sustainable futures in Asia-Pacific 205*
ACE VICTOR FRANCO ACERON
Case 13: Water and urban renewal in North Africa 215
NISREEN LAHHAM
Case 14: Youth leadership and the use of the future 222
ACE VICTOR FRANCO ACERON AND SHERMON CRUZ

PART III
Parallel and convergent developments   231

6   Gaming Futures Literacy: The Thing from the Future   233
STUART CANDY

7   An extended Futures Literacy process: design
lessons from measuring wellbeing   247
STEFAN BERGHEIM

8   Gender and the future: reframing and empowerment   257
IVANA MILOJEVIĆ

Glossary   268
Index   271

Figures

0.1	Futures Literacy Labs 2012–2016	3
1.1	A framework for describing and researching Futures Literacy	24
1.2	Mapping different implementations of the FLL on the FLF	40
3.1	The modelling relation (adapted from Rosen, 1985)	73
3.2	An evolutive system	79
4.1	Dewey cycle of learning	97
4.2	Three phases of the learning cycle	98
5.10.1	Emergence of choice scenarios	193
6.1	An example prompt (no. 1) from The Thing from the Future's original four-card design: Arc, Terrain, Object, and Mood (first edition, revised 2015)	236
6.2	An example prompt (no. 2) from The Thing from the Future's original four-card design	237
6.3	An example prompt (no. 1) from The Thing from the Future's simplified three-card design: Future, Thing, and Theme (Singularity University edition, 2017)	237
6.4	An example prompt (no. 2) from The Thing from the Future's three-card design	238
6.5	An example prompt (no. 3) from The Thing from the Future's three-card design	238
7.1	Four elements of a quality of life process	250
8.1	Examples of retold story narratives	265

Tables

2.1	Foresight Maturity Model (Grim, 2009)	62
5.12.1	Action agendas developed by the five groups	213
5.13.1	Expectations and hopes for water and slums	218
5.14.1	Four types of cards in The Thing from the Future	225
8.1	Three gendered scenarios for the future	262

Contributors

Ace Victor Franco Aceron is Education Officer at UNICEF Philippines. Working in the United Nations system since 2013, Ace has been involved in the UN's education outreach activities with previous engagements at UN Academic Impact, a global initiative for higher education based in the UN Headquarters in New York. In 2015–16, he was project coordinator for UNESCO's Foresight Programme in Asia-Pacific in Bangkok. This was followed by an international consultancy at the UNESCO Office in Hanoi, where he supported the monitoring and evaluation of the *Gender Equality and Girls' Education Initiative in Vietnam*, and the development of Office's country programme and resource mobilization strategy. Ace is a licensed Social Studies teacher in the Philippines and a research fellow in disaster preparedness education at the Japan Foundation-Manila. He has a master's degree in International Relations from the Graduate Institute of Peace Studies, Kyung Hee University, Republic of Korea.

Bayo Akomolafe (PhD) is Chief Curator and Executive Director of The Emergence Network. He is author of *These Wilds Beyond Our Fences: Letters to My Daughter on Humanity's Search for Home* and *We Will Tell Our Own Story*. Lecturer, speaker, father and 'rogue planet saved by the gravitational pull' of his wife Ej, Bayo hopes to inspire a diffractive network of sharing within an ethos of new responsivity – a slowing down, an ethics of entanglement, an activism of inquiry, a 'politics of surprise'. Bayo graduated Summa Cum Laude from Covenant University, Nigeria. Largely trained in a world that increasingly fell short of his yearnings for justice, and in reconciling his internal struggle to reconnect with his community, his doctoral research explored Yoruba indigenous healing.

Adriana Arellano has a master's degree in Social Work and Social Policy Administration and is passionate about evidence-based policy-making in the social and education sectors. She was Education Policy Analyst and Policy Director at the Ecuadorian Coordinating Ministry of Social Development and consultant to the Inter-American Development Bank and UNASUR prior to joining Grupo FARO, Ecuador, as Research and Knowledge Management Director, where she supports first-class research quality, promoting internal knowledge management and implementing research projects. She co-authored several papers and led studies such as 'Más Saber América Latina', 'Manabí Será' and the 'MingaLibro', a methodological innovation to promote collaborative writing.

Mathias Béjean (PhD) is Associate Professor at Paris East University, Créteil, France, and member of the Institut de Recherche en Gestion (IRG). His research focuses on the relationships between innovation, design and management. He is particularly interested in philosophical and formal approaches to design theory, and is presently developing a theoretical approach to design processes, named D-MES, with Andrée Ehresmann, mathematician specialist of category theory. He currently teaches design and innovation management at IAE Gustave Eiffel and ENSCI-Les Ateliers (Paris Design Institute).

Stefan Bergheim (PhD) is the founder and director of the Center for Societal Progress, a non-profit think tank based in Frankfurt, Germany. He holds a doctoral degree in Economics and worked as an economist in the financial industry between 1995 and 2008. He published on topics such as *The Happy Variety of Capitalism*, created a *Progress Index*, and led the working group 'Prosperity, quality of life and progress' in the German Chancellor's 2011/12 'Dialogue on Germany's Future'. Using futures methods, he developed *Quality of Life Processes*, put into practice as *Positive Futures – Forum for Frankfurt* and in the German national well-being strategy.

Cristiano Cagnin (PhD), of the Center for Strategic Studies and Management Science, Technology and Innovation (CGEE), Brazil, was previously a scientific officer at the EU Commission DG Joint Research Centres – Institute for Prospective Technological Studies. He is an industrial engineer involved in research, international collaborative projects and consultancy in innovation, business strategy, environment management and cleaner production, and foresight. He is currently engaged in sustainability, Research, Technology, Development and Innovation (RTDI) and foresight research and practice, active on projects related to sustainability across diverse thematic areas, RTDI and regional coordination and joint programming; and supports policy design and implementation-making through early identification of emerging issues. His research interests include alternative ways of increasing interactions and learning between social stakeholders to bridge the gap between RTDI and individuals in society, leading to inclusive governance and responsible, sustainable innovation, production, consumption and living.

Stuart Candy (PhD) is an Associate Professor in the School of Design at Carnegie Mellon University in Pittsburgh, Pennsylvania, USA. His experiential futures work has appeared worldwide in museums, festivals, conferences and city streets, on the Discovery Channel, and in the pages of *The Economist* and *Wired*. He is a member of the foresight advisory board at the International Federation of Red Cross and Red Crescent Societies (Switzerland), and a Fellow of The Long Now Foundation (USA), INK (India), the World Futures Studies Federation (France) and the Museum of Tomorrow (Brazil).

Orazio Bellettini Cedeño is a graduate of the Kennedy School of Government, Harvard University, United States of America, a social entrepreneur, and a

xiv *Contributors*

policy researcher who has advised international agencies, civil society organizations and governments on strategies to increase knowledge production, enhance education quality and transparency. He has trained graduate students and government officials in local finance, development policies and public reforms at the Catholic University in Ecuador (PUCE), Latin American Faculty of Social Sciences (FLACSO) and the University of Murcia, Spain. Orazio is the Co-founder and Executive Director of Grupo FARO, Ecuador, a think-and-do tank that promotes the participation of citizens in the strengthening of the state and civil society. In 2008, he became an Ashoka and Avina Fellow, and in 2013 was selected by the Rockefeller Foundation as Resident Fellow at the Bellagio Center. He is the first President of the Ecuadorian Council of Civil Society Organizations and member of the Steering Committee of the Latin American Initiative for Applied Policy Research.

Sandra Coulibaly Leroy is Deputy Director of the Programming and Strategic Development Department at the Organisation Internationale de la Francophonie (OIF), helping to strengthen the institution's capacity for strategic thinking. From 2012 to 2014 she was Deputy Permanent Representative of the OIF to the United Nations in Geneva after a stint as the organization's Deputy Director of Cultural Diversity and Development sector. She holds several postgraduate qualifications in international relations focusing on intercultural relations, communication and new technologies including an Executive Master's in international negotiation and policy from the Graduate Institute of International Studies in Geneva (IHEID). She lectures at the Art and Communication School of Paris and University Senghor in Alexandria, Egypt.

Shermon Cruz (PhD) is a professional futurist, a climate reality leader, a certified business continuity professional and founder of the Center for Engaged Foresight, Philippines. He is an active member of the World Futures Studies Federation, the Asia Pacific Futures Network and the Association of Professional Futurists. Shermon specializes in futures education and research, strategic foresight facilitation, planning, governance, city resilience, crisis management and policy management. He was a director of the Philippine Center for Foresight Education and Innovation Research (PhilForesight) and Professor of Futures Studies at Northwestern University in the Philippines. He was a recipient of the 2013 World Social Science Forum Prize and the International Social Science Council's Early Career Social Scientist from the Global South.

Ngarkidané Djidingar is a graduate of the Center of Research and Action for Peace (CERAP), Ivory Coast, and of St Thomas Aquinas University, Burkina Faso. He received a MSc in Ethical and Sustainable Economic Development and a BA in Political and Legal Sciences. Formerly he worked as an international volunteer for the Organisation Internationale de la Francophonie (OIF) as well as, for the FAO, OIF and the Global Alliance against Climate Change. Introduced to foresight research and knowledge laboratories by Sandra Coulibaly (OIF) and Riel Miller (UNESCO), Ngarkidané is 'passionate about the future' and has contributed to several activities in this context with OIF, UNESCO, Futuribles International and the Royal Institute of Strategic Studies, Morocco.

Andrée Ehresmann (PhD) (born Bastiani) is Emeritus Professor of Mathematics at Picardie Jules Verne University, France. She has directed about 50 PhD students and organized numerous international conferences. She has published more than 130 papers in mathematics and in pluri-disciplinary domains: functional analysis and control problems; category theory (development of sketches and higher order categories with Charles Ehresmann); elaboration of the Memory Evolutive Systems (with J.-P. Vanbremeersch), a dynamic model for multi-scale, multi-agent multi-temporality complex systems, with applications to Biomathematics and Cognition (the MENS model), including higher cognitive processes such as creativity and anticipation.

Aidan Eyakuze, an economist, is the Executive Director of Twaweza East Africa, which enables children to learn, citizens to exercise agency and governments to be more open and responsive in Tanzania, Kenya and Uganda. Aidan was appointed to the global Steering Committee of the Open Government Partnership in 2016 and the Board of the Global Partnership for Sustainable Development Data in 2017. Aidan has 15 years' experience as a scenario practitioner in national projects in Kenya, Tanzania, South Africa, Nigeria and East Africa. He co-leads the State of East Africa Reports publication and facilitates futures thinking for private sector, civil society and public organizations.

Jean-Jacques Gouguet (PhD) is Professor Emeritus in Economics and Spatial Planning at the University of Limoges, France. He has been the Scientific Director of Economic Studies for the Centre de Droit et d'Économie du Sport (Centre for Sports Law and Economics, University of Limoges) for over 25 years. He has expertise in professional sports economics, territorial analysis, sectoral analysis and in public policy evaluation. He is a leading expert in the field of economic impact and social benefit studies of major international sporting events. He coordinated studies on the Rugby World Cup in 2007, Euro 2016 (2014 and 2016) and the Olympic and Paralympic Games of Paris 2024 (2016). Founder and Vice-President of the International Association of Sport Economists (IASE), member of the Editorial Board of the *Journal of Sports Economics* (JSE) and of the *Journal of Regional and Urban Economy* (RERU), he has authored 10 books and about 150 articles in collective works or specialized magazines.

Kewulay Kamara is a poet/storyteller, multi-media artist and lecturer. His work has been featured in *The New York Times* and other major media outlets. Kewulay has performed at several prestigious centres including the Cathedral of St John the Divine, the Museum of Natural History and Oxford University, and participated in the People's Poetry Gatherings, and the Geraldine R. Dodge Poetry and Langston Hughes Festivals. He directed the epic poetry documentary, *In Search of Finah Misa Kule*, and the companion book, *Word in the Belly of the Word*. He has published scholarly articles in the *Journal of Future Studies* and xvi *Contributors*

gave a Ted TEDxUNC Talk on the uses of storytelling and foresight. Kewulay conducts Future Literacy workshops, participates in international foresight conferences and uses foresight tools in live performance. Kewulay Kamara is the founder/executive director of Badenya, Inc., an arts-presenting organization in New York, and Dankawalie Secondary School in Sierra Leone.

Geci Karuri-Sebina (PhD) has been Executive Manager at South African Cities Network since 2011. She previously worked with National Treasury, South Africa; the Council for Scientific and Industrial Research, South Africa; Human Sciences Research Council, South Africa; and the University of California Los Angeles (UCLA) Advanced Policy Institute, United States of America. Geci holds master's degrees in Urban Planning and Architecture from UCLA, and a PhD from the University of Witwatersrand, South Africa. Her interests range from development foresight, policy, planning and practice topics, particularly relating to urban governance, the built environment and innovation systems. She has two decades' experience working and publishing in these fields. Her most recent publication is the book *Innovation Africa*.

Per M. Koch is a senior adviser at Innovation Norway, a Norwegian agency for innovation. He has been working on industrial and social innovation and research and innovation policy since 1991, in the Norwegian Ministry of Education and Research and the Research Council of Norway. He was the leader of STEP, a Norwegian research institute for innovation research. He has been a member of the OECD Committee for Science and Technology, and chaired the OECD working party on international S&T collaboration for Global Challenges (STIG). He led the EU research project Publin, on innovation in the public sector.

Nisreen Lahham (PhD) is the founder and Head of Futures Studies Forum for Africa and the Middle East (FSF), and an advisor for GIZ at the programme Adaptation to Climate Change in the Water Sector in the Arab Region (ACCWaM) and the Nexus Dialogue Programme. Previously, she was the Executive Manager of the Center for Futures Studies (CFS) in the Cabinet Office, Government of Egypt. Nisreen is a member of the International Panel of Futurists (PIP), a member of the Egyptian Futures Studies Council, and an editor of North Africa Horizons Newsletter. Her interests relate particularly to environmental planning, sustainable development, water and food security, and green communities. She has BSc in Architecture from the University of Jordan and PhD in Engineering from Ain Shams University in Cairo.

Lydia Garrido Luzardo is a social anthropologist specializing in Social Change, Sustainable Development and Anticipation. She is a research professor at FLACSO Uruguay (Facultad Latinoamericana de Ciencias Sociales) and Associate Director of the Future Laboratory (Laboratorio de Futuros) at FLACSO. As a practitioner of anthropology of anticipation, her focus is on emergent processes in contemporary societies, with the objective of generating knowledge to strengthen decision-making capacities. She is the articulator of the Uruguayan Node of the Think Tank – the Millennium Project, Global Futures Studies & Research, and member of its Planning Committee. A founding member of RIBER (Iberoamerican Foresight Network), she is also involved with the UNESCO Global/Local Anticipatory Capacities Project as researcher and consultant.

Matthew Giuseppe Marasco is a Hallmark Research Scholar at La Trobe University in Melbourne, Australia. He completed an internship with the not-for-profit Australian Futures Project in 2015, was a La Trobe University delegate to the 9th UNESCO Youth Forum in Paris in 2015 and was an intern in the UNESCO Social & Human Sciences Sector in 2016. He is also a consultant in results based planning, monitoring-evaluation and corporate social responsibility.

Edmund Matotay is currently a senior programme management officer and professional advisor currently working with Norwegian Church Aid in Tanzania. NCA works with people and organizations around the world to eradicate poverty and injustice. Before joining NCA Edmund worked with Natural Resource Governance Institute (NRGI) as a Country Officer. NRGI is a global organization dealing with research and policy on petroleum, gas and mining. Prior to NRGI, he worked with the Society for International Development (SID) as a Programme Manager responsible for programmes management, research, training, publications and policy dialogues. Before SID Edmund worked for three and half years with Oxfam GB as a Researcher where he was responsible for programmes research cycles, sector analysis and intellectual support for programmes across the country. Prior to Oxfam GB Edmund spent ten years at Mzumbe University as a lecturer, trainer and a consultant in the Faculty of Public Administration and Management. He has published a book, book chapters, and journal papers in peer-reviewed outlets across a range of fields including: social security, public health, mobile telecommunications for development, agriculture, value chains, voices, inequalities, etc. His most recent publication is in the journal *Development* entitled 'Inequalities and Structural Transformation in Tanzania'. Edmund holds a master's degree in Public Administration from the University of Agder, Kristiansand Norway, and a Postgraduate Diploma in Socioeconomic Analysis for Development from the University of Rotterdam and the Institute of Social Studies, Holland.

Riel Miller (PhD) is one of the world's leading authorities on the theory and practice of 'using-the-future' to change what people see and do. He has pioneered efforts to develop Futures Literacy and Anticipatory Systems thinking as requisite elements of new strategies to enhance humanity's capacity to be free. He is recognized as an innovative and globally experienced teacher and project initiator, designer and manager. Riel started his career at the OECD in 1982. During the mid-1980s he was a senior manager in the Ontario public service (Ministries of Finance; Universities; and Industry). From the mid-1990s to 2004 he returned to the OECD to work in the International Futures

Programme. He founded xperidox, an independent consultancy in 2005. In 2012 he was appointed Head of Foresight at UNESCO.

Ivana Milojević (PhD) is a researcher, writer and educator with a trans-disciplinary professional background in sociology, education, gender, peace and futures studies. Since the early 1990s, she has delivered speeches and facilitated workshops for governmental institutions, international associations and non-governmental organizations. She has been a visiting and adjunct professor at universities in Europe, Asia and Australia and is currently co-director of Metafuture, an educational think tank which explores futures-oriented issues. Milojević is the author of over 70 journal articles and book chapters, as well as the author, co-author and/or co-editor of a number of academic books.

Kacper Nosarzewski (MA) is a partner at Warsaw-based foresight consultancy, 4CF, and a member of the board of the Polish Society for Futures Studies. He works as a consultant in strategic foresight to international institutions such as UNESCO, UNDP, businesses and NGOs. In addition to projects in the field of national security, business strategy and public policy, he is managing a project aimed at introducing future-oriented education components into Polish and European school and university curricula. He is a graduate of the University of Warsaw, where he also taught digital humanities in transdisciplinary liberal arts programmes. He currently teaches strategic foresight and analysis at the Polish Naval Academy.

Roberto Poli (PhD) is the first UNESCO Chair in Anticipatory Systems, University of Trento, Italy. He teaches futures studies and philosophy of science, is President of -skopìa, a start-up of the University of Trento offering anticipation services on a professional basis and is a fellow of WAAS – World Academy of Art and Science and STIAS—Stellenbosch Institute for Advanced Study. Poli is Director of the master's programme in 'Previsione sociale' (Social Foresight) of the Department of Sociology and Social Research at the University of Trento, editor-in-chief of Axiomathes (Springer), editor of the series Categories (De Gruyter) and Anticipation Science (Springer), and member of the editorial board of five journals, including Futures and European Journal of Futures Research. Poli has published five books, edited or co-edited more than 20 books or journal special issues and published more than 250 scientific papers.

Martin Rhisiart † (PhD) was Professor of Strategy and Innovation at the University of South Wales, UK, and Director of the Centre for Research in Futures and Innovation. Martin designed and delivered a range of international research projects on strategic foresight and innovation. His futures work was funded by a range of national and international bodies, including the UK Commission for Employment and Skills, Arts and Humanities Research Council (UK), DG Research (European Union), Department for Enterprise, Jobs and Innovation (Republic of Ireland), and the Welsh Government. Martin died at the age of 43 in June, 2017. A terrible loss for his family and all of his colleagues. We are grateful for his contributions to this volume and for his engagement with the development of Futures Literacy over the last decade.

Pierre Rossel (PhD) is a Swiss anthropologist with 23 years of experience researching and teaching at the Swiss Federal Institute of Technology in Lausanne. His expertise is in the field of technology assessment/technology foresight, with an emphasis on the renewal of foresight methodologies and concepts, in particular, weak signal analysis, 'thick presents', backcasting approaches, anticipatory issues; applications and mandates regarding the emergence of new pervasive forms of ICTs (IoT, blockchain, Big Data, bots, etc.); support for innovative projects in micro-nano technologies, cleantech, the industry 4.0 transition, and related regional and urban management challenges.

Jennifer Rudkin (PhD) is a designer and researcher, trained at the ESADSE (École great Supérieure d'Art et de Design de Saint-Étienne, France) and at RISD (Rhode Island School of Design, Providence, USA). She holds a PhD in Design from the Politecnico di Milano, Italy. Currently working on Design for Policy for the Joint Research Centre of the European Commission (EU Policy Lab), her interests focus on developing a design activity that participates in current emerging social and societal issues. Prior to joining the EU Policy Lab team, she taught design at the Design School of East China Normal University in Shanghai, China and worked on the direction and coordination of international projects, events and workshops at the intersection of Design and Foresight, notably on the Future of Work, on Drawing Food Futures and on the development of Futures Literacy Labs at UNESCO.

Nicolas Simard is a Canadian diplomat with expertise in public policy development, strategic analysis, foresight and strategic planning, managing major development programmes, Sub-Saharan Africa and South Asia. Since 2004, he has worked with the Canadian International Development Agency (CIDA) in the Directorate of Democratic Institutions and Conflict on the Agency's strategy for assisting fragile states and was responsible for coordinating the strategic planning of CIDA's bilateral and regional programmes in West and Central Africa. At the Department of Canadian Heritage (PCH) he designed and implemented the International Strategic Framework. He was Deputy Director of Canada's Assistance Program in Bangladesh and most recently, Director and Head of the Office of the International Organization of La Francophonie (OIF) in Paris where he helped to set up a new strategic oversight and foresight function.

Ilkka Tuomi (PhD) is Founder and Chief Scientist at Meaning Processing Ltd., Finland. He has written books on artificial intelligence, theory and practice of intelligent organizations, information society, computer networks, and innovation theory, as well as over 40 scientific articles. He has a degree in Theoretical Physics from the University of Helsinki, and a PhD in adult education from the same university. His areas of interest include next-generation foresight models, anticipatory systems, knowledge creation theory, innovation and technology studies, R&D&I policy, and the new economics and sociology of informational value production models.

Jean-Paul Vanbremeersch holds a medical degree in Geriatrics-Gerontology and a university diploma in the field of dementia and cognitive disorders. From 1977 to 2015 he ran his own independent medical practice and has served as a coordinating physician in a geriatric institution since 2004. Since 1986, with Mrs A.C. Ehresmann, he has published work on the theory of Evolutionary Memory Systems, with applications to cognition (MENS Model), aging and anticipation. He is also co-author of the book *Memory Evolutive Systems*.

Foreword

Audrey Azoulay, Director-General of UNESCO

There is no debate that we are living at a time of exceptional innovation. In so many areas, human ingenuity is breaking old barriers to invent new cures for disease, new means of communicating, new ways of organizing business and life. We see innovation occur when people face both terrible challenges and inspirational opportunities. In this context, I believe that understanding why and how to 'use-the-future' becomes all the more important.

As the French philosopher and sociologist Edgar Morin pointed out, much pain, even conflict, arises from the contradictions we all experience between living in a complex, dynamic and creative world and the rigid, sometimes deterministic, frameworks we use to understand this reality and its evolution, as well as the choices it offers.

This is why being 'future literate' is so important. This is about understanding the nature of the future and the role it plays in what we see and do. Evidence shows that people can change how and why they think about the future. Developing this capacity to imagine can be a powerful tool for catalysing change today. Becoming more skilled at designing the systems and processes used to imagine tomorrow is an essential part of empowering women and men with the 'capacity to be free', as developed by Martha Nussbaum and Amartya Sen, to craft new approaches to more inclusive and sustainable development.

Transforming the Future: Anticipation in the 21st Century exemplifies UNESCO as the laboratory of ideas for the United Nations, raising new questions today by changing our understanding of tomorrow. There can be no assurances that the choices we make today will create a better tomorrow – but we can become better able to harness our imagination to grasp the potential of the present and craft ways to act that are consistent with our values. This book opens a new field for innovation in exploring how humanity can live better with the uncertainty and creativity of a complex evolving universe for the benefit of all.

Audrey Azoulay, 24 November 2017

Acknowledgements

As with all such endeavours many people have contributed. The project would never have happened without the support of the former Director General of UNESCO, Irina Bokova and the new Director General, Audrey Azoulay. The authors of the chapters and case studies (see the Table of Contents for names) were not only dedicated and generous with their time, ideas and resources but also encouraged me to not give up when the going got tough. They reinforced the powerful support that I deeply appreciate from the hundreds of the people who organized and participated in the Futures Literacy Laboratories-Novelty (FLL-N) all around the world.

Special recognition is in order for Stefan Bergheim and Maree Conway. Stefan read through the entire manuscript and made important contributions to improving the text, including as editor of the case studies. Maree proofread the entire manuscript, offering crucial feedback along the way, as well as providing significant assistance addressing bibliographic issues.

I also want to thank Lydia Garrido Luzardo, Richard Sandford and John Sweeney for their efforts to test and reflect on both the theory and practice of Futures Literacy. Roberto Poli, Pierre Rossel and Ilkka Tuomi have played critical roles in the emergence of this work over the last decade and have also commented on the draft manuscript as it evolved. I have also benefitted from the insights and feedback of Peter Bishop, Loes Damhof, Keri Facer, Ted Fuller, Michel Godet, Roumiana Gotseva, Kais Hamammi, Sohail Inayatullah, Hugues de Jouvenel, Anita Kelleher, Maya Van Leemput, Kacper Nosarzewski, Alioune Sall, Sari Soderland, Stefaan Verhulst, Philine Warnke and Markku Wilenius.

Last, but not least in this list of colleagues, is Martin Rhisiart who not only contributed the first case study reported in this volume but has also been an important collaborator over the last fifteen years. Unexpectedly and tragically, Martin died in June 2017, a terrible loss for us all.

Special thanks are also due to colleagues who worked directly with me at UNESCO, in particular, John Crowley, Maria Linda Tinio-Le Douarin, Jennifer Rudkin, Irianna Lianaki-Dedouli and Abdoulaye Ibrahim. Numerous UNESCO 'interns' made enthusiastic and very practical contributions at specific points in the process: Francesca Ballini, Mackenzie Dickson, Fayruz El Assaad, Olivier Esclauze, Arianna Flores Corral, Leyla Kjazim, Clara Lew-Levy, Matthew

Marasco, Tonya Reznikovich, Omar Sahi, Tigidankay Sannoh, Luciano Scala, Ivan da Souza and April Ward.

The project started when I joined UNESCO in the second half of 2012 as Head of Foresight, working in the Bureau of Strategic Planning (BSP). My colleagues at BSP, Hans d'Orville, Jean-Yves Lesaux and Jacques Plouin, all contributed in different ways to making this happen. In this initial phase, the project was supported financially by The Rockefeller Foundation, with special thanks to Claudia Juech. Additional support was provided by Norway in the form of a special grant to organize Futures Literacy Labs in the field and a meeting of the Research Subcommittee in Oslo, thanks to Per Koch at Innovation Norway as well as Ellen Veie and Elisabeth Guibrandsen at the Research Council of Norway. Per Koch also deserves special credit for Innovation Norway's contribution of most of the funds needed to co-publish this book with Routledge in open access.

Many other organizations provided significant in-kind contributions due to local champions, in particular: the South African Node of the Millennium Project – thanks to Geci Karuri Sabina; CGEE Brazil that ran four Futures Literacy Labs – thanks to Cristiano Cagnin; The ValueWeb – thanks to Svenja Rüger; the Association of Professional Futurists – thanks to Cindy Frewen; and the Millennium Project, thanks to Jerry Glenn. Heide Hackmann of the International Social Science Council and now the merged International Science Council provided numerous opportunities to advance this proof-of-concept phase of the research. The International Organization of Francophonie (OIF) has played a crucial role supporting numerous Futures Literacy Labs and contributed funds for the translation of this book into French. This happened because of the unstinting support of Sandra Coulibaly-Leroy at the OIF. Thanks are also due to the Future Studies Forum for Africa and the Middle East – in particular Nisreen Lahham for her on-going involvement and translation of this book into Arabic, supported by financing from The Rockefeller Foundation.

An important acknowledgement needs to be made to the invaluable contributions of all the participants in the initial Steering Committee and the Bellagio Convening (Miller, 2014), the Oslo meeting of the research methods sub-committee (Miller, 2014), and the How Do We Identify Great Opportunities? gathering in Ispra/Borghi (Miller, 2015).

Contributions to the overall realization of this project were also made by a wide range of UNESCO colleagues, in particular: Lalla Ben Barka, Nada Al Nashif, Dendev Badarch, Vincent Duforney, Vincenzo Fazzino, Ian Dennison, Ronald Kayanja, Cristina Puerta, Mimouna Abderrahmane, Barbara Torggler, Dov Lynch and Matthieu Guevel.

I am grateful to Rebecca Brennan, Charlotte Eandersby and Leila Walker at Routledge for their support for this publication. They have been an encouraging force throughout the process.

I would like to extend my personal gratitude for the encouragement and insights I received from Isabelle Miller, Laurent Dominati, Pankaj Ghemawat, Kewulay Kamara, Jean-Claude Ruano-Borbalan, Michael Storper and, in the earlier stages of this undertaking, the inspiration and creativity of Robin Murray.

Of course, any errors or defects remain my responsibility as the editor and primary author of this book, and the main architect of this research project.

The individual authors are responsible for the choice and the presentation of the facts contained in this report and for the opinions expressed therein, which are not necessarily those of UNESCO and do not commit the Organization.

The designations employed and the presentation of material throughout this book do not imply the expression of any opinion whatsoever on the part of UNESCO concerning the legal status of any country, territory, city or area of its authorities, or concerning the delimitation of its frontiers or boundaries.

Riel Miller, Paris, October 2017

References

Miller, R. (2014) *Networking to Improve Global/Local Anticipatory Capacities – A Scoping Exercise: Narrative Report*. Paris: UNESCO/Rockefeller Foundation.

Miller, R. (2015) *Evaluating and Improving the Use of the Future for Identifying and Choosing Dynamic Opportunities*. Paris: UNESCO.

Introduction

Futures Literacy: transforming the future

Riel Miller

Imagine, for a moment, that you are a physicist doing research in the early years of the 20th century. Your field of study is advancing by leaps and bounds, including new theories about subatomic particles. Only there seems to be no way to test your ideas because you lack the tools needed to conduct the appropriate experiments. Then, some of your colleagues come up with an idea for an 'accelerator' that visibly records the results of particles colliding with other particles. It is an amazing and complicated machine that was invented and refined over a number of years by bringing together many theoretical and technological advances (Bryant, 1994). But once the accelerators start being built you are in possession of a tool for revealing the invisible. You are able to test your hypotheses by running practical experiments. You can even explore new theories by simulating some of the conditions of the universe just moments after the Big Bang.

Now imagine that you are a social scientist in the early years of the 21st century trying to understand a key component of another 'universe', the realm of human decision-making. Specifically, you are interested in the ways in which the future plays a role in choices meant to improve the human condition. The challenge is not exactly the same as testing your theories by smashing atoms, but it is not as far removed as it might seem. Today, like when the accelerator was invented, there appears to be a convergence of different theories and tools that enable a better understanding of why and how people 'use-the-future'.[1] This confluence is made up of many pieces, spanning advances in complexity theory to breakthroughs in the design of innovation processes. But the key for understanding why and how the future is used is anticipatory systems (AS) theory (Rosen, 1985; Poli, 2014; Fuller, 2017; Nadin, 2016).

This piece of the puzzle is central. In a way that parallels the theories that led to efforts to run experiments for detecting sub-atomic particles, anticipatory systems theory proposes the potential existence of different kinds of future, sparking the search for methods to detect these largely unimagined and invisible elements of the world around us. Both are quintessential scientific endeavours (Schneider, 2012), only the future, unlike sub-atomic particles, does not actually exist.[2] In this sense, the hypothesis that there are different kinds of future and that it is feasible to invent ways of generating the evidence needed to test such a hypothesis is more daunting than hypothesising and searching for sub-atomic particles. Hunting for different kinds of futures runs directly into the obstacle that by definition the future cannot exist in the present, since if it did it would no longer be the future but the present. And yet, as everyone knows, the future plays a role in the present. How can something that does not exist have an impact?

One answer to this problem is the idea of anticipation. *The future does not exist in the present but anticipation does. The form the future takes in the present is anticipation.* Thus, the integration of the later-than-now, be it a millisecond or a millennium, into the present is achieved through various kinds of anticipatory systems and processes (Miller and Poli 2010; see also Chapter 2). Taking an anticipatory systems (AS) perspective on the integration of the future into the present is the starting point for the formulation of a framework for connecting the theories and practices of 'using-the-future'. And this in turn is the foundation for defining and exploring the capability to 'use-the-future', for different reasons and in a variety of ways, called here Futures Literacy (FL).

A better understanding of FL depends on advances in both the theory and practice of anticipation. Developments in the theory of anticipatory systems (AS) lead to hypotheses about different kinds of anticipation. Developments in anticipatory practices put AS to use and thereby enable the testing of hypotheses about such systems. As is typical of this kind of gradual and fragmented process of coalescence around a set of shared ideas and observations, the process does not follow a linear sequential path. What it means to be 'futures literate', or capable of understanding and applying AS, is also emergent (Miller 2007, 2011). People's fictions about the later-than-now and the frames they use to invent these imaginary futures are so important for everyday life, so ingrained and so often unremarked, that it is hard to gain the distance needed to observe and analyse what is going on.

Yet, as with all discoveries, it is the world's richness and mystery that confronts the prisons of our minds, helping us to overturn the old frames and create new ones. In such circumstances, at least initially, people often search in vain to understand and overcome a problem that is inherent to the very system they are trying to fix. To cite Wittgenstein,

> Getting hold of the difficulty deep down is what is hard. Because if it is grasped near the surface it simply remains the difficulty it was. It has to be pulled out by the roots; and that involves our beginning to think in a new way. The change is as decisive as, for example, that from the alchemical to the chemical way of thinking. The new way of thinking is what is so hard to establish. Once the new way of thinking has been established, the old problems vanish; indeed, they become hard to recapture. For they go with our way of expressing ourselves and, if we clothe ourselves in a new form of expression, the old problems are discarded along with the old garment.
>
> (Wittgenstein, 1984)

The UNESCO FL Project, started in late 2012, is an ongoing effort to get hold of the difficulty 'deep down' by engaging in the conventional scientific pincer movement – combining theory and practice. Over the course of more than 30 collaborative and innovative on-the-ground experiments (Figure 0.1), combined with relevant expert gatherings in different parts of the world (Miller, 2014, 2015), this project has been able to advance along both theoretical and experimental lines.

The Futures Literacy Framework (FLF) presented in Chapter 1, as a way to understand FL, builds on both the theory of AS, called the Discipline of Anticipation in Chapter 2, and extensive insights from practical experiments in thinking about the future, covered in Chapters 4 and 5. The FLF delivers a clear

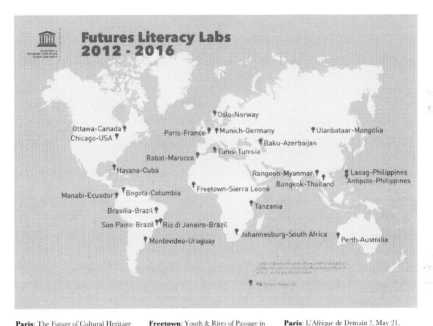

Paris: The Future of Cultural Heritage Research, November 19-20, 2012
Baku: Scoping Global Anticipatory Capacities, June 1, 2013
Paris: Knowlab Design Test Session "Scoping the Know-Lab: Tomorrow's Knowledge, Creation Microscope" A Primer and Images, June 20-21, 2013
Brasilia: The Future of Science, 11-12 July, 2013
Sao Paolo: Changing the Way Universities Use the Future?, July 15, 2013
Chicago: The Future of Futurists, July 19, 2013
Oslo: Innovation as Learning, Knowing as Learning. Knowing as Science: Imagining a Universal Innovation Society in 2040, October 21-22, 2013
Bogota: Using the future to think about local labor markets, November 25-26, 2013
Rio de Janeiro: Imagining the Future of Science in Society, November 28-29, 2013
Paris: Imagining the Future of the Transition from "Youth" to "Adult", January 13-14, 2014

Freetown: Youth & Rites of Passage in Sierra Leone, January 20-21, 2014
Munich: Imagining the Future of Sports in Society, February 5-6, 2014
Paris: Inhabiting Planet Earth 2100: Beyond Cities?, March 27-28, 2014
Calceta, Bahia de Caraquez, Monta: A Series of Future Literacy Knowledge Lab in Ecuador, April 26-May 1, 2014
Rangoon: Addressing the future of education in Myanmar?, May 2-3, 2014
Laoag City: Resilient Cities, Brighter Futures -A Forum-Workshop on Anticipatory Thinking and Strategic Foresight Methods for Sustainable City Futures, May 21-24, 2014
Johannesburg — All Africa Future Forum, May 26-28, 2014
Ottawa: The Future of Innovation Ecosystems in the Public Sector, June 4-5, 2014
Tanzania: Future-Proofing an Entire Nation, September 2013
Brasilia: Joint International Foresight Academy, November 16-21, 2014

Paris: L'Afrique de Demain ?, May 21, 2015
Rabat: Imagining Africa's Future, June 25-26, 2015
Bangkok: Rethinking Education: the Future of Informal Learning, September 1-3, 2015
Ulaanbaatar: The Future of Mongolia, September 20-October 2, 2015
Paris, 9th UNESCO Youth Forum, October 26-28, 2015
Rabat: Futures Literacy: Advancing a Community of Practice in Africa – The Future of Urbanisation and Water in North Africa, December 4-5, 2015
Tunis: Social Transformations, 3-4 March, 2016
Montevideo: What Development for What Uruguay? March 28-30, 2016
Paris, Reframing Mobility and Identity: The Future of Africa, July 4-5, 2016
Havana: Using the Future to Embrace Complexity, July 13, 2016
Antipolo City: Developing the Capacity of Filipino Youth Leaders to Use the Future, November, 13-16, 2016

Figure 0.1 Futures Literacy Labs 2012–2016

analytical approach to defining what a futures literate person is able to do. The FLF does this by providing a descriptive mapping of the ontological and epistemological attributes of anticipatory activities as specific anticipatory assumptions (AA). AA are the most basic component of anticipatory activities: these assumptions are necessary for all 'uses-of-the-future' because 'imagination' can only be elaborated on the basis of the underlying assumptions.[3] Conscious human AA include choices about what kind of future to anticipate and which methods to use to think about a particular kind of future. AA, as will become clear in later pages, may even be applied to non-conscious anticipation. In this universe, anticipation is a ubiquitous activity and the AA needed to describe the diversity of specific 'uses-of-the-future' covers a range of great breadth and depth.

This means that research into AA can be undertaken in many different ways across many different fields, ranging from mathematical biology (Rosen, 1991) and the creative economy (Henry and Bruin, 2011) to psychology (Sutter, 1983) and sociology (International Sociological Association, 2016). The research task undertaken in this book however, does not focus on depicting or analysing AA from a historical or cultural perspective. Rather, the challenge addressed over the following pages is that of describing the AA underpinning FL as it is practised – most often unknowingly (futures illiteracy) – around the world today. These AA, exposed by the research conducted for this project, display a rich diversity of contexts and human participants, but only cover a sub-set of all the AA that can be found in the immense number of anticipatory activities and systems around us.

Transforming the Future: Anticipation in the 21st Century provides a framework and evidence regarding the attributes of FL, as a conscious human capability. The research is concentrated on how to define and assess the extent to which someone has or can become futures literate by collecting evidence of her capacity to understand the nature and role of the AA needed to 'use-the-future' in practice. The task is specified on the basis of the analytical precision made possible by the FLF that was developed for this project. The ambition is to explore the diversity of FL around the world today. With this purpose in mind, as discussed in detail over the following chapters, an innovative 'knowledge laboratory' was developed to produce evidence of people's AA and thereby the extent to which they can become or are already futures literate. This specially designed lab is a practical method for detecting people's AA as they use different anticipatory systems.

The effectiveness of the 'knowledge laboratory' approach, explained in detail over the following chapters, arises from the power of learning processes to expose what people know and can come to know. Conducting scientific research using learning processes is nothing new (Kuhn, 1970; Fleck, 1979; Argyris and Schon, 1996; Knorr Cetina, 1999; Bateson, 2000) but the knowlab approach pioneered here called for the harnessing of a wide range of techniques, from action-learning (Lewin, 1946; Chiu, 2003; Macdonald, 2012) and collective intelligence (Weschsler, 1971; Lévy, 1997; Yu, Nickerson and Sakamoto, 2012) to creativity heuristics (Yilmaz and Seifert, 2011) and the many techniques of 'real world research' (Robson, 2002). Similarly, considerable innovative and inter-disciplinary effort was required to bring together the different and emerging strands connecting AS theory to developments in the theories of complexity, ontology, social science, and human agency (see Chapter 1). But perhaps the most significant contribution of this book is the bringing together of these two strands of social science, the 'knowlabs' methodology for generating evidence of people's AA and AS theory for understanding how people 'use-the-future', in order to invent a new general-purpose research tool, here called Futures Literacy Laboratories (FLL).

This general-purpose tool was then put to the test in a more narrowly focused version, tailored to the needs of the UNESCO FL Project to explore a wide range of AA and in particular those that are outside the boundaries of conventional 'uses-of-the-future'. This customised FLL tool is called an FLL-N. The 'N' stands for 'Novelty' (Bergson, 1913; Bergson and Mitchell, 2005; Tuomi, 2017) and reflects the specific research requirements of the UNESCO FL Project to cover a large range of different AA, including those that generally only appear once people have acquired a certain degree of FL. The FLL-N is just one example of how FLL can be customised, as explained briefly below and in more depth in Chapters 1, 4 and 5. The book as a whole also provides considerable detail on all these issues, including more 'players' from the supporting cast of methods and tools that contributed to the research. But before plunging into the intricacies of the FLF in Chapter 1 and the details of the case studies that explore FL around the world, two stage-setting points merit concise elaboration in this introduction: one is the general-purpose research tool (FLL) and its customised version, the FLL-N, specially designed for conducting experiments targeting AA *and* novelty around the world; the other is a succinct overview of the main findings of the project so far.

An experimental approach: Futures Literacy Laboratories-Novelty (FLL-N)

Building a time-machine, even if such a device were feasible, would not help conduct experiments aimed at discovering and analysing the attributes of conscious human anticipation. This is because FL as a capability is not about the accuracy of predictions or determining the success or failure of efforts to impose, colonial fashion, today's idea of tomorrow on tomorrow. A time machine would be useful for that task. But the attributes that describe when someone is futures literate are not those of prescience, perfect preparation and planning, like somehow always being able to pick the horse that is going to win the race. Rather the task when describing FL is to reveal the anticipatory assumptions (AA) that determine why and how futures are imagined. Anticipatory activities require AA, the basic parameters of the models that make anticipating the future feasible. With respect to 'using-the-future', AA are like the particles exposed by an accelerator in a physics lab – elements of the underlying structure behind the surface of appearances. AA describe in specific terms the contours and functioning of anticipatory systems (AS). Different AA generate different 'imaginary', not-yet-existent futures – including, as will be explained in Chapter 1, different 'kinds' of future.

In order to describe conscious human anticipation AA are essential, even when the AA are tacit and the role played by the imaginary future is obscured by a lack of appreciation of the nature and differences of anticipatory systems (AS). This means that the task of researching FL as a human capability requires some method for arriving at descriptions of people's AA. But, since these AA are often imperceptible, even uninvented and unattainable without prior acquisition of the capability to 'use-the-future', the key methodological step is to find an approach that actually involves learning to be futures literate. As with other capabilities such as reading and writing, FL is a skill that can be revealed and obtained through learning processes. Such learning processes, as Dewey (1997) pointed out long ago, always begin with a disruption or realisation that there is something we do not know or do not understand (Miettinen, 2000; Tuomi, 2005). With respect to FL, what we do not know, or at least do not think about very often or in much depth, are the answers to the questions: "What is the future?", and "What methods do we use to 'know the future'?" Most of the time, given people's 'futures illiteracy', these questions are not even posed.

The following pages touch on many reasons for such 'futures illiteracy' and why in today's world it is difficult to answer the two basic FL questions. But the main point, at the outset of this book, is that it is difficult to study or develop a capability when people rarely ask themselves "What is the future and how do I use it?" They are not well positioned to provide evidence regarding the extent of their capabilities. Their anticipatory assumptions, systems and processes remain implicit, a form of tacit knowledge that frames much of what they see and do, but without them being aware – in this sense it is 'invisible'. Which is why, if the aim is to gain a better understanding of FL, we need to first develop and deploy both a descriptive analytical framework, the Futures Literacy Framework (FLF), and a general-purpose research tool, Futures Literacy Laboratories (FLL). Bringing these two pieces together offers *one* way of rendering largely 'invisible' conscious human anticipation more 'visible' – a way that is particularly well suited to the goals of the UNESCO FL Project (for more detail see Chapter 4).

The appropriateness of FLL for this project should not, however, be construed as a claim that there is only one approach to detecting AA. Many other methods are available for identifying, classifying and analysing AA. For instance, psychologists gather data on hope and fear, drawing attention to basic AA like a person's belief that they will be alive tomorrow. Another common AA is when politicians, voters, economists and educators all imagine the future based on the belief that education is the best stepping stone to tomorrow's jobs. Familiar situations also routinely expose people's AA, as when people flee a location because the weather service predicts the imminent arrival of a hurricane. As already noted, detailing and collecting the many AA that shape the futures people imagine can be done using a wide variety of methods, from historical analysis and anthropological studies to subjective point-of-view surveys and textual analyses. The choice of method depends on the specific scientific goals and the specific contextual relevance/feasibility of deploying one tool as opposed to another. Here, given the focus on the capacity to use-the-future (FL) the emphasis has been on FLL.

Chapters 1 to 5 provide considerable detail regarding FLL as one general-purpose approach to generating evidence of people's AA. FLL are an effective tool for detecting and inventing AA because FLL are designed in such a way that people engage directly with AS as the means for thinking collectively about the future of a topic that is meaningful to them as a group. Because FLL are collective intelligence processes that make tacit AA explicit through learning, it is a process that must always be collaboratively designed to take into account 'local' contexts. This means that independent of the specific research or instrumental goals of a particular FL Lab, for instance the future of the Sustainable Development Goals, the process whereby people are brought together to think about the future must be customised from the perspective of creating a learning environment. FLL as a general-purpose tool for revealing AA can only work if the learning process can tap into what participants in the laboratory believe and feel about the future.

Consequently FLL are only effective when the selection of participants, topic definition, physical setting, sequencing of the agenda, and learning heuristics are co-determined on-location by teams of designers and facilitators (see Chapter 4 for more on design issues). Such customisation is essential if FLL are to generate relevant and observable learning about both the topic of the lab and FL as a capability. The necessity for local customisation is also a virtue if the aim is to develop a tool for revealing AA that can be applied to a very wide and diverse range of settings around the world. Such is the case for FLL and one of the main reasons why it is an appropriate methodology for the UNESCO FL Project. By design, FLL as action-learning processes must be made to measure, adapted for specific contexts, whatever and wherever that might be.

At the same time, on the basis of the specification of process outcomes and research targets made possible by the analytical precision of the FLF, it becomes practical to develop sub-categories of FLL designed to achieve specific goals. The FLL-N deployed by this UNESCO FL Project are a case in point. Extensive details can be found in Chapters 1, 4 and 5. Here, it suffices to note that the FLL-N is built on the foundation of the general-purpose FLL with the additional research task of spanning AA that reach from the conventional to the novel. Once again, over thirty of these FLL-N have been run since 2012 (see Figure 0.1).

Findings so far: proof-of-concept achieved

The exploration of the theory and practice of FL that is reported in this book has produced four clear findings:

1 People around the world do indeed deploy anticipatory systems and processes. The FLL conducted for this project provided evidence that people can identify and change their anticipatory systems and the AA that underpin such systems. In this sense the effort to research the attributes of FL was successful, that around the world and at all levels of decision-making there are communities-of-practice that deploy anticipatory systems and practices in

order to make decisions. For the most part, these decision-makers engage in anticipatory activities without an explicit awareness of the theory and practice of thinking about the future. In other words, they are futures illiterate and the methods applied in order to integrate the future into decision-making are generally ad hoc and lack explicit and tested theories of anticipation and related design principles for applied anticipatory activities.

2   The general analytical Futures Literacy Framework (FLF) that emerged as part of this project does provide an effective theoretical foundation for the practical task of exploring humanity's largely invisible conscious anticipatory activities. The findings in this book show that the FLF provides a coherent analytical terrain that helps reveal and map people's anticipatory activities. The FLF enables: (1) the development of FL (the capacity to anticipate), (2) research into what constitutes FL, and (3) how to assess and improve the design principles used to co-create processes like FLL that are meant to improve both anticipatory practice and research. In addition, the FLF highlights the relevance of anticipatory systems research beyond individual conscious human "use-of-the-future" in fields ranging from political science and economics to biology and psychology.

3   The general purpose FLL tool is effective at identifying AA in a wide variety of contexts and the special purpose tailored FLL-N is effective at generating evidence of AA across a wide range of anticipatory systems. Actually, running over 30 of these experiments also provided important new insights and evidence concerning the design principles that make FLL and FLL-N effective approaches to understanding why and how people anticipate. This latter finding is two-fold, since it shows that the FLF is useful for designing tools for understanding anticipation and that such tools can be custom-designed to reveal specific aspects of people's AA. In this respect, this book both explores the design requirements of processes meant to develop FL and suggests directions for further research into the principles and rules for designing and running such processes. Looked at from the perspective of an innovation cycle, FLL are ready to move from the proof-of-concept phase to the prototyping phase.

4   Building on a preliminary conclusion regarding the current state of FL in the world, it looks like conscious human anticipatory activities fall into two broad and unequal camps. On one side is the large and dominant set of activities composed of an old deterministic and reductionist paradigm for conceiving and organising human agency. On the other side are traces, perhaps weak signals, of a new paradigm for understanding why and how to 'use-the-future' – with significant implications for reconceptualising the nature and exercise of human agency. This implies that there is significant potential for UNESCO and other governmental and civil society organisations to collaborate in the creation of networks capable of undertaking the formalisation and deployment of FL as a new and more effective approach to linking anticipation and decision-making. Even at a proof-of-concept level the findings reported here show the power of FL to overcome poverty of the imagination, a worldwide

scourge at the moment, and develop new sources for the invention of hope, an essential ingredient for peace. The ambitions of Agenda 2030 and the many fears that find expression in today's hate-filled current events point to the importance of stepping-up efforts to conduct the research and build the networks, at global and local levels, needed to foster FL. In this respect UNESCO could play a catalytic leadership role in changing the conditions of change by advancing FL, a new approach to anticipation in the 21st century that might transform the future.

This introduction is not the place to plunge into a detailed discussion of topics that are present throughout this book and call for much further research as well. Suffice it to point out that the evidence collected here confirms, at a proof-of-concept level, that people's anticipatory activities can span distinct anticipatory paradigms. And that revealing this requires tools that are capable of making heretofore-invisible aspects of anticipation perceptible. This, in turn, offers preliminary support for the proposition that humanity could learn how to 'use-the-future' in a more diversified way or become more futures literate. Overall these findings suggest that the theory and practice of anticipation in the 21st century may be poised to transform the way the future is used. Not just by offering improvements in the futures people imagine, but crucially in why and how people anticipate. In short, changing the way the future is used holds out a promise of changing the future.

These overarching findings also point to a more speculative intuition: that the cultivation of FL as a capability has the potential to change the way human agency is conceived and exercised, opening up new opportunities for humanity to take advantage of complexity and emergence in all its forms. This, in turn, points to an even more speculative scenario or imaginary future in which humanity adopts a different frame for understanding its role in the emergence of the collective conditions that provide part of the context for the resilience of our species. The gist is a dual hypothesis: first, that being futures literate improves the ability of people to sense and make-sense of novelty, including the richness of ephemeral time-space unique phenomena; and second, that this enhanced ability to appreciate, even cultivate complexity, for instance as 'ontological expansion' (Tuomi, 2017), might enable humans to adopt strategies intended to improve our prospects for resilience as a species by using the gift of human agency in ways that are more balanced between planning and creative spontaneity, between continuity based insurance of risk and diversification that embraces uncertainty.

Outline of the book

Chapter 1 elaborates the FLF in detail, spelling out the parameters for defining FL and then how such a frame can be used to design relevant research processes and research agendas. Chapter 2 focuses on anticipatory systems issues, developing the idea of a Discipline of Anticipation. Chapter 3 proposes a critical stepping-stone from experiments that offer proof-of-concept evidence of FL to more rigorous prototype testing based on a mathematical approach that formalises what happens in FLL.

This is potentially a breakthrough for both evaluating the accuracy of the FLF as a way to describe FL and assessing the effectiveness of different FLL designs. Chapter 4 explains the design principles that inform the operational co-creation of FLL-N as a tool for revealing and mapping FL. Chapter 5 contains summaries of 14 FLL-N case studies. Chapters 6, 7 and 8 present parallel methodological and analytical developments that reinforce the proposition that the emergence of the theory and practice of FL as a capability is part of humanity's practical efforts to find new ways to reconcile our understanding of human agency with the wonder of our complex emergent universe.

Notes

1 Throughout this book the phrase 'use-the-future' is presented in single-quotes in order to underscore two points. One is that strictly speaking, since the future does not exist in the present, it cannot be used. In other words, this phrase is shorthand for engaging in anticipatory activities. Two, and the reason for still using the phrase despite the risk of sowing confusion, is that it is important to draw attention to the fact that humans instrumentalise the future. Anticipation is used for many purposes and in many ways – this is the meaning of 'use-the-future'.
2 Today there is some speculation about so-called 'block time', in which the past, present and future all coexist. Nevertheless, for the moment, at a practical level even if the future may exist simultaneously with the present, it is not accessible (Tibbs, 2017).
3 In the case of non-conscious anticipation, discussed in greater detail in Chapters 1 and 2, the terms 'imagination' and 'anticipatory assumptions' may seem somewhat inappropriate. How does a tree imagine or have AA? Despite the strangeness of applying such terms to non-conscious living organisms there is a pertinent similarity. The inventiveness of evolutionary processes and the encoding that occurs through genetic and instinctual codes can be seen as being analogues of conscious imagination and assumptions.

References

Argyris, C. and Schon, D. A. (1996) *Organizational Learning: A Theory of Action Perspective*. Boston, MA: Addison-Wesley.
Bateson, G. (2000) *Steps to an Ecology of Mind*. Chicago, IL: University of Chicago Press.
Bergson, H. (1913) *Time and Free Will: An Essay on the Immediate Data of Consciousness*. New York: George Allen and Company.
Bergson, H. and Mitchell, A. (2005) *Creative Evolution*, trans. Arthur Mitchell. New York: Random House Modern Library.
Bryant, P. J. (1994) *A Brief History and Review of Accelerators*. Geneva: CERN. Available at: https://cds.cern.ch/record/261062/files/p1_2.pdf (Accessed: 29 August 2017).
Chiu, L. F. (2003) 'Transformational Potential of Focus Group Practice in Participatory Action Research', *Action Research*, 1(2), pp. 165–183. doi: 10.1177/14767503030012006.
Dewey, J. (1997) *How We Think*. Buffalo, New York: Prometheus Books.
Fleck, L. (1979) *Genesis and Development of a Scientific Fact*. Chicago, IL: The University of Chicago Press.
Fuller, T. (2017) 'Anxious Relationships: The Unmarked Futures for Post-Normal Scenarios in Anticipatory Systems', *Technological Forecasting & Social Change*, 124, pp. 41–50.

Henry, C. and Bruin, A. de (2011) *Entrepreneurship and the Creative Economy: Process, Practice and Policy*. Cheltenham: Edward Elgar Publishing Ltd.

International Sociological Association (2016) *The Futures We Want: Global Sociology and the Struggles for a Better World*. Available at: http://futureswewant.net/about/ (Accessed: 29 August 2017).

Knorr Cetina, K. (1999) *Epistemic Cultures: How the Sciences Make Knowledge*. Cambridge, MA: Harvard University Press.

Kuhn, T. S. (1970) *The Structure of Scientific Revolutions*. Chicago, IL: The University of Chicago Press.

Lewin, K. (1946) 'Action Research and Minority Problems', *Journal of Social Issues*, 2(4), pp. 34–46. doi: 10.1111/j.1540-4560.1946.tb02295.x.

Lévy, P. (1997) *Collective Intelligence: Mankind's Emerging World in Cyberspace*. New York: Plenum Trade.

Macdonald, C. (2012) 'Understanding Participatory Action Research: A Qualitative Research Methodology Option', *Canadian Journal of Action Research*, 13(2), pp. 34–50.

Miettinen, R. (2000) 'The Concept of Experiential Learning and John Dewey's Theory of Reflective Thought and Action', *International Journal of Lifelong Education*, 9(1), pp. 54–72.

Miller, R. (2007) 'Futures Literacy: A Hybrid Strategic Scenario Method', *Futures*, 39(4), pp. 341–362.

Miller, R. (2011) 'Using the Future: A Practical Approach to Embracing Complexity', *Ethos – Journal of the Singapore Civil Service*, Singapore.

Miller, R. (2014) *Networking to Improve Global/Local Anticipatory Capacities – A Scoping Exercise: Narrative Report*. Paris: UNESCO/Rockefeller Foundation.

Miller, R. (2015) *Evaluating and Improving the Use of the Future for Identifying and Choosing Dynamic Opportunities*. Paris: UNESCO/Rockefeller Foundation.

Miller, R. and Poli, R. (2010) 'Anticipatory Systems and the Philosophical Foundations of Futures Studies', *Foresight*, 12(3), pp. 7–17.

Nadin, M. (2016) 'Anticipation and Computation: Is Anticipatory Computing Possible?', in Nadin, M. (ed.) *Anticipation Across Disciplines*. Cham: Springer Publishing, pp. 283–339.

Poli, R. (2014) 'Book Review and Abstracts: Anticipatory Systems: Philosophical, Mathematical and Methodological Foundations', *International Journal of General Systems*, 43(8), pp. 897–901.

Robson, C. (2002) *Real World Research*. 2nd edn. Malden: Blackwell. Available at: http://www.dem.fmed.uc.pt/Bibliografia/Livros_Educacao_Medica/Livro34.pdf. (Accessed: 29 August 2017).

Rosen, R. (1985) *Anticipatory Systems: Philosophical, Mathematical, and Methodological Foundations*. Oxford: Pergamon Press.

Rosen, R. (1991) *Life Itself: A Comprehensive Inquiry into the Nature, Origin, and Fabrication of Life*. New York: Columbia University Press.

Schneider, S. H. (2012) *The Primordial Bond: Exploring Connections between Man and Nature through the Humanities and Sciences*. Cham: Springer Publishing.

Sutter, J. (1983) *L'anticipation: Psychologie et Psychopathologie*. 1st edn. Paris: Presses Universitaires de France.

Tibbs, H. (2017) 'Future Anticipatory Practices', in Poli, R. (ed.) *The Handbook of Anticipation: Theoretical and Applied Aspects of the Use of Future in Decision Making*. Cham: Springer International Publishing, pp. 1–23.

Tuomi, I. (2005) 'The Future of Learning in the Knowledge Society: Disruptive Changes for Europe by 2020', in Punie, Y. and Cabrera, M. (eds) *The Future of ICT and Learning in the Knowledge Society: Report on a Joint DG JRC-DG EAC Workshop Held in Seville, 20–21 October 2005*. Luxemburg: European Commission.

Tuomi, I. (2017) 'Ontological Exapnsion', in Poli, R. (ed.) *Handbook of Anticipation: Theoretical and Applied Aspects of the Use of the Future in Decision Making*. Cham: Springer International Publishing.

Weschsler, D. (1971) 'Concept of Collective Intelligence', *American Psychologist*, 26(10), pp. 904–907. doi: 10.1037/h0032223.

Wittgenstein, L. (translation Peter Winch) (1984) *Culture and Value*. New edition. Chicago, IL: University of Chicago Press.

Yilmaz, S. and Seifert, C. M. (2011) 'Creativity Through Design Heuristics: A Case Study of Expert Product Design', *Design Studies*, 32(4), pp. 384–415. doi: 10.1016/j.destud.2011.01.003.

Yu, L., Nickerson, J. V. and Sakamoto, Y. (2012) 'Collective Creativity: Where We Are and Where We Might Go', Proceedings of *Collective Intelligence Conference 2012 (CI2012)*. Available at: https://ssrn.com/abstract=2037908 (Accessed: 22 January 2018).

Part I
Discovering anticipation in the 21st century

Towards Futures Literacy?

1 Sensing and making-sense of Futures Literacy

Towards a Futures Literacy Framework (FLF)

Riel Miller

Futures Literacy (FL) is a capability. A futures literate person has acquired the skills needed to decide why and how to use their imagination to introduce the non-existent future into the present. These anticipatory activities play an important role in what people see and do. Developing a detailed description of this capability to 'use-the-future' calls for an analytical framework that can clarify the nature of different anticipatory systems and guide both research into FL and its acquisition as a skill. Such a framework is presented in this chapter, focusing on the sub-set of anticipatory systems and processes that humans use when they consciously imagine the future.

The first section briefly presents a case study in order to introduce the key concepts of the Futures Literacy Framework (FLF). The second section spells out some of the main analytical challenges that the FLF is meant to address given that FL is as an emergent and evolving capability. The next section describes the FLF in detail, explaining the different ontological and epistemological categories that are used to map FL. The fourth and final section provides two illustrations of how the FLF can be used. The first part explains how the FLF can be used to situate and design Futures Literacy Laboratories (FLL), a general-purpose tool that reveals anticipatory assumptions (AA), and then a more specific task-oriented sub-category of FLL designed specifically for the research agenda of this project regarding novelty, the FLL-N. The second part discusses how the FLF can be used to situate the theory and practice of Future Studies (FS) in ways that clarify why particular tools are more or less appropriate for specific tasks as well as pointing to the potential to both deepen and enlarge the discipline beyond the boundaries of currently dominant theory and practice.

Searching for Futures Literacy in Sierra Leone

In early 2014, in the aftermath of a horrific civil war, but before the devastation of the Ebola epidemic, UNESCO organised a FLL-N in Freetown, Sierra Leone (Case Study 5 in Chapter 5). The Lab was designed to explore the transition from 'youth' to 'adult' in the Sierra Leone of the future. On the face of it this task involved one of the most universal ways of 'using-the-future': imagining 'growing-up'. Age progression is the familiar model we apply when we imagine that a crawling baby will learn to walk. Personal experience has forged this frame, we all know that in due course – assuming nothing unusual happens – the baby will 'grow-up', which is why we do not chastise a baby for not yet knowing how to walk. Nor do we apply intensive remedial therapy because we are worried that crawling will impede walking. We make sense of the crawling baby through the frame of the temporal journey from infant to child to adolescent to adult.

This 'growing-up' story is accessible and perhaps even the dominant template humans use to imagine the future. The frame of 'growing-up' (Goffman, 1974), with its pictures of the tomorrows we will catch-up with or converge on, enables us to sense and make-sense of what a baby is doing now. And it is a clear illustration of how people 'use-the-future' by deploying an anticipatory system (AS) to understand the present. For most people, this kind of elementary anticipation comes automatically, without the need for explicit awareness. And since they do not need to think explicitly about the anticipatory systems and process they deploy to 'use-the-future', people rarely consider that the future can be 'used' for different reasons and with different methods. For example, in the Sierra Leone FLL-N a diverse group of participants, spanning different ages, origins and professions, were startled when they discovered that by breaking with the simple 'growing-up' frame for imagining the future they could expand what they sense and make sense of in the present.

Through a co-designed, highly context-sensitive collective intelligence process that used different futures, the participants in the Sierra Leone FLL-N became aware of their anticipatory assumptions (AA), making it possible to invent futures less constrained by the frame of catching-up or converging with today's idea of an adult or yesterday's idea of what it meant to 'grow-up'. By undertaking a learning voyage that developed their futures literacy they were able to call into question the frames that confine the transition from youth to adult to a set of pre-existing rites of passage along linear and hierarchical paths to old age. Instead participants in the Sierra Leone FLL-N explored and invented alternative images, definitions and conditions for autonomy, responsibility, trust and wisdom in their specific post-conflict community. They challenged terms like 'youth' and 'adult' that for them obscured more than revealed the actual lived experiences and meanings of people's current roles and positions in their local community.

Initially, participants were surprised that the frame of 'growing-up' turned out to be inadequate, even counter-productive. But as their capacity to 'use-the-future' developed they started to not only imagine different futures but also learn that there are different kinds of anticipation. Both the meaning of 'becoming responsible' and the avenues for getting there changed. Different imaginary futures enabled new ways of seeing the present. As participants started to become futures literate they began to understand the power of anticipation in shaping what they see and do.

The sequence of the FLL-N as an action learning process unfolds as follows.

1 Participants experience and become explicitly conscious of how the future plays a central role in what they perceive and pay attention to in the present.

2   By changing the way they 'use-the-future' participants started to realise that they can anticipate in different ways and thereby imagine different futures.
3   By putting together the first and second insights participants begin to understand that imagining different futures changes what they could see and do in the present.
4   By imagining different futures participants become aware of their own capacity to invent the underlying anticipatory assumptions (AA) that shape their of-necessity fictional descriptions of the later-than-now. By starting to acquire FL they become better at rooting their AA in their own history and specific socio-economic-cultural context. Participants begin to reassess their perceptions of the present, depictions of the past and aspirations for the future.
5   Through engagement in the knowledge co-creation processes of the FLL-N participants begin to acquire the capacity to design this kind of collective intelligence process that enables them to choose why and how to anticipate, contributing to the acquisition of the skills that make up FL.

The structured processes of FLL as a general-purpose tool for revealing AA shows that people can use different kinds of future, for different reasons and by deploying different methods. The FLL-N customised for this project generated evidence that being futures literate facilitates the discovery and invention of novel phenomena in the present. Designing these processes as well as testing different hypotheses about FL requires a systematic and comprehensive analytical framework that enables both practitioners and researchers to distinguish why and how to 'use-the-future' for specific ends in particular contexts. This is the role of the FLF and a key step towards gaining a better understanding of the evolving capability of FL.

The challenge of mapping an emergent and evolving capability

Efforts to conduct research into defining and mapping FL need to take into account its continuously emerging and evolving aspects as well as the acquired stock of what is 'already known' about 'using-the-future'. FL as a capability is reflexive, in the sense that through practice people invent and redefine the way they 'use-the-future', and it is constructive in so far as the constant 'use-of-the-future' plays a role in building up the world around us – including why and how we anticipate (Misuraca, Codagnone and Rossel, 2013). The challenge of developing an analytical framework for understanding FL, already a moving target, is compounded by the fact that many theories such as complexity and anticipatory systems theories, and practices such as action learning and collective intelligence knowledge creation (CIKC) processes that enable people to sense and make-sense of FL are only now starting to appear in explicit and coherent form.

At the outset of this effort to define and map FL then, it is important to note that both the results reported in this book and the FL Framework (FLF), elaborated in order to provide a theoretically and analytically grounded approach to

FL, are necessarily of an exploratory, preliminary, tentative, and even inventive character. Research into such emergent phenomena need to not only seek out the relevant strong- and weak-signals, but also try to account for the possibility that engaging in such inquiry can actually generate or invent new concepts, relationships, processes and even systems. As Popper argues in the following quote:

> Our very understanding of the world changes the conditions of a changing world; and so do our wishes, our preferences, our motivations, our hopes, our dreams, our phantasies, our hypotheses, our theories. Even our erroneous theories change the world, although our correct theories may, as a rule have a more lasting influence. All of this amounts to the fact that *determinism is simply mistaken*: all of its traditional arguments have withered away and indeterminism and free will have become part of the physical and biological sciences.
>
> ('Two New Views of Causality', Popper, 1990, p. 17, emphasis in original)

The FLF sketched over the following pages reflects today's evolving conditions for thinking about the future and picks up on the research and experiences of many people, across many fields of theory and practice. In particular, the research results reported here have benefitted significantly from the work done on: anticipatory systems (Rosen, 1985; Nadin, 2010a, 2010b; Rossel, 2010; Tuomi, 2012; Miller and Poli, 2010); complexity (Ulanowicz, 1979; Rosen, 1986; Ehresmann and Vanbremeersch, 1987; Kauffman, 1995; Delanda, 2006; Poli, 2009); management (Snowden, 2002; Stacey, 2007; Wilenius, 2008; Fuller, 2017); governance (Sen, 1999; Mulgan and Albury, 2003; Unger, 2007; Boyd *et al.*, 2015); knowledge creation/management (Nonaka, 1994; Wegner, 1998; Tuomi, 1999; Lewin and Massini, 2004; Paavola, Lipponen and Hakkarainen, 2004; Latour, 2005); human agency/behaviour (Archer, 2002; Kahneman, 2012); and Futures Studies (Slaughter, 1996; Ogilvy, 2002; Bishop and Hines, 2006; Godet, 2006; Masini, 2006; Miller, 2007b; Inayatullah, 2008; Fuller, 2017; Ramírez and Wilkinson, 2016). Other fields of both practice and research, running from design thinking (Kimbell, 2011) and participatory decision-making (Scharmer, 2007; Kahane, 2012; Hassan, 2014) to the widespread implementation of action learning (Adler and Clark, 1991) and action research (Hult and Lennung, 1980; Robson and Turner, 2007) in many different contexts, have also played an important role in the discovery and elucidation of why and how people 'use-the-future'.

Of course, FL is not the first capability to be analysed by researchers and philosophers. FL, like many such general and regularly practised capabilities, can be described from different perspectives, including philosophical and applied, cognitive and prescriptive (Sen, 1999; Nussbaum, 2011; Poli, 2015). Skills like reading and writing have been defined and analysed on the basis of different theories, such as Piaget's Theory of Cognitive Development (Wadsworth, 1971), and practices like genre-based learning-to-write pedagogies (Rose and Martin, 2012). Widely dispersed social capabilities can also be described in macro-functional terms (Bourdieu and Passeron, 1977; Bauman, 2013; Giddens, 1991; Beck, 1992), as in the case of the general society-wide diffusion of the basic capacity to read and write, a central aspect of the transition from peasant to industrial society (Miller, 2007a). The bottom line is that efforts to describe such cross-cutting and frequently used capabilities must go beyond static approaches that only see repositories of knowledge ready to be downloaded by receptive citizens, consumers or students. Over time, as contexts change and new phenomena emerge, the nature of a capability such as what it means to be 'literate' or in this case futures literate, at personal and societal levels, also evolves (Trilling and Fadel, 2009).

The need to simultaneously detect and invent FL calls for a research methodology that is capable of discerning continuity and difference in the processes and categories of 'using-the-future'. As it turns out, addressing this kind of double or recursive analytical challenge is precisely one of the vocations of FL. 'Using-the-future' to understand the present already attempts to address a chicken-and-egg type conundrum. Or to use another metaphor, the effort to map FL is like having to invent the thief who is then able to catch a thief. Gregory Bateson expresses this notion of engaging in knowledge creation where there is reciprocity between 'product as process and process as product' by inventing a term: "metalogue" (Bateson, 2000, p. 1). Gathering evidence about why and how people 'use-the-future' calls for this type of 'metalogue' methodology, a double movement design that enables researchers "to learn from actors without imposing on them an 'a priori' definition of their world building capacities" (Latour, 1999, p. 20). In other words, research into FL is challenging not only because of its implicit, quasi-hidden status in today's world but also because this type of broad capability is both reflexive and a part of so many other skills, with so many evolving facets.

In the beginning: "what is the future?"

An analysis of FL must start with a definition of what is the future. Then, on that basis, turn to the challenges of why and how to 'use-the-future'. As already touched upon in the introduction to this book, in practical terms the future only exists in the present as some form of anticipation. The future qua future remains the potential that the later-than-now will arrive. But that future cannot exist in the present, since if it did it would no longer be the future.[1] Hence anticipation is the only way that the future is actually expressed in the present. This shifts the focus to the systems and processes that allow anticipation to become an identifiable and active part of the present. The future therefore exists in the present as anticipation and anticipation is generated through active systems and processes.

This ontological perspective on the future matters for FL for at least two reasons. First because differences in the kinds of future being imagined generate differences in both what humans perceive and the meanings they associate with what they perceive. Second because 'what' matters for 'how'. Or, to put it another way, how people try to understand the future depends on what kind of future they are trying to understand. As Poli (2011, p. 75) notes in his important work exploring the ontology of anticipation: ". . . elements of ontology should become part and parcel of the set of categorical tools that any working futurist should have at his or her disposal".

Having identified the need to ground the future at an ontological level invites the next question: what is the basis for distinguishing different kinds of future? Here the work of the mathematical biologist Robert Rosen (Rosen, 1985) offers a crucial insight. His work considers the anticipatory systems of single-celled organisms and makes the case for integrating anticipation into the basic definition of life. Anticipation is the capacity of an organism to incorporate the later-than-now into its functioning in ways that are relevant. Focusing the relevance of the later-than-now on 'functioning' provides an 'actionable dimension' to the definition of anticipation. However, this formulation can encompass rather passive forms of action, like non-conscious sensing and conscious efforts to know – which are actions that may or may not have further consequences related to reactions, like leaves falling, or choices like deciding to take an umbrella if the weather forecast predicts rain.[2]

This perspective throws into relief the ontological difference between conscious and non-conscious anticipation, making it evident that at a fundamental level it is feasible and meaningful to distinguish anticipatory systems that operationalise different kinds of future. The anticipation of trees or protozoa is not the same thing as anticipation by a cat or a human. Rosen's anticipatory systems perspective not only helps to justify and motivate a search for a diversity of responses to the question: 'what is the future?'. It also points to the need for a framework to help guide efforts to distinguish different anticipatory systems (see Chapter 2 for a discussion of the Discipline of Anticipation (DoA)).

Two kinds of future: two different anticipatory systems

When people 'use-the-future', what is the future that they are using? Or as we shall see: what are the futures, plural, that they are using? One fruitful approach to revealing the ontological aspects of conscious human use-of-the-future is to apply Heidegger's "Being versus beings" distinction (Heidegger, 1962) to different kinds of explicit anticipation, specifically the difference between anticipation-for-the-future (AfF) versus anticipation-for-emergence (AfE). The 'being' of AfF is the future as a goal – a planned/desired future that people bet on. There are many 'beings' of this kind of future, ranging from when you take an umbrella to be prepared if it rains to planning to climb Mount Everest. In contrast, the 'being' of AfE is in a sense a non-future, from the dominant AfF perspective. The future of AfE is one that is not a goal or target meant to structure the making of preparatory and planning bets. The later-than-now imagined in AfE is a disposable construct, a throwaway non-goal that need not be constrained by probability or desirability.

AfF is the overwhelmingly prevalent form that the future takes when people use it in their everyday life. For the most part, humans have internalised the relevant anticipatory systems (AS) and related knowledge creation processes (KCP) before they can even speak. For instance, very young babies cry out when hungry, motivated by the expectation that food will then arrive, and are able to project the trajectory of a ball that is rolling along a table (Bower and Paterson, 1973; Wang, Baillargeon and Brueckner, 2004). These anticipatory capabilities are the foundation for everyday tasks, like preparing for rain by deciding to wear a raincoat or planning to sell phones by building the relevant kind of factory. Generally, when people are asked about what kinds of futures they use they are not even aware that they constantly deploy anticipatory systems, even less that the future can be anything other than a goal (AfF).

The current monopoly of AfF as the only way to 'use-the-future' is evident in many different ways, particularly in terms of the frame used for human agency. AfF is what gives meaning and force to today's ubiquitous slogan: 'make a difference'. AfF is the frame that legitimises and incentivises the grandiose claims being made by leaders worldwide that they can impose their will on tomorrow. In a nutshell, the imperative is to colonise tomorrow with today's idea of tomorrow. As a result, the formulation of human agency in terms of decision-making and the responsibilities that go with it focus almost exclusively on the future as a goal (AfF) and so anticipatory activities concentrate on setting and achieving this goal. Given this obsession it is not surprising that almost all the theoretical and practical knowledge that makes up fields like Future Studies (FS) are about AfF.

Of course, it may seem that this is hardly a problem or controversial. 'Using-the-future' in this way has worked fairly well up until now and comes to most people, even babies, quite easily. So why attempt to both discover other kinds of future and expand the kinds of future that people use? Aside from the rationale that the discovery of new or ignored aspects of reality is a worthy scientific endeavour in and of itself, the main reason is that an exclusive focus on AfF narrows human agency in two reductionist ways.

First, people do not practise diversifying their 'uses-of-the-future' and therefore do not develop the capacity to go beyond probability and planning futures, with an exclusive focus on the relevant 'closed' anticipatory systems (AS) and related knowledge creation processes (KCP). Second, by boxing-in the conception of agency AfF biases what people see and do to choices that seem less threatened by uncertainty or more 'reasonably' safe from uncertainty or changes in the conditions of change. Not only does this obscure the richness of complexity and the plethora of experiments that generate novelty all around us, it gives excessive weight to 'robust' options that often take the form of heavy investments that generate legacy systems and the burdens of path dependency.

In other words, despite the fact that the world is non-ergodic (North, 1999; Taleb, 2010; Davidson, 2012) and the conditions of change do indeed change, most AfF assumes the opposite: an ergodic world. The almost exclusive focus on AfF frames human agency in a way that biases what we see and do towards a search for certainty and comforts humanity's currently prevalent delusions of omnipotence. And, of particular relevance here, it inhibits the development of FL because it impedes the search for anticipatory systems and processes that are outside of AfF. In a curious twist, the ergodic assumption that dominates fields like economics – an assumption of no change in the conditions of change – obscures precisely one of the key potential changes in the world around us: the way we anticipate. The 'what-if' being suggested here is that conscious human anticipation may be able to reframe the search for certainty and thereby the framing of human agency.

Walking on two legs

Moving beyond an AfF mono-vision or helping people to 'walk-on-two-legs', to use Mao's dual-paradigm slogan (Mao, 1977) by deploying both forms of anticipation cannot start at an epistemological level because there is an inherent practical contradiction between AfF as a search for certainty and alternatives that instrumentalise a different kind of future for a different purpose. Diversifying the ways in which the future is used, beyond the AfF's planning and preparation, calls for the recognition of another kind of future – one that is distinct at an ontological level from AfF. As already noted, this other future is called here, in an initial terminological foray, anticipation-for-emergence (AfE). Although at first this kind of future may seem quite strange, AfE is not about the future as a goal or instrument for getting to some future – any future. Rather AfE is a use of the future to sense and make sense of aspects of the present, particularly novelty, which tends to be obscured by AfF.

'Walking on two legs' is about becoming better able to engage in spontaneity and improvisation through acquiring the knowledge needed to sense and make-sense of emergent complexity, including its crucial specificity-unique (SU) and ephemeral dimensions. This is a critical step in becoming able to embrace complexity rather than just lamenting it as some cursed and inescapable source of 'wicked problems'. It is about finding ways to reconcile human agency with the origins of our freedom in a creative universe (Bergson, 1998; Kauffman, 2016). Perhaps an infoverse (Wendt, 2015; Wheeler in Kobaysahi and Nihon Butsuri Gakkai, 1990) characterised by ontological expansion (Tuomi, 2017) that invites a new strategic approach to resilience by leveraging complexity and the diversification novelty affords. Clearly not today's everyday way of 'using-the-future' (Miller, 2011; Ogilvy, 2011; Miller, 2015b).

Leaving aside the challenge of how to detect and make practical use of AfE, addressed in some detail in the discussion of FLL in the fourth section below and Chapters 3 to 5, the key point at this stage is that the identification of two broad categories of ontologically distinct kinds of future allows for the specification of the primary hypothesis tested at a proof-of-concept level by the research reported here. The hypothesis is this: when people engage in a knowledge creation process designed to imagine the future in the form of anticipation-for-emergence (AfE) it is easier to: (1) sense and make-sense of existing but otherwise invisible emergent-novelty, and (2) invent or innovate – the actual creation of emergent-novelty. The proposition is that imagining AfE futures makes it easier for people to: invent new words; sense and make-sense of the novel; imagine the potential for the persistence of changes that are always initially locally unique and seemingly ephemeral; and pose questions that are new because they can detect and invent phenomena that make up the emergent present, including new paradigms.

In part, AfE does this by loosening the grip of AfF on what is sensed and made-sense of. Formulated in negative terms the hypothesis is that, at a minimum, using this other kind of future (AfE) helps to deconstruct those aspects of the present that are held in place as repetition by existing expected and desired futures (AfF).

Posed positively, liberating the future through AfE gives direct access to creative novel aspects of the present that are inaccessible through AfF. Initial, proof-of-concept level evidence from efforts to test this hypothesis can be found in Chapter 5 containing the case studies that report on experiments that use AfE to identify and generate novelty. Getting people to engage with these two ways of 'using-the-future' – AfF and AfE – provides an opportunity to test both the negative and positive propositions: that AfF constrains perception of novelty in the present and AfE facilitates it.

The choice of what kind of future to think about also plays a critical role in making epistemological choices, the choice of the knowledge creation processes (KCP) that actually generate different kinds of imaginary futures – AfE and AfF. Furthermore, distinguishing between the 'what' and the 'how', or the ontological and the epistemological aspects of 'using-the-future', provides the foundation for developing a more complete analytical map of FL as a capability. This map, as depicted in Figure 1.1, outlines key aspects of a Futures Literacy Framework (FLF). The FLF is intended to serve as both an analytical structure for generating evidence and testing hypotheses as well as an inclusive 'big tent' for understanding and developing the capability of humans to 'use-the-future' (see second part of the fourth section below for a discussion of the relationship of the FLF to Futures Studies (FS)).

The Futures Literacy Framework (FLF)

The Futures Literacy Framework (FLF) as depicted in Figure 1.1 is an analytical tool for describing the different attributes of FL as a capability. As is evident when looking at Figure 1.1, the FLF being advanced here covers both different kinds of futures (ontology) and how to know these different futures (epistemology) as the basis for describing FL. The ontological categories are on the left-hand side of Figure 1.1 and the epistemological ones are on the upper right. Drawing the intersection between these two sets of characteristics of FL generates six distinct clusters of anticipatory assumptions (AA1 to AA6) in the domain of conscious human 'use-of-the-future'.

This framework for describing why and how people 'use-the-future' is useful because it contributes to:

1 developing FL by helping to construct the learning processes that enable people to 'use-the-future' in different ways depending on aims, means and context;
2 exploring FL by helping to identify existing and new topics for research;
3 determining the best methods to conduct research into FL by helping to select the appropriate design criteria; and
4 FL as a practice by helping to determine which tools for thinking about the future are most appropriate for the kind of future being thought about in a given context.

24 *Riel Miller*

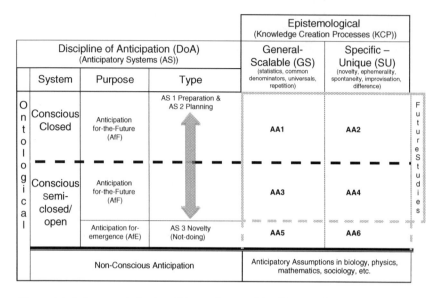

Figure 1.1 A framework for describing and researching Futures Literacy

As already touched upon in the Introduction, AA are the fundamental descriptive and analytical building blocks for understanding FL and 'using-the-future'. The reason that AA are the basic analytical unit of the FLF is that conscious human anticipation can only occur on the basis of AA of one kind or another. AA are what enable people to describe imaginary futures. AA define the frames and models that are used to invent the content of the fictions that are conscious human anticipation. By definition therefore, being futures literate is the capacity to identify, design, target and deploy AA. Giving AA a central role also draws attention to the difference between FL as the conscious human capability to anticipate and non-conscious anticipation. When anticipation occurs without explicit conscious imagining, such as with trees or single-cell creatures or through the functioning of capitalist competition, the AA are of a different, non-volitional character. This is why the bottom of Figure 1.1 designates non-conscious anticipation as the kind of future that is relevant to fields like biology, physics, mathematics, sociology, economics, etc. In these fields, the later-than-now at an ontological, 'what-is-it?' level is defined and incorporated into anticipatory systems, at least up until recently, by exclusively non-volitional evolutionary processes.

Returning to conscious human anticipation, one of the virtues of designating AA as the theoretical and practical core of human anticipatory capabilities (FL) is that AA can be described and situated on the basis of the intersection of different AS and KCP, as per the FLF depicted in Figure 1.1. Such a dual coordinate approach to defining and describing anticipatory capabilities rests on the proposition that conscious human anticipation always depends on the capacity to imagine. In turn, this means that the relationship between AS and KCP that are relevant for FL must, in one way or another, contribute to the invention and description of different kinds of imaginary futures or, in the terms of the FLF: different anticipatory systems (AS). Conscious anticipation is fundamentally about producing fiction. As a result the KCP that are relevant is restricted to those frames (Goffman, 1974; Lakoff, 2006; Kahneman, 2012) that enable meaningful descriptions of imaginary futures.

These three terms – AA, AS and KCP – are defined in detail in this chapter as part of the FLF and used extensively to describe the customised FLL-N design that was used for the case studies presented in this volume. Overall, it is the development of the Futures Literacy Framework (FLF), as a specification of the theory of anticipatory systems (AS), knowledge creation processes (KCP) and the relationship between the two as defined by clusters of anticipatory assumptions (AA), that enables a Bateson (2000) type 'metalogue' approach to researching the emergence and evolution of the human capability to 'use-the-future' (FL).

To set the stage for the rest of the book the following sub-sections offer an initial discussion of the three distinct areas of the FLF as presented in Figure 1.1: (1) ontological; (2) epistemological; and (3) anticipatory assumptions AA1 to AA6. And, as already noted, the fourth section then turns to consideration of two examples of the application of the FLF, first to the design of the FLL-N research tool used in this project, and second to the application of the FLF to advancing the theory and practice of Future Studies (FS).

Ontological side

A framework for describing the capacity to 'use-the-future' needs to start, as already discussed, with the ontological question: what kind of future is being used? A range of answers to this question can be found on the right-hand side of Figure 1.1, covered by the overarching label: The Discipline of Anticipation (DoA). The DoA (see Chapter 2) explores the different kinds of future that are associated with distinctive sets of anticipatory systems (AS) and extends, at the bottom of Figure 1.1, to non-conscious anticipation (Rosen, 1985; Poli, 2010, 2014).

The ontological side of conscious anticipation (DoA) is divided into three categories – system, purpose, type – for defining *what* kind of future or the nature of the subject of the AS humans use when they are consciously 'using-the-future'.

At a *system level*, there are two distinct categories: closed and semi-closed/ semi-open. Closed system anticipation is defined by AA that limit the number and nature of the variables used to imagine the future. The world is assumed to be ergodic, or not subject to changes in the conditions of change (North 1999; Popper, 1990). One of the most familiar forms of this type of closed systems use-of-the-future can be found in the field of macro-economic forecasting where the assumption is explicitly *ceteris paribus* or 'all other things being equal – or constant'. Semi-closed/semi-open systems anticipation is defined by AA that accept that the conditions of change may change and that novelty characterises emergent reality. The difference between semi-closed and semi-open is one of degree and practical choices regarding the different levels of reality – or the extent to which a prior assumption constrains the next level assumptions (Poli, 2001, pp. 261–283). In practice, given current limitations of conscious human AS, which may change in presently unimaginable ways, humans can only use a semi-open kind of future due to our inherent linguistic and cognitive limitations. Conscious 'use-of-the-future' – the explicit imagining of the later-than-now – can only be done at the moment with words and cognitive framing, some of which may originate/be influenced by the 'unconscious'. So even if humans may be capable of imagining being beyond dualisms like mortal/immortal or parts/wholes or finite/infinite we are still constrained when anticipating the future by our current forms of consciousness (Montemayor and Haladjian, 2015). For now, the range from closed to 'semi-open' kind of future is all that conscious human anticipation can access. However, it is worth noting that non-conscious anticipatory systems, like those found in trees or single-celled organisms, 'use-the-future' in a form which is not constrained by the parameters that define humanity's capacity to imagine. Such non-conscious anticipation cannot distinguish between open and closed – instead it incorporates a kind of non-future future. Institutions and social systems may have some similar qualities, but in this book the focus is on direct human agency.

At a teleological or *purpose level*, already discussed above, it is contended here that humans can consciously use two basic kinds of future: anticipation-for-the-future (AfF) and anticipation-for-emergence (AfE). The key feature that distinguishes these two forms of anticipation at the applied level of AA shown in Figure 1.1 is the extent to which the imaginary futures are constrained or unconstrained by the imperatives of probability and desirability. As the discussion of the different fields of AA1 to AA6 will highlight, this is a question of degree and the boundaries are not always razor thin or airtight. Take the widespread example of imagining improvements to existing systems – this is an 'adaptive' or reform-oriented perspective. Imagining the realisation of endogenous changes that result in the 'optimal' school or hospital, one that solves all the problems on today's agenda, can be the outcome of combining both closed and semi-open anticipatory assumptions. But the dividing line between AfF and AfE is precisely on either side of the choice of why to imagine the future and the consequences such a choice has for the selection of different kinds of closed versus more open anticipatory assumptions.

As Figure 1.1 shows, there is no overlap between closed AS and AfE, but there can be some overlap between semi-open AS and AfF. Here the degree of openness is in part a proxy for the desire for 'inventiveness' and in part the extent to which the assumptions used to imagine the future are constrained by continuity. All of this plays a role in determining where the imagining process starts and the extent to which the consideration of 'creative reforms' or 'endogenous innovation' run up against the boundaries of existing systems. Indeed today, given the lack of FL, most efforts to innovate fall into AA3. Turning to AfE, the lack of overlap with closed AS reflects the difference in the fundamental purpose of imagining the future, but as already noted AfE cannot avoid making some closed assumptions due to the inescapable constraint of human framing in the here and now.

The third column under the DoA still organises different anticipatory activities based on differences in the kind of future being used. The three different *types* of anticipatory systems, integrating more operational or practical/organisational AA, are: AS1: Preparatory; AS2: Planning; and AS3: Novel (Miller, 2015b).

- **AS1**: In the case of preparatory futures the key ontological level anticipatory assumption is that the future(s) being imagined is amenable to both ex-ante and closed systemic definition and to preparatory and/or pre-emptive action by human agency, usually on the basis of simulation methods. Simulation is of necessity a closed framework based on given variables, ranges of variation and fixed rules governing dynamics. Ontologically such futures are contingent, occurring when there is a 'disruption' by an external force, which may be positive or negative. The AA in AS1 are selected with the aim of preparing for contingencies, both the 'good' ones and the 'bad'.
- **AS2**: With respect to planning futures, the key ontological level anticipatory assumption is that the past determines the future and hence the conditions of change are assumed to be predictable and so future phenomenon are amenable to closed systems probabilistic estimation and, in most cases, subject to influence by human agency. This type of 'planned future' is defined so that it is practical to calculate the odds of successfully reaching the objective by different paths. Why choose one route over another in order to get to the top of Mount Everest, or which policy is more likely to improve the outcomes of existing school systems? These closed system, ex-ante results-based futures also include normative or 'better/worse tomorrow' anticipation. These are desired futures that motivate through the hope of being able to impose today's ideas of tomorrow on tomorrow. The AA in AS2 are selected with the aim of planning the realisation of a specific future outcome – even if chosen from amongst many different possible futures – to find actionable ways to 'colonise tomorrow'.
- **AS3**: The underpinning anticipatory assumption that defines the third operational type of anticipatory system is that the future is non-actionable from the present or, to put it another way, that actions in the present do not have a significant predictable causal relationship with future outcomes. At the ontological level of what is the future, the AA that make up AS3 constrain the construction of imaginary futures to ones that are not the outcome of probabilistic or normative causal sequential preparation and planning. The dissociation of anticipation from the future as goal (AfF) is not intended to mimic the blind evolutionary processes that shape the AS in 'nature' or strip humans of our capacity to act and consciously imagine. Rather AS3 is focused on the present, 'using-the-future' to reveal complex emergence, rich with previously unknowable unknowns (novelty). This is not meant to deny or exclude the insights into the present generated by AS1 and AS2, just assist with the invention or discovery of phenomena that are novel,

cannot immediately be associated with repetition. The futures imagined in AS3 can contribute to naming the unnamed, sensing and making-sense of the previously unknowable. The AA in AS3 are partly selected in opposition to those of AS1 and AS2 that constrain what is imagined to the preparatory and planned, and partly with the goal of liberating why we imagine the future. AfE is about futures that probe and provoke sensing and making-sense of difference in the present.

AS1 to AS3 provide a basic typology of applied conscious anticipatory systems sorted on the basis of differences of ontological status of the future in each AS. AS1 to AS3 bridge to the 'how-to-know' side of anticipation by offering a practical way of sorting different reasons and methods for 'using-the-future' – in other words different kinds of future. And, of course, it is possible to mix these different kinds of future in practice, for instance taking into account contingency (AS1) futures when thinking about planned (AS2) futures. But, as will become clear in the next section, there is less practical compatibility between AS1/AS2 and AS3.

Epistemological side

The right-hand side of Figure 1.1 covers the epistemological or 'how-to-know' methods that enable someone at a practical level to actually generate and describe different kinds of imagined futures. Like the ontological side, the definition of the epistemological aspects of FL as a capability goes beyond currently dominant and familiar categories. The task is in many ways similar to describing the world we can see, hear, feel or taste as we experience it in the present, only with the added requirement that with conscious human anticipation the future can only be imagined.

The 'tool' for this task as a general, all-encompassing category is knowledge creation processes (KCP).[3] This open term was chosen because different AS and different contexts call for different ways of 'knowing'. The reason for such agnosticism or openness regarding 'how-to-know' arises directly from the imaginary nature of the future as anticipation and the potential diversity of what is imagined and how it is given meaning. Sensing and making-sense of fictional worlds covers not just the physical or institutional contours of imagined tomorrows but also the emotions, colours, sounds, tastes, etc. Conscious anticipation as imagination can make use of a very wide range of methods, from the most fundamental forms of sensing and sense-making linked with basic human cognition, framing and narrative to elaborate expressions of extrapolation, superstition and fantasy. All these KCP and more may be relevant to specific anticipatory activities in specific contexts. The challenge is how, in a specific context, at a particular moment and place, to generate and give meaning to the inherently fictional descriptions of the later-than-now.

Many of the KCP applied to anticipatory activities are part of well-established traditions and sub-fields for generating knowledge about a subject. An example of a recently developed and regularly applied method for describing imaginary futures is the field of statistics. As most people know, statistics is a way to define, gather and interpret information that describes the world according to a particular frame or model. Story-telling is an example of a very old KCP that provides a way to sense and make-sense of the world. Both of these KCP, statistics and story-telling, are familiar methods for describing the imaginary future. For instance, statistics is essential for macro-economic forecasting or climate change modelling aimed at producing probabilistic estimates or predictions of the future. Stories and allegories of gods and spirits were and still are guides to human conduct inspired by what is 'ordained' or in keeping with the wishes of tradition and power. Yet again, as with anticipation and 'using-the-future', humans are so accustomed to engaging with KCP that little attention is paid to the choice of method or how it is related to different AS.

This lack of awareness is also characteristic of the dominant institutions of the industrial era, public or private – all organised along variants of the bureaucratic division of labour and power. These administrative systems deploy a range of AS and KCP to generate imaginary futures. For instance, most people are familiar with the dedicated and highly technical systems that can be found in sectors like the military, finance, technology, health, consumer goods, infrastructure, urban planning, energy, etc. Leaving aside the AS aspects, which are overwhelmingly AfF, what is striking is that there is also a uniformity of KCP. In 'mass-era' descriptions of the world, priority is given to the search for scale on the supply side, and the identification of common denominators on the demand side. Past, present and future all succumb to the same descriptive framing that ignores, discards or denigrates the specific, unique and ephemeral.

Being futures literate calls for being able to cover both the General-Scalable (GS) and the Specific-Unique (SU), as presented in Figure 1.1 under KCP. From an applied perspective of 'how-to-know' the methods needed to generate GS and SU imaginary futures can be described as follows.

- **General-Scalable (GS)**. These are methods of knowing that can range from the micro to the macro, from small-scale to large-scale phenomena, consistent with the aims of aggregation, comparability and affirming continuity (repetition). This is what can be called 'marked-space' (Fuller, 2017) that already has coordinates, variables and frames (Goffman, 1974). The field of statistics is a pre-eminent example of this approach to 'knowing' the world. Trends and forecasts are its most familiar methods for imagining and describing the future. From the perspective of the emergent present GS phenomena are those that repeat (Delanda, 2006), otherwise there is no way of knowing if such phenomena are GS.
- **Specific-Unique (SU)**. These are methods of knowing that discover and invent the meaning of phenomena that are initially of "indeterminate" duration – not recognisable repetition, at least not immediately at the moment of 'local' emergence.[4] Such methods of knowing detect or invent the initial meaning of difference in the emergent present – including ways of sensing and making-sense of process as experience. In part, all knowing contains an element of

novelty insofar as the experience of arriving at one meaning rather than another is a definitive exclusion, at that moment, of that other meaning and of a different experience. An obvious example of this kind of bifurcation, path taken/path not-taken, that alters repetition and difference in the emergent present a moment later (i.e. the future), is a fatal error. More positively 'banal creativity', like the realisation of ignorance or the acquisition of knowing, contains that moment of difference relative to the initial starting point. Methods that enable meaning to be attached to SU phenomena do so despite the potential that such meanings may or may not be transient, may or may not become general, may or may not have been unknowable unknowns (unmarked) prior to emergence. SU phenomena take into account that initially there is no way of knowing future states. Nevertheless, KCP for knowing the SU attach meaning, often without words, to phenomena in the emergent present.

This distinction is particularly important in light of both the deeply experiential-contextual nature of many anticipatory assumptions and the fact that grasping complexity entails a twofold recognition of the inherent time-place specificity (uniqueness) of phenomena and initial indeterminacy or openness of all phenomena from the point-of-view of ephemerality/durability. Embracing both approaches to knowing the world is important, not only because there is already an extensive 'toolkit' for doing so, from statistics and stories to models and intuition. But also, because 'walking on two legs' or 'seeing with both eyes' is a critical enabler for a greater appreciation of the richness of complex emergence, the value of process as experience, and learning as change (Ogilvy, 2011).

The KCP used to imagine the future must be selected on the basis of the specific goals and contexts within which the future is being used. The principle that KCP should be 'fit for purpose' includes the 'rightness' of a tool for a pre-existing task, like a hammer for a nail and screwdriver for a screw, but also extends to the appropriateness of a nail as opposed to a screw or a dowel or glue or something else when designing the storage cabinet. To stretch the metaphor even further and to push into AfE/AS3 territory, why build a storage cabinet at all? Why project one form of storage or way of being, such as a sedentary way of life and hence the need for a cabinet? The selection of KCP depends on the choice of why the future is being used and the associated kind of future, in conjunction with the specific context that determines both the actual sources of knowledge that serve as ingredients for generating the content of an imagined future and the conditions that shape the process. Someone who is highly futures literate is knowledgeable and experienced in the design of KCP that will be effective and efficient for deploying specific AS in specific contexts.

Using Figure 1.1 to map the capabilities of a futures literate person makes it clear that their 'know-how' calls for the ability to determine why the future is being used, what kinds of future are most appropriate for such a purpose, and then how to actually go about 'using-the-future' in situ given the 'why' and 'what' parameters. Readers from different futures studies (FS) and foresight communities will recognise that FL, as the capability to meet the design and implementation requirements of a futures literate approach to 'using-the-future', integrates and builds on the work of FS (World Futures Studies Federation) and the wide-ranging experiences of foresight practitioners (Curry, 2012). Indeed, as discussed in more detail in the fourth section of this chapter, the FLF could assist with a more explicit mapping of current mainstream FS theories and practices to different clusters of AA and thereby enhance the field's research and design efforts.

This book, with its focus on initial, proof-of-concept research into FL, is not the place for an exhaustive review and analysis of either KCP as a field or the relationship of KCP in general to thinking about the future. It is important, however, to underscore the diversity and contextual specificity of the methods that can accompany efforts to become futures literate (see fourth section, first part, and Chapter 4). There is no suggestion here that there is only one approach – on the contrary the thrust of developing the FLF is to enable the diversification of methods in light of a clear theoretical framework and a foundation for conducting experiments that test hypotheses about why and how humans anticipate.

Anticipatory assumptions clusters AA1 to AA6

Having noted this open, task- and context-sensitive approach to how knowledge is created when 'using-the-future', it is equally fundamental to underscore that when consciously 'using-the-future' the KCP humans deploy are determined by their tacit and explicit anticipatory assumptions. AA are to FL what an atom is to physics or the cell to living systems. Without abusing the parallels to other disciplines, it is clearly scientifically useful for both the theory and practice of anticipation to be able to identify a common object of inquiry that serves as a shared reference point for the exploration of different facets of the topic and the development of specialised sub-fields. For economics in the 20th century, the common topic of inquiry for theory and practice was 'resource allocation' (Samuelson, 1951). From macro- and micro-economics to labour market and welfare economics, the starting point for questions, hypotheses, and evidence was the nature and dynamics of the allocation of resources such as land, labour and capital to the production of income (flow) and wealth (stock). Of course, the organisation of a field into sub-disciplines around a core topic takes time. Economics, if one starts counting with Adam Smith, has had well over two centuries. Futures Studies and an understanding of FL as a capability are fields that are still in the early stages of development.

One potentially important step along the path towards building a shared language for research into FL and the FLL-N case studies reported in Chapter 5 is to begin detailing the characteristics of different clusters of AA. The FLF provides a starting point for analysing people's AA on the basis of the six clusters defined by the intersection of the ontological and epistemological categories in the FLF. Looking at Figure 1.1 it is obvious that each cluster can be distinguished based on key assumptions about what kind of future is being imagined and whether it is being imagined in GS or SU terms. Much of the time, given the widespread lack of FL, people do not make explicit choices about which AA to adopt.

32   Riel Miller

They nevertheless can be induced, through the action learning/research processes deployed in FLL, to reveal why and how they anticipate. By getting people to reveal why and how they anticipate, FLL generate indicators that can be associated with different clusters of AA.

AA1 Closed/AfF and General-Scalable: 'forecasting'

In AA1, general aspects of imaginary futures are identified and constructed on the basis of closed models. Typical examples are macro-economic and climate change forecasting that extrapolate from the past. The currently dominant epistemological tools for describing AA1 imaginary futures include statistics and benchmarking that use aggregation type common denominators. Indicators that the ways people are 'using-the-future' fall into AA1 include: point forecasts with risk calculation, actuarial tables, trends/mega-trends, deterministic utopias/dystopias, fortune-telling and expert prognostication, which are all part of imagining generalisable probabilistic or normative futures. Totalising deterministic imagination. *Doing. Colonisation of tomorrow. Insurance for tomorrow.*

AA2 Closed/AfF and Specific-Unique: 'destiny'

In AA2, specific-unique aspects of imaginary futures are generated and assimilated on the basis of existing fatalistic or deterministic stories, preordained outcomes or entrenched myths. The imaginary futures in AA2 are foretold. Indicators that the ways people are 'using-the-future' fall into AA2 include: attributes and content of processes for thinking about the future that are confined to generating signs of congruence or affirmation of religious and/or ideologically pre-determined futures. *Doing. Atrophy of the imagination. Fatalism.*

AA3 Semi-open/AfF and General-Scalable: 'creative reform'

In AA3 imaginary futures are harnessed to solving known, even if 'wicked', problems in innovative ways. Since the problem is given, the focus is on endogenous adaptation/creativity – change but with a given goal (AfF). AA3 futures can be probabilistic or normative from within a given paradigm. Creativity methods can be used to seek generalisable solutions but within the confines of AfF type goals. In AA3 the emphasis is on innovative ways of getting to specific 'continuity futures'. Indicators that the ways people are 'using-the-future' fall into AA3 include: within system (endogenous) reform, focus on organisational unit immortality such as global or national or company resilience as adaptive continuity. Currently most innovation activities are in AA3. *Deterministic creative imagination. Doing. Slogan: 'Make a Difference'.*

AA4 Semi-open/AfF and Specific-Unique: 'self-improvement'

In AA4, imaginary futures are often inward or consciousness oriented, facilitating appreciation of process and ephemerality, but in the service of attaining pre-determined futures. AA4 target endogenous creativity, imagining that is confined to extrapolatory probabilistic or pre-conceived normative futures (AfF). Indicators that the ways people are 'using-the-future' fall into AA4 include: adaptation at personal or organisational culture levels through experience induced attitudinal or consciousness changes. *Introspective adaptive imagination. Doing. Slogan: 'Consciousness raising'.*

AA5 Semi-open/AfE and General-Scalable: 'strategic thinking'

In AA5, imaginary futures take on different characteristics as the purpose of anticipation is for sensing and making-sense of emergence in the present (AfE not AfF) with a focus on identifiably general-scalable attributes of the present (repetition). AA5 seeks to detect and invent novelty with reference to phenomena that repeat (Delanda, 2011), since if the phenomenon is not immediately identifiably repetition there is no way of initially knowing if something is general or scalable. Repetition includes variation, a given variable that increases or decreases. Indicators that the ways people are 'using-the-future' fall into AA5 include: detecting system boundaries, identifying the parameters of paradigms – including existing paradigms (a repetition form of novelty) that were previously invisible or partially hidden, invention of new words or identification of missing terms. *Combines doing and not-doing imagination related to general-scalable repetition.*

AA6 Semi-open/AfE and Specific-Unique: 'wisdom–Tao–being'

In AA6, imaginary futures take on different characteristics as the purpose of anticipation is for sensing and making-sense of emergence in the present (AfE not AfF) with a focus on locally specific-unique attributes of the present (difference). Local is used here in its most basic dictionary sense: as within a limited physical or virtual community such that what appears to be a specific-unique difference at the local, and in this sense isolated level, may turn out to be something that has already been identified as a general-scalable repetition at a more global level. Indicators that the way people are 'using-the-future' fall into AA6 include: discovery or invention of novelty – coining new words and/or identifying missing words, recognising and/or establishing relationships at time-place specific/ephemeral/process levels. *Combines doing and not-doing imagination related to specific-unique difference as being.*

On the basis of these two dimensions – ontological and epistemological – the FLF depicted in Figure 1.1 traces a terrain that can be used to describe and map the attributes of FL as a capability. A futures literate person combines an understanding of the DoA, and therefore an awareness of differences in 'what-is-the-future', with a command of the role and functioning of the KCP that are the 'how-to-know' for a specific kind of imagined future.

Stated actively, a futures literate person can choose the AA that are appropriate to the kind of future they want to know and then design and implement the processes that enable them to acquire such knowledge. In a nutshell, a futures literate person is capable of using anticipation for different ends, in different ways and in different contexts.

Two examples of applying the Futures Literacy Framework

The two sub-sections below offer examples of how the FLF can be applied to specific design and analytical tasks. In the first example, the FLF is applied to defining and designing a research tool – the FLL and a specific customised version, FLL-N that was deployed to realise the goals of the UNESCO FL Project. In the second example, the FLF is used to map the theories and practices that currently dominate the field of Future Studies. This mapping shows the potential of the FLF to assist with the application of FS to specific tasks as well as uncover and/or deepen areas of FS research and practice.

Using the FLF to design the FLL and the FLL-N

The central point of this introductory chapter is to explain the FLF and its role in determining both the UNESCO FL Project's research objectives and following on from these objectives, the criteria for developing and implementing the appropriate research tool. This sub-section provides an initial overview of the two-part response to the challenge of designing a research methodology for discovering, inventing and reporting on the actual AA people are using – worldwide. More detail can be found in Chapters 4 and 5. The first part involved the development of an effective and efficient method capable of revealing a full range of AA in almost all contexts around the world. FLL are such a general-purpose tool. The second part of the response to the research challenges of this project entailed the tailoring of FLL to the specific search for AA from across all six clusters, AA1 to AA6. The FLL-N is such a customisation. Both the FLL and FLL-N were the fruits of extended periods of experimentation and on-the-ground collaborative effort.

The initial experiments that pointed towards an FLL type of collective learning approach to thinking about the future were conducted during a two-year effort, from 1988 to 1990, to explore the future of Ontario's Community Colleges (Miller, 1990). Subsequently a range of different action learning approaches were designed and tested as part of the work of the OECD International Futures Programme from 1995 to 2002 (OECD, 1998, 1999, 2000, 2002) and the OECD Schooling for Tomorrow project from 2003 to the end of 2004 (OECD, 2001). Many of the insights and lessons from these experiments were incorporated into the construction of the 'hybrid strategic scenario method' (Miller, 2007b). From 2005 to 2012 experiments with different configurations of the basic FLL design were run around the world, from the FuturesIreland (Miller *et al.* in Aaltonen, 2010) initiative and a review of Korean foresight (Miller, 2017) to private sector experiments involving a wide range of different sectors, such as finance (Miller and Lepecq, 2006), telecommunications (Miller, 2007a), and education technology suppliers (Miller, Tuomi and Bergheim, 2011).

Work on designing a customised tool for this project started in mid-2012 when UNESCO took the initiative, in its role as a global laboratory of ideas (http://en.unesco.org/about-us/how-we-work), to seek evidence regarding the attributes and status of FL around the world. In keeping with UNESCO's mandate, the aim of these experiments was to assess how developing people's capacity to 'use-the-future' might be linked to the exercise of human agency in the pursuit of societal well-being. With this agenda in mind UNESCO teamed up with numerous foundations, government ministries, NGOs, and universities to develop the customised FLL-N approach and co-create a highly diverse set of proof-of-concept experiments (Miller, 2014, 2015a; Cagnin *et al.*, 2015). The FLL-N builds on the basic design of FLL as a tool for detecting AA in a very wide range of settings in order to target the collection of evidence of AA across all six clusters, AA1 to AA6. The rest of this sub-section gives a summary overview of the FLL and FLL-N in order to provide readers another example of the application of the FLF and to set the stage for the rest of the book.

The challenge of gathering evidence of people's AA

As already noted, one of the primary purposes of the project is to detect and analyse the attributes of conscious human anticipation around the world. But again, as already discussed, any such exploration of the relevance and diffusion of the AS and KCP that underpin FL faces a fundamental obstacle – ignorance. For the most part, despite the fact that people, communities and organisations all use imaginary futures all the time, few pay explicit attention to the why, what and how of these anticipatory activities. In other words, they are futures illiterate. Such illiteracy poses a basic scientific challenge: how to identify or describe AA, including those AA that may depend on already being futures literate? And then, on the basis of an answer to this first question, how to find methods for generating evidence that can test whether or not such descriptions correspond to what people are actually doing or could be doing if they were futures literate?

At a fundamental level, all research is always confronted with this type of chicken-and-egg problem because the universe we are part of is continually evolving and the sensing and sense-making frames and tools that we use to understand it change too – both intentionally and unintentionally. From this perspective, and to recapitulate the path leading to the design and implementation of the FLL-N deployed in this particular project, it is useful to underscore that the FLF starts from the hypothesis that anticipation is possible in this universe but that the conscious capacity of humans to describe and use it can be further elaborated. Practice and theory, theory and practice go together. The FLF is such an outcome, fruit of proof-of-concept and design experimentation that has been going on for more than three decades. The FLF supplies an analytical structure for describing conscious human anticipatory activities, detailing six clusters of AA that define and differentiate dimensions of FL as a capability. Defining these clusters enabled a more detailed specification of the proof-of-concept research challenge of the UNESCO FL Project – as the search for anticipatory activities in all six clusters,

AA1 to AA6. This research goal then sets a more precise challenge for the design of a research tool – it must be capable of generating evidence of FL capabilities in AA1 to AA6 worldwide.

Concretely, this meant that the selected research tool must be able to overcome the 'detection problem' that arises from the lack of awareness of AA and do so in many different places, with different histories and contexts. Hence a necessary requirement was that the tool generate evidence of awareness, or lack thereof, of different AA. Furthermore, to meet the evidentiary targets of the project the attributes of the AA that are rendered comprehensible by the research tool must include analytical markers that display the distinctive DoA and KCP attributes that characterise different AA clusters. In certain cases, such as AA1 to AA4 this challenge does not pose that much of a problem. It is relatively easy to expose the AA of clusters AA1 to AA4 by inviting people to make the move from tacit to explicit since such expressions are confined to relatively conventional and familiar AA. More difficult, because of the obstacles posed by paradigm lock-in and the inertial properties of dominant conventions, is generating evidence of AA5 and AA6. At a minimum, this is a dual challenge. On the one hand, there is the difficulty of creating the conditions in which people acquire the capability to think in a 'strange' way, one that is external to their familiar paradigms. On the other hand, there is the difficulty of capturing or sensing and making-sense of something unfamiliar – how to give the data meaning?

Designing a response to the challenge of gathering evidence of AA

Arriving at a set of design criteria for an effective and efficient research tool for gathering evidence of AA started, as noted above, over three decades ago. What is essential in the context of the UNESCO FL Project is not the history of the method but the practical requirements and responses that shaped the research conducted for this project. Considering the challenges of this project led to the adoption of three key design choices, two of which are basic attributes of FLL in general and one of which is specific to the FLL-N tailored to the needs of this project. The basic distinction between FLL and FLL-N is typical of laboratory specialisation where the specific implementations of a basic design can be customised to be more effective at testing a particular set of hypotheses. This kind of customisation should not be confused with the general and universal design requirement that all FLL need to be jointly conceived and implemented in ways that are adapted to the actual context of each experiment. Every time a lab is run the specific ways that participants learn, the specification of the goals, the time of day and the sunniness or not of the room, for instance, all make a critical difference and must be accounted for in the design and implementation of the lab (for further discussion of these issues see Chapters 4 and 5).

(A) Action learning research. The first design choice informing the elaboration of the FL research tool for this project, one that generated the basic architecture, was to use action learning to overcome the 'detection problem' or the invisibility of AA. In other words, people were invited to engage in a process that called on them to imagine the future and begin articulating the associated AA. As the process unfolded participants started to become futures literate, able to articulate and discern different AA. Selecting action learning as the primary method for making AA explicit also offered the advantage of being ex-ante compatible from a design perspective, with a range of reframing tools that can be used to realise the objective of going beyond AfF as required for this specific project and realised through the third design choice below.

(B) Collective intelligence knowledge creation (CIKC). The second major choice for design of this project's research process was that learning is more likely to occur and occur more efficiently if it is done collectively. The choice of 'collective intelligence knowledge creation' (CIKC) processes from among other potentially workable KCP as a core design element reflected the efficiency of this methodology along four dimensions: (1) properly co-designed CIKC are usually efficient at rapidly moving AA from tacit to explicit; (2) CIKC can also be designed in ways that are strongly conducive to both inspiring creativity and finding meanings for such inventiveness; (3) CIKC processes also have the design-critical[5] virtue, if properly co-created, of being able to integrate tools that can be sensitive to both GS and SU phenomena; and (4) these CIKC methods are highly adaptable to context since the choices of both the most relevant topics, ones that people know and care about, and the narrative eliciting heuristics, the kind that invite people to make their AA explicit in analytically meaningful ways, are as diverse as the diversity of contexts in which such processes can occur. This last attribute of CIKC is essential for meeting the design requirements of a global project such as this one.

Two further attributes of CIKC as a general-purpose KCP merit brief elaboration given its role in the design of FLL.

First, the recent and widely dispersed emergence of CIKC initiatives (Scharmer, 2007; Hassan, 2014; The Grove, 2017; The Value Web, 2017) covering a range of designs, theoretical reference points and goals, seems to be symptomatic of a gap or inadequacy in existing methods for sensing and making-sense of the world around us. In other words, at the current point in time there seems to be a globally dispersed need, in all kinds of different communities, covering a gamut of motivations, to tap into sources for making sense of the world (knowing) from *both* the GS and SU perspectives. This demand for new KCP can be considered, in part, a response to the cognitive dissonance that arises when conceptions of human agency steeped in determinism and reductionism crash headlong into both the reality of complexity and the desire for open creativity and diversity (even diversification).

Second, again symptomatic of our times, the growing appreciation of the importance of understanding and engaging with complexity is slowly nourishing a counter movement to the dominance of systems for perceiving and giving importance to generalities in mass societies described through using common denominator statistical methods. This is what futurists call a 'weak signal' – a phenomenon that at first glance is not particularly significant or general in nature and even seems rather superfluous, since collective intelligence processes that privilege specificity and ephemerality are the opposite of those systems that produce averages and trends. But depending on the way the future is imagined, this new KCP might be like the microscope in the 17th century, making the invisible visible. Only as the history of the microscope shows, it was not clear what this new tool would be good for. Was it a form of entertainment, exposing the monsters lurking in a drop of water but invisible to the naked eye? Or was it to assist with gathering the evidence that would show that bacteria cause infection and lead doctors to start washing their hands?

As usual the question when a new tool is invented is what will be its significance or how will it be used? Here again the results of the UNESCO FL Project point to a key field of inquiry – the unique, including the uniqueness of process as a learning experience and affect, or the emotion associated with a 'situation'. Finding ways of describing and giving meaning to ephemeral experience opens up new possibilities, like the realisation that learning something, as opposed to not learning, is actually a distinct fork in reality, the one of paths taken and paths not-taken. As the quote from Popper at the beginning of this chapter emphasises, a change in the capacity to appreciate the meaning of process is a way of changing the present. Empowering people with the capacity to understand the role of conscious anticipation as imagination in shaping perception of the present – in other words they become futures literate – is therefore a way of continuously changing the present.

A+B = FLL. Action learning/research and CIKC processes are the two foundational design choices that define the basic structure of FLL as a general-purpose research tool for discovering and inventing people's AA. Still taking a general design perspective, it is worth noting that the term 'laboratory' designates precisely that – a place where experiments are conducted in order to test hypotheses. Just like a chemistry or physics or biology or psychology lab, FLL can be customised in order to explore a particular set of issues, similar to when a chemistry lab is tailored for high-temperature experiments. Context-determined implementations of FLL usually add other design requirements and solutions on top of the basic FLL foundation, as is the case with the FLL-N that was tailored specifically to the needs of this project.

What makes FLL a general-purpose tool is that combining action learning with CIKC process can be used to reveal AA across all six clusters, AA1 to AA6. However, on the basis of experience running FLL with the aim of detecting AA in the different clusters, it is crucial to recognise that different AA can require distinct and even incompatible action learning/research and CIKC processes at different stages of the laboratory process. For instance, customised FLL, as depicted in Figure 1.2, may be targeted at AA3 or at AA1 and AA2, using an action learning approach that may or may not be incompatible with the approach adopted for an FLL that just explores AA4.

Sensing and making-sense of FL 39

> This point bears emphasis, the meaning of the FLL as a 'general-purpose' tool is that it has certain basic design attributes that reveal AA but in most circumstances the specific hypotheses to be tested call for customisation. Specific research tasks related to different sets or clusters of AA usually call for research methods adapted to the task. For instance, the customisation of the FLL template to the specific tasks of this Project is achieved by seeking a design customisation that is intended to enable the collection of evidence related to all six clusters, AA1 to AA6.
>
> One other general point worth keeping in mind is that FLL are not the only research tool for exploring AA. As already mentioned in the Introduction, alternative techniques that are familiar to researchers conducting historical, ethnographic, semiotic, anthropological, psychological studies and more all offer viable approaches to collecting evidence regarding AA. The decision to privilege a customised FLL, the FLL-N, for this project was largely determined by the still emergent nature of this field and the need to be able to conduct low-cost and worldwide proof-of-concept experiments that tested the hypothesis that FL is a capability expressed across all six clusters of AA.

(C) Reframing. The third choice informing the design of this project's research methodology is the need to address the design-critical challenge of revealing AA across all six clusters. Building on the prior selection of action learning/research and CIKC processes as the defining design components of FLL as a general-purpose method, the third structuring choice takes advantage of the plasticity of learning/creativity to specify the inclusion of a paradigmatic reframing component. This design criterion calls for the co-creation of a catalyst capable of inducing the learning process to move from AA1 all the way through to AA6. In practical terms, the major hurdle is to find a tool that enables participants to get beyond the frame of AfF. As noted before, such a move is difficult due to paradigm lock-in and convention inertia, but is design-critical for this project since experience has shown that without a tool like reframing that generates sufficient distance from the hold of AfF there is no assurance that FLL will generate evidence related to AfE in clusters AA5 and AA6.

Figure 1.2 illustrates the distinction between the FLL as a general-purpose tool for revealing AA that can span all six clusters and specific implementations designed to test for particular sets of AA. FLL-F is a lab that targets the AA of forecasting. FLL-I is designed to discover the AA related to AfF innovation, such as the processes familiar from design or innovation labs (Kelley and Littman, 2001; Stanford d.school, 2017). FLL-C are tailored action learning and CIKC processes that assist participants to become aware of the AA related to their 'consciousness', sometimes the target of work in the Integral Futures field (Slaughter, 2012).

FLL-N, for Novelty, are FLL that have been custom designed for this project. FLL-N put the three design elements together: action learning/research, CIKC

	Discipline of Anticipation (DoA) (Anticipatory Systems (AS))		Epistemological (Knowledge Creation Processes (KCP))	
			General-Scalable (GS) (statistics, common denominators, universals, repetition)	Specific-Unique (SU) (novelty, ephemerality, spontaneity, improvisation, difference)
	Purpose	Type/System		
Ontological	Anticipation for-the-Future (AfF)	AS 1 Preparation & AS 2 Planning/ Closed	AA1 FLL-F	AA2
		AS 1 Preparation & AS 2 Planning/ Semi-closed	AA3 FLL-I	FLL-C AA4
			FLL-N	
	Anticipation for-emergence (AfE)	AS 3 Novelty/ Semi-open	AA5	AA6
				FLL

Figure 1.2 Mapping different implementations of the FLL on the FLF

and reframing. FLL-N = A + B + C. The FLL-N oval offers a graphical representation of the ambition to seek evidence of AA spanning AA1 to AA6. Chapter 4 provides more detail regarding the specific positioning of FLL-N in terms of the FLF and more detailed account of implementation design issues.

The FLF in perspective. The FLL-N, as an example of the application of FLF to developing and locating the theory and practice of FL, shows how the FLF can help to drill down to isolate specific aspects of FL. It is however, also important to avoid confusing specific applications with the more general attributes of both the FLF and its component parts. At least four points are worth raising in this regard.

First, is that using the FLF to select specific ways of producing knowledge, like action learning/research and CIKC for FLL, does not restrict other KCP from being part of FL as a general capability. On the contrary, it is important to not reduce the KCP relevant to the practice of FL to the specific KCP applied in FLL or FLL-N. The former is a lived activity and a capability while the latter is a specific research tool for exploring FL.

Second, KCP are one axis of the FLF, but KCP also go beyond the FLF. KCP is a synonym for epistemology or all the many different methods for 'knowing' that exist and can be applied well beyond efforts to construct and give meaning to contrasting kinds of imaginary futures. In other words, processes for creating knowledge are essential for anticipatory activities and therefore constitute an axis of the FLF, but although it may seem obvious it is important to keep in mind that knowledge is generated in many other contexts and for many other reasons.

Third, collective intelligence knowledge creation (CIKC) processes are a subset of KCP but are also a general-purpose tool for sensing and making-sense of many forms of both specificity and emergence, including learning. CIKC, as a distinct set of theories and practices, is similar in nature to a trans-disciplinary field like statistics that enables humans to define, detect and make sense of specific phenomenon as well as invent the tools like surveys that make something that is imperceptible, like the average height of the population or Gross National Product, perceptible.

Fourth, it is critical to note that there are plenty of examples of efforts to think about the future that are not based on an FLL methodology but that can be mapped onto the FLF framework. Such methods can be identified fairly easily on the basis of the AA that define the method. In most cases this large panoply of FS tools was not conceived of or designed to reveal AA but rather to explore specific futures. Using the FLF to gain a better analytical grasp of the kinds of AS and KCP connected with these tools is a significant step on the road to being able to anchor the matching of tools to tasks on the basis of an underlying theoretical framework. This is the topic of the next sub-section.

Applying the FLF to the relationship between FL and FS

The second example of how the FLF can be applied to a specific analytical challenge is an exploration of the relationship between FL and FS. The main point is that the FLF, as a way of describing FL as a capability, can be used for two purposes: (1) to be more analytically precise about FS theory and practice, and (2) to identify potential directions for the development of FS theory and practice. For instance, Figure 1.1 shows a mapping of the boundaries of mainstream FS as covering primarily AfF. This is depicted on the far right of Figure 1.1 (thicker line) and covers four out of six AA clusters (AA1 to AA4). The attributes of FL as displayed by Figure 1.1 show that the ontological and epistemological dimensions of the FLF extend beyond the main centres of attention that characterise FS today. In other words, the FLF not only encompasses AfF and AfE but also non-conscious anticipation, whereas FS is focused on AfF.

The point here is not to argue that FS should expand to encompass non-conscious anticipation. The aim here is more neutral and analytical. The hope is to offer a framework for thinking about the application and evolution of FS as a field of knowledge. FS could use the FLF to gain a better understanding of how to match specific tools to specific tasks or to expand or contract or shift the focus of FS to cover different issues and points-of-view as theories change and practices adapt. Situating FS in terms of the FLF illustrates how the FLF can be used to describe FL as a capability as well as a guide for research into aspects of FL that have been invisible or ignored up until now. This is not the place to speculate about the future trajectories of FS as a field and the extent to which it may or may not incorporate new or relatively neglected reasons and methods for 'using-the-future' into its dominant discourses and practices. However, it is worth noting that research into FL generates evidence about what people are actually doing, or can do both inside and outside the current boundaries of most of FS, and as a result could inspire an expansion and/or reallocation of the centres of attention of FS.

There are other reasons to use the FLF to examine the relationship between FL and FS. In particular, mainstream FS offers insights into different descriptive labels that can be meaningfully attached to different AA, and methods for imagining the future that can inspire the discovery and invention of AA. FS brings a large inventory of theories and practices related to human use-of-the-future. The range covers many distinct tools and rationales for anticipatory activities – from formal forecasting for risk assessment to creative scenarios meant to evoke a range of possible strategic options – all of which is accompanied by a rich literature that ranges from the dynamics of societal change (Slaughter, 2000, 2003; Inayatullah, 2008) and corporate strategy (Wack, 1985; Van der Heijden, 2005; Ramírez and Wilkinson, 2016) to specific tools like Delphi (Gordon, 1994), morphological analysis (Godet, 2006) and Causal Layered Analysis (Inayatullah, 1998). All these theories and methods can be deployed in the different clusters of AA depending on the context and can be used to describe different aspects of FL. These tools can also be used to design customised FLL aimed at researching specific AA and building FL. Indeed, the design of FLL-Ns called for the use of many of these tools and theories to conduct 'futures thinking' as part of an action learning/research process aimed at discovering and inventing different clusters of AA.

Lest there be any confusion, the exploration into the nature and application of FL undertaken in this book is an attempt to create a shared discourse for the theory and practice of 'using-the-future'. As already noted, the UNESCO FL Project has drawn attention to the idea that AA can be taken as a common starting point for efforts to understand FL as a capability. Up until now most of the academic literature and actual practices in the field of FS have not been able to take advantage of a common analytical vocabulary or shared points-of-reference like AA. This lack of a shared terrain for initiating and connecting collaborative scientific inquiry and application is in some ways not surprising given the weak and largely peripheral position of FS. But the case for a shared disciplinary terrain may also seem somewhat stronger now if there is a general recognition that conscious human anticipation depends on imagining the later-than-now and that all explicit imagining requires making assumptions related to the purpose, nature and implementation of some form of model and/or structured process, even if many of these assumptions are often left implicit.

Putting forward AA and the FLF as constructs for encouraging a shared analytical effort to understand FL is not intended to replace or exclude FS. On the contrary, the aim is to encourage the development of FS by enabling deeper and wider research and application through traditional scientific, experimentation based methods. Again, the adoption of a hypothesis testing approach, in the case of the work in this book at the proof-of-concept level, is not meant to suggest that FLL or FLL-Ns offer or impose some kind of procedural or methodological exclusivity. Quite the opposite, the hope is that by detailing the design principles of FLL as one general-purpose tool for experiencing AA and providing an example of a customised version, the FLL-N, researchers will be able to make their own assessments. The point of these experiments is to explore the limits of these action learning/research tools with respect to exposing specific AA clusters and different aspects of FL. The vocation here is neither to be exclusive or all encompassing, although the premise of generating evidence related to explicit hypotheses is taken as the universal starting point for the specification and conduct of the research. The whole point of the FLF is to push the frontiers or boundaries of the understanding of anticipation, without claiming closure or exhaustivity.

Even the claim of 'disciplinarity' can and should only be tentative. The status of FS as a discipline remains controversial, and the proposition that the FLF offers the prospect of disciplinarity by potentially providing FS with shared ontological and epistemological reference points, remains to be seen. Disciplines, defined as common frameworks for pursuing research and developing practice, are not born full-grown, nor outside of a specific context. Today FS and FL are being pushed and pulled by current conditions and complex evolutionary emergence. One of the main virtues of disciplinarity is that by establishing the boundaries and attributes of the field it becomes feasible to research, debate, and practise in ways that can be compared and contrasted in an 'apple to apple' rather than 'apple to orange' way. One of the main drawbacks is that such disciplinarity can exclude alternative formulations from outside and suppress heretical ideas on the inside. There is no denying that the claim of disciplinarity for FL as a capability based on the FLF does run the risk of exclusion, but it is a risk that needs to be assessed in context.

Currently there are at least two mitigating factors that seem worth taking into consideration. First, the serious lack of scientific capacity and status with respect to understanding the nature and role of the future in theory and practice. This is a serious problem if one accepts the hypothesis that motivates the work presented in this book: that understanding anticipation better may be a necessary but not sufficient condition for reframing the relationship between human agency and complexity. Second, some guardians of a particular foresight methodology or those who lay claim to specific and exclusive purpose for 'using-the-future' may argue either that their theories or frameworks already offer a shared terrain for disciplinarity or that their theories and practices do not fit within the FLF.

Such disputes are inherent to this kind of exercise and may seem wasteful and risky, particularly since up until now FS has been unable to forge a shared terrain. But the hope here is that through careful design and inclusive processes, the UNESCO FL Project is managing to build a 'big tent' that might reduce the costs of collaboration and produce some of the benefits expected from the efforts of an organisation like UNESCO that serves as a global laboratory of ideas. So far, the results seem positive. The UNESCO FL Project has successfully engaged with academics and practitioners from across the global FS community, making common cause in seeking a more coherent foundation for the field's different ontological and epistemological strands. Admittedly there is a risk of creating divergent, even paradigmatically distinct terrains for thinking about the future. Even if such debates do have the virtue of sustaining competitive inquiry into the world around us, there is the downside risk of costly internecine and/or tangential conflicts. Yet, at this proof-of-concept stage of the research the signs remain promising. As the evidence from the case studies show, the FLF as defined by specific theories of anticipation and knowledge creation can make sense of and put to use a wide range of different ways of 'using-the-future' – from forecasting (Tetlock and Gardner, 2016) and Delphi (The Millennium Project, 2017) to Causal Layered Analysis (Inayatullah, 1998) and Theory U (Scharmer, 2007).

In part, this reflects the fact that the FLF is about making it practical to 'walk-on-two-legs' – one deterministic and the other non-deterministic. This is mostly because both becoming futures literate and 'using-the-future' to appreciate novelty require an understanding of the goals and methods of preparation and planning. Detailing these more technical aspects of the UNESCO FL Project is helpful for separating out conclusions regarding the general aspects of the FLF as an analytical scaffolding, from the specific focus of this project on testing the parameters of the discipline by pushing the research process to detect novelty, specificity, and the design attributes of processes that explicitly 'use-the-future' in a number of different ways. This last point merits being underscored in light of the delicate question noted above regarding both the inclusiveness of the FLF and the relationship between FS and the FLF.

Conclusion

So far during this project no specific heuristics, tools and purposes for 'using-the-future' have failed to find a place within the FLF. To reiterate, the focus in the UNESCO FL Project on specificity, empowerment, novelty, collective intelligence and knowledge laboratories, does not mean that the FLF is confined to these topics and tools. The selection for this project of particular theoretical, analytical, and practical issues and approaches reflects the priorities of UNESCO and its partners to develop and clarify FL as a capability that may be able to contribute to human resilience. For this reason, the UNESCO FL Project set out to: map how people around the world 'use-the-future'; discern different kinds of future; invent and assess processes that help people to become futures literate; test design principles for 'using-the-future' in a futures literate fashion; and explore in-depth the relationship between 'using-the-future' and appreciating complexity.

With these objectives in mind, the research process for the UNESCO FL Project was designed to focus on the main parameters of the FLF, not to provide an inventory of all the theories and methods that fit within that framework. For instance, although forecasting using probabilistic methods fits entirely with the FLF, the way that predictive methods for imagining the future were used in this project was to reveal people's AA – rendering the tacit explicit – and to start the process of developing their capacity to use different futures in different ways. The hope is that the FLF, as a collaborative work in progress, can contribute to the construction of a shared scientific foundation and that this process will not be played out as an insider–outsider game. The UNESCO FL Project is intended and designed to invite different communities with an interest in advancing humanity's understanding of anticipation to join together to propose, test and refine elements of a framework that coherently encompasses as full a range of ontological and epistemological components as is possible.

As is typical of such a scientific endeavour, the research process and findings are not necessarily the same thing, even if the tools often take on considerable prominence. Put another way, the research process as designed and implemented so far uses the future as part of an action research/learning approach. However, the topic of this research is FL as a capability. Deploying anticipatory systems and processes in order to understand FL makes disentangling the two somewhat tricky, but as elaborated in detail over the following chapters, testing the relevance of a framework for making sense of how people anticipate by engaging in anticipation is quite effective. In particular, there are many attributes of FL, such as those related to complexity and indeterminism, which can only be discerned by getting people to actually anticipate in different ways. Working in this direction, the research and experimentation into the FLF reported in this book confirm the critical role of advances both within and across the fields of anticipation and knowledge creation. Later chapters go into greater depth on specific topics while the case studies deliver considerable detail on what happens when designing and implementing processes to test the FLF in a range of different contexts.

Notes

1 Hadin Tibbs, in his chapter in the *Handbook of Anticipation* (ref Poli, 2017) discusses the implications of 'block-time' for the ontology of the future. Such efforts to reveal aspects of our universe are of fundamental importance and no judgment is made here one way or the other. The only assumptions I make here, in the context of the effort to better understand human agency, is that at a practical level the future is always inaccessible when the observer is 'in-time' as opposed to outside looking at 'block-time'. Such an assumption also seems to be compatible with a view of creativity and unknowability that posits the potential for invention to enlarge the universe of possibilities, while forgetting may shrink it. I want to thank Hardin for the conversation regarding this topic, but do not hold him in any way accountable for the interpretation presented here.
2 Focusing the relevance of the later-than-now on 'functioning' provides an important component of the definition of anticipation because it includes an 'actionable' dimension. However, this formulation can encompass rather passive forms of action, like efforts to know – which is an action that may or may not have further consequences related to reactions, like leaves falling, or choices like deciding to take an umbrella if the weather forecast predicts rain.
3 One of the factors that made research into anticipation and the different ways of 'using-the-future' difficult was the related yet distinct issue of the dominant approaches to 'knowing'. In the same way that it became necessary to open up the ontological field of what-is-the-future it also became necessary to distinguish methods for knowing the unique/specific from the general/common. Indeed, work on FL not only draws attention to the epistemic bias towards generalities, common denominators and scalability of much social science and everyday frames for describing the world but also calls rather directly for the recognition of knowledge creation processes (KCP) that can sense and make-sense of the unique, specific and ephemeral. This suggests that the epistemological sphere also needs rebalancing, particularly if the richness of time-place specificity as an inherent part of complex emergence is to be taken into account.
4 The local nature of novelty is related to the issue of the moment of discovery and/or invention, which is inherently time/place specific. The ability or inability to recognise repetition is limited by what is known there (location) and then (present) and in this sense the recognition of repetition or difference is always initially limited by what is known locally – or the point of origin.

5 The term 'design-critical' as used here means that the goals that the design is meant to achieve cannot be fulfilled if a 'design-critical' element is not addressed. In this specific case, the necessity that the research tool be able to reveal the use of KCP from both the GS and SU categories.

References

Aaltonen, M. (2010) *Robustness: Anticipatory and Adaptive Human Systems*. Marblehead: Emergent Publications.

Adler, P. S. and Clark, K. B. (1991) 'Behind the Learning Curve: A Sketch of the Learning Process', *Management Science*, 37(3), pp. 267–281.

Archer, M. (2002) 'Realism and the Problem of Agency', *Alethia*, 5(1), pp. 11–20.

Bateson, G. (2000) *Steps to an Ecology of Mind*. Chicago, IL: University of Chicago Press.

Bauman, Z. (2013) *Liquid Modernity*. Cambridge: Polity Press.

Beck, U. (1992) *Risk Society: Towards a New Modernity*. Thousand Oaks, CA: Sage.

Bergson, H. (1998) *Creative Evolution*. Mineola: Dover.

Bishop, P. C. and Hines, A. (2006) *Thinking about the Future*. Washington, DC: Social Technologies.

Bourdieu, P. and Passeron, J.-C. (1977) *Reproduction in Education, Culture and Society*. London: Sage.

Bower, T. G. R. and Paterson, J. G. (1973) 'The Separation of Place, Movement, and Object in the World of the Infant', *Journal of Experimental Child Psychology*, 15(1), pp. 161–168.

Boyd, E., Nykvist, B., Borgstrom, S. and Stacewicz, I. A. (2015) 'Anticipatory Governance for Social-Ecological Resilience', *Ambio*, 44(1), pp. 149–161.

Cagnin, C., Frewen, C., Garrido, L. Miller, R. and Nosarzewski, K. (2015) *The Future of Science in Society: Report on the CGEE – UNESCO Futures Literacy Workshop*. Brasilia.

Curry, A. (ed.) (2012) *The Future of Futures*. Houston, TX: Association of Professional Futurists. Available at: https://drive.google.com/file/d/0B7Bn-eBPZZX7Ty1fS3JsMTFqbjQ/view (Accessed: 8 August 2017).

Davidson, P. (2012) 'Is Economics a Science? Should Economics Be Rigorous?', *Real-World Economics Review*, 59, pp. 58–66.

Delanda, M. (2006) *A New Philosophy of Society: Assemblage Theory and Social Complexity*. 1st edn. London / New York: Continuum.

Delanda, M. (2011) *Philosophy and Simulation: The Emergence of Synthetic Reason*. London / New York: Continuum.

Ehresmann, A. C. and Vanbremeersch, J.-P. (1987) 'Hierarchical Evolutive Systems: A Mathematical Model for Complex Systems', *Bulletin of Mathematical Biology*, 49(1), pp. 13–50. Available at: http://www.sciencedirect.com/science/article/pii/S0092824087800332 (Accessed: 18 December 2017).

Fuller, T. (2017) 'Anxious Relationships: The Unmarked Futures for Post-Normal Scenarios in Anticipatory Systems', *Technological Forecasting & Social Change*, 124, pp. 41–50.

Giddens, A. (1991) *The Consequences of Modernity*. Redwood City, CA: Stanford University Press.

Godet, M. (2006) *Creating Futures: Scenario Planning as a Strategic Management Tool*. 2nd edn. London: Economica.

Goffman, E. (1974) *Frame Analysis: An Essay on the Organization of Experience*. 1st edn. Boston, MA: Northeastern University Press

Gordon, T. J. (1994) 'The Delphi Method', *Futures Research Methodology*. Washington, DC: The Millennium Project.

Hassan, Z. (2014) *The Social Labs Revolution: A New Approach to Solving Our Most Complex Problems*. San Francisco, CA: Berrett-Koehler Publishers.

Heidegger, M. (1962) *Being and Time*. Translated by John Macquarrie & Edward Robinson. Oxford: Blackwell Publishers.

Hult, M. and Lennung, S. (1980) 'Towards a Definition of Action Research: A Note and Bibliography', *Journal of Management Studies*, 17(2), pp. 241–250.

Inayatullah, S. (1998) 'Causal Layered Analysis: Poststructuralism as Method', *Futures*, 30(8), pp. 815–829. Available at: http://www.sciencedirect.com/science/article/pii/S001632879800086X (Accessed: 18 December 2017).

Inayatullah, S. (2008) 'Six Pillars: Futures Thinking for Transforming', *Foresight*, 10(1), pp. 4–21.

Kahane, A. (2012) 'Transformative Scenario Planning: Changing the Future by Exploring Alternatives', *Strategy & Leadership*, 40(5), pp. 19–23. doi: 10.1108/10878571211257140.

Kahneman, D. (2012) *Thinking, Fast and Slow*. London: Penguin Press.

Kauffman, S. A. (1995) *At Home in the Universe: The Search for the Laws of Self-Organization and Complexity*. 1st edn. Oxford: Oxford University Press.

Kauffman, S. A. (2016) *Humanity in A Creative Universe*. Oxford: Oxford University Press.

Kelley, T. and Littman, J. (2001) *The Art of Innovation: Lessons in Creativity from IDEO, America's Leading Design Firm*. New York, NY: Doubleday.

Kimbell, L. (2011) 'Rethinking Design Thinking: Part 1', *Design and Culture*, 3(3), pp. 285–306. Available at: http://caa.tandfonline.com/doi/abs/10.2752/175470811X13071166525216 (Accessed: 18 December 2017).

Kobaysahi, S. and Nihon Butsuri Gakkai. (1990) *Proceedings of the 3rd International Symposium Foundations of Quantum Mechanics in the Light of New Technology: Central Research Laboratory, Hitachi, Ltd., Kokubunji, Tokyo, Japan, August 28–31, 1989*. Tokyo: Physical Society of Japan.

Lakoff, G. (2006) *Simple Framing: An Introduction to Framing and Its Uses in Politics, Rockridge Institute*. Available at: http://archives.evergreen.edu/webpages/curricular/2006-2007/languageofpolitics/files/languageofpolitics/SimpleFramingRockridgeInstitute.pdf (Accessed: 1 August 2017).

Latour, B. (1999) 'On Recalling ANT', *The Sociological Review*, 47, pp. 15–15.

Latour, B. (2005) *Reassembling the Social: An Introduction to Actor-Network-Theory*. Oxford: Oxford University Press.

Lewin, A. Y. and Massini, S. (2004) 'Knowledge Creation and Organizational Capabilities of Innovating and Imitating Firms', in Tsoukas, H. and Mylonopoulos, N. (eds) *Organizations as Knowledge Systems: Knowledge, Learning and Dynamic Capabilities*. London: Palgrave Macmillan, pp. 209–237.

Mao, Z. (1977) *A Critique of Soviet Economics*. New York: Monthly Review Press.

Masini, E. (2006) 'Rethinking Futures Studies', *Futures*, 38(10), pp. 1158–1168. Available at: http://www.sciencedirect.com/science/article/pii/S0016328706000486 (Accessed: 18 December 2017).

Miller, R. (1990) *Vision 2000: Quality and Opportunity*. Toronto: Ministry of Colleges and Universities Ontario.

Miller, R. (2007a) 'Education and Economic Growth: From the 19th to the 21st Century'. San Jose, CA: CISCO Systems.

Miller, R. (2007b) 'Futures Literacy: A Hybrid Strategic Scenario Method', *Futures*, 39(4), pp. 341–362.

Miller, R. (2011) 'Being Without Existing: The Futures Community at a Turning Point? A Comment on Jay Ogilvy's "Facing the Fold"', *Foresight*, 13(4), pp. 24–34.

Miller, R. (2014) *Networking to Improve Global/Local Anticipatory Capacities – A Scoping Exercise: Narrative Report*. Paris: UNESCO/Rockefeller Foundation.

Miller, R. (2015a) *Evaluating and Improving the Use of the Future for Identifying and Choosing Dynamic Opportunities*. Paris: UNESCO/Rockefeller Foundation.

Miller, R. (2015b) 'Learning, the Future, and Complexity. An Essay on the Emergence of Futures Literacy', *European Journal of Education*, 50(4), pp. 513–523.

Miller, R. (2017) 'The Challenge of Systemic Change. Is it Time to Change the Way Governments Use the Future? Questions Inspired by the Republic of Korea's Strategic Foresight Initiatives from 1999 to 2010', *Emergence: Complexity and Organization*. doi: 10.emerg/10.17357.99297bb988774f37d01d1edd6c986870.

Miller, R. and Lepecq, G. (2006) *The Future of Smart Payments*. Seville: Gemalto.

Miller, R. and Poli, R. (2010) 'Anticipatory Systems and the Philosophical Foundations of Futures Studies', *Foresight*, 12(3), pp. 3–6.

Miller, R., Tuomi, I. and Bergheim, S. (2011) *Learning Productivity: It Is Time for a Breakthrough*. 2. Promethean Thinking Deeper Research Papers Series. Seattle, USA: Promethean Incorporated.

Misuraca, G., Codagnone, C. and Rossel, P. (2013) 'From Practice to Theory and Back to Practice: Reflexivity in Measurement and Evaluation for Evidence-Based Policy Making in the Information Society', in *Government Information Quarterly*, Vol. 30, Supplement 1, pages S1–S110 (January 2013), ICEGOV 2011 Supplement. Edited by Marijn Jansen and Elsa Estevez.

Montemayor, C. and Haladjian, H. H. (2015) *Consciousness, Attention, and Conscious Attention*. Cambridge, MA: MIT Press.

Mulgan, G. and Albury, D. (2003) 'Innovation in the Public Sector', London: Strategy Unit, Cabinet Office, pp. 1–40.

Nadin, M. (2010a) 'Anticipation: Annotated Bibliography', *International Journal of General Systems*, 39(1), pp. 35–133.

Nadin, M. (2010b) 'Anticipation and Dynamics: Rosen's Anticipation in the Perspective of Time', *International Journal of General Systems*, 39(1), pp. 3–33.

Nonaka, I. (1994) 'A Dynamic Theory of Organizational Knowledge Creation', *Organization Science*, 5(1), pp. 14–37.

North, D. C. (1999) 'Dealing with a Non-Ergodic World: Institutional Economics, Property Rights, and the Global Environment', *Duke Environmental Law and Policy Forum*, 10(1–12), p. 1. Available at: https://scholarship.law.duke.edu/delpf/vol10/iss1/2.

Nussbaum, M. C. (2011) *Creating Capabilities: The Human Development Approach*. Cambridge, MA: Harvard University Press.

OECD (1998) *21st Century Technologies: Promises and Perils of a Dynamic Future*. Paris: OECD Publishing.

OECD (1999) *The Future of The Global Economy: Towards a Long Boom*. Paris: OECD Publishing.

OECD (2000) *The Creative Society of the 21st Century*. Paris: OECD Publishing.

OECD (2001) *What Schools for the Future*. Paris: OECD Publishing.

OECD (2002) *Governance in the 21st Century*. Paris: OECD Publishing.

Ogilvy, J. (2002) 'Futures Studies and the Human Sciences: The Case for Normative Scenarios', in Slaughter, R. A. (ed.) *New Thinking for a New Millennium: The Knowledge Base of Futures Studies*. New York: Routledge, pp. 26–83.

Ogilvy, J. (2011) 'Facing the Fold: From the Eclipse of Utopia to the Restoration of Hope', *Foresight*, 13(4), pp. 7–23.

Paavola, S., Lipponen, L. and Hakkarainen, K. (2004) 'Models of Innovative Knowledge Communities and Three Metaphors of Learning', *Review of Educational Research*, 74(4), pp. 557–576.

Poli, R. (2001) 'The Basic Problem of the Theory of Levels of Reality', *Axiomathes*, 12(3–4), pp. 261–283.

Poli, R. (2009) 'The Complexity of Anticipation', *Balkan Journal of Philosophy*, 1(1), pp. 19–29.

Poli, R. (2010) 'An Introduction to the Ontology of Anticipation', *Futures*, 42(7), pp. 769–776.

Poli, R. (2011) 'Steps Toward an Explicit Ontology of the Future', *Journal of Futures Studies*, 16(1), pp. 67–78.

Poli, R. (2014) 'Anticipation: What About Turning the Human and Social Sciences Upside Down?', *Futures*, 64, pp. 15–18.

Poli, R. (2015) 'Introduction: Relational Science, Complexity and Anticipation', in Poli, R. and Rosen, J. (eds) *Robert Rosen: Selected Papers on Social Systems*. Berlin: De Gruyter.

Poli, R. (ed.) (2017) *Handbook of Anticipation: Theoretical and Applied Aspects of the Use of the Future in Decision Making*. Cham: Springer International Publishing.

Popper, K. (1990) *A World of Propensities*. Bristol: Thoemmes Press.

Ramírez, R. and Wilkinson, A. (2016) *Strategic Reframing: The Oxford Scenario Planning Approach*. Oxford: Oxford University Press.

Robson, S. and Turner, Y. (2007) '"Teaching Is a Co-Learning Experience": Academics Reflecting on Learning and Teaching in an "Internationalized" Faculty', *Teaching in Higher Education*, 12(1), pp. 41–54.

Rose, D. and Martin, J. R. (2012) *Learning to Write, Reading to Learn*. Sheffield: Equinox.

Rosen, R. (1985) *Anticipatory Systems: Philosophical, Mathematical, and Methodological Foundations*. Oxford: Permagon Press.

Rosen, R. (1986) 'On Information and Complexity', in Casti, J. L. and Karlqvist, A. (eds) *Complexity, Language, and Life: Mathematical Approaches*. Berlin: Springer Publishing, pp. 174–196.

Rossel, P. (2010) 'Making Anticipatory Systems More Robust', *Foresight*, 12(3), pp. 72–85.

Samuelson, P. A. (1951) *Economics – An Introductory Analysis*. New York: McGraw-Hill.

Scharmer, C. O. (2007) *Theory U: Leading From the Future as It Emerges*. Cambridge, MA: The Society for Organizational Learning.

Sen, A. (1999) *Development as Freedom*. Oxford: Oxford University Press.

Slaughter, R. A. (1996) 'Futures Studies: From Individual to Social Capacity', *Futures*, 28(8), pp. 751–762.

Slaughter, R. A. (2000) *Futures for the Third Millennium: Enabling the Forward View*. Sydney: Prospect Media.

Slaughter, R. A. (2003) *Futures Beyond Dystopia: Creating Social Foresight*. London: Routledge.

Slaughter, R. A. (2012) *To See with Fresh Eyes: Integral Futures and the Global Emergency*. Indooroopilly, Queensland: Foresight International.

Snowden, D. (2002) 'Complex Acts of Knowing: Paradox and Descriptive Self-Awareness', *Journal of Knowledge Management*, 6(2), pp. 100–111.

Stacey, R. D. (2007) *Strategic Management and Organisational Dynamics: The Challenge of Complexity*. 5th edn. Harlow: Prentice Hall.

Stanford d.school (2017) *Stanford d.school*. Available at: https://dschool.stanford.edu/ (Accessed: 28 August 2017).

Taleb, N. N. (2010) *The Black Swan: The Impact of the Highly Improbable: With a New Section:'On Robustness and Fragility'*. London: Random House.

Tetlock, P. E. and Gardner, D. (2016) *Superforecasting: The Art and Science of Prediction*. London: Random House.

The Grove (2017) *Experience the Advantage of Working Visually*. Available at: http://www.grove.com/ (Accessed: 28 August 2017).

The Millennium Project (2017) *The Millennium Project*. Available at: http://www.millennium-project.org/ (Accessed: 30 August 2017).

The Value Web (2017) *Transforming Decision Making for the Common Good*. Available at: http://thevalueweb.org/ (Accessed: 20 August 2017).

Trilling, B. and Fadel, C. (2009) *21st Century Skills: Learning for Life in Our Times*. San Francisco, CA: Jossey Bass.

Tuomi, I. (1999) *Corporate Knowledge. Theory and Practice of Intelligent Organizations*. Helsinki: Metaxis.

Tuomi, I. (2012) 'Foresight in an Unpredictable World', *Technology Analysis & Strategic Management*, 24(8), pp. 735–751.

Tuomi, I. (2017) 'Ontological Exapnsion', in Poli, R. (ed.) *Handbook of Anticipation: Theoretical and Applied Aspects of the Use of the Future in Decision Making*. Cham: Springer International Publishing.

Ulanowicz, R. E. (1979) 'Complexity, Stability and Self-Organization in Natural Communities', *Oecologia*, 43(3), pp. 295–298. doi: 10.1007/BF00344956.

Unger, R. M. (2007) *The Self-Awakened: Pragmatism Unbound*. 1st edn. Cambridge, MA: Havard University Press.

Van der Heijden, K. (2005) *Scenarios: The Art of Strategic Conversation*. New York: John Wiley & Sons.

Wack, P. (1985) *Scenarios: Uncharted Waters Ahead, Harvard Business Review*. Cambridge, MA: Harvard Business Publishing. Available at: https://hbr.org/1985/09/scenarios-uncharted-waters-ahead (Accessed: 30 August 2017).

Wadsworth, B. J. (1971) *Piaget's Theory of Cognitive Development: An Introduction for Students of Psychology and Education*. New York: McKay.

Wang, S., Baillargeon, R. and Brueckner, L. (2004) 'Young Infants' Reasoning about Hidden Objects: Evidence from Violation-of-Expectation Tasks with Test Trials Only', *Cognition*, 93(3), pp. 167–198.

Wegner, E. (1998) *Communities of Practice: Learning, Meaning, and Identity*. 1st edn. Cambridge: Cambridge University Press.

Wendt, A. (2015) *Quantum Mind and Social Science*. Cambridge: Cambridge University Press.

Wilenius, M. (2008) 'Taming the Dragon: How to Tackle the Challenge of Future Foresight', *Business Strategy Series*, 9(2), pp. 65–77.

World Future Society (2017) *World Future Society*. Available at: http://wfs.site-ym.com/ (Accessed: 30 August 2017).

2 The Discipline of Anticipation

Foundations for Futures Literacy[1]

Riel Miller, Roberto Poli and Pierre Rossel

Introduction

Over the past few decades questions have periodically surfaced regarding the nature and basic features of Futures Studies (FS). Fruitful initial answers have been provided by what have now become classics of the field, such as the pioneering *Art of Conjecture* by De Jouvenel (1967) or the extensive *Foundations of Future Studies* by Bell (2011). Poli (2011) provides a more detailed reconstruction of the field. More recently a series of five workshops, called the Futures Meeting (FuMee, 2013) used the European COST initiative on foresight methodologies (2011) as a springboard for research into the founding principles, cross-cutting foundations and key concepts that define the evolving field of Futures Studies (see Miller and Poli, 2010 for papers published from the first FuMee). A recent issue of *On the Horizon* (Poli, 2013, p. 1) adds further elements to the discussion. In addition, the Association of Professional Futurists (APF) published *The Future of Futures* (Curry, 2012), seeking to clarify how to define Futures Studies (see for example, Miller, 2012).

Most recently research into anticipation as a concept that is relevant across a wide range of fields has taken off through a newly established series of international conferences and a *Handbook of Anticipation* edited by Poli (2017). The first International Anticipation Conference took place at the University of Trento in 2015 (Project Anticipation, 2015) and the second one took place in London in November 2017 (*Anticipation 2017*, 2017). Since 2012 the exploration of anticipatory systems and efforts to advance FS worldwide have been encouraged by Riel Miller's work at UNESCO. He played an instrumental role in the establishment of three new UNESCO Chairs, with Roberto Poli at the University of Trento, Italy, Markku Wilenius at the University of Turku, Finland, and Sohail Inayatullah at the University of Sains Islam, Malaysia.

The analysis presented in this chapter reflects the discussions and debates that have been underway for almost a decade now, involving a number of other colleagues, particularly the members of the FuMee Steering Committee (The FuMee Network, 2013). The discussion of the Discipline of Anticipation (DoA) proposed in this chapter starts from the proposition that any effort to straightjacket FS into the boundaries of a single discipline will fail to capture the diversity of the field.

The exploration of DoA offered over the following pages does not therefore claim to encompass the entire field of FS, rather it pursues certain key dimensions of what it means to 'use-the-future'.

The Discipline of Anticipation

We discuss the DoA firstly by focusing our attention on the 'Anticipation' component, then moving to the 'Discipline' component.

Knowing the future

All efforts to 'know the future' in the sense of thinking about and 'using-the-future' are forms of anticipation. Equally the future is incorporated into all phenomena, conscious or unconscious, physical or ideational, as anticipation.

The DoA covers all 'ways of knowing' the later-than-now as anticipation, from those forms of anticipation that are observed, for instance, in a tree that loses its leaves in the Autumn to human planning that attempts to colonize the future and efforts to make sense of emergent novelty in the present by finding inspiration in systemically discontinuous imaginary futures. Looked at as a 'way-of-knowing' the DoA addresses the codification of the myriad of systems of anticipation, both conscious and non-conscious. The DoA develops, sorts, and diffuses descriptions of the processes/systems of anticipation or how the later-than-now enters into reality.

One important rationale for investing in the DoA is that it may improve the conscious use of the future in the present (Rossel, 2010). This rationale takes as its starting point the contention that perfect anticipation of change is both practically and theoretically not achievable in our universe.[2] On the practical side the trouble is the unavoidable incompleteness of both the data and models used to attempt to predict the future. On the theoretical side, the impediment to predicting tomorrow is that our universe is 'creative' in the sense that novelty happens – provided that suitable enabling pre-conditions are given. If we accept this latter reason as part of the explanation for the change that characterizes our universe then humanity's conscious relationship to reality faces an additional challenge – how to take novelty into account in our perceptions of the present. This is where the DoA has a particularly important contribution to make.

Specifically, the DoA provides ideas and tools that can alter and expand the role of anticipation in shaping what humans perceive, including our capacity to make sense of novelty. This is because the theory and practice of the DoA develops and extends the categories and methods of anticipation that can be used to improve discovery and sense making. By enlarging and enhancing the analytical and operational approaches to incorporating the later-than-now into our thinking the DoA can improve anticipatory capacities in a wide range of circumstances. Initially the DoA helps anticipatory thinking to move beyond the approaches that most humans acquire without effort or reflection, such as our 'natural' aptitude for understanding both the future trajectory of objects in motion, helping us to avoid being hit by cars, and direct cause and effect, helping us to avoid putting our hand on a hot stove.

Subsequently, as the reach and refinement of the discipline benefits from more reflection and purposeful experimentation it may help to create the conditions for other novel changes. In this respect, the DoA is like other disciplines; it is an effort to develop a fuller classification of various types of anticipation and a more systematic inventory of the ways in which anticipation is understood by different sciences and disciplines in the service of human knowledge. Like all such efforts to gain a better understanding of a subject there is no assurance that the knowledge so acquired will of necessity serve good or ill, nor generate only intended consequences.

While anticipation has been widely studied within a number of different disciplines – including biology, anthropology, cognitive and social sciences – to date nobody has collected and systematically compared the results. A preliminary survey by Poli (2010) and a bibliography by Nadin (2010) signal the scale of the task. So far two figures stand out as central contributors to the Discipline of Anticipation: the mathematical biologist Robert Rosen (1985, 2000) and the anthropologist John W. Bennett (1996). The former established the theory of anticipatory systems, the latter the connection between anticipation and resilience. The issue of anticipation is presently a hot topic. The following are a few selected recent references to anticipation (for a more extensive list, see Poli, 2010):

- Anticipation in biological, psychological, economic and social systems – aka the theory of anticipatory systems (Louie, 2009; Poli, 2009, 2010, 2011; Louie and Poli, 2011);
- Anticipation and resilience (Almedom *et al.*, 2007; Almedom, 2009; Rossel, 2012; Zolli and Healy, 2013);
- Anticipation and Futures Literacy (Miller, 2006, 2007, 2011b, 2012);
- Anticipatory governance (Fuerth, 2009, 2011; Karinen and Guston, 2009; Fuerth and Faber, 2012).

Not surprisingly, from the point of view of FS and the DoA, the primary focus of attention falls on explicit anticipation as a combination of capacities that allow human beings to consider and evaluate the present in light of the way they imagine the future. In this sense, explicit anticipation (individual and collective) can be considered a key element or contributor to the human activity of decision-making. Anticipatory activities play a key role in both the search for available choices in the present and the form of agency in which such choices are conceived and eventually acted upon.

One use of anticipation is as a means to imagine how actions might play out in the future, although such simulations can only be tested once future realities happen. Simulations of this kind can be useful to think about the consequences of decisions, including errors that could turn out to be irrevocable. As Fuerth and Faber (2012) aptly note: "reality has no 'do over' function", and therefore, "the ability to experiment in a virtual setting safely, without suffering real-world consequences of trial-and-error, is an invaluable tool". Clearly it calls attention to the potentially unforgiving nature of reality and the costs arising from what may turn out to be wrong decisions, either in the short or the longer term. But excessive fear of actual error, the desire to always be so well prepared, so perfectly planned, that the target is never under- or over-shot, can crowd out one of the other strands of anticipation, learning from failed or mistaken experiments by reconsidering the anticipatory assumptions that help us make sense and evaluate the present. This strand of anticipation can be obscured when we lose sight of the fact that conscious efforts to prepare for the future or shape it are but part of a larger mix of elements that make up difference and repetition in the emergent present, including novelty that cannot be known in advance.

The importance of the DoA may well be that it enables a more explicit and considered approach to these two strands of anticipation – bringing additional perspectives and systematic knowledge, not only to efforts at preparing for external events that are assumed to be predictable and to planning that aims to achieve specific goals in the future, but also to the less familiar challenge of grasping the meaning of what may look like a failed experiment yet turns out to be an emergent success when judged against a new framework. One may be thought of as conscious anticipation that addresses closed systems and the other anticipation that addresses open systems, as discussed in Chapter 1 with respect to Anticipation for the Future (AfF) and Anticipation for Emergence (AfE) (see also Ogilvy, 2011; Miller, 2011a).

Both are obviously important as part of humanity's effort to make choices in the present, but the anticipatory systems that make up the former strand are much more familiar than the latter.

In conclusion to this section it is worth noting that much of our understanding of anticipation remains cursory and fragmentary. Yet even if this leads us to refrain at this point from making strong or general claims regarding the nature and role of the DoA it seems fair to note that anticipation does play a basic role in many different fields from biology, sociology, and economics to medicine and architecture, and politics. Thus, developing our understanding of anticipation and the DoA would seem to be of general relevance to humanity's endeavour to better sense and make sense of our reality.

Disciplinarity

Human efforts to appreciate the nature and functioning of anticipation in the world around us are undertaken on the basis of specific concepts and practices, either tacit or explicit. This is the field of knowledge that explores, invents, accumulates, and transmits the frameworks and information that make up our understanding and experience of anticipation. The DoA as a field of knowledge is made up of the many different 'ways of knowing' anticipation. The term DoA can be applied to both the practice of a skill (an apprentice learns a discipline from a master) and the parameters that define or delimit a body of knowledge that is 'studied' (a student acquires the knowledge of a discipline).

As a field of knowledge, the DoA can be sustained and improved through scientific effort. Like similar fields of practice and theory of knowledge, such as economics or sociology but also more applied crafts, the field of knowledge provides specific ways of knowing-describing-understanding such activities. Anticipation is pervasive, but there are specific anticipatory processes that can be identified, used, and made the subject of hypothesis testing through experimentation and analytical efforts. A better understanding of different forms of anticipation is helpful for engaging in economic and sociological analysis, just as theories and practices that help to understand economic and sociological phenomena can clarify aspects of anticipation.

The DoA, like other fields of knowledge, has sub-fields and a history and weighting of different sub-fields. Additionally, certain sub-fields are more preponderant in other fields of knowledge, such as forecasting in economics or climate science. Also, as with the emergence of other fields of knowledge, historical context matters. In the case of DoA a series of factors have served to both push and pull and enable and demand the development of a more sophisticated body of knowledge. For example, a push might be complexity theory offering new tools for thinking about the future, while a pull might be practical efforts to solve the problems presented by changes in the condition of change by inventing new approaches and frameworks.

Apart from the content side (to which we shall soon return), a complementary way to characterize the DoA is to take into consideration the accountability criteria that its practitioners should follow. The simplest way to summarize this aspect is to take FS as the covering term, the most general umbrella including all the ways to study, think and 'use-the-future' – ranging from visionary and utopian futures and pop futurism to participatory, critical or integral futurism and the extrapolatory projections of simulations, formal modelling and forecasting. FS is inclusive. Every aspect, type, and way of including the future within one's analysis, theories or actions is a legitimate component of FS.

Some components of FS are more subject than others to constraints, however. In particular, futures exercises conducted by professionals and futures teaching require forms of accountability that may be inappropriate for the field of FS as a whole – such as responsibility toward clients and students, and basic research. We shall adopt the expression DoA for this sub-field of FS.

Two further demarcations help in distinguishing different versions of the DoA, or differently nuanced DoAs. First, the needs of professionals and academics may differ, in part, and respond to different accountability criteria. Second, two preponderant foci can be distinguished when looking across current theory and practice within the DoA. Using familiar labels from the foresight community, futures generated by closed anticipatory assumptions are part of the 'forecasting' strand, futures invented by combining open and closed anticipatory assumptions are part of the 'foresight' strand. While these terms do not fully capture all the nuances of FS as practice, in particular the nature and range of open futures, the current discourse falls roughly into these two camps.

Much forecasting practice rests on the well-established modelling approach that tests predictive hypotheses using past data. If the model and data are deemed to accurately describe past behaviour of the variable(s) being predicted the model is considered more or less robust for extrapolatory purposes. Economic and climate change forecasts work along these lines. Sophisticated forecasters, working within the carefully developed and tested closed models used for extrapolation of variance, can find ways to integrate advanced systems theory into their reasoning and conclusions – together with the implied issues of multi-stability, discontinuity, phase transitions, etc. These simulations however, circumscribe the imaginary future within the probabilistic premises required to use models to project the past into the future.

Foresight as a practice, when distinguished from forecasting, is formally premised on the unknowability of the future and hence attempts to be more systematic in imagining futures that are not constrained by projecting the past. This does not mean that foresight practitioners do not use extrapolation and models to imagine the future. Indeed, they can use probabilistic statements as spring-boards for imagining the future and can even, in certain circumstances, aim to provide a probabilistic assessment of the future. Foresight processes however, usually take a different path from that of the forecaster. In general, foresight claims both a more creative and participatory mission, aimed at discovering new options and exploiting different forms of knowledge. As a result, foresight as a practice has experimented, somewhat haphazardly as is to be expected at the outset of new frameworks, with the challenge of both inventing and making sense of numerous new methods for generating and interpreting anticipatory assumptions and imaginary futures (Bishop, Hines and Collins, 2007; Wilkinson, 2009; Rossel, 2012).

Given the divergent priorities of these two groups of practitioners it is not surprising that there has been relatively little cross-fertilization or joint efforts. Overcoming this divide could be quite productive since there are numerous issues such as Futures Literacy and complexity (see section on complexity below) that are of relevance to both groups.

Summarizing, a discipline offers at least three advantages:

- **Depth**: by distinguishing its focus, a discipline can develop an expertise (specialization), deepening its theory and practice;
- **Identity**: through such specialization, both the practitioner and the layperson can identify the discipline as concerned with a specific subject-matter and why it is trustworthy;
- **Legitimacy**: depth and identity help to foster responsibility and legitimacy (which include reputational assets and attention to excellence) (Miller, 2012, 39–40).

Deciding whether the DoA, as we see it, is a discipline and what makes us think so and with what degree of legitimacy, is a challenging task. As an initial contribution, the following section addresses three questions:

1   What is a discipline, what do we mean by that?
2   Is what we call the DoA a discipline? What would qualify it for that claim?
3   What are the key components of the DoA as a discipline?

The idea of a discipline and the issue of disciplinarity

Etymologically, 'discipline' is related to the 'code of conduct' of a 'discipulus', a person subjected to an explicit training. With the coming of age of modern science, the term 'discipline' started to encompass the idea of a sub-field of knowledge, bearing its own focus, knowledge models, procedures and set of issues to work upon. The DoA is a discipline precisely because it has its own territory of knowledge (the future, or better, the future-as-linked-to-the-present). The disciplinarity of the DoA includes both the clarification of the relevant models, procedures and issues – which to some extent may overlap with those of FS and eventually with those of other disciplines too – and the criteria of accountability mentioned above.

If we push this proposition further, we must specify the knowledge territory addressed by a discipline and the ways to address this knowledge territory. The following are some general features we are aware of that are presented by most if not all the disciplines.

- **A focus (or a variety of foci)** characterizing the discipline. Clarifying the foci of interest is more relevant than establishing clear-cut boundaries, because the latter can overlap with an endless number of other disciplines.
- **Key theories**, explanatory of some real-world references or issues.
- **Public traces**, in the form of documents that can be analysed and discussed, and eventually revisited and reused years afterwards. In this sense, building a discipline is a historical process that may or may not be cumulative, combining creation and destruction as well as preservation or maintenance – which determines that status of the discipline's assets at any point in time. Furthermore, the process itself of generating traces is valuable and enables different learning dynamics to be distinguished and addressed.
- **Peer-evaluation** of some kind regarding the work of participants by other participants, occasionally participants from other disciplines. The habit of referencing the work of others upon which, or in contrast to which, one attempts to build new knowledge is considered a fair code of conduct. Two sets of criteria apply: (1) standard practices for complying with scientific debating and evaluation patterns; and (2) practices specific to the discipline, to be identified and discussed within the DoA arena, and related to the particular issues and challenges of the DoA.
- **Assessment**. This is perhaps the most demanding aspect, in part because there are at least two relevant paradigms. Taking the dominant view of the relationship between prediction and agency, embodied in planning, there is a dual problem for assessing the performance of foresight activities: (1) strictly speaking there are no current data about the future and therefore evaluations

of futures exercises cannot be based on the realization or not of pre-defined outcomes; and (2) there is no way to know if by making a prediction in the present (e.g. the "year 2000 bug" or "Y2K bug" (Quigley, 2005)) the future outcome will be altered – was there or was there not an actual Y2K threat to begin with? An alternative paradigm for evaluation starts from a different conception of the use of the future and its relationship to agency. This might be called the anti-planning paradigm. Here the evaluation of anticipatory activity is not related to plan fulfilment or the accuracy of predictions in divining outcomes. Instead success is based on the constant diversification of imagined futures, including non-predictive and non-normative descriptions of tomorrow, with the outcome being the expansion of sensing and sense-making in the present. Despite, or perhaps because of these difficulties in assessing foresight practice, the DoA may offer a number of solutions by enhancing the viability of input-based assessment, checking to see if the ingredients and processes respect state-of-the-art knowledge. Like all disciplines, the DoA is one approach to 'quality control' based assessment, including critical reflections on the assumptions of the discipline.

Key theoretical components of the DoA

As with every other discipline, the DoA exploits a variety of methods. This chapter, however, intentionally leaves aside discussion of these diverse methods in order to remain focused on the meta-level disciplinary aspects. In other words, we are concerned with how our understanding of the functioning of the discipline can be organized. Here, as a preliminary proposition, we present two ways of understanding how the DoA is organized, namely Futures Literacy (FL) and complexity.

Futures Literacy

Skipping over the history of anticipatory thinking, the current situation is one where the capacity to understand anticipation is becoming both more operationally doable and desirable. The emergence of this capacity, in a way that may be compared to the push and pull of the emergence of the universal capability to read and write during the industrial revolution, can be called Futures Literacy (FL) (Miller, 2006, 2007, 2011b, 2012). As with reading and writing, FL entails the capacity to decipher and categorize as well as produce (design, conduct and interpret) explicit (volitional and intentional) processes of anticipatory knowledge creation, as a necessary and ordinary skill. FL, like language literacy, involves the acquisition of the know-what, know-how, know-who and know-why – to which we could also add problems of know-when – that are required to deploy anticipatory systems appropriately – i.e. to be fit for purpose. FL is the knowledge and skill of how to 'use-the-future', it is a familiarity with anticipatory systems and processes. As noted in Chapter 1, to 'use-the-future' is, strictly speaking, not possible since the future does not exist as an object or tool to be used. The future as anticipation however, is continuously instrumentalized; the point of this phrase is to draw attention to this common and important activity.

What distinguishes FL from the common everyday capability to 'use-the-future' to cross the street without being hit by a car or planning to go to the movies with friends is that it requires an explicit awareness of distinctive anticipatory systems and the associated logic that connects specific tools to specific tasks. At a general level, conscious human anticipatory activities, either explicit or implicit, are a way of generating the imaginary futures needed to understand and act in the present. Concerning explicit anticipation, three main uses can be distinguished: optimization, contingency, and novelty. Optimization futures can be used to 'colonize' the future on the basis of closed anticipatory assumptions that inform extrapolation; contingent futures can be used to prepare for anticipated surprises, but as preparation cannot, by definition, take into account unknowable novelty this type of anticipation is also closed; finally, open or novel futures have the potential to expand perceptions of the present beyond what is apparent on the basis of closed optimization or contingency futures (see Chapter 1 and Miller, 2012, p. 41).

The point of distinguishing these three categories is to assist with the challenge of linking specific tasks to specific methods or approaches for both thinking about and attempting to shape the future (see section below). Because optimization actively attempts to impose patterns from the past on the future it privileges causal-predictive methods, often implemented through formal (usually equation-based) models running historical data. Contingency planning is how we try to prepare for already recognized possible surprises, often with the aim of 'surviving' or continuing with a minimum of systemic disruption. Using novel futures to discover new ways of making sense of the emergent present provides one way of taking advantage of the unknowable as it starts to become knowable, enhancing the capacity to discover the present. Novelty includes objects and processes emerging from our activities and the subsequent actions we exert upon and with them.

These three ways of 'using-the-future' are manifested in the world around us in distinctive ways. People 'using-the-future' to achieve some optimal outcome tend to understand reality as deterministic and manipulable – in the sense that future goals and problems are perceptible and can be directly influenced. Many of the familiar and most trusted tools deployed by those 'using-the-future' for optimization involve explicitly closed system dynamics and trend extrapolation – all close to forecasting and predictive scenario building. Contingency planning often deploys a broader range of methods such as the Delphi method and simulations. Preparation of this sort can include within system innovation and openness as rehearsing a crisis can reveal endogenous unknown unknowns. Finally, efforts to invent and appreciate emergent novelty call, on the one hand, for more modesty about what is knowable in the present and expected in the future, and on the other hand, more ambition in imagining the future in order to assist with the appreciation of exogenous unknown unknowns. Making sense of novelty calls for a greater capacity to invent and explore openness in all its forms. This is what makes the DoA timely, it reflects the needs and resources currently pulling and pushing the development of the capacity to embrace novelty.

Distinguishing three ways of 'using-the-future' provides a practical analytical framework for thinking about the future. By analysing how people are 'using-the-future' this framework makes it easier to match tools to tasks. However, clearer criteria for assessing how and to what end the future is being used does not mean that at any given time people, communities or institutions use only one approach. In daily life, a multiplicity of ways of 'using-the-future', a range of distinct anticipatory systems and processes, are deployed simultaneously. Differentiating three main types of future is a conceptual tool for better classifying and understanding the way in which communities and other relevant subjects 'use-the-future'.

All three uses of anticipation can serve human intention and volition, including the desire to assure individual, organizational and species resilience. By providing distinct categories and methods for integrating the future in the present, knowledge of the DoA may enhance Futures Literacy, enabling people, communities and organizations to manage and take advantage of the stress and excitement generated by the only certainty we know – constant change.

While these three categories are derived from extensive experience in concrete anticipatory activities, they are in need of some theoretical polishing. As they stand, these three categories guide practitioners, providing clues for varying perspectives and levels of analysis. As the DoA develops we hope to provide a more comprehensive analysis of the structural features (including other ways of 'using-the-future' still to be documented), overlapping practices, and dynamic inter-connections.

Complexity

During the past 60 years complexity has been defined in so many different ways that the term risks becoming meaningless. Furthermore, complexity is one of those issues that quickly veers into difficult technicalities. For the DoA the importance of complexity is that it calls for an awareness of different anticipatory systems. One of the simplest ways to define complexity is to distinguish 'complex' from 'complicated' problems and systems. Complicated problems originate from causes that can be individually distinguished; can be addressed piece-by-piece; for each input to the system there is a proportionate output; the relevant systems can be controlled and the problems they present admit permanent solutions. Complex problems and systems result from networks of multiple interacting causes that cannot be individually distinguished and must be addressed as entire systems; that is, they cannot be addressed in a piecemeal way; they are such that small inputs may result in disproportionate effects; the problems they present cannot be solved once and forever, but require to be systematically managed and typically any intervention merges into new problems as the result of the interventions to deal with them; and the relevant systems cannot be controlled – the best one can do is to influence them, learn to "dance with them" as Donella Meadows aptly said (Meadows, 1999).

A more detailed analysis of the differences between 'complicated' and 'complex' has to consider: (1) the 'complicated' perspective tends to work with closed systems, while the 'complex' perspective works with open systems; (2) the former naturally adopts a zero-sum framework, while the latter can adopt a positive-sum framework; (3) the former relies on first-order systems, while the latter includes second-order systems, that is, systems able to observe themselves – which is one of the sources of their complexity.

The traditional, bureaucratic structure adopted by organizations and institutions derives from an understanding of systems and problems that precedes the discovery of complexity. These structures are tailored to addressing 'complicated' – not 'complex' – systems and problems: they work as if problems could be addressed individually and in a piecemeal way, with outputs systematically proportionate to relevant inputs, and aim to manage and control underlying systems. Additionally, if we expand our consideration of change to incorporate novelty – discontinuity that is unknowable in advance – there is the challenge of being in two or more frames at once. How to develop the capacity to see and act in ways that take into account incompatible but coexisting systems? These are situations where taking the point of view of one system not only renders the other invisible but often expresses an existential conflict with the new system. The problem that surfaces here is dramatically urgent: while there is considerable expertise and experience with the invention and implementation of bureaucratic structures meant to act within the existing framework of agency – how to 'use-the-future' for optimization and contingency – we still are in the deepest fog about how to build up anticipatory structures able to organically deal with complex problems and systems (see Poli (2014) on Anticipatory Governance and Miller (2011b) on changing the way governments 'use-the-future').

Is the DoA an improvement?

One of the main justifications for further developing the DoA is the contention that it may improve the way humanity 'uses-the-future'. In order to determine if it does or does not calls for some way of assessing if the DoA actually enhances use of the future by foresight practitioners and others. The obvious problem from within the existing paradigm, as already noted above, is how to assess what has still to become actual. From the point of view of the present, like when a decision-maker makes a choice regarding how to 'use-the-future', it is not very comforting that the only way to know if one particular anticipatory system or set of anticipatory systems is superior to another is once it is too late, i.e. a long time later. Although such ex-post assessment may partially work to build up a track record in dealing with 'optimization' and 'contingency' futures, such approaches shed no light on false-negatives (futures that did not occur because the prediction altered the outcome) nor on what went unseen or remained incomprehensible because imagining closed futures obscured phenomena in the emergent present.

The intractable nature of this assessment problem emerges clearly if we examine the Foresight Maturity Model (FMM) (Grim, 2009). The FMM is designed to help identify the areas where foresight focus could bring the most benefit, allowing resources to be optimized for the most overall benefit. Furthermore, the FMM provides a means to assess progress in a measurable way. The two main features of FMM are: (1) devising the main steps of a foresight exercise, as developed by Bishop and Hines (2006); and (2) identifying the series of basic maturity levels (Table 2.1). The main purpose of FMM is to assess the capability of organizations and institutions to develop strategic foresight by relying on the concept of best practice, a concept that is often elusive (for discussions of the problems surrounding 'best practice' see Auspos and Kubisch, 2004; Coote, Allen and Woodhead, 2004; Foot *et al.*, 2011). Apart from efficiency issues however – i.e. debates on performance measurement problems – the very idea of 'best practice' seems to make little sense for FS, because 'best practices' can obstruct efforts to find innovative ways to make sense of emerging challenges.

One very important blind spot is the absence of complexity in the picture, leading to rather optimistic explanations, in particular for framing, scanning and forecasting activities.

For these reasons, we need a more nuanced framework. Let us call it the 'Anticipatory Capability Profile' (ACP). ACP is composed of the three components in its name: the **Anticipatory** component distinguishes among the different ways of 'using-the-future' (for instance, the different anticipatory systems and processes that define FL). The **Capability** component distinguishes among the different frameworks adopted by professional futurists for performing their exercises. As a preliminary approximation, one can exploit the difference between

Table 2.1 Foresight Maturity Model (Grim, 2009)

Disciplines of a Foresight Exercise	*Basic Maturity Levels for Each Discipline*
Leadership (capacity to translate foresight into action on an ongoing basis)	**Ad Hoc** (being only marginally aware of processes; most work is done without plans or expertise)
Framing (capacity to identify and solve the right problems)	**Aware** (being aware that there are best practices in the field; learning from external input and past experiences)
Scanning (capacity to understand what's going on in the immediate environment and in the world at large)	**Capable** (having a consistent approach for a practice, used across the organization, which delivers an acceptable level of performance and return on investment)
Forecasting (capacity to consider a range of future possibilities)	**Mature** (investing additional resources to develop expertise and advanced processes for a practice)
Visioning (capacity to decide what the organization wants in the future)	**World-class** (being a leader in its field, often creating and disseminating new methods)
Planning (capacity to develop plans, skills, and processes that support the organization's vision)	

'modelling' and 'reframing' mentioned in the first section above. Finally, the **Profile** component puts together the components characterizing Anticipation and Capability, specifying which constraints they should respect. Needless to say, the above is only a rough skeleton. Much work will be needed before being able to construct an effective assessment framework by seeking, inventing and experimenting with different ways to operationalize the distinct dimensions.

Conclusion

The DoA is in its early stages of development. In this regard, the DoA is not different from any other discipline – or science for that matter. Changing conditions give rise to changing needs and capabilities. The DoA reflects a range of convergent and divergent aspects of the present. There is the ascendance of new theories of anticipation and complexity. There is the decline in the effectiveness, both in terms of outcomes and perceptions, of old ways of 'using-the-future'. The DoA is not born full-blown; it will require considerable work to enhance both the theory and practice – a fertile dialectic. Efforts are already underway in a wide variety of places and institutions, including the UNESCO Chairs and Anticipation conferences mentioned at the outset of this chapter. There are also many practical experiments taking place, as described in this book, covering Africa, Europe, Latin America and Asia, as a global network begins to take shape. Like all such efforts there is no way to tell in advance if the effort will be for good or ill; what can be affirmed is that such an effort is intended to contribute to the scientific aspiration of gaining a better understanding of the world.

Notes

1 This chapter was initially commissioned to assist the deliberations of the Steering Committee of the Networking to Improve Local/Global Anticipatory Capacities: A Scoping Exercise (Miller, 2014). The current version has been slightly revised and some of the terminology updated to help the reader understand references across different chapters in this book.
2 Raising awareness of the limitations of the forecasting approach does not mean that we negate the reality of common practices and the myriads of situations where an immediate or less immediate future is anticipated using probabilistic approaches with 'reasonable success'. The fact that excessive dependence on these methods not only generates the costs of false-negatives and false-positives but also blinds us to the fruit of non-probabilistic or complex ways of thinking does not erase the utility of this currently dominant approach.

References

Almedom, A. M. (2009) *A Call for a Resilience Index for Health and Social Systems in Africa*. Boston, MA: Pardee Center for the Study of the Long-Range Future.
Almedom, A. M., Tesfamichael, B., Saeed Mohammed, Z., Mascie-Taylor, C. and Alemu, Z. (2007) 'Use of "Sense of Choherence" (SOC) Scale to Measure Resilience in Eritrea: Interrogating both the Data and the Scale', *Journal of Biosocial Science*, 39(1), pp. 91–107.

Anticipation 2017 (2017). Available at: http://anticipation2017.org (Accessed: 8 October 2017).

Auspos, P. and Kubisch, A. C. (2004) *Building Knowledge About Community Change: Moving Beyond Evaluations*. Washington, D.C.: Aspen Institute Roundtable on Community Change.

Bell, W. (2011) *Foundations of Futures Studies: Human Science for a New Era: Values, Objectivity, and the Good Society*. London: Transaction Publishers.

Bennett, J. W. (1996) *Human Ecology as Human Behavior: Essays in Environmental and Development Anthropology*. 2nd edn. London: Transaction Publishers.

Bishop, P. C. and Hines, A. (2006) *Thinking About the Future*. Washington, D.C.: Social Technologies.

Bishop, P. C., Hines, A. and Collins, T. (2007) 'The Current State of Scenario Development: An Overview of Techniques', *Foresight*, 9(1), pp. 5–25.

Coote, A., Allen, J. and Woodhead, D. (2004) *Finding Out What Works: Building Knowledge About Complex, Community-Based Initiatives*. London: King's Fund.

Curry, A. (ed.) (2012) *The Future of Futures*. Houston, TX: Association of Professional Futurists.

European Cooperation in Science and Technology (COST) (2011) *Foresight Methodologies: Exploring New Ways to Explore the Future*. Available at: http://www.cost.eu/COST_Actions/isch/A22 (Accessed: 8 August 2017).

Foot, C., Raleigh, V., Ross, S. and Lyscom, T. (2011) *How Do Quality Accounts Measure Up? Findings from the First Year*. London: King's Fund.

Fuerth, L. S. (2009) 'Foresight and Anticipatory Governance', *Foresight*, 11(4), pp. 14–32.

Fuerth, L. S. (2011) 'Operationalizing Anticipatory Governance', *Prism*, 2, pp. 31–34.

Fuerth, L. S. and Faber, E. M. H. (2012) *Anticipatory Governance Practical Upgrades: Equipping the Executive Branch to Cope with Increasing Speed and Complexity of Major Challenges*. Washington, D.C.: National Defense University Press.

Grim, T. (2009) 'Foresight Maturity Model (FMM): Achieving Best Practices in the Foresight Field', *Journal of Futures Studies*, 13(4), pp. 69–80.

de Jouvenel, B. (1967) *The Art of Conjecture*. New York: Basic Books Inc.

Karinen, R. and Guston, D. H. (2009) 'Toward Anticipatory Governance: The Experience with Nanotechnology', in *Governing Future Technologies: Nonotechnology and the Rise of an Assessment Regime*. Dordrecht: Springer Publishing, pp. 217–232.

Louie, A. H.-Y. (2009) *More Than Life Itself: A Synthetic Continuation in Relational Biology*. Frankfurt: Ontos Verlag.

Louie, A. H.-Y. and Poli, R. (2011) 'The Spread of Hierarchical Cycles', *International Journal of General Systems*, 40(3), pp. 237–261.

Meadows, D. (1999) *Leverage Points: Places to Intervene in a System*. Hartland, VT: Sustainability Institute.

Miller, R. (2006) *From Trends to Futures Literacy: Reclaiming the Future*. Melbourne: The Centre for Strategic Education.

Miller, R. (2007) 'Futures Literacy: A Hybrid Strategic Scenario Method', *Futures*, 39(4), pp. 341–362.

Miller, R. (2011a) 'Being Without Existing: The Futures Community at a Turning Point? A Comment on Jay Ogilvy's "Facing the Fold"', *Foresight*, 13(4), pp. 24–34.

Miller, R. (2011b) 'Futures Literacy – Embracing Complexity and Using the Future', *Ethos*, 10, pp. 23–28.

Miller, R. (2012) 'Anticipation: The Discipline of Uncertainty', in Curry, A. (ed.) *The Futures of Futures*. Houston, TX: Association of Professional Futurists.

Miller, R. (2014) *Networking to Improve Global/Local Anticipatory Capacities – A Scoping Exercise: Narrative Report*. Paris: UNESCO/Rockefeller Foundation.

Miller, R. and Poli, R. (2010) 'Anticipatory Systems and the Philosophical Foundations of Futures Studies', *Foresight*, 12(3), pp. 7–17.

Nadin, M. (2010) 'Anticipation: Annotated Bibliography', *International Journal of General Systems*, 39(1), pp. 35–133.

Ogilvy, J. (2011) 'Facing the Fold: From the Eclipse of Utopia to the Restoration of Hope', *Foresight*, 13(4), pp. 7–23.

Poli, R. (2009) 'The Complexity of Anticipation', *Balkan Journal of Philosophy*, 1(1), pp. 19–29.

Poli, R. (2010) 'The Many Aspects of Anticipation', *Foresight*, 12(3), pp. 7–17.

Poli, R. (2011) 'Steps Toward an Explicit Ontology of the Future', *Journal of Futures Studies*, 16(1), pp. 67–78.

Poli, R. (2013) 'Overcoming Divides', *On the Horizon*, 12(1), pp. 3–14.

Poli, R. (2014) 'Book Review and Abstracts: Anticipatory Systems: Philosophical, Mathematical and Methodological Foundations', *International Journal of General Systems*, 43(8), pp. 897–901.

Poli, R. (ed.) (2017) *Handbook of Anticipation: Theoretical and Applied Aspects of the Use of the Future in Decision Making*. Cham: Springer Publishing.

Project Anticipation (2015) *First International Anticipation Conference*. Available at: http://www.projectanticipation.org/index.php?option=com_content&view=category&layout=blog&id=31&Itemid=598 (Accessed: 8 October 2017).

Quigley, K. F. (2005) 'Bug Reactions: Considering US Government and UK Government Y2K Operations in Light of Media Coverage and Public Opinion Polls', *Health, Risk and Society*, 7(3), pp. 267–291.

Rosen, R. (1985) *Anticipatory Systems: Philosophical, Mathematical, and Methodological Foundations*. Oxford: Pergamon Press.

Rosen, R. (2000) *Essays on Life Itself*. Chicago, IL: Columbia University Press.

Rossel, P. (2010) 'Making Anticipatory Systems More Robust', *Foresight*, 12(3), pp. 72–85.

Rossel, P. (2012) 'Early Detection, Warnings, Weak Signals and Seeds of Change: A Turbulent Domain of Futures Studies', *Futures*, 44(3), pp. 229–239.

The FuMee Network (2013). Available at: http://www.fumee.org/ (Accessed: 8 August 2017).

Wilkinson, A. (2009) 'Scenarios Practices: In Search of Theory', *Journal of Futures Studies*, 13(3), pp. 107–114.

Zolli, A. and Healy, A. M. (2013) *Resilience: Why Things Bounce Back*. New York: Simon & Schuster.

3 Towards a formal framework for describing collective intelligence knowledge creation processes that 'use-the-future'

*Andrée Ehresmann, Ilkka Tuomi,
Riel Miller, Mathias Béjean and
Jean-Paul Vanbremeersch*

Introduction

One of the key claims for Futures Literacy (FL) as a capability is that it potentially enhances our capacity to act in ways that are consistent with our values and aspirations. Beyond the important virtues conferred on anticipation that arise when preparation and planning are successful, there are two other specific advantages – proposed as hypotheses – that are of particular interest in this book. The first is that a greater capacity to 'use-the-future' makes it easier to sense and make-sense of the world around us. This hypothesis rests on the proposition that a better understanding of anticipatory assumptions, including those related to distinct anticipatory systems, empowers people to grasp why and how the imaginary future influences what they see and do in the present. If this hypothesis holds it means that a futures literate person is better able to detect and attribute meaning to novelty and complex emergence than someone who is futures illiterate. The value being expressed here is that it is better to understand the world than to remain ignorant. The second hypothesis is that FL, because it enhances the capacity to appreciate complexity, makes it easier to take advantage of change, to deploy everyday forms of contextual creativity, and to embrace a diversification strategy towards resilience. The value expressed here is, in summary form, the desire for 'freedom' understood as a capability (Sen, 2009; Nussbaum, 2011).

Testing these hypotheses requires, at a minimum, the ability to collect two sets of 'evidence'. The first is the extent of a person's FL – how futures literate are they? And second is the extent to which differences in this capacity to 'use-the-future' alter a person's ability to sense and make-sense of our complex emergent world. Collecting this evidence depends on being able to define and observe the two main variables – the extent to which someone is futures literate and their ability to appreciate complexity. The starting point for measurement is always a definition, be it grounded in empirical observation or theoretically derived reasoning or both. For the first variable, the capacity to 'use-the-future', i.e. FL as a capability, elements of a definition have been sketched in the Futures Literacy Framework (FLF) presented in Chapter 1 where the attributes of distinctive sets of anticipatory assumptions are specified. For the second variable, appreciation of complexity, there is a wide range of definitions to choose from and this is not the place to enter into an in-depth exploration of the topic. Instead, the focus here is on a dimension of complexity that is directly implicated in the formulation of the FLF, specifically the term 'novelty' (Bergson, 1913; Kauffman, 2008; North, 2013; Stubbe, 2017; Tuomi, 2017), with the working definition being a person's capacity to detect or invent novelty as difference, a metric that is specified, from a practical collection of evidence perspective, as being able to ask 'new' questions.

Defining the experience of appreciating complexity through a proxy such as being able to ask 'new' questions sets up three metrics. First is a binary metric, an either/or choice. On one side of the binary metric is when no new questions occur. An example of this situation might be when people imagine the future and arrive at no new questions, perhaps as seen subjectively, by their own estimation, or by a third-party observer (or perhaps both). On the other side of the binary, when imagining the future does generate new questions, there are two more metrics. One is about assessing the differences in the kind of 'newness' of the questions being asked and then from within a particular category of new question the extent to which such a question might be considered to 'push the envelope' of 'newness'. Here again there is much to explore and once more a pragmatic shortcut is provided by the primary focus in this book on understanding FL. Thus, from an anticipatory systems perspective the key attribute of 'new' and the basis for determining thresholds and metrics is the relationship between the kind of future people imagine and what they perceive.

In the context of the FLF this gives a fairly precise meaning to the differences in degree and kind that can be used to describe 'new' questions. When people imagine the future do they ask new questions at all? If not, then it is the first case of the binary measure. If yes, then the kind and extent of 'new' needs to be referenced to the anticipatory assumptions that frame the imaginary future. Looking at the FLF mapping to provide bearings, the kind of 'newness' depends on the fundamental difference between anticipation-for-the-future (AfF) and anticipation-for-emergence (AfE). This means that discerning what kind of new question is being asked is based on determining if the question arises from a future imagined on the basis of the AfF anticipatory systems – preparation (AS1) or planning (AS2) – versus the AfE anticipatory systems – novelty (AS3). In the terms used in Chapter 1 it depends on which 'leg' one is walking. As for degrees of 'newness' the theory and evidence contained in this book are only preliminary, but what this work suggests is that the critical factor is endogenous to the evidence creating process in so far as the effort of being futures literate entails a constant identification of the 'box' made up by one's anticipatory assumptions and it is this constant identification of boxes that provides the basis for assessing not only if one is moving outside of a particular box but in what ways and how far.

Subsequent chapters in this book begin to fill in a few more details regarding the ongoing effort to understand the nature and implications of FL. The task in this chapter is to point towards one critical stepping stone that has not yet been put in place but appears to be a highly promising direction if the aim is to move from the proof-of-concept phase that enquires into the resonance of basic concepts to the testing of prototypes phase that renders operational what it means to 'master' FL as a capability. This chapter outlines a formal mathematical model that can assist with gathering evidence and testing hypotheses by rendering what takes place in FLL more detailed and explicit. The purpose of applying this formal mathematical model is not to mimic other sciences or seek legitimacy in what is erroneously considered the superior veracity of quantitative depictions of 'reality'. Rather, the role of the category theoretic model of Memory Evolutive Systems (MES), developed by Ehresmann and Vanbremeersch (1987, 2007) is to describe what happens in *collective intelligence knowledge creation (CIKC) processes that use anticipatory systems (AS) and related knowledge creation processes (KCP)* – in other words in an FLL.[1]

The MES model is a tool for formalizing what happens in FLL (Tuomi, 2014). One of the strengths of the MES model is that it builds on a 'dynamic' category theoretic formalism that can model impredicative or self-referencing systems, including biological, social, and cognitive evolutionary systems that cannot be captured using more conventional mathematical approaches. Applying MES to FLL is a way to achieve greater precision in describing the attributes and functioning of the actual experiments as learning processes. For a number of reasons, discussed below, the MES is capable of specifying and tracking the complex emergent processes of FLL. This MES formalization is made possible by building on the development of both the comprehensive analytical definitions of FL provided by the FLF (Chapter 1) and the design principles that specify FLL as a means to generate evidence regarding different aspects of FL (Chapters 4 and 5). Formal descriptions of this kind provide a crucial next step along a path of scientific inquiry into FL.

In the past, mathematical frameworks, like the MES, have played a key role in advancing understanding in many fields, from physics and chemistry to economics and statistics. With respect to FL much remains to be done. For instance, the application of the MES to FLL underscores the critical importance of further research into how to connect the actual performativity of the labs as action-learning/research and the collection of meaningful evidence that corresponds to the necessarily more abstract formalization of the MES. In other words, how do we measure what is actually happening in the FLL so that it can be used to fill in a formal MES rendering? Still, at this stage of research into FL and anticipatory systems, the potential application of MES to FLL offers a critical stepping stone for scientific assessment of the performance of different specific FLL designs as well as helping to test the critical hypotheses motivating research into FL: that becoming *more* futures literate can *enhance* human efforts to sense and make-sense of complexity.

As already noted, the MES has not actually been applied to FLL yet, so this chapter is not reporting the results of direct tests. The purpose of this chapter is, in part, to signal what needs to be done as the FL research agenda advances from the proof-of-concept to the prototyping phases of the innovation cycle (Murray, Caulier-Grice and Mulgan, 2010). This chapter also provides an initial mapping, for those so inclined, of the MES to FLL. Even more technically oriented readers are referred to a forthcoming article (UNESCO MOST publications) that will provide a full specification of the MES-FLL, including relevant mathematical proofs. For now, the goal is to explain how the MES model enables FLL to be described in greater detail with respect to the different positions and roles of the actors, relationships, and shared ideas and memory that constitute the AS and KCP that emerge from specific implementations of FLL.

The MES and FLL

In Chapter 1 FLL were presented as an example of how the Futures Literacy Framework (FLF) can be used to select design criteria for a research tool meant to expose anticipatory assumptions (AA). FLL, as touched upon in Chapter 1 and developed in more detail in Chapter 4, deploy two knowledge creation processes (KCP) sub-categories: action-learning/research and 'collective intelligence knowledge creation' (CIKC). FLL combine these two rather multi-purpose KCP in order to enable the discovery and invention of AA. MES modelling provides a way to formalize what happens when running the KCP in FLL in general as well as in specific implementations that are customized for particular research goals and laboratory contexts, such as the FLL-N deployed by the UNESCO FL Project. This application of MES mathematics to FLL generates insights in at least three distinct fields of analysis.

First, it enhances the ability to identify changes in the degree and nature of complexity that are generated by FLL thereby allowing for more sophisticated approaches to the testing of hypotheses related to FL. For instance, an MES tracking of the action-learning taking place in an FLL makes it easier to establish to what extent becoming more futures literate is associated with sensing and making-sense of different kinds and degrees of novelty.

Second, MES formalization of the specific KCP used to conduct FLL can help to disentangle the ontological from epistemic aspects of what is happening, making it easier to ascertain the effectiveness and efficiency of choosing different sets of design principles and contexts when running FLL. For example, by comparing different implementations of FLL formalized by applying MES it becomes easier to expose how differences in sequencing the action-learning process or the timing of the introduction of specific heuristics for activities like reframing might alter the effectiveness and/or efficiency with which FLL generate specific sets of AA.

Third, the fact that the category theoretic approach that informs the MES is also an approach to modelling so-called 'impredicative' anticipatory systems introduces an important potential synergy between efforts to enhance research into FL through the application of the MES to FLL and the discovery and invention of paradigmatically different perspectives on human agency. Here the potential for the MES to add value is not the same as in the two domains above that focus respectively on assessing what is happening and improving the design of a particular process. The promise in this third field is speculative and is inspired by imagining what could emerge from paradigmatic-type changes in the conditions of change. An example in this third field might be something along the lines of what becomes possible due to transformations in underlying social paradigms, for example, the kind of change in basic societal frames that occurred in conjunction with what is often called the 'first scientific revolution'. Right now, there is no way to know what changes in the conditions of change might emerge if high levels of FL were widely diffused throughout society, along with the relevant methods, like FLL, and the relevant mathematics, like category theory.

The potential for generating important insights into FL across these three fields of inquiry illustrates the utility of combining the MES with FLL. But it merits noting, the contributions of category theory and the MES approach are not confined to discussions of anticipatory systems-type research or activities like FLL. Category theory and the MES are broad mathematical approaches that apply to an open set of topics such as: evolution of biological systems (Simeonov, Smith and Ehresmann, 2012); cognition and development of higher cognitive processes (Ehresmann, 2012; Ehresmann and Gomez-Ramirez, 2015); design (Béjean and Ehresmann, 2015); and anticipation (Ehresmann, 2017). In this respect, it is crucial to keep in mind two points arising out of the discussion in Chapter 1 of the so-called 'microscope of the 21st century'. The first is that CIKC are a general methodology and should not be reduced or conflated with the application of this method in FLL. Second, the general application of MES to both action-learning/research and CIKC processes might give a considerable boost to the design and application of the 'microscope of the 21st century'. Chapter 1 already flagged the observation that today's widespread experimentation and innovation around these KCP may be a symptom of a broad, cross-disciplinary challenge – inventing tools and conceptual frames that enhance our capacity to appreciate the specific, unique and ephemeral. Indeed, the application of the MES to FLL is in part a step in this direction.

Why FLL are suitable for MES formalization

The primary purpose of FLL is to reveal and articulate people's AA. Given that currently AA are largely tacit and latent in nature (Nonaka, 1994), FLL must be designed as processes that make AA explicit. The basic observation that underpins the FLL design is that at a given time each participant has their own stock of knowledge, stories, frames and interpretations (Polanyi, 1962). They provide the 'raw material' or inputs for a process that follows design principles meant to access what participants know and believe about a particular topic. These personal stocks of knowledge get mixed into a conversation that is structured to generate shared meanings as well as new knowledge flows that may restructure existing systems of meaning. In other words, learning.

This is how FLL can make tacit or even previously unknowable knowledge evident and meaningful. At the same time, by drawing the participants' attention to the fact that they are 'using-the-future' in specific ways, FLL also provide participants with tangible experience of 'using-the-future'. This is how FLL launch participants along the path of learning how and why to use anticipatory systems and processes (the future) in increasingly sophisticated and productive ways. FLL engage specific stocks of knowledge that are rooted in participants' experiences with underlying communities of practice and interest. The knowledge, often tacit, that participants possess as a part of these communities is intricately embedded in social conditions of the community. The stocks and flows of knowledge are (re)produced and renewed through ongoing social practices and social learning where the participants can progress towards greater degrees of understanding and new forms of meaningful action.

In the formal model described below, we call these stocks of community-specific knowledge the 'Archetypal Core' of the community. It provides the conceptual categories and standard procedures that form the foundation of practical action and sense-making. Below we show how the emergence of new elements in this Archetypal Core can be formally modelled. This emergence of new imagined realities, therefore, can be interpreted as collective concept formation, as expansive learning, and as knowledge creation. When several such Archetypal Cores are brought together, 'boundary objects' can become archetypal objects by linking the infrastructures, and, in some cases, several Archetypal Cores can fuse into a shared collective system of meaning (Bowker and Star, 1999; Star, 2010).

From the point of view of a member of a community of practice, she or he needs to be able to move beyond the current system of meaning and, accounting for latent realities in his/her landscape, create knowledge that is anticipatory in nature and in this sense 'create the future' by imagining the future. FLL, however, do not just aim to generate new knowledge about imaginable futures; they also aim to make explicit the different ways in which imaginary futures frame what we see and do. FLL, therefore, also develop capabilities to 'use-the-future' for different reasons and with different methods. As a result of participating in a FLL, participants can see how different uses of the future structure everyday discourses in their specific environments. The participants, therefore, gain improved capacity to 'use-the-future' at a level of abstraction that makes these capabilities transferable across situations and domains.

The specific attributes of FLL mean that arriving at a formal model of the process must take into account three fundamental challenges at the leading edges of complexity theory. First, to be able to model learning, innovation, and knowledge creation, a formalism is needed that enables rigorous definitions of emergence. Second, to describe how the present is influenced by imagined futures it is necessary to understand the nature and functioning of anticipatory systems and processes. Third, to describe the emergence and operation of shared collective systems of meaning it is crucial to show how multiple models can be linked together and form shared Archetypal Cores.

Conventional modelling approaches are too weak for this task. To model such processes in a rigorous way requires formalisms that are stronger than those traditionally used in physics, economics, and the social sciences. Fortunately, category theory and MES can provide the required strength. But before diving into the application of MES to FLL it is necessary to pause for a moment to understand the impredicativity of anticipatory systems and the role of category theory mathematics.

But first, the relevance of the impredicativity of anticipatory systems

One of the very first applications of category theoretic ideas beyond pure mathematics was in describing how living organisms are different from inorganic matter. Towards the mid-1950s, the pioneer of mathematical biology Nicholas Rashevsky concluded that the conventional approach to study biological systems as physical systems had fundamental limitations (Rashevsky, 1954). Physics is based on an approach where the characteristics of systems are derived from the characteristics of their constituent elements. The essence of living beings, however, is that they are functionally organized systems. A human heart, for example, can only be understood in relation to a body where it fulfils its function. When scientific analysis tries to study living organisms, it focuses on their constituent components and particles but in so doing loses information about the organization that underpins the phenomenon of life. Science, as it were, squeezes living organisms through a tight sieve and searches for the secrets of life from the resulting mass of cells and molecules. According to Rashevsky, biology cannot be found there as the organism has been killed in the process. The test tubes of biologists need to capture not the matter but its organization.

Rashevsky suggested that if we want to study living systems, we have to focus on their functional organization. This suggestion became the starting point for what is now known as *relational biology*. In 1958 his student Robert Rosen formulated a ground-breaking formal model of a living cell using category theory, showing that all living systems have an underlying structure of functional dependencies that allow the system to maintain its organization (Rosen, 1958a, 1958b).

For conventional scientific modelling, Rosen's model of the simplest living organism poses a problem. If living systems are systems that can regenerate their functional organization, they need to be modelled as systems that have an internal model of their own functional organization. This leads to 'impredicative' models that classical physics excludes from the start. Newtonian differential equations require recursion where states follow each other in a same 'phase space' and previous states determine the next. This Newtonian formalization does not apply to impredicative systems, in which "the phase space itself changes persistently" (Longo, Montévil and Kauffman, 2012).

This has obvious importance far beyond mathematical biology. Organization is a key element in human bodies, as well as in societies, cultures and economies. Rosen understood well the general importance of the relational approach and since the 1970s extended these relational ideas into a general theory of anticipatory systems (Rosen 1985; see also Louie (2009) for the definitive mathematical exposition of relational biology and Rosen's work). Rosen defined an *anticipatory system* as a system that acts based on a model of itself and its environment. An internal model allows the system to 'predict' future consequences and the system can therefore 'react' to the future. The simplest cells do this through their functional organization that constantly generates the components that are needed to regenerate the organism. As living beings, humans are composed of a multitude of such anticipatory systems; in addition, they can also have cognitive and theoretical models that allow them to act in the present based on anticipated futures. As soon as we describe a system that contains a model of itself, we enter the domain of impredicative systems, and category theoretic formalism becomes necessary.

Although Rosen discussed adaptation and evolution in biological systems (Rosen 1973, 1991) his work on anticipatory systems mainly focused on the organization of living beings in an invariant state. Category theory, however, also provides a rigorous formal way to describe change and emergence when time is incorporated in it. Furthermore, as category theory can help to compare formal models, including the relational, non-mechanistic ones that interested Rosen (1991), it also provides a solid foundation for understanding systems where action is based on anticipatory models of the future.

In general, modelling is a relation between a system that is modelled and its model. A model is 'good' if the entailments in the system, for example, causal influences in a physical system, and the entailments in its model, for example, functional mappings from a set of observed values to predicted measurable values, are in congruence. In other words, there has to be a 'closure' of entailment in the modelling relation. For a typical inanimate physical system, the modelling relation, therefore, looks as in the Figure 3.1 below.

An inanimate system can be modelled using a formal system that represents the system as system states and transitions from one system state to another. For example, text-book examples of physics belong to this class. In physics, there are formal models where the evolution of the system and its future can be determined through a sequence of system states defined on the same phase space, and these changes can be described using differential equations. Biological, cognitive, social and economic systems are 'impredicative' and, as already noted, cannot be modelled as classical dynamical systems or as algorithmic computation. Because of this difficulty such systems are rarely discussed in standard science text-books.

As discussed below, the MES model uses a hybrid approach that describes systems that can have impredicative characteristics. It represents system evolution by a family of configuration categories indexed by time, with transitions from one configuration to another generated by decomplexification processes accounting for structural changes of the kinds: suppression, addition or combination of components.

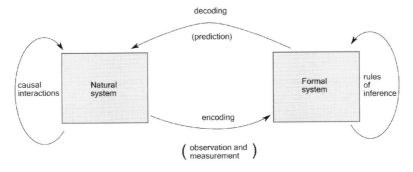

Figure 3.1 The modelling relation (adapted from Rosen, 1985)

This 'dynamic' variant of category theory therefore, re-introduces the possibility of a dynamic description at a level where the underlying complexity can be effectively captured.

This distinction between classical dynamical systems and impredicative systems is important as it leads to different ways of 'using-the-future'. Dynamical systems, although often highly complicated, can at least in principle be deterministic. As their evolution is essentially recursively determined by earlier states of the system, the future can be predicted and computed using well-defined algorithms. Although prediction even in closed systems can be difficult, for example, due to chaotic dynamics or errors in observation and measurement, there are clear rules for inferring future states of the system. When it is assumed that a system can be modelled using a closed dynamical system its future can be imagined by closed system forecasting. The problem of anticipation, then, becomes a problem of devising 'accurate' closed system models and about gathering data that can be used to make predictions with these models. In the FLF presented in Chapter 1 such anticipation covers AA1 and AA2.

For impredicative systems, classical dynamical models cannot, in general, capture the global evolution of the system. Although such models may provide predictions that match system behaviour within confined parameters such as short-time periods, the predictions are bound to have increasing errors if they are extrapolated outside of the specified limits. Additionally, and perhaps more importantly in the context of trying to understand the implications of anticipatory systems and processes, the goal is not only to imagine the future using predictive means but also to understand the present which is full of impredicative systems. Thus, the problem is not only that the future states cannot be inferred based on classical dynamic models but also that the present state of the environment would be obscured by a reliance on futures defined exclusively through a deterministic approach.

This is the core of what is at stake here in terms of the scientific nature and utility of the Discipline of Anticipation (DoA). A lack of awareness of the DoA that reduces the future to classical predictive modelling obscures aspects of reality, in particular novelty and changes in the conditions of change, that can only be discerned/invented through the application of impredicative modelling. This underscores the utility of the category theory-based MES approach, not only for describing the complex evolutionary-type emergence of CIKC processes but also for describing FLL that are designed to improve the capacity to make sense of and invent novelty by going beyond a misplaced trust and reliance on imagining the future exclusively based on predictive dynamical models.

The MES formalization of FLL makes it clear that part of what happens in this kind of CIKC is to probe the actual system to find out what are its constraints and relationships. Discerning more fully the local state of an open and evolving complex system may, in certain circumstances, also facilitate making improvements to probabilistic forecasts conducted within closed systems. But this need not be the sole purpose, instead it becomes practical to design processes that explicitly move beyond 'using-the-future' exclusively as an instrument of prediction or 'realizability' to incorporate the anticipatory systems and processes of impredicative modelling. FLL can be designed in order to create conditions that foster invention (local ontological expansion) by explicitly using the imaginary future to probe, disturb and reframe anticipatory assumptions (AA).

Applying an MES formalization to the design and analysis of FLL as a process generates indicators of how FLL improve the use of anticipatory systems and processes in two different ways. First the Archetypal Cores of the participants can, on the basis of becoming futures literate, distinguish between predictive and impredicative models of themselves and their environments. For example, using the terms of the FLF, this could mean distinguishing Anticipation for the Future (AfF) from Anticipation for Emergence (AfE) – or being able to 'walk-on-two-legs' as described in Chapter 1. This means that people, by becoming futures literate, are able to decide how to 'use-the-future' in ways that make it easier to discern the full range of constraints, dependencies and relations that make up emergent complex reality in the present. Second, on the basis of understanding the essential difference, as depicted by the FLF in Chapter 1, between the AfF of closed dynamic systems and the AfE of semi-open novel systems, a futures literate person is better able to make choices regarding how to best 'use-the-future' in a specific context or phase of a process. Looked at in terms of the dimensions in the FLF and the role of FLL process in developing FL, an MES-based FLL makes it practical to trace the specific attributes of changes in why people 'use-the-future' and which techniques are best suited for producing different imaginary futures.

The MES is a way to analyse what is occurring in an FLL, for example as discussed in more detail below, by observing the emergence of new archetypal objects in the Archetypal Core expressed, in the terminology of MES, as colimits that consolidate underpinning patterns, and by discussing the role of 'changes in the conditions of change' which, in MES, result from the formation of 'complex links' between 'multi-faceted' objects (see below). In the following sections, we introduce some of the key ideas and mathematical constructs that underpin the MES model (full exposition of the model and its mathematical foundations is provided by Ehresmann and Vanbremeersch (2007)).

Graphs and categories

A social system can be represented by a social network, that is, a *graph*[2] in which the network nodes or 'objects' are individuals and groups of different kinds, and arrows between the nodes represent relations between the network objects. Instead of simple graphs, below we consider *categories*, which have some additional structure. This allows us to be able to use the tools of the mathematical category theory. Category theory, introduced by Eilenberg and MacLane (1945), is a form of relational mathematics. A category is first a graph, in which information is encoded in the links or arrows between objects rather than in the objects themselves. The properties of the objects are therefore fully deduced from their interactions in the category. This is in clear contrast to the standard approach in physics, where all information about a system is encoded in the objects and their attributes, and where relations between the objects are expected to result from the internal states of the objects.

Category theory is often presented as an abstracted version of the most basic characteristics of functional mapping in mathematics, namely composition and associativity. When a function maps values to other values and these are further mapped, we can define a composite function that does the mapping from the original values to the final ones. Furthermore, if we have a sequence of such mappings, we get to the same end points independent of the way we combine the mappings. In mathematical terms, the composition of functions is associative, and we can write, for example f(gh) = (fg)h where gh is the composite function of g and h, and, similarly, fg the composite of f and g.

More generally, a *category* consists of a graph on which there is a given *composition law* which associates a 'composite' arrow to each path of the graph (= sequence of consecutive arrows). This composition further needs to satisfy the associativity axiom which implies that a path has a unique composite and a unity axiom associating an 'identity arrow' to each vertex.[3] Category theory has been described as mathematical structuralism since it makes a general concept of structure possible, thus unifying many domains of mathematics. In the late fifties, its foundational role in mathematics was made apparent through the introduction by Kan (1958) of adjoint functors, and in particular the concept of colimit (or inductive limit). In MES, the notion of colimit is essential in order to internally distinguish different levels of complexity among the components of the system. For instance, the object representing an institutionalized social group (say the groups of people in FLL) will appear as the colimit of the pattern consisting of its interacting members.

Category theory has increasing applications in other sciences, including logic, computer science, physics, and biology. In a category modelling of a 'concrete' system, the arrows represent channels through which the objects interact, and paths with the same composite correspond to 'operationally equivalent' paths. The next sections offer a brief introduction to the 'dynamic' category theory MES model. This approach allows the modelling of evolutionary multi-scale systems, with components of increasing complexity that vary over time, and are self-organized. The dynamic of MES is modulated by the interactions between specialized subsystems, called *co-regulators*, each operating at its own rhythm with the help of a flexible long-term 'memory' allowing for learning and adaptation. Examples are biological, social, and cognitive systems.

Memory Evolutive System applied to a social system

The MES methodology is based on a 'dynamic' category theory, that also takes into account the different dynamic 'physical' constraints to which the system is subjected. As an example, we first recall the main characteristics of a social system.

The structural and dynamic organization of a social system

A social system has a multi-level internal organization into components and links between them, and its evolution depends on dynamic and structural changes.

There are several kinds of components, and they may vary over time, with possible suppression or addition.

1. **Individuals and groups** of interacting individuals of different complexities, up to large institutions, such as groups of individuals interested in learning and developing anticipation skills through FLL.
2. **Memory components**: Knowledge of any nature about the system, its environment and past events. The memory also includes non-conscious and tacit knowledge such as ad hoc methods, cultural values and symbolic systems, affects and emotions. All these components form the flexible memory of the MES. Of particular importance for modelling FLL, the memory allows people to move tacit AA to explicit and for the acquisition of FL through the process to change the conditions of change.
3. **Observation and measurement tools**. These components are inter-related by (directed) links that render interactions and communications of different sorts possible. For instance, an individual can recall memories, send instructions to other individuals or to a computer, and participate in the negotiation of shared sense-making that is at the core of a CIKC process.

The system has an internal organization in which the components have themselves a more or less elaborated internal organization; it is "a system of systems; itself an element of a higher-order system" (Jacob, 1970). More precisely, the system has a hierarchical organization in which the components are classified into disjoint increasing *complexity*[4] *levels* numbered 0, 1, . . . *m*:

- a component of level 0 (e.g. an individual) is said to be *atomic*; and
- a component C of level $n+1$ is *n-complex* in the sense that C combines and consolidates at least one pattern P of components of levels $\leq n$ interacting in a coordinated way, so that C has the same operational role as P acting collectively; in the category setting, C will be represented by the colimit of the pattern P. For instance, a FLL is a 1-complex component while its participants are of level 0.

The emergence problem will consist in constructing more complex components. For instance, in the memory there is formation of records of increasing complexity which sum up a large quantity of information.

A social system can be considered as a 'living entity', which is not invariant but evolves, with both its structure (components and links) and its organization varying over time. To account for this evolution in a MES model, two types of changes have to be considered.

78 *Andrée Ehresmann et al.*

First, there are internal changes in the components and the links due to different dynamic 'physical' constraints (e.g. temporal, energetic) which must be respected. In particular, a link from a component A to a component B has a propagation delay (i.e. the period necessary to transmit information from A to B) and a strength at t, and a component or a link can be active or passive at t (depending if information is transmitted or not at t).

Second, there are systemic structural changes such as loss of components and links (e.g. death, suppression of obsolete interaction); addition of new components (e.g. by birth, learning, invention of new knowledge); formation of a new complex component obtained by transforming a pattern P of lower order components which interact informally into a component C 'formalizing' the pattern; in time C may take its own identity and act as such, despite the possible departure of some members and the arrival of new ones. For instance, an FLL 'formalizes' the collective work of its participants with their more or less specific roles.

The system as an evolutive system

As the components and links of a system vary over time, the evolution of the system in the MES approach cannot be represented by a unique category, but by what we call an *Evolutive System* **K** defined as follows:

1   For each t during the life of the system the *configuration* of the system at t is modelled by a category K_t. An object of K_t represents the state $C(t)$ at t of a component C of the system existing at t.
2   The configuration K_t of the system varies over time. The change of configuration from t to $t' > t$, is measured by a functor[5] from a sub-category $K_{tt'}$ of K_t to $K_{t'}$, called a *transition*.
3   The transitions satisfy a *transitivity condition* (T).[6]
4   A *component* C of the system is a maximal family (C_t) of objects of K_t related by transitions. A *link* s: B → B' between components B and B' is a maximal family of morphisms s_t : B(t) → B'(t) of K_t related by transitions.

Figure 3.2 shows several successive configurations of the Evolutive System **K**, beginning from an initial configuration K_{t0} at time t_0, the transitions between them and different components.

Such an evolutive system provides a 'hybrid' representation: the relational and organized aspects of the system are captured in the structure of the successive configuration categories which give a snapshot of the state of the system at a given time, and the internal dynamics are captured by the 'transitions' between configurations which measure both the dynamic changes of states and the structural changes (such as loss, or addition of components).

A transition is therefore not a deterministic transformation between configurations, but a way of mapping change across time as it might be seen from an external point of view. Likewise, this definition does not refer to a reductionist point of view of change as if it could occur with the 'same' category configuration

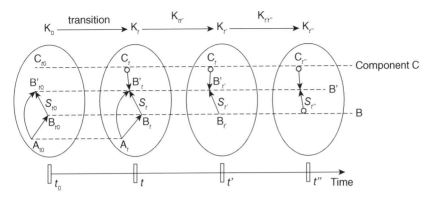

Figure 3.2 An evolutive system

persisting over time. It also accounts for the loss of elements (components or links) between t and t' by being defined only on the sub-category $K_{tt'}$ of K_t consisting of the elements which still exist at t'. For a component C which still exists at t', the transition maps the state $C(t)$ of C at t to its new state $C(t')$ at t', and the same for the links. The 'new' elements at t' are those that are not in the image of this functor. It is thus a way of formalizing a rich mapping of change that goes beyond deterministic and reductionist views of evolution.

The transitivity condition satisfied by the transitions implies that a component C of the system, e.g. the interactions and knowledge generated by, for instance, a specific team of participants in an FLL, is represented by the family of its successive states $C(t)$ in the successive configuration categories while it exists; as such, it is a maximal family of objects of successive configurations connected by transitions. The links between components, which represent the relations that components share over time between each other, are defined similarly as maximal families of arrows connected by transitions.

Organization in complexity levels: simple and complex links

In the section above, we have classified the components of a social system into a hierarchy of disjoint complexity levels: a component C is *n*-complex if it combines a pattern P of interacting components of lower levels.

This hierarchical structure can be translated in MES (using the categorical notion of colimit) as follows: a component is *n*-complex at a time t if it is the colimit of a pattern of interacting components of levels < n. Such an *n*-complex component C has then at least one *ramification* of length $\leq n$ down to level 0 obtained by taking a lower level pattern P of which C is a colimit, then, for each component P_i of P, a lower level pattern of which P_i is the colimit and so on down to level 0. In fact, C may have several such ramifications and we define the *complexity order* of C as the smallest length of its ramifications (it can be < n).

Over time, the number of complexity levels can increase with the formation of 'more complex' components.

In particular, it occurs in the development of the 'memory' of the MES (modelled by a hierarchical subsystem) that represents the knowledge of any nature of the system, including information on its past experiences, the procedures then used to respond and their results.

If we think of the complexity order of a component as measuring a kind of 'vertical' complexity, in MES we have also complex components, said to be *multi-faceted*, with a kind of 'horizontal extension'. These components take up the 'challenge of being in two or more frames at once' (see Chapter 2); for example, groups of people able to operate with different capabilities, ambiguous objects and polysemous concepts in the memory.

A component M is *multi-faceted* if M is the colimit at t of at least two lower level patterns P and Q which are *structurally non-connected*.[7] The fact that P and Q have the same colimit is not a local property at their level but 'emerges' at the higher level of M, to reflect global properties of these lower levels (due to the 'universal' property of a colimit). At a specific time t of the life or duration of a multi-faceted component M, it also has several structurally non-connected ramifications (which can be interpreted as its different 'facets'), and it can play a different role in possibly heterogeneous developments depending on the facet through which it operates. Over time M may lose some of its facets and/or acquire new ones while preserving its own identity, thus undergoing individuation.

The existence of multi-faceted components is called the *multiplicity principle* (MP); it generalizes what Edelman and Gally (2001) called the "degeneracy" in biological systems: "the ability of elements that are structurally different to perform the same function or yield the same output..." It ensures a kind of 'operational redundancy' and gives flexibility to the system, in particular allowing for a robust and flexible enough memory to keep track of changes in the environment, to adapt to diverse circumstances and to develop collective intelligence knowledge creation (CIKC) processes.

If C and C' are n-complex components respectively colimits of lower levels patterns P and P', there are *n-simple links* from C to C' which bind a cluster of links between the components of P and P'. Such links just reflect local properties of C and C'. An important consequence of MP is the existence of *n-complex links* which represent new properties emerging at the level $n+1$ from the global structure of lower levels. Such a link is the composite of n-simple links binding non-adjacent clusters, separated by a switch so that it does not bind a cluster of lower level links. In the next section, we show that complex links are necessary for the emergence of components of increasing complexity orders, in particular in the memory, and, in FLF, for introducing 'change in the conditions of change' at the root of novelty.

Local and global dynamics of the system

In an evolutive system, transitions indicate changes between two instants, but these transitions do not provide information regarding the dynamics underlying the changes that "result from networks of multiple interacting causes that cannot be individually distinguished" (Poli, 2017) in relation with the flux of information between the components and the exchanges or constraints originating from the environment. The dynamics of the system are strongly influenced by the elements of its 'memory', in particular information of its past, and it also allows for the development of this memory by storing new experiences of the system and the procedures used to respond. The system can be described in a recursive fashion, where the changes in the system result not only from previous states of its components and linkages, but also from the anticipated results of previously used procedures. In effect, this introduces conventional dynamics back to the system description, but with a crucial difference: in the MES model preceding states are not necessarily states of elementary components as in conventional dynamic systems; instead, they can be complex memory components emerging to combine relational, functionally organized and non-local patterns.

The introduction of such components, therefore, generates a hybrid representation that can capture both relational complexity that results from the organization of the components as well as dynamics that shape the evolution of the system from one system configuration to another by taking account of memorized previously used procedures. Anticipation can enter the picture. In the MES framework, the dynamic is internally regulated by the local dynamics of a network of functional subsystems, called *co-regulators*, which have a differential access to the global memory, in particular to recall procedures relative to their function. The global dynamic of the MES results from the interplay among the local dynamics of these co-regulators. This interplay is not deterministic because of the impredicativity of the system.

Each co-regulator, say CR, operates stepwise at its own rhythm, a step corresponding to its 'thick present' (Poli, 2011). At each step, CR only receives partial information from the system through the links arriving to it during the step. The part of the system that is accessible in this way to a specific co-regulator is called its *landscape*, modelled by an evolutive system. Based on this information and with the help of the memory, CR selects a procedure that it tries to implement for the next transition, by developing a *Complexification-Decomplexification Process* (CDP) (see below). The results are evaluated at the beginning of the next step, possibly revealing a failure.

The Complexification-Decomplexification Process at the basis of emergence

The transition from t to t' results both from the dynamic change of states of the components and the structural changes of the configuration of the system at t. These last changes correspond to the 'standard changes' emphasized by Thom (1975): birth, death, collision, and scission. In a social system like an FLL they become: addition and suppression of some elements, combination of some patterns to form a complex component, decomposition of a complex element. The aim of the *Complexification-Decomplexification Process* (CDP) is to anticipate what will be the new configuration of the system after realization of a procedure Pr having objectives of these types which, naturally, also induce other changes. As the results have important consequences for FL (see section below) the mathematical conclusions are detailed below (for proofs see Ehresmann and Vanbremeersch, 2007; Ehresmann, 2017).

Emergence Theorem. Let Pr = (S, B) be a procedure on a hierarchical category K with the following data:

- a set S of elements of K to suppress;
- a set B of patterns P to bind so that P admits a colimit cP.

  (i) The CDP with respect to Pr allows to explicitly construct the 'optimal' new category K' after such changes have been effected.
  (ii) The colimit cP in K' of a pattern P in B has a higher complexity order than P if and only if some of the links of P are complex links.

It follows that, if a procedure Pr = (S, B) verifying the condition (NE): at least one of the patterns in B has some complex links, then the CDP leads to a non-ergodic system. In this case, the procedure will be said to be non-ergodic. Otherwise Pr is ergodic.

In FLF, a consequence of the Theorem is the possibility of classification of the cluster of Anticipation Assumptions AA_i (see Chapter 1), depending on the characteristics of the procedures they use. Another consequence is that the evolution of the system through successive CDPs can allow the emergence of components of increasing complexity order and complex links between them which play the role of 'changes in the condition of change', and render the system impredictable. The MES model, therefore, can capture some emergent properties of the system and, thanks to its memory, develop anticipatory assumptions allowing for AfE. We will now study these operations in the particular case of Futures Literacy specific MES (FL-MES).

Futures Literacy – Memory Evolutive System (FL-MES)

We have defined a Memory Evolutive System as a hierarchical evolutive system that satisfies the multiplicity principle, equipped with a hierarchical evolutive subsystem representing the memory and a network of co-regulators. In the process of its evolution, new components of higher complexity order and new complex links between them can emerge through CDPs. Building an FL-MES admitting as co-regulators the different participants to a specific FLL as well as the FLL itself will therefore provide an understanding of how the various participants in an FLL process can collectively progressively figure out novel futures, namely that could not have been deduced from the existing individual and collective knowledge of the participants at the beginning of the collective process.

In FL-MES the landscape of a participant (considered as a co-regulator) corresponds to the mental space of the participant, while the landscape of FLL corresponds to their collective mental space, and will be called the macro-landscape (ML). While CDPs occur in different ways across a given MES, in the FL-MES the focus is on the CDPs occurring in the 'local' landscapes of the participants and in the macro-landscape. Thus FL-MES concentrates on the emergence of new mental objects and/or relations between them over time. This includes so-called 'rational knowledge' as well as emotional and non-conscious evocations. In this way, the FL-MES helps with understanding how the various participants in a given FLL process can enrich the way they anticipate. In other words, the FL-MES formalizes how different co-regulators can form collective macro-landscapes by activating and developing a richer FL-Archetypal Pattern. The FL-MES enables the tracking of the unpredictable 'interplay' in FLL that generates, identifies and makes use of emerging complex links to formulate imaginary futures based on different anticipatory assumptions. The changes that occur as people become futures literate can be defined and traced, providing the evidence for testing hypotheses about the nature of FL and the design of processes to acquire it.

The Archetypal Core

We have seen above that a MES develops a hierarchical memory. Its components are called *records*. Over time, multi-faceted records with increasing complexity order can emerge through CDP (see above). These higher-order records constitute an evolving nexus of memory, its Archetypal Core. It consists of multi-faceted polysemous records integrating knowledge of various modalities (motor, sensorial, epistemological, emotive), with several ramifications through which they can often be recalled.

The records of the Archetypal Core are strongly interconnected by complex links. In the MES model it is assumed that the links between such records form self-activating loops that maintain the activation of an archetypal record for a period of time, and where activation propagates to lower levels. Thus, when an archetypal record A is recalled, its activation propagates to others through archetypal loops which maintain it for some time; from there it diffuses to lower level records through unfolding of ramifications and switches between them; thus, large domains of the memory are activated.

In a social system, the Archetypal Core can be understood as the nexus of the collective (Halbwachs, 1980) or institutional memory (Douglas, 1986) of the social system, which is constantly reproduced through communicative and practical action (Giddens, 1986; Luhmann, 1995). In sociocultural theories of learning, Archetypal Memory is represented as those cultural stocks of knowledge that provide the foundations for sense-making and learning (Vygotskiĭ and Cole, 1978), thus providing the identity of the community in question (Lave and Wenger, 1991). In the context of an FLL it leads to the development of a FL Archetypal Pattern that enables choices with respect to the specific use to which the future is put.

FLL – combining AS and KCP

FLL, as described using the FLF developed in Chapter 1, are general-purpose tools for revealing AA that combine action-learning and CIKC processes that involve a number of people thinking together about the future. Each participant brings special knowledge and experience, in both tacit and explicit forms, as well as their capacity to invent and imagine, debate and discern. In FL-MES, the knowledge and capacities are embedded in the individual memories and Archetypal Cores of the participants. As the participants share their historical and cultural stocks of knowledge, their Archetypal Cores have common elements, possibly with different ramifications. In the process of collective sense-making and knowledge creation, the participants exchange their ramifications of archetypal objects, which lead to the gradual formation of a shared FL-Archetypal Pattern which allows for the formation and extension of the macro-landscape.

When FLL are modelled as MES the process can be traced through the gradual formation of a FL-Archetypal Pattern which allows for the formation and extension of the macro-landscapes (ML). The formation of the Pattern helps with the sharing of explicit knowledge as well as some tacit knowledge (e.g. tacit procedures, skills), and emotions. The Pattern can even follow the transformation of tacit into explicit, thus providing formal descriptions of knowledge generating collective intelligence. The partially overlapping landscapes of the different participants are united in the macro-landscape. As archetypal loops are self-maintained, their activation sustains that of the ML, so that ML persists over a longer period of time and may be progressively extended as the process unfolds. The participants can then select different procedures on ML for anticipating the results of the corresponding CDPs.

Distinguishing ergodic and non-ergodic uses of the future

When analysing the design and implementation of a FLL as a process of ML formation and evolution through the framework of FL-MES, it is particularly important, given the specific role of 'using-the-future' and distinguishing different kinds of anticipatory assumptions, to differentiate between situations where anticipation is used to identify 'realizable' or 'practically desirable' futures (AfF in the FLF)[8] and situations where the future is used to gain a better understanding of the present without being overly limited by realizability or desirability (AfE in FLF).[9] The FL-MES formalization provides an analytical framework for tracking how the formation of FL-Archetypal Patterns and the choice of AA play a role in detecting/inventing/co-creating the richness of reality. *Ergodic anticipation* involves making sense of the present situation through references to the past and the futures imagined from the past, as defined by known trends and given or already familiar images of the future. It is defined by (1) a search for futures that are deemed 'realizable' or 'realistically desirable' on the basis of already known or familiar anticipatory assumptions; and (2) the aim is given. In other words, in the terms of the FLF this is AfF; the anticipatory systems and processes are deployed with the aim of attaching probabilities to the realization of a future on the basis of already known, i.e. familiar, descriptions of the future.[10] In FL-MES, it follows from the Emergence Theorem that the procedures selected for CDP should be ergodic in the sense of without use of complex links.

Here the ML represents a common mental space for the group in which current observations and already expected trends can be related to past situations in order to make sense of them. New aspects of the present and future, including weak signals, may be detected as participants share and discover more about the existing landscape. But it is important to stress that the distinction between ergodic and non-ergodic anticipation draws attention to differences in anticipatory systems (AS). From the perspective of the FLF presented in Chapter 1 this is the difference between those AA that are part of AS1/AS2 and those that are in AS3.

As discussed in Chapter 1, the AS that is used in ergodic anticipation is imagined from the vantage of the past – in this sense ergodic anticipation is defined by the use of models and processes that treat the future as an extrapolation of the past. Non-ergodic anticipation takes a different vantage point, one that attempts to relax the constraint of the past on imagining the future – AA that are found in the AA5 and AA6 clusters of the FLF. In FL-MES it means that the selected procedures for CDP on the ML introduce complex links which ensure change in the conditions of change. Depending on the circumstances ergodic versus non-ergodic anticipation involve different degrees of openness, the suspension of existing assumptions and the invention of new frames or paradigmatically incompatible anticipatory assumptions. Ergodic and non-ergodic anticipation are constructed on the basis of different intentions, AfF versus AfE, and call for methods (KCP) that differ on the basis of the kinds of anticipatory assumptions that are used.[11]

FL-MES formalization exposes the extent to which the design of FLL, for instance at a particular stage in the process when there is ergodic anticipation (Phase 1 as described in Chapter 4), do or do not give rise to CDPs leading to the emergence of complex links. Additionally, the FL-MES formalization helps to reveal the linkages between different phases of the FLL process and the role of ergodic versus non-ergodic anticipation. For instance, it should be evident that in many contexts non-ergodic anticipation involves the construction/selection of different anticipatory assumptions from those of ergodic anticipation and that non-ergodic anticipation will – in most cases – generate different imaginary futures from ergodic anticipation. In both cases the critical evidence will be found in the distinct attributes of the anticipatory assumptions, the primary data generated by FLL.

For the most part, given today's dominant approaches to ergodic anticipation, the choice of anticipatory assumptions will be based on a desire to produce so-called realizable scenarios. As discussed in Chapter 1 these are probabilistic 'stories' or pictures of tomorrow that are usually meant to facilitate imposing today's idea of the future on the future, what might be called a colonization of the future. Thus, the characteristics of the macro-landscape (ML) in this phase of the FL-MES formalization of FLL corresponds to the search for procedures that generate imaginary futures that are believed to be realizable and are meant to reveal the steps necessary for such colonization; as seen in the section on CDP above, it requires the selection of procedures that avoid the use of complex links. Otherwise, the use of complex links in the selected procedures leads to non-ergodic anticipation. So far, however, due to a lack of extensive experimentation with different anticipatory assumptions and with the formalization of FLL, it is too early to tell if only certain assumptions are compatible, or not, with the potentially different aims and methods of ergodic and non-ergodic anticipation. Still, with respect to the FLL cases presented in Chapter 5 of this volume two points that distinguish this research into FL are worth noting. One is that the FLL conducted for the UNESCO FL Project were explicitly designed to go beyond the ergodic anticipation that dominates most current foresight exercises, including CIKC processes. Most of these efforts to think about the future use anticipatory assumptions that are meant to generate realizable futures on the basis of trend extrapolation and/ or preferences. Two, by way of contrast, the design principles used to construct and implement the FLL that serve as case studies in this volume go through three phases, with phase one using conventional ergodic anticipation, phase two using anticipatory assumptions that are considered more compatible with non-ergodic anticipation, and phase three contrasting the anticipatory assumptions generated in the first two phases (for more detail see Chapter 4 and 5).

FLL in practice

The formalization of the FL-MES can help to ensure that the design of the different phases of the FLL respect the goal of differentiating ergodic from non-ergodic anticipation and to gather and interpret the outcomes generated during and after the process. As already discussed in Chapter 1 these design principles are anchored in a theory of different kinds of future. The starting premise is that the future only exists as anticipation and hence ontological differences are defined by differences in AS. This results in the identification of three kinds of future that can then serve as differential starting points, distinct clusters of anticipatory assumptions, that can be used to design the steps and tools that are used in context specific FLL. The three different kinds of future – contingency, optimization, and novel – fit easily into an FL-MES approach. The first two are fundamentally retrospective extrapolatory, using the past to predict the future, even at low levels of probability, while the third is impredicative and calls for modelling that is semi-open.[12] At a practical level, leaning on the experience of the proof-of-concept case studies in this volume, novel futures can be generated by FLL through the deployment of anticipatory assumptions in an action-learning CIKC process that builds participants' FL by passing through successive phases of ergodic and non-ergodic anticipation.

As will be laid out in more detail in Chapter 4, FLL start in Phase 1 with the identification of ergodic prospective assumptions that generate the familiar MLs of expected and hoped-for imaginary futures. Then in Phase 2, the process moves on to generate anticipatory assumptions that are 'relatively' non-ergodic,[13] giving rise to equally 'strange' MLs. In Phase 3, there is a recursive contrasting of the MLs produced in Phase 1 versus Phase 2 such that participants can discern the procedures leading to both complexification versus decomplexification versus complication with respect to their ML of the present. The future is used to understand the present and then, if so desired, to continue on from the search for choices to the making of choices, sometimes on the basis of closed system predictions.

The FL-MES formalization makes it possible to trace the changes that occur as participants collaborate in an action-learning CIKC process like the FLL. The succession of ML during the different phases tracks how collaboration to describe imaginary futures gets participants to reveal their initial or existing AS. The FL-MES provides an analytical window on the changes that occur in people's AA and how this is associated with different AS as well as specific design choices, like particular heuristics. This is crucial for testing the proposition that when participants experience constructing their own AA, developing their capacity to control and invent assumptions, they can contrast ergodic with non-ergodic anticipation, AfF and AfE. An FL-MES formalization of the process could also help participants and observing researchers to discern the boundaries and relationships that allow for the identification of complexification versus decomplexification and (de)complication of descriptions of the present. On this basis FLL produce data, in the form of participants' AA and descriptions of the present, that can be observed and collected by external third-party researchers.

Part of the reason that the FL-MES may be able to play such a key role in the design and analysis of FLL is, as already noted in Chapter 1, that FLL are 'laboratories'. By applying the same criteria that characterize scientific laboratories since the 16th century (Hannaway, 1986) FLL aim to achieve three objectives: making sense of complexity; building futures literacy; and generating data on anticipatory assumptions. More detail regarding the nature of FLL as labs and related design issues are discussed in Chapter 4.

Conclusion

This chapter has started an exploration of the potential for category theoretic concepts to rigorously model important aspects of the FLL process. It has also shown that a 'dynamic' category theoretic description is necessary for evolutive anticipatory systems. Evolutive anticipatory systems are systems that have flexible models of themselves and their environment, and which perceive and act based on these models. Their 'dynamic' is impredicative, and therefore cannot be described using conventional dynamical systems found in the text-books of physics, economics, and social sciences. Category theory, however, provides a stronger formalism that shows great promise in modelling complex systems characterized by emergence and novelty. Novelty, emergence and innovation are natural phenomena in the category theoretic model of Memory Evolutive Systems (Ehresmann and Vanbremeersch, 2007). This has important applications to situations of creativity and learning, such as FLL.

Notes

1 The Futures Literacy Lab (FLL) can be defined as the combination, through application of explicit design principles, of a collective intelligence knowledge creation (CIKC) process with anticipatory systems and processes (ASP). Thus FLL=CIKC + ASP.
2 In this chapter, a graph (or more precisely directed multi-graph) consists of a set of objects (its vertices) and a set of arrows (or directed edges) between them.

3   A category K is a graph equipped with an internal *composition law* which maps a path (f: A → B, g: B → C) from A to C on an arrow gf: A → C (called its *composite*) and which satisfies the conditions: it is associative and each vertex A has an identity id_A: A → A; a vertex of the graph is called an *object* of K, and an arrow a *morphism* or a *link*. The standard reference for mathematicians on Category Theory is Mac Lane (1978).

4   As the concept of complexity is used in various ways by different authors, it is useful to note that the MES model has a less global interpretation of complexity than Rosen. In Rosen's terminology, impredicative systems are complex as they cannot be described using a finite algorithmic model. For Rosen, systems either are complex or not. For a more detailed discussion, see Louie (2009). See also the relations between Rosen and MES in Ehresmann and Vanbremeersch (2007, end of chapters 4 and 6) and in Axiomathes (Baianu, 2006). In MES, the components are distributed in a hierarchy of complexity levels so that a component C of level n+1 is the colimit of at least a pattern of interacting components of levels < n+1.

5   A *functor k* from K to K' is a map which associates to each object A of K – an object $k(A)$ of K', to each arrow from A to B in K an arrow from $k(A)$ to $k(B)$ in K' and which preserves identities and composition. A partial functor from K to K' is a functor from a sub-category of K to K'.

6   (T) If $C(t')$ exists, then $C(t'')$ exists if and only if $C(t')$ has $C(t'')$ for state at t''.

7   In a category, two patterns with the same colimit M are *structurally non-connected* if they are not isomorphic and there is no cluster between them binding into the identity of M. In this case, M is said to be *multi-faceted*.

8   Ergodic anticipation cannot dispense with the necessity of imagining the future. Nor can it escape from the fact that past futures also required a set of anticipatory assumptions, typically ones that were tacitly extrapolatory/probabilistic (projections on the basis of already familiar ensembles of past/future). These ensembles are part of the Archetypal Core.

9   Nothing can be imagined without making certain assumptions. And no assumptions can be formulated without the past and the present providing the conceptual and experiential foundations. It is therefore impossible to imagine the future without making assumptions. This means that there is no way to imagine the future without making at least minimal assumptions that are rooted in past realizability and/or desirability (or opposites). In this sense, there is an ergodic component to the non-ergodic. Nevertheless, the distinction, even if only one of degree and/or levels, remains pertinent with respect to the relationship between imaginary futures and sensing/sense-making of the complex emergent present. The threshold may differ in different circumstances, but it remains true that there are novel phenomena that are obscured, even unimaginable, from within probabilistic or utopian anticipatory frames.

10   In effect, the nature or attributes of the de/complexification generated by ergodic and non-ergodic anticipation are different (see section above on CDP). These differences are due to the difference in anticipatory assumptions that structure ergodic and non-ergodic anticipation.

11   One of the issues here relates to creativity and invention – relative to the starting point of each person/group. Both ergodic and non-ergodic anticipation can involve creativity, invention and discovery, but the underlying anticipatory assumptions are different.

12   Of course, there is no way to know unknown unknowns or to pre-empt genuine uncertainty, and phenomena must emerge first in order to be sensed and made-sense of. But the anticipatory assumptions that are used to generate the futures that then play a role in shaping what can be perceived or invented given reality and our interaction with it can be designed in ways that are more or less conducive.

13   At a theoretical level, there is no inherent impediment to generating scenarios that describe a 'change in the conditions of change' through AfF or AfE. Although, once ergodic non-ergodic anticipation scenarios start painting 'paradigmatic level change', there is a contradiction that emerges between the anticipatory assumptions related to

the instrumental colonizing purpose of retrospective ASP and the nature of complex evolution as a process full of novelty (unknowable unknowns). In other words, ergodic anticipation can project discontinuities as being necessary to arrive at some utopian or dystopian outcome, but such speculation remains within a deterministic and 'realizable' logic, thereby constraining the anticipatory assumptions to this end. Non-ergodic anticipation, by relaxing requirements related to probability and realizability, invites exploration of configurations that lie outside the past.

References

Baianu, I. C. (2006) 'Robert Rosen's Work and Complex Systems Biology', *Axiomathes*, 16(1–2), pp. 25–34.

Béjean, M. and Ehresmann, A. (2015) 'D-MES: Conceptualizing the Working Designers', *International Journal of Design Management and Professional Practice*, 9(4), pp. 1–20.

Bergson, H. (1913) *Time and Free Will: An Essay on the Immediate Data of Consciousness*. New York: George Allen and Company.

Bowker, G. C. and Star, S. L. (1999) *Sorting Things Out: Classification and Its Consequences*. Boston, MA: MIT Press.

Douglas, M. (1986) *How Institutions Think*. Syracuse, NY: Syracuse University Press.

Edelman, G. M. and Gally, J. A. (2001) 'Degeneracy and Complexity in Biological Systems', *Proceedings of the National Academy of Sciences of the United States of America. National Academy of Sciences*, 98(24), pp. 13763–768.

Ehresmann, A. (2017) 'Anticipation in MES – Memory Evolutive Systems', in Poli, R. (ed.) *Handbook of Anticipation: Theoretical and Applied Aspects of the Use of the Future in Decision Making*. Cham: Springer Publishing, pp. 1–31.

Ehresmann, A. C. (2012) 'MENS, an Info-Computational Model for (Neuro-) Cognitive Systems Capable of Creativity', *Entropy*, 14(12), pp. 1703–1716.

Ehresmann, A. C. and Gomez-Ramirez, J. (2015) 'Conciliating Neuroscience and Phenomenology via Category Theory', *Progress in Biophysics and Molecular Biology*, 119(3), pp. 347–359.

Ehresmann, A. C. and Vanbremeersch, J.-P. (1987) 'Hierarchical Evolutive Systems: A Mathematical Model for Complex Systems', *Bulletin of Mathematical Biology*, 49(1), pp. 13–50.

Ehresmann, A. C. and Vanbremeersch, J.-P. (2007) *Memory Evolutive Systems: Hierarchy, Emergence, Cognition*. Amsterdam: Elsevier Science.

Eilenberg, S. and MacLane, S. (1945) 'General Theory of Natural Equivalences', *Transactions of the American Mathematical Society*, 58, pp. 231–294.

Giddens, A. (1986) *The Constitution of Society: Outline of the Theory of Structuration*. Berkeley, CA: University of California Press.

Halbwachs, M. (1980) *The Collective Memory*. New York: Harper & Row.

Hannaway, O. (1986) 'Laboratory Design and the Aim of Science: Andreas Libavius versus Tycho Brahe', *Isis*, 77(4), pp. 585–610.

Jacob, F. (1970) *La logique du vivant*. Paris: Gallimard.

Kan, D. (1958) 'Adjoint Functors', *Transactions of the American Mathematical Society*, 87, pp. 294–329.

Kauffman, S. A. (2008) *Reinventing the Sacred: A New View of Science, Reason and Religion*. New York: Basic Books.

Mac Lane, S. (1978) *Categories for the Working Mathematician*. New York: Springer Publishing (Graduate Texts in Mathematics).

Lave, J. and Wenger, E. (1991) *Situated Learning: Legitimate Peripheral Participation*. Cambridge, MA: Cambridge University Press.

Longo, G., Montévil, M. and Kauffman, S. (2012) 'Enablement in the Evolution of the Biosphere', in *Proceedings of the Fourteenth International Conference on Genetic and Evolutionary Computation Conference Companion – GECCO Companion 2012*. New York: ACM Press.

Louie, A. H.-Y. (2009) *More Than Life Itself: A Synthetic Continuation in Relational Biology*. Frankfurt: Ontos Verlag.

Luhmann, N. (1995) *Social Systems*. San Francisco, CA: Stanford University Press.

Murray, R., Caulier-Grice, J. and Mulgan, G. (2010) *The Open Book of Social Innovation*. London: NESTA. Available at: https://www.nesta.org.uk/sites/default/files/the_open_book_of_social_innovation.pdf (Accessed: 21 January 2018).

Nonaka, I. (1994) 'A Dynamic Theory of Organizational Knowledge Creation', *Organization Science*, 5(1), pp. 14–37.

North, M. (2013) *Novelty: A History of the New*. Chicago, IL: University of Chicago Press.

Nussbaum, M. C. (2011) *Creating Capabilities: The Human Development Approach*. Cambridge, MA: Harvard University Press.

Polanyi, M. (1962) *Personal Knowledge: Towards a Post-Critical Philosophy*. Chicago, IL: University of Chicago Press.

Poli, R. (2011) 'Steps Toward an Explicit Ontology of the Future', *Journal of Futures Studies*, 16(1), pp. 67–78.

Poli, R. (2017) 'Introducting Anticipation', in Poli, R. (ed.) *Handbook of Anticipation: Theoretical and Applied Aspects of the Use of the Future in Decision Making*. Cham: Springer International Publishing.

Rashevsky, N. (1954) 'Topology and Life: In Search of General Mathematical Principles in Biology and Sociology', *Bulletin of Mathematical Biophysics*, 16(4), pp. 317–341.

Rosen, R. (1958a) 'A Relational Theory of Biological Systems', *The Bulletin of Mathematical Biophysics*, 20(3), pp. 245–260.

Rosen, R. (1958b) 'The Representation of Biological Systems from the Standpoint of the Theory of Categories', *The Bulletin of Mathematical Biophysics*, 20(4), pp. 317–341.

Rosen, R. (1973) 'On the Dynamical Realization of (M, R)-Systems', *Bulletin of Mathematical Biology*, 35(1–2), pp. 1–9.

Rosen, R. (1985) *Anticipatory Systems: Philosophical, Mathematical, and Methodological Foundations*. Oxford: Pergamon Press.

Rosen, R. (1991) *Life Itself: A Comprehensive Inquiry into the Nature, Origin, and Fabrication of Life*. New York: Columbia University Press.

Sen, A. (2009) *The Idea of Justice*. Boston, MA: Belknap Press of Harvard University Press.

Simeonov, P. L., Smith, L. S. and Ehresmann, A. C. (2012) *Integral Biomathics: Tracing the Road to Reality*. Cham: Springer Publishing.

Star, S. L. (2010) 'This Is Not a Boundary Object: Reflections on the Origin of a Concept', *Science, Technology, & Human Values*, 35(5), pp. 601–617.

Stubbe, J. (2017) *Articulating Novelty in Science and Art: The Comparative Technography of a Robotic Hand and a Media Art Installation*. Cham: Springer Publishing.

Thom, R. (1975) *Structural Stability and Morphogenesis: An Outline of a General Theory of Models*. Reading, MA: W.A. Benjamin.

Tuomi, I. (2014) 'Something New Under the Sun: A Category Theoretic View on Innovation and Unpredictability', in *5th International Conference on Future-Oriented Technology

Analysis (FTA) Engage Today to Shape Tomorrow. Brussels: Joint Research Centre, European Commission.

Tuomi, I. (2017) 'Ontological Exapnsion', in Poli, R. (ed.) *Handbook of Anticipation: Theoretical and Applied Aspects of the Use of the Future in Decision Making*. Cham: Springer Publishing.

Vygotskiĭ, L. S. and Cole, M. (1978) *Mind in Society: The Development of Higher Psychological Processes*. Cambridge, MA: Harvard University Press.

Part II
Futures Literacy Laboratories
Design principles and case studies

4 Futures Literacy Laboratories (FLL) in practice

An overview of key design and implementation issues

Riel Miller

Introduction

The first goal of any process meant to research or develop Futures Literacy (FL) as a capability must be to find a way to make anticipatory assumptions (AA) explicit and observable. The solution to this challenge, after considerable reflection and debate in the early stages of the UNESCO FL Project (Miller, 2014), was to design and deploy a tool that eventually came to be called Futures Literacy Laboratories-Novelty (FLL-N). As discussed in Chapter 1, FLL-N is a sub-set of a more general FLL design meta-framework. The difference between FLL and FLL-N is that the former consists of a set of design principles for processes that enable the discovery and invention of AA, from just one to many, and the latter is a specific implementation designed with the goal of ensuring that participants explore a broad range of AA, specifically those that encompass 'extra-systemic' or outside-the-box kinds of novelty (Tuomi, 2017).

Succinctly, the UNESCO FL Project's research and development instrument, and the design principles underpinning this instrument, needed to be effective and efficient at delivering the following outcomes:

1. A process that would be highly adaptable and easily applied across a vast range of contexts around the world, involving very different sets of participants, topics, durations, resources, lead times, output requirements, etc.
2. Observable AA covering the full spectrum as specified in the Futures Literacy Framework (FLF) elaborated in Chapter 1, from AA1 to AA6, in all of the potential practical situations for running experiments noted in the previous point.
3. Enhancements to the capacity of participants to 'use-the-future', i.e. to become more futures literate.
4. Proof-of-concept level evidence of the relationship between the development of FL as a capacity and the ability to sense and make-sense of novelty, where novelty is a form of complex emergence.
5. Proof-of-concept level evidence of an enhanced appreciation of time-place specificity/uniqueness arising from the combination of 'collective intelligence knowledge creation' (CIKC) processes and 'using-the-future'.

6 Experimentation with different designs and the testing of different design principles for developing and implementing processes for using-the-future and developing FL as a capacity – in other words, provide an opportunity to refine the methods being used.
7 Improvements in the capacity of local communities to 'use-the-future', i.e. to become more futures literate, in order to encourage sustainability, equity and peace by opening up new ways of framing hope and action locally and globally.
8 Initiate networks and communities of practice at the local and global levels related to advancing the theory and practice of 'using-the-future' – i.e. FL.
9 Assist UNESCO to be an innovative organization capable of taking a leadership role in addressing the changing nature of the challenges humanity faces by seeking a more effective alignment between, on the one hand, applying human agency to the desire for resilience through sustainability, equity and peace and, on the other hand, understanding and acting with a fuller appreciation of complexity as a fundamental resource for achieving these goals.
10 The means to overcome 'poverty-of-the-imagination' (Popper, 2002) and thereby provide a sustainable source of hope for a 'better life' in the future; a necessary if not sufficient condition for humanity to find the will and motivation to take the risk of making changes intended to realize its constantly evolving aspirations.

The set of design principles that enabled the UNESCO FL project to create and run processes that met these objectives emerged from three decades of experimentation with 'using-the-future' for different ends, in different ways and in different contexts (Miller, 1990, 2001, 2007; Miller, O'Connell and O'Donnell, 2010). This FLL meta-framework for designing processes that reveal and invent AA provided the starting point for the refinement and adaptation of FLL-N tailored to meet the goals of the UNESCO FL Project, while respecting both the stringent resource constraints and imperative of ensuring global coverage.

Since 2012 over 36 different FLL-N have been conducted in more than 20 countries. Chapter 5 presents a sample of 14 case studies. Covering such a breadth of topics and scope of communities, while aiming for the goals noted above and sticking to the time and budget constraints of the project, set very rigorous parameters for FLL-N. These practical parameters account, in large part, for the choice of short-duration 'collective intelligence knowledge creation' (CIKC) processes, usually one to two days, and highly compressed lead-up and follow-through phases. The adoption of this time-limited format was a pragmatic response to the constraints of the UNESCO FL project and should not be construed as being inherent to the design principles or constituting some kind of 'norm' bounding FLL or FLL-N. CIKC processes that 'use-the-future', of which FLL are an example, can last a few hours or a couple of years – it all depends on the context.

The aim of this chapter is to set the stage for the sample of case studies presented in Chapter 5 by providing readers with a succinct overview of the generic meta-framework for designing and implementing FLL-N, without going all the way to providing a full-fledged 'do-it-yourself' (DIY) guide. Developing such

Futures Literacy Laboratories in practice   97

DIY instructions (see, for instance, Knapp, Zeratsky and Kowitz, 2016) and the associated principles is one of the goals of the next phase of the UNESCO FL Project aimed at testing FLL-N prototypes, called the 'Imagining Africa's Futures' project (UNESCO, 2017). This next prototyping phase of the innovation cycle involves experimenting with different FLL-N designs, under carefully constructed and monitored research conditions, in order to produce more precise and robust rules and templates as a means to advance the theory and practice of FL around the world.

FLL and FLL-N in practice: a brief and general overview

The general structure – a learning process

FLL are designed so that people make their anticipatory assumptions explicit and thereby reveal not only the determinants of the futures they imagine but also the attributes of the anticipatory systems (AS) and knowledge creation processes (KCP) that they use when thinking about the future. FLL expose why and how people use-the-future. This data emerges from their inter-actions as participants learn to 'use-the-future'. At the most basic level, FLL, as a design meta-framework, are shaped by the proposition that a learning processes, in the sense of Dewey (1997), follow a cycle along the lines of Figure 4.1. The starting point for perceiving and understanding AA is to interrupt the routine action of 'using-the-future' to provoke a sense that there is a problem when imagining the future. This realization kicks-off the learning cycle that serves as the skeleton for building an FLL, and most action-learning CIKC processes (Almirall, Lee and Wareham, 2012).

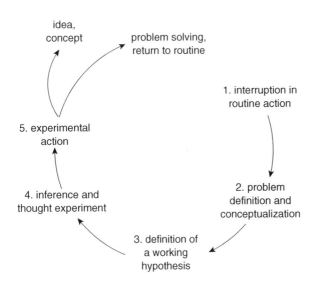

Figure 4.1 Dewey cycle of learning

Source: Tuomi, 2005

The importance of underscoring the Dewey learning cycle in Figure 4.1 is the centrality of finding a way to spark this inquisitive and reflective human process in order to nurture the development of FL. A FLL or FLL-N without an 'interruption of routine action' is like a chemistry lab without a catalyst. And, to stretch the comparison a bit further, like the catalyst used in a chemistry lab there are many different ways to initiate and sustain the learning cycle. What is essential is for this moment to occur – that instant of realization when someone is inspired to ask a 'new' question. Then, once again taking the designer's perspective, the process needs to continue as an experimentation-based approach to problem solving and thereby sustaining the learning cycle as it is depicted in Figure 4.1.

Although the learning cycle framework is a highly useful guide for the FLL and FLL-N designer, it does not solve the key challenge of how to spark the learning process. There are, of course, a quite infinite set of circumstances that can initiate learning and many potentially relevant theories and pedagogical methods. The practical approach adopted to help design the action-learning of FLL rests on the idea of a learning curve depicted in Figure 4.2. The S-shaped learning curve, familiar to most people from their own experiences, is quite helpful for guiding the designers and implementers of CIKC processes because it sets out basic parameters for each phase. Phase 1: Reveal: tacit to explicit – easy; Phase 2: Reframe: creative, inventive, experimental – difficult: Phase 3: Rethink: compare, reflect, consolidate – easier.

Following from the choice of the S-curve approach to structuring the learning process, FLL generally kick off the learning cycle by conducting exercises, which will be different in different contexts, that take advantage of the ability of humans to shift tacit knowledge to explicit by sharing it with others. This phase needs to

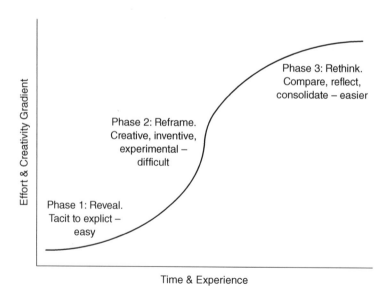

Figure 4.2 Three phases of the learning cycle

be designed to arrive at that moment when participants start to suspect that there is a problem with their 'routine action'. CIKC processes can be particularly effective at leveraging the capacity of a group to reveal such 'gaps' through an initial task that is both easy to do and, in the case of FLL, relevant to exposing the tacit AA of participants in the process. Towards the end of this phase, participants start to become sceptical of their capacity to 'use-the-future'. This is one of the 'ah ha!' moments of the learning cycle. Participants are no long sure of why and how to think about the future. This sets the stage for the more difficult Phase 2, which in turn prepares participants for Phase 3.

The point being made here, since a more detailed discussion of the three phases of FLL-N is in the next section, is that the S-curve learning sequence helps guide the designer's ordering of different steps and the selection of different tools/heuristics that make up FLL. In particular it ties most design choices to the requirement that selected processes and tools engage people in learning about something they know enough about to be able to make their thoughts explicit, be creative and meaningfully consolidate what they have learned. Awareness of the criteria for creating the conditions that enable learning, combined with the requirements for knowledge sharing that make CIKC functional, are also crucial for determining the selection of participants, the specification of the topic – how it is defined and framed – and the kinds of activities that will enable participants to 'use-the-future' in ways that are creative and facilitate learning.

Designing a successful FLL rests on paying careful attention to the process as a whole since each phase is tightly linked to the next one. All of the phases need to bring AA to the forefront, not only in order to realize the research and 'problem solving' objectives, but crucially to ensure the participants move along the FL learning curve. Furthermore, in order that the AA discerned by participants in one phase contribute to those that emerge in the next one it is crucial to design the processes and facilitation so participants do not get trapped into debating claims that one assumption or set of assumptions is better or more positive than another. FLL could be designed to invite people to argue that one set of assumptions or a particular reframing heuristic merits precedence over others. But in most cases, given that participants generally start from a low level of FL, the primary task is to build up a basic understanding of what it means to 'use-the-future'. Debates over one set of AA or another is not the purpose of the exercise.

On the contrary the aim is to open participants up to the notion of a diversity of reasons and methods for 'using-the-future'. The FLL design, particularly in the FLL-N implementation, calls for the selection of learning processes that do not lock participants into claiming there is one 'correct' set of AA, even if the search for AA must involve surfacing the rich cultural and historical heritage that is beneath participants' usually tacit AA. All this means that considerable attention has to be paid to the choice and implementation of the heuristics and reframing processes, particularly in Phase 2. From a designer's perspective the aim is to seek processes, usually sourced from within the community, that tap into the participants' own power to distance themselves from their frames, whatever that frame happens to be and however they happen to be able to develop such distance.

In the beginning... a spark within

Given the goals of the UNESCO FL project and the design criteria of FLL-N it is an important requirement that the spark of curiosity and desire to think and rethink the future comes from within a community. Concretely this means that the FLL-N process begins, in most cases, when a local champion or specific initiator of the activity is searching for ways to think about the future. This point of departure is a spark from within, not a match lit from outside. And even in situations, more common than not given low levels of FL, where it is not very clear why and how to think about the future, what matters is a willingness to think in 'new' ways. This is one of the reasons that almost all of the FLL-N conducted so far have been initiated and driven by communities seeking to innovate, a group that implicitly or explicitly is trying to appreciate complex emergence.

Efforts to initiate an FLL-N from outside the relevant community and without an expressed appetite for innovative thinking run the risk that the process will fail to evoke or 'surface' (Scharmer, 2007) the community-specific attributes of how people 'use-the-future'. To meet the objectives of the UNESCO FL Project it is essential that the inception of FLL-N and the premises for collaboration avoid locking in external AA or those AA people expect that others expect. Starting and then co-creating a process that is meant to 'surface' and invent the AA that are authentic to the participants is a delicate task. The reasons and methods people use to bring the future into what they see and do are central to daily life and wellbeing. Drawing participants into a process that alerts them to their own futures illiteracy (not someone else's) can be destabilizing and inimical to learning.

Starting on the wrong foot, using inappropriate language or procedures or CIKC tools can reduce participants' willingness to dig within to find their AA and reinforce the tendency to take someone else's reasons and methods for 'using-the-future'. This means that from a design perspective it is essential from the outset to take into account, beginning with the very first conversation that starts the journey, the importance of a non-subordinating approach to setting out the terms for collaboration, specification of the topic, selection and manner of inviting the participants, continuous joint creation of the process – including during the running of the Lab, and the determination of outcomes.

Establishing the foundations for undertaking a process to (re)think why and how to 'use-the-future' also demands building up an initial degree of FL within the core group. Without a basic grasp of FL it is impossible for those leading the effort at the community level to engage in a joint-design process that generates FLL. Developing this shared understanding of the basics of FL takes time and significant attention to seeking and validating local history and the many different ways of framing the future (AA). In the vast majority of cases this start-up period requires running a simulation or test-run FLL with key players. This provides an opportunity to experiment with a range of different ways of formulating the topic of the FLL, testing different tools/heuristics that can be used during the action-learning CIKC process, and how to best craft a learning environment that welcomes and inspires engagement and creativity.

Every context will have different conditions for constructing a safe space for participants to express and negotiate shared meaning. Other critical questions during start-up are: who to invite to participate, how to invite them, where to run the process – paying careful attention to the important physical conditions or "the stage" for expression and the unfolding of the dramatic narrative thread of CIKC, for how long, with what kind of facilitation, how to best alternate small group and full-group work, etc. Eventually a detailed agenda for the FLL emerges and the roadmap for preparing the event falls into place – and it is no longer a generic FLL based on the meta-framework design principles but a specific implementation like the FLL-N.

One of the key challenges worth flagging is the selection of a topic for a CIKC process like FLL. This choice usually flows out of a discussion around the pressing challenges or so-called 'wicked problems' that the community is not only grappling with but is also willing to formulate with an openness to rethinking the nature of the problem. Although some FLL demand only endogenous creativity and so the invitation and topic can be quite closed from a systemic perspective (AA1 and AA2 as spelled out in Chapter 1), when it comes to FLL-N it is clear that both the acquisition of FL and its application to detecting or inventing novelty call for the selection of a topic and goal that embrace complexity by seeking to extend beyond the boundaries of currently imaginable systems/processes. It is, of course, quite feasible to design FLL around highly specific planning targets or contingency preparedness, situations where the topic is fixed and systems are closed; confining the conversations in this way means that participants will not be exposed to using-the-future beyond the search for deterministic certitudes. This is not the case with FLL-N. With FLL-N, specification of the topic and the tasks for exploring it need to be invitations to be open and creative in searching and inventing the imaginary future. Participants in an FLL-N need to seek AA that include anticipation for emergence (AfE) (see the discussion in Chapter 1 of the distinction between anticipation for the future (AfF) and AfE).

Once this start-up phase is completed, with the specification of a topic, the goals of the process, and the basic attributes of the participants to be recruited, it is time to begin sketching the actual laboratory process. As is evident from the case studies in Chapter 5 and as has been emphasized already, each FLL-N is unique. It is therefore somewhat misleading to provide a general overview of the design of the three-phase learning voyages, the CIKC processes that 'use-the-future', which were developed and actually deployed during the proof-of-concept phase of the UNESCO FL Project. In important ways, there is no 'average' FLL-N since it is central to the methodology to adapt the learning process to context and not expect that the same steps, heuristics, terminology, reframing devices, etc. will generate evidence of the diversity of AA. Uniformity of procedures makes sense when conducting a test in a chemistry lab or when seeking to understand a psychological or political response to a standard question in an appropriately specified, usually relatively homogeneous target population. But when the goal is to delve into the specificity of AA in a particular community at a given point in time, the techniques must be adapted to the task, not the other way around.

102 *Riel Miller*

With this caveat in mind, the next sub-sections do offer a general overview of the three-phase learning-curve FLL process as applied to the UNESCO FL Project's FLL-N.

Phase 1: Reveal – expectations and hopes

Following the learning curve of the FLL meta-framework this first phase is the 'easy' part, as participants shift what they already think about the future from implicit to explicit and build shared meaning, usually working in small break-out groups. Successful designs for this first phase use heuristics that facilitate making anticipatory assumptions explicit, such as the realization that their default way of imagining the future is deterministic. Achieving these goals raises a number of design challenges. One of the first is that the heuristic selected to engage people in a conversation about the future of the topic chosen for the FLL-N should invite them to appreciate what they know and give permission to an open expression of expectations, hopes, and fears. In this phase priority needs to be given to keeping the task of moving from tacit to explicit manageable and unintimidating.

In Phase 1 most FLL-N opted for the sometimes difficult but pedagogically useful differentiation of expectations from hopes, with the work usually conducted in that order. Structuring the Phase 1 process to distinguish the probable from the desirable typically enabled participants to begin to understand that there are different kinds of future. In most FLL-N the initial focus was on predictions, often considered a more 'technocratic' task, and only then in the second round of Phase 1 on hopes. Part of the motivation for selecting this design, expectations then hopes rather than the other way around, is that in many contexts it gave participants an opportunity to disentangle delicate and emotional aspects of the future like pessimism and optimism. Teasing out the difference between expectations and hopes also draws attention to the role of AA. In the prediction round, it is common for participants to recognize, even if only in passing, that the ceteris paribus premises required to make probabilistic forecasts are not convincing. In the aspirations round, liberated from the conventional imperative of thinking about the future probabilistically, participants also begin to see that their hopes are shaped by AA. At the end of this first phase participants know they can deploy their knowledge of the topic to generate imaginary futures while it dawns on them that these pictures depend on their analytical and narrative framing assumptions, including AA (Miller, 2007).

As always, specific design choices depend on the nature of the group, topic, available time, setting, etc. For most FLL-N, due to time constraints and the primary aim of helping people to perceive their anticipatory assumptions in a way that is relevant to the local topic, the facilitators were instructed to steer the conversations away from dystopian futures and time-series or 'movie' type descriptions of how a particular future came to be. This design choice reflects the view that catastrophe scenarios and the recounting of causal chains that determined some final outcome tend to distract from the efficient and effective realization of the goals of FLL-N. Breakdown futures are in many ways too easy to invent and often do not induce people to discuss their assumptions in much depth, since everything just falls apart. As for the elaboration of scenarios that are the outcome of a deterministic cause and effect, these stories tend to be highly time-consuming to produce, and are technical and difficult to manage in CIKC processes. In part this is because predictive 'accuracy' for complex topics is unattainable, although detailed fictions with strong advocates are common, leading groups into pointed but inconclusive debates. Thus, from the perspective of designing a process that helps both observers and participants to perceive the group's AA, it is usually more effective and efficient if the small group facilitators guide the conversation away from discussions of dystopias and paths to tomorrow to focus instead on describing in detail relatively positive day-in-the-life snapshots deemed probable or desirable in a specific year in the future.

Two further design issues usually come up when putting together and running Phase 1. The first, just alluded to, is: when in the future? Here the typical response is far enough into the future that people relax their desire and anxiety to engage in 'accurate' predictions. This varies depending on the group and the topic. The relaxing effect of pushing the time horizon out to the long-term is really a sort of ruse, meant to get participants beyond the ingrained expectation that they should be able to predict the short-run. Being asked to think long-term is a way of 'giving permission', reducing the anxiety of being wrong about the future. Although often draped in the gravitas of thinking about future generations, long-term thinking is often a way of trying to reassure ourselves by colonizing the future, believing that we can and should impose today's idea of tomorrow on tomorrow. At the end of Phase 1 participants are usually open to questioning this typically unquestioned hubris. As Phase 1 wraps up it usually does not seem strange to point out that from the perspective of a non-deterministic complex emergent universe, non-predictability starts immediately. Complexity thinking provides permission to embrace uncertainty, to be open to complex emergence, at all points in time, even right now.

The second design issue is how to help participants to develop and share a meaningful narrative, a description of the future they imagine together. Here there are many potential tools/heuristics, again depending on the group and context. One of the tools that was used in numerous FLL-N conducted as part of the UNESCO FL Project was Sohail Inayatullah's Causal Layered Analysis (CLA) process (Inayatullah, 1998). This tool is well adapted to short-duration, highly diverse FLL-N because it assists participants to deepen their descriptions of the futures they have imagined. In most cases the procedure involved an initial step in which each participant in a break-out group silently notes down three or four bullet points describing their snapshot of expected or hoped-for futures, next the facilitator invites each participant to share these glimpses of tomorrow, and then the facilitator introduces the four levels of CLA: litany, systems, protagonists, metaphor. The discussion of these different levels or perspectives is used to enrich the narrative that describes the different attributes of the future evoked by the group. It is important to note that in most cases the design did not call for the facilitators to ask the group to find a consensus or a shared 'vision' but rather to capture the diversity of perspectives, including outlier aspects, in order to provide a rich picture.

Phase 2: Reframing – playing with AA

The learning curve is much steeper in Phase 2, in part because reframing involves a triple estrangement. First, people have little experience of 'using-the-future' other than for preparation or planning, i.e. for deterministic purposes. Asking participants to leave behind the comfort zone of this AA can feel quite disturbing, particularly since preparation and planning are so deeply rooted in the dominant ways of thinking about survival. Second, most people do not know how to imagine the future without using probabilistic framings, even for desirable/undesirable futures. Practically speaking, when participants are asked to let go of extrapolation of the past into the future, including utopias deemed 'unrealistic' but based on projecting yesterday's values on tomorrow, they are unable to get their imaginations in gear. Denied their habitual imagining spaces (see Chapter 1 and Miller, 2007), lacking variables and motivation (why think about the future if not to plan or prepare?) participants do not have the source material or scaffoldings necessary for describing imaginary futures.

Third, reframing calls for a dual movement that seems to go in two opposing directions, one towards abstraction and the other towards concretization. The abstraction occurs when participants are asked to let go of familiar fixtures in the world around them, opening up a distance between the specific ways things are done in the present, like education that happens in schools, and the general nature or function of an activity, like learning that can happen anywhere. The concretization occurs when participants are supposed to describe how things work but in a world imagined on the basis of strange AA. All of this is hard because participants are usually not accustomed to using their imaginations in this way.

A quick illustration might help to grasp the challenge here. In this fictional example imagine that a group of FLL-N participants have found a time-machine and are able to go back in time to a period when there was no universal compulsory schooling. Then, from that context, they are asked to imagine what the world would be like at a 'day-in-the-life' level if they were to imagine a future world where there has been a full implementation of universal compulsory schooling. In this illustrative case, since the participants know full well what it is like to live in a society with compulsory universal schooling it is actually hard for them to describe what can be called 'past futures'. Still, what this exercise shows is that it is easy to describe the future of schooling and how it functions when, as time travellers, the present is available as a guide. But our ancestors had no such advantage. Now get into their shoes for the reframing exercise: leap forward 30 years and imagine a world where schools have become marginal, but learning has become really central to everything. The challenge for participants in this example is to use the general category of learning as a human activity for framing and then describing in practical detail an imaginary tomorrow. Both tasks are difficult – how has learning changed and how has daily life changed in this 'reframed' playground for the imagination?

Given the difficulty of imagining the future with unfamiliar AA, particularly the adoption of a non-deterministic purpose for the future, Phase 2 faces significant design challenges. For the reframing to succeed the FLL-N designers need to find contextually specific ways to induce and sustain the estrangement that arises from disrupting participants' AA, yet maintain a connection to what the participants find meaningful and within reasonable reach of an intensive exercise in creative thinking. This is one of the reasons why CIKC was chosen as an approach to guide the organization and tools for Phase 2. Diversity and processes for negotiating shared sense making can spark the creativity needed to elaborate descriptions of daily life in a future imagined on the basis of unfamiliar frames and AA. The process needs to invite and inspire participants to question the way they use the future; in other words, introduce alternative ways of thinking about emergent reality – repetition and difference. By playing with unfamiliar futures in an unfamiliar way, participants confront the limits of using-the-future exclusively to prepare and plan. They begin to move into the realm of 'anticipation for emergence' (AfE) not just 'anticipation for the future' (AfF). In this way Phase 2 moves the group beyond assumptions about deterministic causality so that they begin to experience what it is like to be more futures literate by developing the capacity to use a wider range of anticipatory systems and processes.

In practical terms, for much of the UNESCO FL Project, a specific source of reframing was used as the basis for adaptation to the specific FLL-N context: the Learning Intensive Society (LIS) scenario (Miller, 2004). The advantage of using this scenario was that it had been elaborated by suspending key sets of AA, including the ways in which people 'use-the-future' – a change in the conditions of change. The LIS also covered a wide range of currently dominant models/frames used to describe economic, social, political, technological, ecological and gender functioning. Using the LIS for the FLL-N Phase 2 process enabled relatively rapid customization and created the kind of alternative AA playground that seemed reasonably likely to encourage participants to engage in their own reframing. The serious disadvantage of adapting an off-the-shelf reframed world was its lack of genuine roots in the specific context of the community undertaking the FLL-N. Optimally the reframing frames, narrative and analytical (Miller, 2007), should be developed from within the community. However, in practice – at least so far – it has been hard to find a way to do this given the constraints of the UNESCO FL Project. The results of the proof-of-concept phase, as presented in the case studies in Chapter 5, underscore a series of ongoing research tasks, including how to best design and implement reframing. Further hints on approaches to reframing and CIKC can also be found in the discussions of efforts to explore wellbeing (Chapter 7), the use of gaming (Chapter 6) and gender (Chapter 8). Seeking answers to a wide range of research questions, including approaches to reframing, is one of the main goals of the next stage of the UNESCO FL Project that focuses on FLL-N prototyping.

Phase 3: New questions – next steps

In most FLL-N conducted so far Phase 3 has been constructed around a comparison and contrast exercise between Phases 1 and 2. This part of the process is designed to identify, invent, and reinforce observations about differences in AA and how this provides insight into both why and what the future can be used for. In large part this is what can be called a form of meta-cognitive process (Dunlosky and Metcalfe, 2009; Metcalfe and Shimamura, 1994) that on the one hand, leverages the similarities and differences in AA to build an understanding of the practice of FL and on the other hand, involves thinking about thinking about the future to build an understanding of the theory of FL. Phase 3 teases out different aspects of FL as a capacity. Different FLL and FLL-N will of course generate different degrees and mixtures of understanding of FL. Often, although not all of the time, participants manage to begin to feel comfortable differentiating deterministic from non-deterministic 'uses-of-the-future'. They begin to see the box for their imagination created by deterministic uses of the future, and start to imagine what it would be like to be able to invent different anticipatory assumptions, including ones where the reasons for 'using-the-future' might be different.

In addition, because the FLL-N is focussed on a specific and meaningful topic, participants recognize that they have been thinking about their problem or hope or issue on the basis of imaginary futures framed by a particular set of AA. Most of the time this leads to understanding their topic in new ways because they have achieved some distance from their usual, and typically tacit framing, and can begin to work with alternative framings. In many cases there is a realization that their anticipatory assumptions, often 'past futures' like the trajectory of industrialization experienced by most of the world's rich countries, are constraining the way they see the present. Participants begin to understand how a particular image of the future, rooted in a specific set of anticipatory assumptions, brings them to focus too narrowly on those aspects of the present that seem important for planning to converge or catch-up with someone else's past or present.

Like the other phases of the FLL-N this one is highly context dependent. The aims of the process as determined by the community play a key role in determining how far the discussion will go. Generally, at the end of Phase 3 there is a deeper appreciation of the role of imaginary futures and the underpinning AA in determining what participants sense and make-sense of in the complex emergent present. This realization that using-the-future in different ways, for preparation or planning or novelty, reveals different attributes of the present is a key takeaway from the FLL-N. But the power of this realization is amplified when it is accompanied by two other insights. First is that the AA that open up part of the novel emergent present do not 'use-the-future' for preparation or planning, but enlarging perception. Second is that there is an important distinction between what might be called 'search' and 'choice'. In other words, efforts to sense and make-sense of the complex emergent present need to be separated, at least in part, from efforts to act on bets or engage human agency to secure specific imaginary futures. Here then is one of the central attributes of FL as a capacity – it entails the ability to distinguish the different anticipatory systems and processes that are relevant to perception and action, even if both are interdependent and relationally constituted.

What this means in practice is that Phase 3 can be easily followed by a Phase 4 that is more about choice than search, even if this phase was not often designed into FLL-N conducted for the UNESCO FL Project, due to many different constraints, including time and resources. Drawing a line between the more reflective Phase 3 and a more action oriented Phase 4 and beyond is also justified by the learning curve design meta-framework. Phase 3 is meant to achieve a certain closure and satisfaction, the familiar denouement of a theatrical or dramatic process that is also an important design referent for CIKC processes of all kinds. As discussed in Chapter 1 and with respect to the 'microscope of the 21st century', the content of imaginary futures and of participants' perceptions of the present and past include emotions and ephemeral, even illogical guesses. These are food for thought and creativity, wisps of the fleeting and maybe heretofore unimagined possibilities that can only be sensed and made-sense of through new words, concepts, fears and hopes. If the design of an FLL-N is meant to include these aspects of complex, time- and place-specific emergence, then the fullness of what people articulate, including emotions and dreams, needs to be able to surface. Having invited this kind of sharing to occur, the process needs to respect the engagement and visceral nature of the learning that is taking place by concluding in a way that empowers participants through some form of closure. Asking new questions, ones that constitute an ontological expansion for the participants, i.e. relative to their starting point, generally does the trick.

Conclusion

Stepping outside the perspective of FL as a theory and practice for embracing complexity, which is perhaps the most novel message – at a proof-of-concept level – of this book, the long-road of developing and testing FLL offers three additional messages worth noting at this point.

One is that CIKC are, as the 'microscope of the 21st century', a fundamental breakthrough in two distinct and crucial ways. The first way is as a means to shared sense making and negotiated meaning. In UNESCO speak, this is often called inter-cultural dialogue, but in many circumstances, this may be both too grandiose and misleading. CIKC processes enable people, at a specific place and time, with their unique mixture of communities and cultures – past, present and imagined futures – to work together to create knowledge by shifting tacit to explicit and finding space to invent and negotiate meaning. This is much the same as any effective team building process, if seen from today's dominant organizational perspective, and could be considered 'diplomacy' and hand-shaking across cultures if you take the reductionist objectivist perspective on boundaries and an aggregative perspective on the relationship of micro to macro. But if you adopt a relational ontology (Tuomi, 2017) and an assemblages perspective on parts and wholes (Delanda, 2006), then CIKC processes can be more than building bridges between distinct, objective and autonomous 'others'. CIKC can be a tool for playing and creating with what we know and do not yet know as relational anticipatory living entities, which is why category theory and the Memory Evolutive Systems approach, as discussed in Chapter 3, can help us to describe more formally what happens in an FLL.

Two is that as a 'laboratory catalyst' getting people to think about the future is a powerful way to make CIKC processes function. In other words, there are certainly processes, called even more generically 'innovation laboratories' (Gryszkiewicz, Lykourentzou and Toivonen, 2016; Murray, Caulier-Grice and Mulgan, 2010; Scharmer, 2007), that build an awareness and knowledge with very little explicit and theoretically grounded understanding of what is the future. This kind of CIKC is certainly viable – the future is just the later-than-now. But in the case of FLL design, what is striking is the role of understanding and taking into account anticipatory systems and processes. In a general way the future is a powerful way to invite and incite people to share and create, and it is particularly effective and efficient for running CIKC processes. But what the UNESCO FL Project proof-of-concept experiments show is that designs like the FLL and FLL-N that take into account the attributes of FL, particularly engaging with diversity of why and how to 'use-the-future', provide a more systematic and coherent approach to sensing and making-sense of the complex emergent present. FLL, unlike generic 'innovation laboratories', undertake a process that builds up FL, going through the stages of learning about anticipatory systems and processes. Like someone who learns the alphabet then moves on to reading and writing and literature, someone who is futures literate is able to generate an entirely new set of imaginaries or 'possibility spaces' (Miller, 2007). FLL are a powerful type of CIKC because the future is integrated into the process, not just as the 'later-than-now' – some ontologically formless proposition hence epistemologically ambiguous – but rather as a conceptually powerful springboard to 'using-the-future' for different ends and with different means selected on the basis of a theory of FL.

Three is that the by combining the creative power of CIKC with learning and scaffolding up FL is what makes FLL-N effective and efficient at leveraging or inspiring what might be called relative ontological expansion (Tuomi, 2017). Here relative means that the starting point for the ontological expansion is where participants begin when they dive into the process. From this perspective absolute ontological expansion is adding something entirely new to the universe while relative ontological expansion is when people 'discover' or 'invent' an idea that is new to them – much novelty is of this specific kind. FLL-N are thus in part about becoming better able to discover and invent novelty in all its forms, which is why cultivating FL is one way of turning the uncertainty inherent in our complex emerging universe from a threat into an asset, from a disruptive force into a source of meaning.

In closing, much experimentation, research and exploration remain to be done. The work undertaken so far by the UNESCO FL Project and in the case studies presented in the next chapter have only begun to scratch the surface.

References

Almirall, E., Lee, M. and Wareham, J. (2012). Mapping Living Labs in the Landscape of Innovation Methodologies. *Technology Innovation Management Review*, 2. Retrieved from http://www.timreview.ca/article/603.

Delanda, M. (2006). *A New Philosophy of Society: Assemblage Theory and Social Complexity* (1st ed.). London / New York: Continuum.

Dewey, J. (1997). *How We Think*. Buffalo, NY: Prometheus Books.

Dunlosky, J. and Metcalfe, J. (2009). *Metacognition*. Thousand Oaks, CA: SAGE.

Gryszkiewicz, L., Lykourentzou, I. and Toivonen, T. (2016). 'Innovation Labs: Leveraging Openness for Radical Innovation?' Available at: https://ssrn.com/abstract=2556692 (Accessed: 21 January 2018).

Inayatullah, S. (1998). Causal Layered Analysis: Poststructuralism as Method. *Futures*, *30*(8), 815–829. Retrieved from http://www.sciencedirect.com/science/article/pii/S001632879800086X.

Knapp, J., Zeratsky, J. and Kowitz, B. (2016). *Sprint: How to Solve Big Problems and Test New Ideas in Just Five Days*. New York: Simon & Schuster.

Metcalfe, J. and Shimamura, A. P. (1994). *Metacognition: Knowing about Knowing*. Cambridge, MA: MIT Press.

Miller, R. (1990). *Vision 2000: Quality and Opportunity*. Toronto: Ministry of Colleges and Universities Ontario.

Miller, R. (2001). 21st Century Transitions: Opportunities, Risks and Strategies for Governments and Schools. In *What Schools for the Future?* (pp. 147–155). Paris: OECD. Retrieved from http://www.oecd-ilibrary.org/education/what-schools-for-the-future_9789264195004-en.

Miller, R. (2004). Imagining a Learning Intensive Society. In J. Coolahan (Ed.), *Learning in the 21st Century: Towards Personalisation* (pp. 27–74). Dublin: Information Society Commission. Retrieved from https://www.researchgate.net/publication/310803202_Imagining_a_Learning_Intensive_Society.

Miller, R. (2007). Futures Literacy: A Hybrid Strategic Scenario Method. *Futures*, *39*(4), 341–362.

Miller, R. (2014). *Networking to Improve Global/Local Anticipatory Capacities – A Scoping Exercise: Narrative Report*. Paris: UNESCO/Rockefeller Foundation.

Miller, R., O'Connell, L. and O'Donnell, R. (2010). Futures Ireland: A Case Study in Building Futures Literacy. In M. Aaltonen (Ed.), *Robustness: Anticipatory and Adaptive Human Systems*. American Emergent Publications. Retrieved from https://www.researchgate.net/publication/285131731_Futures_Ireland_A_Case_Study_in_Building_Futures_Literacy.

Murray, R., Caulier-Grice, J. and Mulgan, G. (2010). *The Open Book of Social Innovation*. London: NESTA. Available at: https://www.nesta.org.uk/sites/default/files/the_open_book_of_social_innovation.pdf (Accessed: 21 January 2018).

Popper, K. R. (2002). *The Poverty of Historicism*. London: Routledge.

Scharmer, C. O. (2007). *Theory U: Leading from the Future as It Emerges*. Cambridge, MA: The Society for Organizational Learning.

Tuomi, I. (2017). Ontological Expansion. In R. Poli (Ed.), *Handbook of Anticipation: Theoretical and Applied Aspects of the Use of the Future in Decision Making*. Cham: Springer Publishing.

UNESCO. (2017). Signing of a Memorandum of Understanding between UNESCO and the OCP Foundation. Retrieved from http://www.unesco.org/new/en/member-states/single-view/news/signing_of_a_memorandum_of_understanding_between_unesco_and/ (Accessed: 30 October 2017).

5 The Futures Literacy Laboratory-Novelty (FLL-N) case studies

Edited by Stefan Bergheim

Case 1: Cultural heritage research and the future

Martin Rhisiart

Efforts to recognise and preserve cultural heritage, in all its forms, are fundamentally linked to views of the past, present and future. As a result, the anticipatory assumptions that form the foundation for imagining the future play a determinant role in understanding what cultural heritage is, which aspects are deemed worth preserving and how to attempt to assure durability or continuity. In keeping with the general design principles for Futures Literacy Laboratories (FLL) and the specific targets of the Future Literacy Laboratory-Novel (FLL-N), as detailed in Chapter 4, the co-creation of the process for this customised lab needed to take into account the specific nature of the link between anticipation and cultural heritage.

This led to a re-articulation of the topic to ensure that both the identification of cultural heritage and its temporal dimensions were amenable to being understood from an anticipatory perspective. This specification of the topic, the approach to reframing and the type of questions all facilitated the surfacing of intra- and extra-systemic anticipatory assumptions. This, in turn, allowed participants to sense and make-sense of distinct strategic perspectives and ensuing implications for their research agenda. Senior researchers participating in this FLL, according to feedback collected during and after the event, found the process was exceptionally effective at revealing both key assumptions and new directions that might shape the selection of strategic research priorities in the field of cultural heritage preservation. The design lessons from this case study provide insights into how FLL can assist researchers working in a highly technical and specific field to both better understand and invent items for their strategic agenda.

This FLL-N was organised as part of a larger project sponsored by the European Commission's Joint Programming Initiative on Cultural Heritage and Global Change: a New Challenge for Europe. The goal of the overall project was to develop a Strategic Research Agenda (SRA) for the field of cultural heritage, with a horizon of 10–20 years. Futures methods were widely used throughout the project (Miller, 2007a), including the FLL-N described below as a case study in using the future. Two other approaches for thinking about the future were also used: a drivers meta-analysis covering scientific and grey literature; and a real-time Delphi Study that explored the views of cultural heritage experts on drivers and potential changes in the field/impacting on the field.

The aim of the FLL-N was to push the boundaries of conventional thinking, with the hope of revealing and inventing innovative strategic policy choices in the area of cultural heritage research. The FLL-N methodology was chosen on the grounds that it was designed to go beyond the parameters of traditional futures exercises – to explore novelty as defined by the Futures Literacy Framework (FLF) presented in Chapter 1. A collaborative design process was undertaken, following the general design principles for FLL and specifically for a FLL-N as outlined in Chapter 4. By the end of the design phase it was clear that the aim of this FLL-N was to mobilise the collective intelligence of a group of cultural heritage research experts to push the boundaries of strategic thinking about their field, paying particular attention to the challenges facing Europe.

This case study summarises the three-phase FLL-N process followed by participants and concludes with overall comments on how an enhanced understanding of the potential of the present that surfaced in the discussions reveals strategic issues and choices for cultural heritage research. The richness and subtlety of the discussions that occur during an action-learning collective intelligence knowledge creation process, like the FLL-N, makes it challenging to fully record and describe what occurred. The following summary offers highlights of the conversations that took place during this FLL-N with an emphasis on the research priorities of the UNESCO FL Project and the goals of this specific exercise on the future of cultural heritage research.

Participants were selected on the basis of their contributions to the Scientific Committee of the Joint Programming Initiative and represented interests across the field of cultural heritage research. Most of the 17 participants were well established and senior researchers, with affiliations to national and international scientific communities. The participants were drawn from ten European Union countries.

Workshop programme and methodology

The FLL-N methodology was used to co-design and facilitate a two-day lab in November 2012, with a strong emphasis on the FLL-N action-learning/research approach. The participants were divided into two groups and worked through the three FLL-N phases, with plenary feedback and discussion after each level. The group work was facilitated by Dr Martin Rhisiart and Mr Meirion Thomas. The plenary sessions were facilitated by Dr Riel Miller. A customised FLL workbook was distributed to participants that included materials intended to encourage a more open and creative discussion. In particular, there were some initial thoughts on re-defining the meaning of the key term *preservation* within cultural heritage research. Questioning such a basic concept was meant to provoke reflection on how contemporary societies engage with the continuous processes of cultural reproduction, including through digital means.

Phase 1: The future of cultural heritage research: values and expectations

Participants spent approximately one and a half hours discussing their values and expectations for cultural heritage research in 2032. The two breakout groups were asked to discuss their views regarding the probable future of cultural heritage research in 2032. As per the standard FLL design, the main objective in Phase 1 of the process is to identify expectations (what people think *will probably* happen), and hopes and preferences (what they would *like to see* happen by 2032). One of a number of aspects customised for this FLL-N, in light of the participants' high level of technical knowledge, was to start the group work with an initial invitation to question some of the basic terms used to discuss cultural heritage research.

The first question for group discussion was: what is research? In response to the question, participants stated that knowledge creation in society is changing, and that the validity and role of the research process will be different. The enquiry process or practice of research is changing and in some cases, the validity of research is also changing. One other important perspective raised was the difference between science and research. It was noted that in several countries, the focus is primarily on natural and not social sciences and humanities. This leads to a lack of integration; the arts need to be tied to science to get recognition and funding.

DEFINITIONS

Group 1: Cultural heritage can be many different things – including memory, skills, materials, and technologies. It is about 'dealing with old stuff' – evoking the passage of time between past and present.

Group 2: Cultural heritage institutions have several roles: to collect; to research; to preserve; to disseminate. It was emphasised that 'what is not functional is lost'; part of the role is to give function to the artefact.

EXPECTATIONS FOR 2032

Group 1: Cultural heritage research will be more interdisciplinary but practice will remain ahead of structures and institutions. This will cause a continued lag in support for interdisciplinary funding.

Europe will be more multicultural: a challenge for cultural heritage research is to better reflect that diversity and what it means for individuals. Cultural heritage research will have a positive role as a bridge between diversity and social identities. Relevance will be a critical challenge: cultural heritage research needs to reflect diversity or there will be declines in funding and in relevance. It is unclear whether problems of funding cycles will be overcome; this will depend on progress in educating decision-makers. The economic situation further undermines prospects for continuity of funding.

Group 2: The task of cultural heritage curators will be to decide what stays and what goes. However, the role will be redefined – to make intelligent linkages (maybe digital more than physical). The paradigmatic shifts ensuing from globalisation (e.g. China; Islam) will force reinterpretation of cultural heritage. There will be an open science of cultural heritage research, with greater participation from citizens and consumers; cultural heritage research will be more integrated into society.

PREFERRED 2032 FOR CULTURAL HERITAGE RESEARCH

Group 1: There will be recognition of the need for funding, and increased recognition, awareness and interest from the public. Cultural heritage research should be closer to the people; it should be more decentralised and networked. Cultural heritage research has the capacity to empower individuals to participate in cultural heritage; education and awareness across society will be central to this vision. This preferred vision brings the public into the process, partially because it will be a necessity since professional resources (e.g. conservation) will not be sufficient. The boundary between the digital and the physical in cultural heritage research will disappear. Cultural heritage research should become a continuous act of creation as opposed to a static stand-alone effort at preservation. Careers in cultural heritage research should become more entrepreneurial – embracing a portfolio approach that combines periods in the private, public and philanthropic sectors.

Group 2: In the preferred future cultural heritage research will be depoliticised and unifying. It will not be driven by political correctness but rather by academic freedom. Funding for cultural heritage research will be evaluated more effectively. It will be valued more generally socially and economically. There will be less 'Tivolisation' – less akin to a theme park attraction. Cultural heritage research should be recognised as a discipline.

PRESENTATIONS OF RECENT DEVELOPMENTS IN FORESIGHT AND FL

Following Phase 1 group work and plenary presentations, participants were provided with an overview of recent developments in the field of foresight, its role in national research prioritisation and in addressing grand challenges in the European Union. They were then introduced to the idea of FL in general and the Learning Intensive Society reframing tool that they would use in Phase 2 of the FLL-N.

Phase 2: Reframing cultural heritage research

Using the Learning Intensive Society (LIS) as a model for imagining cultural heritage research in 2032, the groups were challenged to describe their work under a different set of framework conditions – social, economic and cultural. Participants had approximately three hours during the afternoon of the first day

114 *FLL-N case studies*

and the morning of the second day to complete Phase 2. The objective of the Phase 2 discussions was to produce a 2032 scenario for cultural heritage research. In accordance with the typical FLL-N design their task was to provide a snapshot of how the knowledge production and scientific enquiry process functioned under an alternative set of boundaries and conditions.

From the perspective of design and facilitation, participants were asked to consider the economic, social and cultural dimensions of this transition. What could be the new nature, purpose and direction of research? How could this move beyond Mode 1 and Mode 2 research (Gibbons *et al.*, 1994)? This might move towards an open, distributed research and knowledge production system. What might be the implications of a shift from private ownership to collective availability for institutions and infrastructure? How could cultural heritage research become a more dynamic field, where there is real-time reflexivity and interpretation? What do culture, heritage and preservation mean in a LIS 2032 world?

The following brief scenario summaries convey some of the main aspects of cultural heritage research in 2032 as imagined by the groups. Although the groups followed a common facilitation process, the outputs reflect the dynamics of each group. It is interesting that the two scenarios are different, although both share common elements.

GROUP 1: ATHENA SCENARIO

Athena is our friend – 30 years old – with a lot of skills and ambition. She is a practitioner, a craftsperson and an aspiring researcher. She would like to get into more research – in a LIS, the main value is exchange of knowledge as part of the social fabric. Cultural heritage is an important feature in her society where old and new are both valued. The old brings accumulation of knowledge and experience and can inform new knowledge so cultural heritage is a representation of knowledge. Athena is a questioner and is looking for new horizons. Craft knowledge and high-end research are equally valued and allow for different and varied career development opportunities.

Government is the guarantor of knowledge and institutions, and the ability to acquire and develop knowledge, including high level knowledge through universities. But Athena is not sure that she wants to be in this realm. Athena asks questions and becomes part of the team as a researcher; however, she is not embedded within institutions. Society allows her to do both pure and applied research – knowledge is the prime value creator and people are valued by their portfolio of knowledge. People can pick and choose. Education is a mix of science and the arts to develop a palette of skills; practice is open to research and research is open to practice.

Shared value is mediated through collective appreciation of the worth of knowledge. When people retire, their knowledge is not dispersed; they can still bring their knowledge into the economy and society. Society supports Athena to learn and practise; she will be supported if and when she has children. Society values her knowledge and skills and will support her to fulfil her learning ambitions. Cultural heritage research is more fluid – Athena can enter the field at various stages as suits her circumstances and ambitions. Open access to knowledge and national institutions will act as mediators of that knowledge.

GROUP 2: CULTURAL DIVERSITY IN EUROPE EVENT SCENARIO

We are a researcher in a digital hub centre focusing on 2012 heritage and we are organising an exhibition/conference 'Cultural Diversity in Europe'. The context for the event is that cultural rights are enacted and 'work' well; there is a strong focus in cultural research on global connections among cultural groups, and the drive in cultural heritage research is to find unifying concepts. For the conference, machine translation is a key tool to allow Chinese etc. translation. This is a virtual exhibition based around digital technologies challenging the virtual realities for cultural heritage and research – what is the role of the *original*? The event is strongly participatory – participants use ambient computing that enables them to see, feel, smell and experience the exhibits.

Knowledge is a commodity of value so in the world of 2032 cultural heritage research is a generalised activity: 'Everyone is a researcher now'. People do their own research and produce learning intensive products. Virtual experiences and participatory cultural heritage research mean that paradoxically, there is enhanced meaning and value assigned to original artefacts. There is an increased role for validation and reference points – cultural heritage institutions that curate – and for cultural heritage institutions as intermediaries between knowledge and private funders. Institutions are strongly educational, entertainment-focused and demonstrative – enabling touching, feeling and experiencing.

Phase 3: Rethinking cultural heritage research

In the Level 3 discussions, the groups reassessed anticipatory assumptions surfaced in Phases 1 and 2. In particular, the group work was guided by the following question: What are the anticipatory assumptions around cultural heritage research – and the social, economic, cultural conditions that frame them? Participants had approximately two hours to do Phase 3.

GROUP 1

How cultural heritage is valued more broadly
In the current situation, there is an assumption that cultural heritage is valued in policy because there may be an economic value – cultural enterprise, creative industries, etc. There is a separation of researchers and users/consumers and producer; they are independent of one another. Much but not all 'engagement' is on the basis of dissemination of results once research has been completed, that is, post-hoc engagement.

Empowerment and democratisation
How can cultural heritage research support empowerment? One dimension where people feel more comfortable is intra-systemic empowerment, where

116   FLL-N case studies

constraints are removed within the research community to enable cross disciplinary working. This is a process of collaboration and reform.

How can cultural heritage research support empowerment on a social level? What would this really mean? It seems that there are two dimensions. The first is the removal of constraints – the permission to act. The second is ownership of the creating process.

How can cultural heritage research support and anticipate policy discussions? How can cultural heritage research be ahead of the game in respect of economic instrumentality?

Creating new structures and infrastructure – there could be better, shared ownership of infrastructure across institutions, which would also facilitate cross-disciplinary working.

Intrinsic role and value of cultural heritage in society
In order to realise the potential of cultural heritage at a societal level, a lot of progress needs to be made in – and through – education. A more holistic and personalised approach to education would help to remove false choices between sciences and arts.

GROUP 2

Cultural heritage matters to society at large – this is the fundamental and underlying assumption. Increasing participation beyond passive forms of 'consumption' is good.

Everyone is a researcher now – how developed is that? How much of that is already apparent in programmes and activities now? There are some good signs in the present, e.g. programmes have requirements for dissemination plans and for digital distribution of outputs.

Knowledge is a commodity with value – this has implications for evaluation and funding of research in cultural heritage. Evaluation of knowledge and artefacts needs to improve. Evaluation of research outputs and decisions on research funding need to be on 'net new content' – new, original and valuable content – rather than simply looking at citations.

Important role of technology – digital technologies and access, but materiality also matters, alongside the digital and the intangible.

Cultural heritage research helps integration of communities and societies – enables further understanding and is a unifying factor. A precondition to this is the first assumption – that cultural heritage is valued by society at large.

Producers/consumers drive cultural heritage research – society establishes key strategies for cultural heritage – undertaken from a broad political and cultural context, but also responds to problems such as natural environment. Consumers also become producers; everybody becomes a researcher, and increasingly they will drive cultural heritage research.

Conclusions

In concluding the workshop – particularly drawing on the points made during the third phase of the process – the final plenary session focused on insights and implications for strategic policy choices for cultural heritage research. This part of the workshop lasted approximately one hour. Four key considerations for developing a strategic research agenda emerged.

Empowerment – how can cultural heritage research support empowerment and democratisation within society? There are two distinct dimensions to the social empowerment question from a cultural heritage research/practice perspective. The first is giving people permission to act by removing constraints, e.g. allowing people to access artefacts/conservation. The second is enabling ownership in the research process.

Co-creation – how can policy be designed in a way that genuinely uses the knowledge and capacity distributed in society? This is a large question for research policy more broadly, and one in which cultural heritage research may be able to lead the way. Engagement in this sense is not disseminating the results of closed research processes after they have finished but rather co-creating research and knowledge through a distributed and participatory model of enquiry and practice.

Importance of values – the crucial role of values in cultural heritage research was recognised. First, cultural heritage research should be reflective of values in society. Second, values should be explicitly addressed in judgements on what is worth preserving/how to make the choice of what is preserving. Without societal recognition and valuing of cultural heritage, discussions on options for cultural heritage research will be largely futile. Cultural heritage research needs to address the intrinsic value of cultural heritage in society generally – touching on issues of continuity, discontinuity and identity.

Valuing knowledge and the allocation of resources – new methods of evaluating research are needed, which will serve as the basis of allocating resources. Evaluation of research outputs and decisions on research funding need to be done on the basis of producing net new content/knowledge rather than simply looking at citations.

As outlined in the introductory section to this case study, this FLL-N was part of a Joint Programming Initiative (JPI) to support the development of a Strategic Research Agenda (SRA) for Cultural Heritage Research in Europe. The results of the FLL-N and the other elements of the Foresight study (Joint Programming Initiative (JPI) on Cultural Heritage, 2013), directly informed the shape and content of the SRA report, published in June 2014 (JPI on Cultural Heritage and Global Change, 2014). The SRA highlights the four strategic considerations for cultural heritage research policy that flowed directly from the FL workshop: empowerment; co-creation; the importance of values; and valuing knowledge and the allocation of resources. In this case, one objective for the FLL-N – to elicit fresh policy-oriented thinking and options – was realised through the subsequent work of the SRA. This is due in large part to the collective endeavour and commitment of the participating institutions. One of the interesting results of the workshop is the shaping of institutional goals and the allocation of resources towards cultural heritage research in the years to come.

The realisation of the FLL-N on Cultural Heritage Research was partially funded by a Coordination and Support Action from the European Commission (JHEP CSA - Contract number 277606) and the contributions, in kind, by UNESCO.

References

Gibbons, M., Limoges, C., Nowotny, H., Schwartzman, S., Scott, P. and Trow, M. (1994) *The New Production of Knowledge: The Dynamics of Science and Research in Contemporary Societies*. London: Sage.

Joint Programming Initiative (JPI) on Cultural Heritage (2013) *Foresight Study and Technological Capability Report: Futures Literacy Scenarios Workshop – The Future of Cultural Heritage Research*. Available at: http://www.jpi-culturalheritage.eu/wp-content/uploads/JHEP_D2.4_Part3.pdf (Accessed: 30 August 2017).

JPI on Cultural Heritage and Global Change (2014) *Strategic Research Agenda*. Rome: JPI Cultural Heritage.

Miller, R. (2007a) 'Futures Literacy: A Hybrid Strategic Scenario Method', *Futures*, 39(4), pp. 341–362.

Case 2: The future of science in society

Cristiano Cagnin and Lydia Garrido Luzardo

What is science? What is knowledge creation? There are many answers. The aim of this Futures Literacy Lab-Novelty (FLL-N) on the future of science and society was not to debate definitions but to find starting points for collaborative exploration of how our ideas about the future influence our understanding of the present. The working definition, proposed to serve as a basis for starting conversations, was science as a set of specific methods and relationships that enable humans to continuously negotiate their understanding of the world around them (see for example, Understanding Science 2017; Anon 2017a, Anon 2017b). Sense making and making sense is a key pillar of knowledge creation that encompasses a learning process, both internal and external, which produces knowing in all its forms. The way the future is used in science defines which science and its place in society.

Hence, we need to dig into the assumptions embedded in knowledge creation and in our capacity to invent novelty.

This also relates to decision making. Making decisions to embrace complexity and treating uncertainty as a resource for exploration of new possibilities calls for a significantly enhanced comprehension to use the future to understand the present. Building this greater capacity rests on bringing anticipation out into the open as the way the future exists in the present. Doing so makes clear that conscious human search and choice deploy a range of different anticipatory systems to invent and apply the future to practical decision making. An applied anticipatory systems approach to using the future provides policy and decision makers as well as individuals with an enhanced capacity to both question and invent the anticipatory assumptions that inform their choices.

The above is in line with the Centre for Strategic Studies and Management's (CGEE) mission to promote Science, Technology and Innovation (STI) to advance economic growth, competitiveness and wellbeing in Brazil. It does so by carrying out foresight and strategic evaluation studies in combination with information and knowledge management approaches and systems. At the core of its activities is its position and ability to articulate and coordinate diverse actors within the Brazilian National Innovation System (NIS). One of the CGEE's institutional objectives linked to its mission is to lead foresight studies that generate anticipatory intelligence for both the Brazilian NIS and the STI Ministry and its agencies.

During the past five years, CGEE has been changing its approach to developing and addressing new strategic questions and in recognising new issues which deserve further investigation via systemic and systematic observations and dialogue. It is doing so to evolve its foresight practice to combine generations one to five of foresight development (Georghiou, 2001, 2007; Johnston, 2002, 2007; Cuhls, 2003) as well as foresight modes 1 (Eriksson and Weber, 2006; Havas, Schartinger and Weber, 2007) and 2 (Da Costa et al., 2008), and to enable its results to be better positioned to support reorienting the Brazilian NIS. The aim is to move from a normative and prescriptive approach to one that embraces complexity, emergence and novelty. Such a move is being sought by fostering an improvement in CGEE's capability to use systematic approaches and to develop recommendations for policy design and implementation based on shared insights and perceptions as well as evidence. Several tools and approaches are being explored to enable CGEE to advance in this direction and to use the future to inspire and expand collective imagination and understanding of the present. Ultimately, the aim of foresight at CGEE is to balance contextualised design with systemic and systematic qualitative and quantitative approaches, and to welcome unknowability and uncertainty as sources of novelty, thus also providing an invitation to creativity and improvisation.

In this context, this specific FLL-N was designed to assist the participants to collectively identify and invent new anticipatory assumptions. Anticipatory assumptions cover a range of different elements that enable conscious thought to allow us to imagine the future and make choices in the present. Our conversation

120 FLL-N case studies

in the FLL was contextually specific, not only because we were a distinctive group of people, meeting in a particular place and at given moment in time, but also because from a wide range of perspectives, the idea and practice of science was evolving.

Movement towards new forms and relationships of knowledge creation, spanning efforts to redesign societal innovation systems and embrace unknowability are altering, reconfiguring and inventing new ways of thinking and doing science. This all points towards the importance of opening up what we imagine to be the future of science as one of the ways to assist with a fuller appreciation of the potential of the present. The workshop was carefully designed to achieve this objective.

During the workshop, participants went through a FLL-N process. This experience enabled them to more fully explore the potential of the present and thereby advance their capacity to make strategic decisions in contexts of ambiguity. This ensured that diversity and complexity could serve as sources of inspiration; a way to embrace the dazzling heterogeneity of the world as well as to respect the creative spontaneity of freedom and serendipity.

The workshop: imagine the future of science in society

The Future of Science in Society workshop, co-organised by CGEE and what was then called the UNESCO Foresight Unit, took place as a satellite event of the World Science Forum in Rio de Janeiro on 28 and 29 November 2013. The workshop had three primary goals: (1) guide participants through a learning-by-doing process that challenged the implicit and explicit anticipatory assumptions they use to think about the future; (2) test and refine the Futures Literacy methodology being globally shaped through the UNESCO project 'Networking to Improve Global/Local Anticipatory Capacities – A Scoping Exercise'; and (3) support CGEE in changing its approach to developing and addressing new strategic questions, recognising new issues that merit further investigation via systemic and systematic observations and dialogue, and transforming its way of designing, organising, implementing, managing and evaluating its foresight and strategic studies.

Participants in this FLL-N workshop included representatives from government, industry, academy and youth. They were selected to represent a wide range of viewpoints in their understanding of science and its roles in society. Overall, the 25 participants varied in age from 20 to 60+ years old and represented a number of different organisations, including: CGEE, UNESCO, UNIDO, Department of Economic and Social Affairs of the United Nations Secretariat, University of North Carolina, Academy of Sciences of both Hungary and Cuba, Max Planck Institute, Embraer, Petrobras, Vale, Association of Professional Futurists, Millennium Project, Getúlio Vargas Foundation, Pontificia Universidade Católica do Rio de Janeiro, Institute of Pure and Applied Mathematics, Faculdade Latino-Americana de Ciências Sociais, Secretariat of Strategic Matters of the Brazilian Presidency, and Ministry of Science, Technology and Innovation.

Participants were divided into four working groups, each with a facilitator and an observer whose role was to back up the facilitator, support the organisation of group discussions into Post-its and/or flip charts and to take notes on the process and its main results. Despite having similar guidelines on how to operate in each of the three main workshop phases, working groups had the freedom and flexibility to adapt group dynamics, since the idea was to experiment with different moderation approaches and test what might work best for each context. Each phase took roughly two and a half hours plus an hour for reporting back in plenary sessions and discussions.

Phase 1: Reveal

The exercise started by asking participants to think about their predictions about and hopes for the different roles of science in society. The main objective was to build temporal and situational awareness. Self-awareness is related to experience. For pedagogical purposes, the design placed these experiences in a frame through shifting both expectations/predictions and values/hopes from tacit to explicit. This took place via a facilitated group discussion about the future of science in society in 2040.

Generally, participants' main assumptions centred on the relationship of science to technological development. Within this science-technology nexus they tended to focus on how, in the future, science-technology would resolve a vast range of existing challenges and problems and enable knowledge sharing that empowered individuals and societies. In this phase, the work and results were quite conventional. They did not find it too surprising, thrilling, or shocking. Their imaginations were engaged and they built well on each other's ideas, having fun, learning together, showing respect, and playing along.

During the exercise, many participants found that some anticipated changes had both positive and negative aspects. For instance, more open access to data might produce innovations and new security and privacy risks. Participants were challenged by the facilitator to think beyond an extrapolation of 'business as usual', noting concerns with progress and growth paradigms, which made them build more negative outcomes and contingencies but not radically different scenarios. They looked backward and agreed that the future is not the present anymore, but remained anchored in present experiences and ways of framing them.

In the second segment on desired futures (hopes and dreams for 2040), many participants took the positives from their expectations and built on them, which they called 'new frontiers' for science. Education, health, environment and technological breakthroughs would open new opportunities. In terms of risks such as the military and cyber-security, they explored solutions and contingencies for overcoming possible problems.

Even though participants were well versed in cutting-edge topics like transhumanism, the singularity, environmental issues and other technological futures, the discussion did not stray far from what they already saw as likely outcomes. This kind of extrapolation changed substantially by the time the process reached Phase 3.

122 *FLL-N case studies*

The main outcomes of Phase 1 for all four groups were similar in terms of overall assumptions regarding participants' expectations and desires related to the future roles of science in society. Outcomes were summarised as follows.

Science as technology fix – the main attributes being:

- biotechnology and information and communication technologies are pervasive across all realms of society;
- clean energy (e.g. nuclear fusion) becomes more affordable to all as it does for health systems (cancer solved; nanotechnology, genetic and bionic medicine, etc.), water and all other means necessary for societies' quality of life;
- science can address all global challenges (the reach of a sustainable world with the Millennium Goals achieved and businesses competing for remaining garbage) and to bring about greater social justice, as well as to enable global peace and quality of life through new innovations (STI breakthroughs), knowledge at new frontiers and unknown technologies;
- STI controlling nature leading to a bridge between machines, humans and nature;
- extension of human life through reengineering of cells and genetic enhancements;
- first child born in space and ability to travel to neighbouring galaxies; and
- more productivity, efficiency and access to services.

Science/knowledge empowering individuals and societies – the main attributes being:

- integration between science and society leads to empowerment of citizens and greater democracy;
- science becomes international, transdisciplinary and collaborative and is embedded early in education with equal access and opportunities for all;
- science serving and responding to social needs as well as an input to policy and decision making – policy informed by scientific evidence with political systems accountable to scientific decisions and public judgement/outreach;
- gender equality and balance as well as recognition making scientific careers of greater interest (considering youth needs and expectations) and leveraging overall investments in research (the EU applies 5 per cent of GDP on R&D investments);
- citizens become more informed making better decisions individually and collectively (thinking globally, acting locally); all citizens are scientifically literate;
- the scientific method is pervasive for individuals in their daily life and at all educational levels, bringing about a new kind of spirituality, with new values and ethics (e.g. no more science for war), as well as leading to both admiration and fear of science and its achievements;
- human and social values become means of exchange, and diversity becomes the main driver for innovation;

- borderless world governance and increased communication, with fewer corporations and more networks globally leading to open and free access to and sharing of knowledge;
- conflict between marketing and government as regulators, driving scientific developments – either way there are risks of manipulation to overcome due to hidden agendas;
- conflict between indigenous and scientific knowledge and cyberterrorism remain unresolved; and
- 'Big Brother' as STI controls data and information of all individuals.

Phase 2: Reframe

Phase 2, in keeping with the standard FLL-N design, calls for a reframing exercise that uses 'rigorous imagining' in order to take on two distinct challenges: inspiring participants to imagine anticipatory assumptions that are outside the boundaries of their existing frameworks and deploying a systematic creative procedure that generates awareness of anticipatory assumptions. To meet these challenges participants engage with a disruptive tool that invites them to articulate detailed descriptions of a reframed imaginary future society. Participants were provided with an adapted reframing model – a version of the Learning Intensive Society discussed in Chapter 4 – that they could use as inspiration for describing a disruptive or systemically discontinuous imaginary future. The Learning Intensive Society is a societal model that embraces novel, emergent complexity and treats uncertainty as a resource not a threat. This model was designed without reference to probability or desirability. There was no suggestion that this alternative future is likely to happen or is even desirable; the point was to experience the power of our anticipatory assumptions in shaping the futures we imagine, and the potential to address the creative challenge of inventing paradigmatically different futures. Participants engaged in a rigorous imagining process that enabled the development of systemically discontinuous but operationally detailed descriptions of organisations/functions.

The point of the reframing model is to give participants a few descriptive variables and functional relationships that depart from existing dominant societal attributes and organisational forms. The model is designed to equip participants with new or unfamiliar elements for describing the future and provides inspiration for creative thinking about the nature, role and organisation of knowledge production in general and scientific activities. The main assumptions of this alternative future world are that the conditions for fluid communication, rapid sense-making, spontaneous innovation and unique creation make organisational and governance systems more open, diverse and dynamic, thus open for renewal, birth and death.

Groups moved differently through the process. One group determined collectively that a new reputation process could replace some current institutional barriers, eventually working beyond objections from entrenched systems. They likened it to a clearly defined, open-edge network. Networks were seen more like mountain peaks and valleys with concentrations of high activity across an otherwise flat landscape. Exploring this potential, they soon had a Facebook-like network for science where access and players were continually evolving, reputations based on peer-acknowledged contributions, and co-creating innovations. Participants imagined a new work/life relationship described as 'productive leisure'. While they would perhaps enjoy more free time, they would never be completely away from work due to mobile interconnectivity. Under the rubric of uncertainties, data would be open to all for both access and input, thus potentially subject to malicious meddling. Ethics would be impossible to manage due to different sensibilities and a lack of responsibility among amateurs: 'not everybody is good' was a comment from one scientist inferring that ethics could be difficult to control in an open shared new system. In what the group defined as a 'new frontier' scenario, qualifications and resources faced unknown pressures and needed new systems for continuous sorting. New avenues and new players would be constants, which is, in effect, saying that change is constant. Finally, the metaphor 'open Olympics in science' explains the scenario where it would be possible to identify outstanding persons at an early age and/or in isolated places.

A second group decided to re-think some of the dimensions and descriptions of variables of the Learning Intensive Society model. Their scenario model was called 'Creative Society, Science and Arts – Bridging the Gap: Scientific Culture, Artistic Culture'. It included the following aspects: activities organised for life; flexible networks; interchange of knowledge; zero material differences; open clusters; cooperative work; cognitive capability identity; no money but human values; and no corporations. Science is associated with spirituality and education: Spirituality, Education and Science. Social dynamism was based on freedom and the capacity of ethical responsibility, transactional exchange-relations was flexible, new universal rights for living and non-living beings (human, animal, plants, post-human); there is no need for gender issues. In terms of governance dynamism, some of the highlights were: individual values based on social contribution; culture of individual and collective rights; no state, only alliances; and open data for government participation.

In another group, participants engaged in a very energetic discussion about the specificities of the Learning Intensive Society model. They started thinking about systemic reforms for achieving better science within the model's framework, including specific, rigorous proposals for building less formal, more project-oriented, international teams composed of individual researchers and sponsors of research, thanks to technology-enhanced networks of research cooperation. One particularly interesting feature of this proposition was to move from using universities and institutes as brokers to facilitating ad hoc networks of scientists and financing institutions. Still, threats for the scientific community in terms of maintaining their prestige and social status were highlighted, and a certain sense of ambiguity about educational priorities to be redefined in the future indicated hesitation about the changes from the status quo that would stem from a potential future expansion of a Learning Intensive Society in the real world. One person also noted that the Learning Intensive Society was, at least to a certain extent, and in given aspects of the model, already in place. The metaphor chosen by the group however, one of 'crossing the mirror and following the white rabbit', clearly indicated the exploratory conscience of the group in the reframing phase.

In yet another group, all participants were excited to either contribute to the Learning Intensive Society or to go against it by anchoring their ideas in how they were seeing the present. Their scenario included the following aspects: humans would be able to connect to their inner voice and to nature; there would be no expectations about what needs to be done as reality unfolds with no need for control; and everything would be interconnected, so what materialises would be exactly what would be needed at each particular moment in time. Physical spaces would be designed for multiple purposes and uses, and communications would happen 'on the go' via telepathy or an avatar. Technology would be pervasive and embedded, interconnecting everything (i.e. ambient intelligence). There would be no need for life in biological terms as there would be many forms of being alive with no waste of energy in connecting people and things. A repository of thoughts and emotions in a sort of cloud connected to everything would allow people to refrain from storing 'facts' as all knowledge would be automatically accessible to anyone at any time. Individuals would be able to live-the-present since there would exist no attachment to past or future. Everyone would be immortal since mind, thoughts and emotions would somehow survive forever in the cloud. Hence, a physical or material space as well as body would not be a constraint. Systems would be flexible, self-organising and self-governing with no central control or organisation according to the needs of the moment. Physical systems would manifest as other systems self-organise and everything is embedded with intelligence. The human body would exist for leisure, experimentation and dreaming; dreams which would be automatically prototyped in personal printers and then produced as a customised unique creation for everyone. In this context, identity would be defined both by history and interactions with one another, and with the environment in the present. Good or bad would cease to exist as experimentation and interactions become the only important activity. Ethics would be embedded in everyone since we would only exist in interaction with the system and others, which brings to the fore mutual respect, trust and appreciation. Wealth would be measured by creativity in interaction, which would lead to unique creation.

Overall assumptions identified in Phase 2 can be summarised as follows.

Networked life and science with embedded technology:

- spontaneous innovation is co-created in interaction with others and unique creation is linked to individual customisation of any product stemming automatically from individuals' dreams;
- productive leisure linked to continual work, experimentation and dreams that become physical reality at any given moment and are designed for multiple purposes and needs;
- seamless communication with no waste of energy and with knowledge automatically accessible to anyone at any time;
- life beyond biology for repository of minds, thoughts and emotions.

Self-organised and self-governing systems – the main attributes being:

- change is constant, life and science are complex, and systems are flexible, able to self-organise and self-govern according to needs of the moment;
- ethics embedded in every interaction, bringing to the fore mutual respect, trust and appreciation, and leading to peer-acknowledged contributions and reputation.

Phase 3: Rethink

Phase 3 is the natural conclusion of the process. The aim was to allow participants to appropriate for themselves key ideas from the overall experience and learning process.

Generally, groups departed from either an operational problem in the present to understand the ways in which this would be operationalised in their developed scenarios, or from a few questions which became relevant only after going through Phases 1 and 2, and that had to be analysed in the scenarios. The two previous phases were steps in the process rather than outcomes. In Phase 3 we searched for a shift in participants' understanding of their use of the future.

Participants identified new questions, especially those which might have been considered unimportant or incomprehensible without going through the process. These included questions around the role and identity of scientists, their way of working and their beliefs, the ways in which science is performed, evaluated and communicated, the ways in which science and constant learning/education can become ambient and evolve towards capacity-based systems, as well as the roles and configurations of government and countries.

During the exercise, one group discussed the opportunities and responsibilities for future generations, individualised laboratory and access systems to resources, new avenues and new images, and working as entrepreneurs, peer to peer rather than at jobs in organisations. Scientists could grow beyond research, innovation and education to more public functions as diplomats and change agents. In summary, participants moved from exploring content in Phase 1 and external abstraction, to living the future in Phase 3: "How will this future affect me, what do I think about it, and what will I do now about it?"

Another group started the debate by identifying questions that apparently had no relevance before going through Phases 1 and 2. These were: (1) What and who is a scientist? (2) How is science performed? (3) How is science evaluated or how to ensure quality? and (4) How is science and its results communicated and to whom? The group then debated these questions and tried to find answers in the developed scenario. It is interesting that the third group was divided with half of the participants trying to look for answers anchored in the present and with what they felt comfortable.

Participants were asked to look back at the whole process (Phases 1 to 3) and to once again identify questions that might have been considered unimportant or incomprehensible at the beginning of the workshop, and that now they thought would be relevant if they were asked to look at the future role of science in society today. New questions started emerging:

- How to democratise science?
- How to evolve from a diploma to a capability-based system?
- Will the educational system as we know it survive?
- How to include informal learning into the current or a new system?
- How will continuous education be provided and made available to all and at any age?
- Is there a need for choice between different or parallel evaluation systems?
- What will be the role and configuration of government and countries to ensure free access and use of information?

In another case, participants engaged in a discussion around the fundamentals of defining the scientific method and the profession of a scientist, and some assumptions from Phases 1 and 2 were also revisited. The subject of the interface between industry and science was also discussed energetically before the group could agree on a common vision of how the corporate world responds to global challenges and encourages/discourages innovation. Crowdsourcing and scientific-sourcing proved to be important axes of discussion about the changing conditions of scientific research and the redefinition of research vocation. Peer-review models were also challenged in the discussion. The group expressed a number of different perspectives without arriving at a consensus. Some thought that there would be different possibilities for transcending the current paradigm, while others were less sure. Everyone recognised that the shortcomings of current approaches would require significant shifts in the science/society relationship, at a minimum because of the unprecedented growth in numbers of the research community. Unexpected outlier results were also presented, such as one participant representing a governmental institution suggesting they would design and experiment with implementing a participatory budgeting project for research financing, an initiative inspired by the workshop.

Another group chose to further explore the ways in which the society imagined in Phase 2 could be operationalised. They presented a short documentary as a prototype to show through images the evolution of life on earth: a self-organised world with no central power and with flexible organisation. Participants made explicit their assumptions: complete capillarity; complete personalisation; complete freedom. The core ideas were: no nations; no boundaries; universal respect for human and non-human values; the whole-net, instead of the internet; and a flexible society. Instead of the philosophy of 'use it and throw it away' they proposed 'pick and use it': shared goods; shared transportation; shared housing, organised through sharing platforms. This is a society of freelancing where the most common job types they imagined would be platforms to share completeness. They realised the need to reframe human behaviour and change mindsets towards a society functioning in networks. They also proposed reframing the nature and the role of science, including social sciences, into a knowledge and cultural creative activity.

128 FLL-N case studies

The description of Phase 3, with outcomes of a different nature from the previous two phases, highlights the new questions identified by participants after moving through the three phases. These may be relevant for anyone interested in better understanding possible roles of science in society as well as that of knowledge creation and exploitation. The new questions are organised around the role and identity of scientists, their way of working and their beliefs, the ways in which science is performed, evaluated and communicated, the ways in which science and continuous education can be democratised and evolve towards capacity-based systems, as well as the roles and configurations of government and countries.

On the facilitation process

Simultaneous processes were taking place during this particular FLL-N – the experiential and cognitive processes of learning, and ones associated with different levels of interaction of individuals. As a group, these processes followed the three phases in the universal group dynamics cycle with a start, middle and end, and its three stages – orientation, conflict and cohesion – with different relative weights in each phase. The learning curve sequence was intended to ease the engagement of the participants in the experiential and cognitive learning process (experience, reflection, conceptualisation, experimentation).

Every group was a system, where four interdependent levels of experience interacted: individual, interpersonal, subgroup and group. During the FLL, the facilitator respected the frontiers of these levels and avoided being invasive. The aim was to ease the process for participants with facilitators 'lighting the phenomena', rather than working with individuals or interpreting the contents directly.

Facilitators also had to be alert to the fact that change and resistance are not two conflicting aspects; instead, they are determined and necessary to each other. All change involves a preservation strategy and respect for the resistance. Bearing this in mind reminded facilitators to be careful to not intervene directly in the group process, instead intervening closer to the borders when resistance arose. Welcoming the resistance was essential to generate a confident environment, an essential step for participants engaging with the process of change.

The facilitator supports the process with the objective of maintaining interaction and co-participation in knowledge creation in accordance with the general design principles of FLL. The aim was to conduct small group exercises following a research protocol while ensuring that the group could perform the task. It was not the objective of the facilitators to intervene in content generation but to observe and take note of results.

Different approaches and tools were used during the process to move knowledge from tacit to explicit and for inventing new hypotheses, variables and models. One of the approaches used to deepen and broaden the content of the structured conversations working with assumptions in Phases 1 and 2 was the Causal Layered Analysis (CLA) method (Inayatullah, 2004) which is a powerful tool for helping participants to make sense of their narratives by organising and communicating attributes of the imaginary futures they described during the workshop. Other methods, such as role-playing, storytelling and using different media for communicating results, were also used in both breakout groups and plenary sessions, allowing for experiments with different kinds of group dynamics and imaginative processes. Such diversity in the design of the knowledge laboratory processes was key to sparking creativity within the groups. Beyond increasing creativity, this approach also made the workshop more pleasant and helped to energise the process. Ensuring that individuals can make personal contributions in an interactive, shared sense-making context is critical for tapping into the collective intelligence of the group and required a strong emphasis on customising the FLL-N design in advance and ensuring that during the process there was a capacity to engage in real-time facilitation of the group dynamics.

Follow-up

The experience of this FLL-N has enabled CGEE to adapt the process and dynamics to undertake several Labs. In 2014, the organisation rethought its strategy and market position with its collaborators through a process involving 12 short and lively encounters of around two hours each. This built directly on both the methodological insights and content generated by the Future of Science FLL-N.

In 2015, CGEE applied the FLL approach to a project looking at the future of sustainable cities commissioned by the Brazilian STI Ministry (MSTI). The FLL workshop brought together people with divergent points of view from research, industry and government, as well as students, religious groups, NGOs and people from different societal groups. In parallel, a discussion took place with children from 6 to 16 years during the Science and Technology Week that is organised every year by MSTI for all schools in cities across the country. The results were combined, exposing the similarities and differences that these two groups (i.e. pupils and adults) expect for liveable and sustainable cities in Brazil. There was convergence in themes such as water, education, energy, mobility, green areas, food systems and health. However, in two themes – governance and security – expectations and proposed actions were quite divergent. Options for innovation policy were then developed for MSTI, to both provide a positive environment for discussion related to the converging themes and to offer a policy mix required to dig deeper into identified issues, thus generating more understanding among stakeholders and coordinating actions with different Ministries. CGEE foresees using and adapting the FLL approach from 2017 onwards in several projects dealing both with sustainability and innovation in cities and regions.

Finally, it is important to highlight that going through several FL Labs has enabled CGEE to test the approach and unlock specific methods which are continually embedded in the ongoing development of foresight methods and applications at CGEE. It has also assisted the institution to disrupt an entrenched top-down approach to making internal decisions. By bringing all staff together, mutual learning has become possible. The discovery of both similar and opposing assumptions and expectations was a very powerful instrument to bring about an open in-house dialogue, which exposed personal biases and expanded the possibility of moving towards a jointly developed vision of what CGEE as an institution wants to be in the future. In a nutshell, it did put in motion a collective change regarding the ways in which the institution relates to its clients and carries out its projects and strategic studies.

As a result, it has been moving from a normative and prescriptive approach alone to one that aims to embrace complexity, emergence and novelty (Cagnin, 2017). This implies developing the ability to 'walk on two legs': improve or optimise the current system at the same time as it moves towards new and/or disruptive system configurations. Being able to operate both in known systems (inside-in, inside-out, and outside-in), with more efficiency and efficacy, as well as to operate in unknown systems (outside-out), will support the institution in crafting strategic questions for itself and its clients. In other words, looking outside systems that we are familiar with will support not only developing and addressing new strategic questions, but also in recognising new issues (e.g. challenges, technologies, social transformations, among others) through systematic observations and dialogue, and selecting those which are worth investigating further in order to identify new opportunities.

References

Anon (2017a) 'Constructivist Epistemology', Wikipedia. Available at: https://en.wikipedia.org/wiki/Constructivist_epistemology (Accessed: 8 April 2017).

Anon (2017b) 'Science', Wikipedia. Available at: http://www.etymonline.com/index.php?term=science&allowed_in_frame=0 (Accessed: 8 April 2017).

Cagnin, C. (2017) 'Developing a Transformative Business Strategy through the Combination of Design Thinking and Futures Literacy', *Technology Analysis & Strategic Management*. Taylor&Francis Online. Available at: http://www.tandfonline.com/doi/abs/10.1080/09537325.2017.1340638 (Accessed: 8 April 2017).

Da Costa, O., Warnke, P., Cagnin, C. and Scapolo, F. (2008) 'The Impact of Foresight on Policy-Making: Insights from the FORLEARN Mutual Learning Process', *Technology Analysis & Strategic Management*, 20(3), pp. 369–387.

Cuhls, K. (2003) 'From Forecasting to Foresight Processes? New Participative Foresight Activities in Germany', *Journal of Forecasting*, 22(2–3), pp. 93–111. doi: 10.1002/for.848.

Eriksson, E. A. and Weber, M. (2006) 'Adaptive Foresight: Navigating the Complex Landscape of Policy Strategies', *Technological Forecasting and Social Change*, 75(4), pp. 462–482.

Georghiou, L. (2001) 'Third Generation Foresight - Integrating the Socio-Economic Dimension', in *International Conference on Technology Foresight - The Approach to and the Potential for New Technology Foresight*. Tokyo: Science and Technology Foresight Center, National Institute of Science and Technology Policy (NISTEP), Ministry of Education, Culture, Sports, Science and Technology.

Georghiou, L. (2007) 'Future of Forecasting for Economic Development', paper presented at UNIDO Technology Foresight Summit 2007, Budapest, 27–29 September.

Havas, A., Schartinger, D. and Weber, K. M. (2007) 'Experiences and Practices of Technology Foresight in the European Region', paper presented at UNIDO Technology Foresight Summit 2007, Budapest, 27–29 September.
Inayatullah, S. (2004) *The Causal Layered Analysis (CLA) Reader*. Taipei: Tamkang University Press.
Johnston, R. (2002) 'The State and Contribution of International Foresight: New Challenges', in *The Role of Foresight in the Selection of Research Policy Priorities*. Seville: JRC-IPTS.
Johnston, R. (2007) 'Future Critical and Key Industrial Technologies as Driving Forces for Economic Development and Competiveness', paper presented at UNIDO Technology Foresight Summit 2007, Budapest, 27–29 September.
Understanding Science (2017) *A Science Checklist*. Berkeley, CA: University of California Museum of Paleontology. Available at: http://undsci.berkeley.edu/article/whatisscience_03 (Accessed: 8 April 2017).

Case 3: Using the future for local labor markets

Kacper Nosarzewski and Lydia Garrido Luzardo

The Futures Literacy Laboratory-Novelty (FLL-N) on Using the Future for Local Labor Markets was conducted on November 25–26, 2013, in Bogotá, Republic of Colombia, with a group of 28 participants from Regional Labor Observatories (Red de Observatorios Regionales de Mercado de Trabajo, RED ORMET), the Ministry of Labor, the National Apprenticeship Service (SENA), and the United Nations Development Program (UNDP). The event was designed as a 'knowledge laboratory,' a learning-by-doing process that engages the collective intelligence of the participants to generate new knowledge. For reasons of effectiveness and efficiency in achieving the participants' goals the future was used as the main reference point for structuring the conversations. When used in the context of a knowledge laboratory, the future is a particularly powerful tool for revealing underlying systemic assumptions and providing new analytical insights, often beyond existing frameworks.

Participants in this FLL-N were able to analyze and question the methods and goals that inform their current on-the-ground efforts to assist with allocation of investments, sharing of information and coordination of organizational activities in local labor markets. Participants also started to increase their own capacity to both use the future and conduct scientific research by gaining practical familiarity with the Discipline of Anticipation and FLL-N design and practice. Lastly, in the context of ongoing action research being conducted by UNESCO, this event contributed to the advancement of innovative approaches to both knowledge creation and the use of the future to formulate collective choices.

The design of the event, with a clear training objective and foresight theme, was prepared by an international group of Future Studies experts: Dr. Riel Miller, Head of Foresight at UNESCO, Paris; Mrs. Lydia Garrido Luzardo, Head of The Millennium Project Uruguayan Node, Montevideo; Mr. Kacper Nosarzewski, Partner at 4CF sp. z o. o., Warsaw, in close collaboration with Mr. Javier García

Estevéz of UNDP Colombia and with important inputs from the regional labor observatories and Ministry of Labor in Colombia. The event was hosted by the Ministry of Labor and UNDP at Grand House Hotel Bogotá.

The transformation of labor markets

A new series of emergent global political, economic and social phenomena are currently generating new categories of value-creation, altering the nature and organization of work, enlarging the role of learning, changing the meaning and practice of age-based landmarks like retirement, and diversifying the objectives of, and means for making investments. Part of this moving landscape involves changes in the conception and construction of collective efforts to understand and influence the world around us.

Today the field of labor policy is being transformed by changes taking place in the nature of work, the systems for organizing the allocation of time to value-creating activities, and the methods used to understand and share the meaning of changes in the distribution of human activity in daily life. Such innovations call for new research methods as well as a capacity to explore new avenues for expressing and organizing human agency. Disruptive changes, ones that signal the inadequacy of existing paradigms, also mark the emergence of new ones. This means that government policy and policy makers are faced with a dual challenge – improving the old and inventing the new.

With respect to labor market foresight that attempts to discern the future of employment and skills, the old can be understood as processes that extrapolate economic change with sufficient detail and sufficient accuracy to undertake supply side planning and demand side adaptation. However, as decades of experience have demonstrated, medium and long-run labor market forecasting is not a particularly useful way to think about the future of work. This is not only because of significant lags in training systems and technical difficulties in meeting rigorous data and modeling specifications, but is also and more importantly due to the fundamentally complex evolutionary nature of economic systems. Recognition of this reality partly accounted for the shift away from labor market planning to framework-type policies in the 1980s and 1990s for OECD countries. Currently the expansion or catch-up/convergence of industrializing countries and the crisis of de-industrialization of developed countries makes it tempting to return to old planning illusions – using forecasting approaches to think about the future nature and structure of human work activity, while at the same time suggesting that something more is needed.

Designing the experience

This two-day FLL-N was designed to assist participants with making sense of the changes taking place around them as well as helping them to see that they can use the future in new ways. Through learning-by-doing knowledge creation, an action research approach to understanding local labor markets, participants recognized: (1) the developments taking place that influence the way the future is integrated into efforts to understand the world today, and (2) the emergence of new approaches to the mutual design and creation of knowledge and work. Participants expanded the range of their analysis without abandoning important and still significant tools for thinking about the future and informing policies that can make existing systems work better.

Through the FLL-N participants enhanced their capacity to detect and make sense of repetition and difference, the old and the new, which are at the core of policy making. At the end of the process participants were better able to 'walk on two legs,' understanding the difference between closed and open systems thinking, between efforts to improve or optimize already existing systems and efforts to perceive and invent new and/or disruptive system configurations. This FLL-N focused the collective intelligence of participants and made their anticipatory assumptions explicit. They came to see how these assumptions play a key role in defining systemic boundaries, thereby shaping the ability to be able to distinguish between endogenous and exogenous continuity and change. By deepening and enlarging participants' capacity to use the future and generate time-place specific knowledge, this FLL-N enabled policy makers to be innovative and context sensitive.

Participating in the FLL-N also provided an opportunity to learn about anticipatory systems and how to use the future, by considering an important topic – the future of local labor markets in Colombia. The FLL-N followed a learning curve sequence intended to engage the collective intelligence of participants. Through this conversational process information is revealed, new meanings and even phenomena discovered and shared sense-making emerges – which is not the same as consensus or agreement; indeed, there can be a clarification of disagreement. Of course, this search process is incomplete and biased in many ways, but since it is collective it is also more diverse, at a minimum in terms of different points of view due to age or gender or personal history, and it offers the potential of making explicit specific, time-place unique information that participants carry with them into the conversation. This is why the creation of knowledge through collective intelligence knowledge creation (CIKC) processes such as in the general FLL design is one of the main ways to research the anticipatory assumptions that we use to imagine the future.

The design of this specific FLL-N agenda involved both learning by doing and learning by viewing techniques, with intertwining lectures and workshop exercises in groups, and with emphasis on the practical dimension of foresight applied to labor market studies and labor policy. Exploring developments taking place in the Discipline of Anticipation and how such advances can be applied to labor market policy analysis and implementation was a key result of this Futures Literacy development process.

134 FLL-N case studies

Aims of the FLL-N

The FLL-N covered four specific objectives:

- develop participants' practical capability to use anticipatory systems to identify and analyze today's emergent phenomena for policy purposes;
- gain a deeper understanding of the latest development in the field of foresight, including the different tools and networks that are advancing the field;
- address current pressing policy issues through a hands-on foresight process;
- invent, design and discuss prototype anticipatory systems projects for Colombia.

Both English and Spanish languages were used during the event with the support of simultaneous interpretation provided by the host.

On the morning of the workshop, the FLL-N design was customized in real-time in order to incorporate insights regarding the participants' context and goals. These specifics were provided by the Vice-Minister for Employment & Pensions, Hon. Juan Carlos Cortés González, the Director of Regional Labor Markets, Mrs. Juana Paola Bustamante, and Mr. Javier García Estevéz of UNDP Colombia.

Lead-up to Phase 1

Based on prior desk research and first-hand research into anticipatory systems and frameworks that had been the benchmark for future-oriented activities of labor market observatories and labor policy-making in Colombia, the team designing and implementing the lab decided to dedicate a substantial portion of the first day to pre-FL activities. The apparent uniformity of local participants revealed in fact a deep disparity of background and experience, with participants bridging the social sciences ranging from economists to social policy analysts to public management specialists. However, the formal homogeneity of the group and relatively flat hierarchical distribution demanded a special effort at appreciative inquiry to prepare the group to explore its anticipatory assumptions.

Starting the FLL-N with a set of introductory lectures was intended to assist the participants in connecting the dots linking their own futures research and forecasting knowledge and the big picture, state-of-the-art thinking about the Discipline of Anticipation and Futures Literacy. At the outset Riel Miller gave a lecture on recent developments in the field of Future Studies and lessons learned from the latest research into the Discipline of Anticipation, Futures Literacy and complexity studies. Next Lydia Garrido Luzardo gave a presentation on the epistemology and ontology of futures work. Then Kacper Nosarzewski provided a review of foresight tools, from probabilistic forecasting to scenario thinking, to early warning systems, and rigorous imagining. These introductory talks were seen as a context-relevant approach to laying down important reference points for the participants and an effective way to set a stage that would be inviting for participants being asked to engage in a challenging collective intelligence process.

Phase 1: Reveal

The standard general FLL-N Phase 1 started with group work focused on the futures of the labor market in Colombia. Participants were invited to speak Spanish in their groups, with report back to plenary simultaneously translated into English to allow for the international facilitation team to discuss and investigate the lab work as it progressed. Phase 1 followed the usual expectations and hopes pattern to revealing anticipatory assumptions. The report back collected evidence of a wide consensus on the place and meaning of notions such as informal economy, labor supply and demand drivers, unemployment taxonomy and relations between policy and workforce. Participants also revealed a set of shared anticipatory assumptions underpinning the futures they imagined related to causality and agency in labor-market analysis and policy-making. Analysis of the imaginary futures created using the Causal Layered Analysis (CLA) method, facilitated by the international team, produced contrasting pictures. On one side the participants displayed considerable consensus on how the economy and labor markets work in general or from an abstract 'economists' point of view. On the other side, particularly when exploring imaginary futures related to the *metaphor* and *headline* layers of CLA, participants depicted the future outside of the 'standard-model,' recognizing the significance of local and regional specificity. These latter images did not coincide with the conventional picture of labor markets based on generalizing and extrapolating a framework derived ex-post from the experiences of already 'developed' countries. The design decision to use Causal Layered Analysis for structuring within group imaging and facilitate meaningful reporting back turned out to be appropriate. As the discussions unfolded the facilitators and observers witnessed strong sensing and sense-making collaboration within the groups as well as learning by doing.

Phase 2: Reframe

The basic FLL-N design was used to conduct the reframing exercise, involving a discontinuous scenario aimed at creating a disruptive context for imagining the future. First, participants were presented with an adaptation of the OECD Learning Intensive Society (LIS) (Miller, 2006) model used for the purpose of stretching beyond the business-as-usual horizon and to question assumptions and incumbent models. Questions about the model and clarifications of its iso-probabilistic nature followed. As was typically the case, the biggest challenge for the groups is to grasp the model as a tool rather than a prediction. With this risk in mind this FLL-N was designed to ensure an opportunity for discussions in plenary and in groups in order to get beyond the idea that the LIS was a solution or forecast. To assist the group in tackling this key hurdle the presentation of the reframing model was followed by a case study of Anticipatory Governance theory presented by Kacper Nosarzewski. The anticipatory administration concept, as laid out by Fuerth and Faber (2012), enables endogenous reframing for innovation within a closed system. The differences between closed and open systems in the context of governance and public administration was further deepened to allow participants to operationalize nuances of the LIS with its important meta-level characteristics as both a model and as a tool. Closed systems are not a favorable environment for exploratory activities from within and often do not allow change unless under strict control and without questioning systemic assumptions. That is why it is a challenging task to get policy makers to recognize and then start to invent anticipatory assumptions that are not just aimed at planning and begin to embrace complexity, including novelty. Once these two presentations were concluded and further debated over lunch, the actual Phase 2 took place over a two-hour session.

Phase 2 was typically framed as learning-by-doing exercises: Prototype and Test, but customized to this specific context. In this FLL-N groups were assigned the task of writing a report from the future to UNESCO about the role of the Observatories in the LIS in Colombia. Effort was devoted to describing specific anticipatory processes/projects to pursue strategic objectives for Colombia and its regions in the present. The aim was to develop prototypes that illustrate and test an anticipatory systems approach. Plenary presentations, reflections and discussions provided a platform for scoping the results of Phase 2. As it turned out, the assignment was not perfectly suited to the analysis and communication habits of most of the participants. Writing a report to UNESCO was interpreted either as a showcase activity or a request for help, with less focus on producing new knowledge and more on attractive framing of current challenges extrapolated into the future or quasi-promotional messages using LIS as a tool, but not as reframing. Only a few participants successfully identified anticipatory assumptions and explicitly presented a reframed vision.

As a consequence, to enable an effective Phase 3 exercise, the facilitation team addressed the challenges and limitations of each group's deliverable, unwrapping and debating specific pieces of knowledge, assumptions and predictions with the participants. This turned out to be a worthwhile activity, leveling up the general understanding of futures literacy and helping participants to confront received ideas about the methods and narrative frameworks for using the future.

Phase 3: Rethink

Due to the extra time invested in debate and clarification after Phase 2, the third phase of FLL was limited to a 45-minute slot and focused on receiving and processing feedback. Participants discussed their improved understanding of the potential of anticipation to enhance the capacity of policy makers to reach societal objectives. Individual testimonies and take-away ideas were presented by willing participants. In general, the evidence of a greater focus on specificity and complexity in relation to local and regional labor markets was gathered and noted. Several participants thought that this kind of FLL-N could be used as a participatory tool for engaging local employers and employees in the work of the Labor Market Observatories. This approach could provide both new sources for analyzing the specific labor market issues in their community and for rethinking practice.

An overview of key application issues and follow-through learning was given by Riel Miller. An open discussion followed for half an hour providing feedback and follow-up ideas. The idea of deploying Futures Literacy task groups to regions throughout Colombia to train additional trainers and local champions was considered a worthy follow-up activity.

Main outcomes and findings

The participants, working at the local level on labor market challenges in Colombia, and the event's sponsors, the UNDP in Colombia and the Ministry of Labor, are all concerned with advancing socio-economic development, and were able to leave the FLL with important conclusions.

First, they received clear confirmation of the intuition that led them to invest in this event – that there was indeed a need to assess and enrich the tools being used to formulate and implement labor market policies by gaining a deeper understanding of how to use the future.

Second, there was important recognition, directly related to existing activities and practices, that to achieve local labor market objectives as well as broader regional and national aspirations it is necessary to acquire new capabilities throughout the community, including for policy makers and researchers. In particular, there is a need to cultivate the capacity to use the future and collective intelligence processes that are efficient in generating locally specific knowledge that enables the invention and deployment of new methods for formulating and implementing collective action.

Third, there are clear and readily available methods for enhancing the practical capacity to use anticipatory systems to identify and analyze today's emergent phenomena for policy purposes through learning-by-doing processes such as the FLL-N.

In summary, participants in this FLL-N acquired both new skills and a new understanding of their current activities that will enable them to move forward in applying the latest developments in the field of foresight to the challenges they face. The experiment, as intended, provided context specific meaning for the newest policy-oriented foresight techniques. Participants gained an appreciation of the role of the future and collective intelligence action-research in producing the sense-making necessary for collective action – the new approach to creating and enacting public policy.

Current pressing policy issues were identified through this FLL-N. Key elements of the RED ORMET (Red de Observatorios Regionales de Mercado de Trabajo) epistemic landscape took on new meaning and became sources of inspiration for new questions and potentially new solutions. Participants were able to reconsider such central issues as the relationship between formal and informal activities, exogenous and endogenous growth, education-employment planning, and knowledge-sharing processes/content among diverse actors at all levels – local, regional and national. The ensemble of methods, carefully designed as a learning voyage, allowed participants to discover and appreciate the repetitions and differences that characterize the emergent and evolving context for value creation at the local, national and global levels. Participants started a process of developing new goals and capabilities for sense making, data processing, analysis and reporting.

Prototype anticipatory systems projects for Colombian labor market observatories were tested during the last session exercise. This exercise offered an opportunity to display new vantage points that had been provoked by the reframing process and reflected the creative dynamic among groups and individual participants. Participants called into question existing definitions and organizational forms of welfare-provision, examining the biases introduced by conceptual and organizational frameworks that reflect paternalism and the eternal dominance of the supply–demand dualism. Participants also started to seek new systemic solutions, pushing the frontiers of the RED ORMET current theory and practice.

Some of the collectively built outputs with strategic implications were:

- building the capacity to generate real-time profiles of productive activity – enhancing the quality of information available for both initiating new value-added activity and improving the efficiency of existing activities/recruitment/networking;
- redefining the expected and operational relationship between the so-called skill supply side in education, and the demand side, beyond the narrow job market definitions in order to escape from a planning approach to the creation and deployment of wealth-creating capacity in contexts dominated by informal work;
- engaging and making sense of cultural assets, the locally specific knowledge and traditions that generate in-situ meaning, in order to enhance the efficiency of information sharing for creating wealth;
- giving a clearer productive meaning to human and social rights, including transparency and openness;
- finding ways of giving local meaning to global connectivity, of all kinds;
- empowering local self-organization and self-management;
- building new bases, crafted out of jointly invented aspirations and collective intelligence based understanding, for cross boundary partnerships, for instance between workers and employees;
- enabling new information-creation processes and places – building time, space and permission for the articulation and negotiation of sense making amongst diverse actors, public, private and social across communities at all levels;
- building up new infrastructure that enables real-time information creation and access beyond current barriers and conflicts.

The notions of temporality, multiple futures, reframing, desirable and probable futures, plausibility, ontological status of present and future, optimization, contingency, novelty, exploratory approaches were all evoked and discussed through a hands-on deliberative process. Participants were able to express and debate a range of strongly held systemic perspectives, providing a large conceptual space for thinking about the ongoing transformation of socio-economic models.

The group was very cooperative and participated in the assignments in a disciplined manner, also asking questions about the details of tasks freely. Much of the process was conducted in the local language and when there were terminological or translation questions there were sufficient resources available to successfully arrive at shared understandings. Cooperation within groups was enthusiastic, with different participants taking turns in presenting and changing roles within the teams.

Regional economic and cultural identity (e.g. impact of the coffee industry) and regional specificity of the observatories played an important role in discussions, demonstrating the ability to evoke and give meaning to specificity in a broader, often international discussion. Spontaneous feedback from participants was collected, including inquiries into technical aspects of exploratory foresight methods and practical upgrades to the existing methodology employed by the RED ORMET members. Some of the participants were able to make direct connections between what they were learning in the workshop and their existing models and knowledge creation systems, i.e. macroeconomics, regional development, etc.

Finally, a clear desire was expressed by participants and sponsors to further develop Futures Literacy and apply the Discipline of Anticipation to the work they are doing at both the local level and at national/global levels. Interest was also expressed in finding ways to design and implement advanced anticipatory processes such as the FLL-N for specific sectors. Subsequent to the event a set of follow-up options were developed and were subject to detailed implementation discussion with the Ministry of Labor.

References

Fuerth, L. and Faber, E. M. H. (2012) *Anticipatory Governance Practical Upgrades: Equipping the Executive Branch to Cope with Increasing Speed and Complexity of Major Challenges*. Washington D.C.: National Defense University Press.

Miller, R. (2006) 'Equity in a Twenty-First Century Learning Intensive Society: Is Schooling Part of the Solution?,' *Foresight*, 8(4), pp. 13–22.

Case 4: Using the future for innovation policy learning in Norway

Per M. Koch

This case study was part of Innovation Norway's effort to introduce advanced methods for thinking about the future into national innovation policy learning. The report reflects the work undertaken between 2013 and 2017. Innovation Norway collaborated with UNESCO, using the Futures Literacy approach to engage in policy learning and policy development.

Innovation Norway is Norway's central agency for encouraging industrial innovation and entrepreneurship. The company also functions as a policy adviser for its owners, the Ministry of Innovation and Trade, and the counties, and for Norwegian society at large. Because of this the institution has to develop efficient arenas for policy learning and policy communication. In this case study, I will look at how Innovation Norway enhanced its capacity to use-the-future by taking a Futures Literacy approach.

Learning potential

Innovation Norway has some 700 employees, distributed between the Oslo headquarters, 15 county offices and 35 offices abroad. Given employees' close contact with industry, and the fact that Innovation Norway has extensive regional, national and international networks, the institution should be uniquely positioned to generate economic, industrial and social intelligence for both policy makers and industry.

Even if the system generates relevant data and knowledge regarding existing policy instruments and challenges that Norwegian individual companies are facing right now, this does not automatically lead to insights into (1) how the instruments and services interact, (2) a broad-based analysis of the innovation system as a whole, and (3) ideas about future challenges and opportunities, both for Norwegian society as a whole and for Innovation Norway.

Policy learning about how to 'use-the-future' as anticipation

In the latest white paper on industrial policy Innovation Norway and the Industrial Development Corporation of Norway (SIVA) underlined Innovation Norway's role as a policy adviser (The Norwegian Ministry of Industry and Trade, 2012, p. 87; The Research Council of Norway, 2017) and also emphasized the role of Innovation Norway as a listening post vis-à-vis industrial development and international opportunities.

If advice is to be provided on innovation policy, one has to have ideas about how imaginary futures are influencing what people see and do in the present. In this context, the point is not to predict the future, as that is impossible, but to identify the kinds of anticipatory assumptions that are being used, including social, political, economic, technological and environmental factors and trends. Decision-makers are using these assumptions to imagine changes in the rules of the game and how companies and policy institutions may need to adapt at tactical and strategic levels.

Societal challenges and sustainability

Policy makers in the field of innovation policy have for a long time made use of the future in their policy discussions. Norwegian policy makers in this field make active use of economic predictions and mapping of emerging technologies.

But both approaches are limited in the sense that they are anchored in current social, political and economic structures. By taking part in the UNESCO Future Literacy Laboratory network, Innovation Norway has tried to achieve two important objectives: (1) to widen the scope of factors and phenomena included when imagining different futures; and (2) to make participants consciously aware of why and how the future is being used and can be used.

One example of a widening of scope is the move from a simplistic technology *push* approach to innovation, where research and technology deliver new inventions and society accepts them uncritically, to a societal *pull* approach, where stakeholders identify global challenges to sustainability and try to develop technical, social and cultural solutions while taking possible negative effects of innovation into consideration. These developments are reflected, for instance, in the EU Horizon 2020 programme for research and innovation, which is targeting several societal challenges facing Europe and the world, including health, demographic change, food security, climate action and more.

In other words, there is a shift taking place from yesterday's dominant approach in which research and innovation agencies were meant to focus exclusively on providing generic policy instruments potentially beneficial to all companies, such as a bottom-up approach where the agencies do not 'pick winners' or judge the social value of projects. Now there seems to be a turn underway towards an approach where ministries and agencies do provide some top-down strategic direction and align public investments to reinforce these choices.

Over the last couple of years, Innovation Norway has gradually shifted its practice and its policy advice in a more challenge-oriented and sustainable direction. Innovation Norway has discussed an innovation policy that will help Norway transform its economy, partly to respond to global challenges and the market opportunities they represent, and partly to replace the current oil and gas dependency with new, future-oriented and sustainable activities. The use of the Futures Literacy Lab methodology is partly in response to this development. These changes are part of why Innovation Norway has pursued new and innovative methods for understanding why and how the future enters into decision-making.

Learning from Futures Literacy

In 2013 Innovation Norway started a new project on the development of the organization as an innovation policy adviser. As part of this project, Innovation Norway decided to test Futures Literacy (FL) as an approach to policy learning, at both national and regional levels. Innovation Norway decided to work collaboratively with UNESCO's FL Project in order to take advantage of the project's cutting-edge research, networking and experimentation around the world.

The process started with a two-day workshop in Oslo on 21 and 22 October 2013, with Riel Miller, members of the UNESCO futures literacy expert group, and representatives of Innovation Norway, the Research Council of Norway and the Norwegian Board of Technology.

142 FLL-N case studies

We had some intense and fruitful discussions on the use of the future in research and innovation policy development. At this workshop, the participants also tested the Futures Literacy Laboratories (FLL) methodology, specifically the FLL-Novelty (FLL-N), designed to introduce participants to a range of anticipatory systems and knowledge creation practices, as outlined in Chapters 1 and 4 of this book.

Subsequently, after the experiment in developing FL and testing the FLL-N methodology, Innovation Norway produced a specially tailored version for deployment in Norway. The main difference between the FLL-N run in Oslo and the version used across Norway is in the time-span for running the exercise. Participation in a two- or three-day laboratory was unlikely given the dominance of existing ways of generating insights and the tight agendas of Innovation Norway employees and its business partners. Working from the basic design principles of FLL it was decided to put together a five- to six-hour process. There was considerable awareness of the risks involved with such an approach, not least being the lack of time for a more fundamental reframing of the topic at hand.

FLL-Innovation Norway (FLL-IN)

We arranged six FLL-IN in 2013 and 2014, testing out different types of challenges, industry areas and participation.

26 November 2013: Internal alpha-test of methodology, Oslo headquarters.

- o   *Topic: Future opportunities and challenges for Norwegian industry.*

28 January 2014: The County of Sogn and Fjordane on the West Coast of Norway.

- o   *Topic: To identify possible future challenges and opportunities for local industry.*

21 March 2014: Internal workshop on Innovation Norway as a policy adviser.

- o   *Topic: Generating ideas regarding the future organization of Innovation Norway's policy adviser function.*

23 and 24 April 2014: The South-East Asia regional group of Innovation Norway, meeting in Bangkok, Thailand.

- o   *Topic: Energy, including energy production, transport and efficiency: What can Norwegian industry achieve in South East Asia?*

26 November 2014: Fremtidsmat (Future Food), Mathallen, Oslo.

- o   *Fremtidsmat is a regional collaboration aimed at developing sustainable food production and products. An implicit goal was to prepare the ground for an application for cluster support from Innovation Norway.*
- o   *Topic: Future opportunities for the development, production and sale of food and beverages in the Oslo Fjord region.*

10 June 2014: The fruit and berry cluster around the Oslo Fjord, Drammen.

o   *This workshop was part of an attempt at establishing formal collaboration between fruit and berry producers around the Oslo Fjord. The workshop was to identify future potential and challenges regarding the use of their products.*

We were very careful to introduce a wide variety of social, economic, technological and environmental factors into the discussions, in order to avoid 'lock in' into existing technologies, policies or cultural paradigms.

Participants were asked to see the world from the year 2030. Longer time spans were considered as they encourage participants to imagine more radically different scenarios but in the end, we decided to go for the middle ground: the distance into the future was far enough for us to be able to introduce serious shifts in framework conditions, while at the same time close enough to make participants see the relevance to their present tasks.

Structure

We learned that the following workshop structure, which is very similar to the FLL-N sequence, functions well. In general, the workshops had some 15 to 20 participants, facilitators included, which allowed us to establish three break-out groups at each event.

INTRODUCTION

The facilitators presented the purpose of the workshop as well as the procedure in a plenary session. The participants were then divided into groups, each with its own facilitator.

HOPE

Using Post-it notes, participants were asked to illustrate their hopes for the future, answering the request: "Give us stories, headlines, quotes and/or concepts from the year 2030." We underlined that these hopes did not have to be realistic. The point was to reveal their dreams and visions for the future, stopping them from being caught up in realistic expectations of what might happen. By asking participants to present their Post-it notes, everyone was included in the discussion.

REALISTIC EXPECTATIONS

Session 2 was similar to Session 1, the only difference being that this time the participants were asked to express their expectations as to what they truly believed would or could happen. In this way, they were able to map their preconceptions, and make themselves aware of these preconceptions. This is what Riel Miller calls "shifting knowledge from tacit to the explicit form" (Miller, 2007).

LUNCH

Including informal and open networking and discussion.

REFRAMING

The facilitators prepared several alternative radical scenarios, which were all designed to force the participants to cope with the unexpected and think outside their safety zone. The facilitators presented one of these reframing scenarios, using elements from the hopes and expectations discussion to help inspire creativity and open thinking. The groups then used the Post-it note process, as in the previous sessions, to generate snap-shot descriptions of the reframed world.

PLENARY SESSION

Given the time limitations of a five- to six-hour workshop it was not possible to get the groups to present their results in plenary session. Instead the facilitators, who had followed the group discussions, brought up some critical points for debate.

Results

Given the condensed timeframe for this kind of collective intelligence knowledge creation process the groups could not really develop highly detailed and coherent scenarios for the year 2030. However, they did manage to sufficiently describe different attributes of their imaginary futures in order to begin posing new questions and exploring innovative perspectives on their current situation. They also started to consider how it might be useful to think further about their imaginary futures, including what it means for location- and industry-specific collaboration and policy.

The fact that all participants were required to present their Post-it notes in the groups meant that we managed to engage them all, including those who were shy and sceptical. In the two first workshops, we started with the expectations session and followed up with the hope session. We realized that the realism of the first restricted their ability to think freely and more positively in the hope session, so we decided to move the hope session to the beginning of the workshops. Many of the participants reported that they found the possibility to dream freely both liberating and useful.

In the standard FLL-N design, quite some time is spent developing and then presenting an alternative, coherent, vision of the future that is radically different from what the participants are accustomed to. Doing this invited participants to adopt a new frame of mind, where it is not only permitted to question assumptions – they are forced to do so. This helps participants come up with new and more radical ideas outside the box. Again, this is not done to predict the future, but to give participants new concepts and ideas they can use in their own learning and strategy development.

The main problem with reducing the length of the workshops to five or six hours is that there is not enough time to explain such a radically different future. Instead we decided to change some of the most essential variables in the relevant innovation system (i.e. factors related to trade, economics, technology, culture, policy or institutional setting).

In the fruit and berry workshop (Oslo Fjord, Drammen) we described a 2030 scenario where the big supermarket-chains had replaced their products with imports. This worked well as participants came up with many ideas for new export-oriented products, green and ecological branding and new sales channels, and they were able to put these innovations into the framework of a different kind of Norwegian and global society.

The counter-factual scenario at the workshop in Sogn and Fjordane did not work equally well. We took two of the main local industries out of the equation: salmon aquaculture had collapsed due to disease and local aluminium production had been moved out of the county. In this case, a local culture characterized by optimism and self-confidence made the participants dismiss these problems as minor nuisances. Instead they continued discussing ideas from Sessions 1 and 2 or, in the terms used in Chapters 1 and 4, they stayed at the FLL-N Phase 1 level, anticipation for the future. These were useful discussions, but not the radical rethinking that was planned.

Our experience from using this short version of the FLL-N methodology is that it works very well as a tool for making participants aware of anticipatory assumptions. In all our workshops, it generated a lot of enthusiasm and energy, and brought up many ideas that were new to participants. The workshops did lead to learning and networking both internally and in the clusters or groups taking part in the exercises. They definitely contributed to Innovation Norway's own strategic thinking by identifying potential challenges and opportunities for Norwegian industry and society and for Innovation Norway. Given the time span allotted it was, however, not always possible to shift the fundamental framework of the participants' thinking in a more radical way.

The dream commitment

Innovation Norway also made use of the experience gained from running these customised FLL-N when carrying out the so-called 'Dream Commitment' (*Drømmeløftet*) in the spring of 2015. Drømmeløftet was in itself a radical innovation for Innovation Norway, a process proposed and initiated by the CEO, Anita Krohn Traaseth. The objective of the exercise was to bring people from Norwegian industry, public sector and civil life together to brainstorm around the need for change, both in reference to societal challenges and the need for moving the Norwegian economy away from its oil and gas dependency.

There was little time for preparations, so we went for a 'lean and mean' organization, asking regional offices and the units abroad to arrange at least one workshop, meeting or conference on a topic of relevance for the future of Norwegian industry and society in a changing global context. Other companies and institutions were also invited to arrange their own Drømmeløftet events, and many did. In total, there were more than 80 different events with more than 3,500 participants, generating many ideas about future challenges and opportunities. Results were published on a separate website, as were several reports based on the process (Innovation Norway, 2016).

These events also gave us valuable insight into current shifts in how participants understand the role of industry in society. We noted, for instance, that many company representatives now expressed great concern for the future of the country and the planet, and argued for a more strategic approach towards a sustainable future. This strengthened Innovation Norway's resolve to make sustainability an integrated part of everything we do. The project led to a mobilization for the future and a challenge-oriented innovation policy, engaging the most important stakeholders, including strong media interest.

With no common methodology for carrying out the events, there was no way we could ensure a more radical reframing of perceptions and ideas in all of them. That being said, the exercise did lead to some radical rethinking. The most important deliverable was, however, that the need for a reorientation of policy development towards the future is now seen as self-evident.

Futures Literacy Lab used in Innovation Norway's own strategic processes

In December 2016 and January 2017 Innovation Norway used the agency's version of the Futures Literacy Labs methodology to stimulate a rethink of future challenges and opportunities among upper and middle managers, as well as by the Board. The processes were designed to help participants reframe their assumptions about the future of Norwegian industry and society on the one hand and the innovation policy system on the other.

The following exercises took place:

> 6 December 2016: the Leadership Group (including the CEO and the leaders of the divisions);
>
> 17 January 2017: the heads of Innovation Norway's regional offices;
>
> 19 January 2017: all members of the Board of Innovation Norway.

Having three exercises with three different groups helped us triangulate assumptions as well as ideas about the future. The labs revealed that there is some uncertainty about the identity of Innovation Norway. Many of the participants found it hard to present a common narrative about what kind of organization Innovation Norway is and what it wants to achieve. There was also uncertainty about the division of labour in the Norwegian innovation policy system, including the relationship to other agencies and institutions and the ministerial level.

The processes generated some intense discussion on future challenges and opportunities and the main drivers involved. Many of the visions presented were quite radical compared to the present. This also applied to ideas about the future organization of Norway's innovation policy system and the role of Innovation Norway. Many participants envisaged futures where Innovation Norway had changed dramatically or where the organization had been replaced by other instruments.

In general, we have found that the Futures Literacy Lab model represents an efficient tool for policy learning. It generates a lot of interest and enthusiasm, and has helped us change the way we think and work as an organization. We see a strong awareness of the need to include the future in the development of instruments as well as for a more strategic, forward-looking, innovation policy.

References

Innovation Norway (2016) *The Dream Commitment – Ideas and Proposals*, Blog. Available at: http://www.drømmeløftet.no/the-dream-commitment-ideas-and-proposals/ (Accessed: 9 August 2017).

Miller, R. (2007) 'Futures Literacy: A Hybrid Strategic Scenario Method', *Futures*, 39(4), pp. 341–362.

The Norwegian Ministry of Industry and Trade (2012) 'Meld. St. 22 (2011–2012) Tools for Growth – About Innovation Norway and SIVA SF'. Oslo: regjeringen.no.

The Research Council of Norway (2017) *New White Paper on Industrial Policy Focuses on Innovation*, News. Available at: https://www.forskningsradet.no/en/Newsarticle/New_white_paper_on_industrial_policy_focuses_on_innovation/1254026273601/p1177315753918 (Accessed: 9 August 2017).

Case 5: Imagining the future of the transition from 'youth' to 'adult' in Sierra Leone

Kewulay Kamara

Introduction

Young people represent the majority of the population in Sierra Leone. Yet, as this Futures Literacy Laboratory-Novelty (FLL-N) demonstrated, they are struggling to find meaning and identity. They are having trouble constructing the social relationships, inter-dependencies and responsibilities that give substance to adulthood. By using the future to examine the present the participants in this FLL-N were able to look at the potential around them with new eyes and tell stories that identify pathways to hope. In Freetown the means for engaging participants' collective intelligence pass through forms of expression and inter-action that are deeply rooted in the specific realities of Sierra Leone today.

The FLL-N offered a privileged and contextualized space for negotiating shared meaning by using the open, imaginary and imaginative future to reflect on the assumptions and questions that underpin policies and expectations. Building on design insights provided by an FLL-N on the same topic run with young people in Paris the week before, the experience in Sierra Leone demonstrated how a diverse group of people can at once develop their capacity to use the future, discover and invent rich stories about the past, present and future, and provide policy relevant analysis pointing to new initiatives and next steps.

The participants, the design and implementation

The Freetown FLL-N was held on 20–21 January 2014 at the Hill Valley Hotel in Freetown and was facilitated by Mr Kewulay Kamara. The FLL-N participants were seven young participants all under the age of 30, none of whom earns a regular salary: one college graduate (male), one college student (male), one drummer and traditional performance artist from the Sierra Leone National Dance Troupe (male), one singer-actress (female), one model and youth leader (female), one journalist and social entrepreneur (female), and one visual artist (male); the remaining participants were adults: one junior secondary school principal and social service worker (male), one former director of the American International School of Freetown and current director of an NGO (SELI) dedicated to teaching writing in English and indigenous languages in several districts in Sierra Leone (female), one participating observer from UNESCO Regional Office in Abuja, Nigeria (male), one facilitator (male), one reporter from the Sierra Leone Broadcasting Corporation; and four student observers from the Capstone Program at the Wagner School, New York University (all female).

The FLL-N was structured around introducing foresight tools, working with these tools in groups, presenting group work to the workshop, and discussions. Each day opened with a ritual of libation-infused music, poetry and dance to maintain excitement and participation, but also to validate the relevance of local traditions for sense-making in the workshop. Abundant use was made of storytelling which included: personal stories; stories about the myths of 'youth' and 'adult' that underlie teenage out-of-wedlock pregnancies and anti-social behaviours; and stories (myths) about country (economy, government and society), ethnicity, ethnic conflicts, rural-urban migration and education. The design of the FLL-N and the facilitation rested on a collaborative approach to learning, collective intelligence knowledge creation and 'using-the-future'. The direction taken by discussions reflected the views and knowledge of the participants.

An important part of public ceremony in Sierra Leone involves conducting a prayer ritual at the outset, usually following Muslim or Christian traditions. However, undertaking a libation as an opening ritual is also rooted in many African traditions. Such calling on the ancestral spirits is still an important practice in families and communities in Sierra Leone today. This traditional libation is an offering that brings together the three essential elements of storytelling. It begins by identifying the community and its ancestors (history); it proceeds to a discussion of the present; and then looks towards the future. The intimacy of the exercise builds trust. A facilitator, possibly a traditional community 'storyteller', strives for maximum participation of all who gather in the circle. Underlying the ritual is an appreciation of the power of words to create and transform reality, a salient part of African philosophical and religious traditions.

In Sierra Leone the design of the FLL-N process was customized to reflect local culture and practices, as well as the specific attributes of the actual participants and the topic under consideration. The entire process started with a questionnaire given to participants to assess their awareness of future methods and to set the stage for thinking about the future. Immediately after the survey participants were introduced to the libation. Next a series of futures methods, each prefaced by an appropriately chosen story, poem, song or music, was used to engage the collective intelligence of the group in deepening, inventing and articulating descriptions of the future. The process concluded with a conversation around metaphors that captured the richness of the imagined futures and a final, closing libation to the future.

This design of a FLL-N uses storytelling as the key heuristic for the knowledge creation process (KCP) that is at the heart of a collective intelligence knowledge laboratory. The selection of a storytelling approach to meeting the FLL-N design principles reflected the specific participants and topic: the 'Youth' to 'Adult' Transition in Sierra Leone. The libation was followed by an exercise using the Futures Triangle (Inayatullah, 2008), which extends the exploration, already initiated by the libation, of the past, present and future. Work on the Futures Triangle was followed by an exercise using the Futures Wheel (Glenn and Gordon, 2009). The Futures Wheel had the advantage of opening participants up to seeing how individual stories are interrelated but with disparate outcomes for individuals and groups. At this point, the group was ready to engage in a Causal Layered Analysis (CLA) (Inayatullah, 1998) exercise.

CLA is important for further deepening the participant's understanding of the present and demonstrating the power of words by revealing the relationship between inner metaphors, individual and group actions, and societal outcomes. This enables the group to begin to see the link between different futures and metaphors. Imagining alternative futures helps build awareness of anticipatory assumptions. By making explicit different scenarios, including the least to the most preferred, old local metaphors and new metaphors rooted in the local culture began to emerge. Participants started to tell new future stories as they began to distinguish 'colonized' and 'discarded' futures. In reframing the original stories participants engaged in a developmental process that facilitated the articulation of stories that past colonialist and future colonizing lenses obscured or distorted. A flood of new local and international stories about the imaginary future enabled the participants – personally and collectively – to see the present with different eyes.

The governing myth

As a result, participants engaged in lengthy discussions of the history of Sierra Leone, including the nature of corruption over time. Stories were told that revealed the ambiguities that call into question familiar hierarchies such as age and status as well as the stifling effect of gender discrimination in the current context. The intangible yet governing myths of family, responsibility and rights combined with these hierarchies seem to perpetuate existing institutions, pervasive dependency and legitimize 'corruption'.

According to participants corruption is not confined to business and politics. Corruption can also be of cultural values such as those of the extended family which oblige the more fortunate to shoulder responsibility for the perpetuation of 'traditions' that exploit others: less fortunate relatives could be subject to near servitude in the name of 'helping to raise' them, and invasive practices that traumatize young girls so that they expect little more than exploitation from men are carried out in the name of protecting chastity. Rituals such as circumcision, which once occurred in the context of a learning process that spanned many years, are now reduced to children being awoken in the night and whisked away for circumcision. Not long ago, circumcision for men and women represented the final stage of 'adulthood' training. Not any more. Some are obliged to 'carry the basket' of the practice of 'circumciser' as the family tradition is passed down from mother to daughter largely because of the material rewards it brings.

'Youth': a moving target

Efforts by participants to imagine the future spurred much reflection and discussion of the conditions of post-civil-war youth. In fact it was noted that the contemporary meaning of the concept of youth in Sierra Leone had been significantly shaped through neighbourhood watch activities during the war. Back then many of the unemployed were teenage and twenty-somethings who are now in their 30s and 40s. Some were combatants. Many are now still unemployed or marginally employed. They still continue to be regarded as 'youth'. In a country where adulthood has come to be subtly defined by the ability to gain independent sustenance, the span of youth has effectively been extended. While some younger people might have reached responsible 'adulthood' because they can provide for themselves, other much older individuals are still regarded as youth because they cannot 'provide', while others might believe that they express their manhood by being 'a baby father'. And young girls subtly internalize the culture of dependence for survival: i.e. they get impregnated by a man so he can take responsibility for them.

Telling all of these stories within the group, as part of imagining the future, helped to develop a deeper understanding of the present challenges facing this youthful population. By mingling the future and stories of individuals and groups in Sierra Leone and throughout Africa the group were inspired to innovate and invent. Reflecting on their stories the participants gained a greater appreciation of the capacity for ritual, storytelling traditions and imaginary futures to deepen our understanding of issues and create new knowledge. The process made clear the transformative power of using the future to reframe the stories and myths that help people sense and make-sense of their world. Participants also gained an appreciation for the diversity of stories that are told about governance, individual responsibility and awareness-raising. Many of these points were dramatized in skits created and performed by workshop groups.

A set of recurring stories related to the relationship between food security and unemployment. Many pointed out that the price of domestically produced rice is so low that farmers prefer to sell their produce to the Republic of Guinea and Liberia. They cannot compete with imported rice, or food aid. Yet others pointed to the poor road infrastructure and food shortages in the cities, and low incentives for agriculture. In these stories, the state of the agricultural sector is related to rural-urban migration, unemployment and prostitution and other anti-social activities that were seen as being exacerbated by the social media. The same analysis suggested that the alarming exploitation of youth in the mining sector is also related to the poor state of agriculture in combination with government action or inaction and the deeper metaphors that govern people's lives.

The old metaphors

Three interlocking sets of myths/metaphors seem to define the current malaise. One myth revolves around the people in authority as family members, 'Pa' and 'Mamy', as providers who are presumed to act in the best interest of the people around them. They 'take care' of their dependents. Their mere position elevates them to an unquestionable pedestal with little need for accountability. Those who are less well off often give their children to be educated by relatives that exploit these children in every way with impunity. All members of the family turn to the Pa to solve his/her immediate, usually financial, problems. Pa is expected to put the family, which could extend to the clan and 'tribe', above the interest of the public in general. This provides a perfect segue into the next interrelated and enabling metaphor for corruption: 'wherever you tie a cow, that is where it will graze.' So the public official uses his/her office to 'take care' of his own with impunity. All these factors interact to perpetuate a culture of dependence. To complete the circle of metaphors, the 'adult' as 'provider', at the very least, provides for themselves regardless of age or means. What happens when a younger person in the family is the 'provider?' The tables are turned. Just as they were turned during the war when the young had access to guns and power and can command their elders. You are a 'youth' if you do not provide for yourself and others. In this evolving culture wealth trumps age, supported by the globalized consumer society and social media's bypassing of old channels of power and communication. As a result, respect for age and other cultural values formerly vested in the community and family fall by the wayside.

The new metaphors

Writing about the results to this approach, Ronald Kayanja writes:

> Probably most striking was how the young people freely expressed themselves with such passion and tears. It showed some deep-seated need for them to 'explode' and understand themselves before they can reconstruct their reality. This is crucial in a society still reeling from the bloody conflict that shocked the world.

While the early part of the workshop exposed different preconceptions of different ethnic groups, of men and women, the unfolding of the processes enabled the emergence of personal stories that carried messages of commonalty, interrelationships, and relief. There are indeed parallel, alternative metaphors buried under the surface. One of the metaphors says in Krio, the lingua franca of Sierra Leone: "we all na wan", or "we are all one". Looking forward, the workshop considered myths such 'we all are one', which promotes unity in the face of ethnic, religious, and social diversity. These conversations and the reframed images of the future produced through the group's collective intelligence began to deconstruct so called 'wicked problems'. Participants evoked the potential of new 'communities of interest' to build alliances and shared understanding. They started to explore avenues for redefining the basic terms and dynamics of the standard versions of the 'youth to adult transition'. Participants were able to ask new questions, redefining the problems, opening up horizons for entirely new solutions.

During and after the workshop there was considerable print and broadcast media attention.

Reflections on storytelling and ritual: observations from the Sierra Leone Futures Literacy Laboratory-Novelty experience

Ronald Kayanja, an observer from the UNESCO Regional office in Abuja, Nigeria, summed up the workshop thus:

> The workshop followed a participatory approach, with the facilitator using what the young people know and are passionate about to enable them to reflect on their personal lives and their country. The discussions brought out issues that concern them most: adulthood and how the war impacted on the definition (with child soldiers and teenage parents etc); youth unemployment; teenage sexual activity and the consequences; challenges of urbanization; trauma from the war; and the challenge of inclusion. Those issues were discussed in depth, with the young people providing causes, effects and possible solutions.

It is easy to imagine that the experience can be adapted to other localities. The experience focused on storytelling as an important tool. Storytelling taps the inner need to tell our story. Telling stories opens us up to conversations that help us make sense of our situation. It builds bonds amongst participants. Storytelling helps transcend different backgrounds and training. A person who creates and tells their story is exploring their past and setting the stage for seeing the importance of anticipation. Stories that tell of the past reveal more about the present, the filter for making sense of past events. Therefore, a storytelling session in any community can be used to reveal how people of that community are 'using-the-future' to understand the past.

People live the present through the myths and legends that frame their world, even when recounted as history and biography. This is layered on to current concerns and states of mind when people start telling their stories. Using storytelling as a heuristic for collective intelligence knowledge creation elicits all of these elements of context as well as the limits created by depictions of the past and imaginary futures. Storytelling sessions also expose underlying tensions and limitations of our understanding of the past and future in the current context. Stories guide our lives, in part by imposing limits and in part by taking us outside those limits. Stories can bring the future into the present.

At the heart of most rituals and ceremonies are stories. These rituals can add weight to the stories that are told in ways that go well beyond the advantages due to the ease of communicating through a process that has a familiar structure and often a strong 'entertainment value'. In this way rituals help participants in FLL-N to appreciate the importance and role of moving their story from tacit to explicit, of sharing their story. They experience the power of their knowledge for the success of an exercise aimed at negotiating shared meaning and the development of their own capabilities, including improving their capacity to 'use-the-future'. Clearly the rituals need to be rooted in the local culture in order to inspire authentic engagement and deep resonance with the community's experiences.

The libation ritual used in the Sierra Leone FLL-N is a good example of this type of local ritual that invites very specific aspects of a community's past to be part of an exploration of why and how to 'use-the-future'. In Sierra Leone the libation created a spirit for the exercise. On the one hand, it opened up participants to tell stories that made them comfortable. On the other hand, these stories were sufficiently familiar to also make participants uncomfortable. When the FLL-N puts such heavy emphasis on storytelling it is important to balance the desire of every participant to tell their story and the need to move the agenda along as the collective learning process unfolds. To make this work it really helps if, as was the case in Sierra Leone, the facilitator loves stories.

Next steps

Sierra Leone foresight network

At the conclusion of the second day, participants expressed interest in 'spreading the word' to other youth throughout the country. Aware of the plethora of NGOs and 'youth organizations' that have sprung up in response to the variety of problems, but without much positive impact so far, the participants decided not to create a new body but to continue their work through a local foresight network in association with UNESCO and Baden Partners in Sierra Leone. This network could provide the structure for spreading knowledge about Futures Literacy and new ways of 'using-the future' to build foresight capacity throughout Sierra Leone with specific attention to youth in transition.

Partners

Both Mr Konneh, Commissioner, Sierra Leone National Commission on UNESCO, and Mr Koroma, Commissioner, Sierra Leone Youth Commission, expressed regret that they could not attend but reaffirmed their willingness to

154 *FLL-N case studies*

continue to work together with UNESCO to 'use-the-future' to build local capacity and empower specific solutions. Part of the follow-through from this first event involves Mr Kewulay Kamara working with Mr Konneh and Mr Koroma to draft a proposal for a foresight conference and FLL-N throughout the country to be funded by the government of Sierra Leone through its Ministry of Finance and Economic Development.

Materials

Some participants noted the absence of audio/visual tools. Futures Literacy Laboratories could greatly benefit from multi-media technology. Such materials in conjunction with the refined rituals could enhance the quality of the experience. The current members of the evolving Sierra Leone Foresight Network could develop such materials.

Sharing the Sierra Leone experience

Mr Ronald Kayanja of the UNESCO Regional Office in Abuja voiced the possibility that the experience of the FLL in Sierra Leone might help with healing and rehabilitation in other post-conflict zones in Africa.

References

Glenn, J. C. and Gordon, T. J. (2009). *Futures Research Methodology*. Washington D.C.: The Millennium Project.

Inayatullah, S. (2008). Six Pillars: Futures Thinking for Transforming. *Foresight*, 10(1), 4–21. Available at: https://doi.org/10.1108/14636680810855991.

Case 6: Imagining the future of sports

Jean-Jacques Gouguet

The Executive Master in European Sport Governance (MESGO) was created by the Center for the Law and Economics of Sport (CDES) in Limoges, with the support of UEFA. The MESGO aims to fill a gap in training options offered to the sports movement. Specifically designed for senior managers in the sports sector, the MESGO brings together representatives of the main stakeholders in European sports to consider the critical challenges it faces and to reflect on regulatory measures that could be put in place to ensure European sport's future prosperity. Jointly organized by five internationally renowned universities and research centres and supported by six major European and international team sport federations, the MESGO is based on a multidisciplinary approach and uses practice-oriented teaching methods to combine academic background information, knowledge sharing and networking.

The MESGO aims to encourage strategic thinking among participants who already occupy or are going to take on high-level positions within sport governing

FLL-N case studies 155

bodies, and to provide them with a framework for reflection and some tools which may help them to address complex change as it emerges. Today, the political, economic, societal and ecological complexity in Europe and the world means that leaders of the European sports sector must seek concerted and sustainable decisions in collaboration with their main stakeholders. Finding innovative solutions and building sustainable governance calls for global collaboration and ethics.

The MESGO's programme is composed of nine sessions of one week each. The final session is dedicated to the future of sport governance. The aim of this workshop is to explore different sets of assumptions about the nature and functioning of sport in the future. What might the sport organization of 2040 be like? What kind of rules regulate global sports and with what kind of enforcement systems? With this session in mind the organisers of the MESGO decided to join forces with UNESCO to co-design a Futures Literacy (FL) approach to this final phase. The MESGO Futures Literacy Lab-Novelty (FLL-N) was custom designed for the specific context of the course. Following the basic FLL-N design, as discussed in Chapters 1 and 4, the process invited participants to take part in structured conversation and reflection in order to collectively identify and invent their anticipatory assumptions and become more futures literate.

For the first time in 2014, the final session of the MESGO programme was divided into two parts. The first part involved traditional-style presentations of recent thinking on the topic of the future of sport and the second part was dedicated to the FLL-N. As usual FLL-N was co-designed in order to ensure appropriate customisation. This tailoring of the process took into account the fact that although participants in the course had been working together for the past 18 months they were nevertheless a highly diverse group: 14 nationalities with a range of employers' structures, sports backgrounds and positions held. The key to the design was to ensure that the individuals, belonging to radically different cultures, compared their visions of the future of sports in a challenging yet exciting exercise.

The FLL-N design, which included a strong level of real-time facilitation, succeeded in generating rich content, more than can be described in this short case-study summary. With brevity in mind, the reporting of this FLL-N has been narrowed down to a description of the work of only one of the three break-out groups. This group offers a reasonable window on the kind of action-learning that occurred during this FLL-N. After a consideration of this sample of the discussion, there is a brief section looking at key lessons from the overall process.

The sport FLL-N

The FLL-N started with a detailed description by Riel Miller of the FL approach and the collective intelligence methodology that underpinned the design of the process. The three phases were presented as follows.

Phase 1: Definition of a possible future for sports through the predictions and hopes of the group members. Predictions are about what you think is most likely

156 FLL-N case studies

to take place, a snapshot of sport in the long-run future. Hopes are about values. For instance, would you like to see changes in how sport is integrated and organized in the society around us?

Phase 2: Development of a model to conceptualize the future of sports. The point is to first liberate our imaginations from the constraints of prediction and current norms by playing with paradigmatically discontinuous futures and second, to experience more fully the power of our anticipatory assumptions in shaping not only the futures we imagine but our perceptions of the present.

Phase 3: Thinking about changing the current vision on the basis of questioning anticipatory assumptions: what are the implications of changing the imagined future of sports?

Phase 1: Reveal – sport in 2040?

This exercise in collective intelligence knowledge creation involved working through a modified Causal Layered Analysis (CLA) process where each participant's ideas about the future of sport were captured as future media headlines, stakeholder perspectives, institutional set-ups and underlying societal myths. In the working group of eight students, each participant wrote a Post-it note about what they imagined as being most likely for sport in the future. Then, in a roundtable, each person presented their ideas before the group discussion. The same procedure was applied to deal with key aspects of a desired future for sport.

It is difficult to synthesize very different visions, but the following themes were consistently mentioned:

- the importance of amateur sport;
- the need for access to sport for all;
- the need to strike a balance between competition, performance and the higher values that are a constitutive element of sport;
- the end of the cult of performance at all costs, the end of the heroic model;
- the importance of defending the integrity of competition;
- revising the institutional sports pyramid.

On this basis, the group agreed on the following representation of the future of sport.

Fear: the future is uncertain and controversial but many experts agree that current global problems are threatening the very survival of the human species. These phenomena will inevitably have consequences for the organization of sport.

Universality: sport has become global to the point that one wonders if it cannot be viewed as a global public good such as health, safety or the environment. From this perspective, there then arises the problem of global governance of such a public good.

Technology: technical progress is deeply ambivalent, it may be the best and the worst thing. Sport does not escape such a risk with, for example, the use of biotechnology leading to the enhanced human and more, to cyber-athletes, mixing man, animal and machine.

Ubiquity: we live at a time of a widespread mobile society, just-in-time long distance humans, goods, capital. Similarly, sport is now present everywhere on the planet, even in traditional societies which were little affected until recently.

Responsibility: in the face of global risks that threaten the very survival of humanity, everyone must ask what he or she is responsible for, in particular, for future generations. Sport cannot escape such a reflection both on its responsibilities in the current global crisis and in the solutions it can provide as a vector of values compatible with sustainable development.

Environment: the central question is whether we are going to reach the thresholds of irreversibility due to the limits of the planet, given that it is man who is the cause of all these global problems (the Anthropocene). In this perspective, the organization of major sporting events must be rethought as both factors contributing to and victims of the degradation of the planet's resources.

These are all external factors that will influence the organization of sport in years to come. In terms of factors internal to sport, the group agreed on the following:

Social Values: sport fulfils many social functions that are beginning to be recognized (health, education, social links, citizenship, etc). It will be interesting to know how, in the future, these features will complement the search for performance through sports competition.

Professional/Passion: one of the main characteristics of sport is the passion and professionalism that inspire practitioners. These fundamental values must be defended.

Organization: the sports organization model will oscillate between US closed leagues and European open leagues. Work is still required on the effectiveness of control instruments to promote one or other of the two models.

Responsibility: the integrity of sporting competition is threatened by numerous abuses: match fixing, betting, doping, money laundering, corruption, etc. It is the responsibility of sports authorities to eradicate such abuses to maintain the image of sport that can serve as a model for respect for the values at the heart of sports ethics.

Trends: the place of sport in society is constantly changing. We must be able to anticipate what will be the place of sport in the society of tomorrow to be able to adapt today.

Finally, we cannot forget an element common to both external and internal trends: conflicts of interest. This is, of course, the state of the balance of power between all stakeholders that determines the nature and extent of the mentioned phenomena.

Phase 2: Reframe: how to make sense of the imaginary futures?

Based on the presentation of a reframing context, participants then worked for over two hours on building a model for imagining a 'discontinuous' tomorrow. They opted for the model of the tree and the forest as a visual way of presenting their findings.

- First, the tree has roots, a trunk, branches and leaves. The roots are the values such as solidarity, integrity and respect that sustain sports. The trunk represents each stakeholder, branches and leaves are the products, including the functions performed by sports. Cycles can be introduced as seasons: in the autumn the leaves fall, and in the spring the leaves return.
- Second, there is the forest as a system; that is, all the trees are interacting, communicating and developing synergies.
- Third, the forest is still in a precarious dynamic equilibrium and may experience crises in terms of its ability to adapt to external shocks (resilience).

Such a model allows us to think about the design and need for a global governance of the sport systems in response to external threats, such as those described above, that may disturb the overall balance.

- **Attacks on the integrity of competition**. Various cheats (money laundering, match fixing, betting, corrupt referees, doping, etc.) maintain a suspicion that ultimately may seriously question the existence of the sporting spectacle. This is a problem of confidence in the integrity of the competition. If that integrity disappears, it creates a risk of public and sponsor disaffection vis-à-vis an activity that is not morally credible. From there, two scenarios for the future of the sporting spectacle can be considered: a scenario of the systematic use of scientifically assisted performance; and a scenario of the death of the sporting spectacle and the renewal of the game.
- **Cult of performance at all costs**. Could we imagine today a professional sport without the systematic search for performance improvement, despite the fact we eventually get to the edge of human limits? That would risk depriving sport of its supporters, sponsors and media access. Thanks to science and technology, we can always push the limits of sport performance and records. Could we avoid turning sport into circus games as a result of inevitable abuses linked to economic, financial, political pressures from the world spectacle that it has become?
- **Ignoring the limits of the planet.** In an absolute impossible context of infinite growth in a finite world, new principles of social organization should be developed and applied in a phase of ecological transition. This questioning of infinite growth will inevitably lead to the questioning of a sport without limits. Faced with the gigantic nature of major sports events, combined with rushing ahead in overcoming human limitations, consideration should be given to the rehabilitation of 'authentic' sports.

Only concerted collective action will provide solutions.

Phase 3: Rethink: how to use new visions of sport?

In the end, the future visions of sports generated by the participants could be seen as influencing their present visions and their concerns regarding local and systemic sustainability. Their vision of sports can be summarized around four pillars of sustainable development.

- **Economy: sport for development.** It is known that sport can be an engine of economic development, a factor creating jobs and added value for urban and rural areas. Hosting regular or occasional sporting events delivers short-term economic benefits but can also leave a longer-term legacy on hosting territories.
- **Social: sport at the service of society.** With so many externalities linked to its practice, sport can generate considerable social benefits. One of the best ways to evaluate this contribution is to calculate the avoided social disutility such as the decrease in delinquency, consumption and drug traffic, improved school results, etc. We should consider incentive systems to promote sport in ways that bring benefits from these externalities.
- **Ecological: sport in the service of environmental protection.** It is difficult to anticipate the way our societies will develop but whatever the strategy is, our lifestyles are likely to be deeply transformed. Sport will not escape such challenges and sports institutions and public actors must prepare for this kind of societal change. It appears especially that sport can be part of the eco-friendly activities that do not contribute to the degradation of the planet.
- **Culture: sport for all.** What might be the consequences of increasing insecurity for entire layers of society? Will we see a reduction in supervised sport? What does it take to attract vulnerable social categories? Are we going to see a segmentation of practitioners? A real issue is to improve accessibility to sport for people who are deprived: the disabled, women, immigrants, seniors, young people from deprived areas, etc.

For sports to play these roles and serve the general interest it will be essential to consider the underlying principles of transparency, accountability, democracy and sustainability. These are the principles that must be implemented today to prepare sport for tomorrow.

Main observations

Three observations summarize the results of this Futures Literacy exercise. First, it is important to consider how the characteristics of the participants affect the functioning of the laboratory. Second, there are important theoretical underpinnings to the process, and third, what makes this process an effective approach to understanding sports systems and policies.

A diversity of sport cultures

The workshop's participants belonged to different cultures because of their nationality. This resulted in a difference of opinions relating to their values, administrative culture, and history. This diversity was particularly felt in the difficulties experienced in reaching common views on sports. Two themes that illustrate these differences are:

- divisions regarding the merits and demerits of centralized decisions versus decentralized, and authoritarian versus democratic organization and processes; and
- divisions regarding the demarcation of amateurs as distinguished from professionals – is there a continuity or rupture between these two segments of sport? Which is more important?

The first theme specifically, provoked deep divisions among the participants. In particular, given the trends that they believe may threaten our societies in the future, it is essential to reflect on the defence of democracy. It is too tempting, in difficult times, to advocate the use of authoritarian methods.

Relevance of results

It is very difficult to summarize the wealth of all the discussions, but an important conclusion is that the students succeeded in identifying fundamental questions. All points of contention in sports today seem to have been addressed: the impact of new technologies, the social value of sport, the integrity of competition, and democratization between amateur and professional sports for all, etc.

These issues reflect the general theoretical analyses that were presented in the first two days of the course, when priority was given to consideration of analytical approaches to thinking about the future of sport. In particular, the manner in which regulation theory distinguishes long-run changes in historical context from specific adaptations, successful or not, of sports institutions. The potential for this disconnect between long-run historical changes and institutional adaptation helps to explain why today's systems enter crisis:

- historical long-term trends are known; they are related to demographics, technology, globalization and the environment;
- sporting institutions and systems are struggling to adapt given legacy characteristics such as bureaucratic structures, lack of transparency and democracy, problems with integrity, etc.

Emerging out of these discussions two points require further consideration. First, the issue of competition, the starting point for most abuses in sports through striving for victory and high performance at any cost. Participants concluded that it was difficult to find a balance between competition and respect for the fundamental values of sport.

Second was the question of the dominant economic system. What is capitalism in the future? Can it survive or is there a need to establish another, less destructive system for the planet? The group did not reach any conclusions on this subject.

Efficiency of the method

The exercise was completed to the satisfaction of all participants due to the very high efficiency of the method. If properly facilitated, it is possible to generate a very creative collective intelligence exercise. The experience for participants was evaluated as follows.

- They all played the game, even if they were surprised in the beginning;
- They all enjoyed the exercise, despite being a little unsettled sometimes as they were not familiar with projecting into the future or developing an analytical model;
- They would have preferred a less extensive theme than the future of sports;
- They greatly appreciated the opportunity to consider recommendations. They were however, somewhat frustrated by the lack of time to deepen this part of the process. Indeed, they expressed a desire to add a work session. The goal should have been to develop a charter for the future of sports by students in this second promotion of MESGO programme.

In conclusion, this prospective exercise is well suited to generating questions that will challenge the sports sector in coming years, and thus is useful for efforts to adapt sport institutions to changing historical circumstances.

Case 7: All Africa Futures Forum: transforming Africa's futures

Geci Karuri-Sebina and Riel Miller[1]

A three-day 'collective intelligence knowledge laboratory' was convened in Johannesburg to address the question of how people think about Africa's future, and how this might relate to prospects for Africa's transformation. It was titled the 'All Africa Futures Forum' and themed 'Transforming Africa's Futures'. The convening built upon two prior international Futures Forums held in 2013 in Paris by the UNESCO Foresight Unit with linkages to some of the same African partners. The Forums were entitled: 'Imagining Africa's Future #1: Beyond Models of Catch-up and Convergence', and 'Imagining Africa's Future #2: Decolonizing African Futures'. This third forum was aimed specifically at bringing together a range of leading African futures thinkers and practitioners to explore developments in the Discipline of Anticipation and its implications for imagining African futures (SAMPNODE, 2014; UNESCO, 2014).

Impetus for the Forum

A fundamental change is taking place in the way people look at the world around them as they strive to embrace complexity, foster their capacity to be free and appreciate the important strengths and weaknesses that make up the legacy systems around them. Their complicated and sometimes painful histories can often incite impatience and urgency for change that can make quick-fixes and old means seem more responsive and promising. There is however, in many cases, the recognition that things may not be quite that simple. The desire to explore these changing ideas and ideals served as inspiration for the All Africa Futures Forum.

In the 1960s in Africa, like elsewhere, there was considerable enthusiasm for long-term thinking. Arguably, in the African case the enthusiasms of post-colonial construction and the rapid economic growth occurring in many parts of the world fuelled a particular set of expectations, many of which are today seen in a different light due to so much disappointment. This history ought to serve as a cautionary tale about the dangers of extrapolation for those who try to think about the future today. The previous Africa Future Forum on 'Decolonizing African Futures: Exploring and Realigning Alternative Systems' in Paris examined the narrowness of the approaches to the future that simply try to colonise tomorrow with today's ideas. The speakers and ensuing discussions at that forum in Paris made clear that efforts to think about the future of Africa must encompass a range of anticipatory systems and processes capable of not only cultivating the strength of local cultures that use the future in a diversity of different ways, but also moving beyond dominant ideas and models of industrial catch-up and convergence.

One of the keys to inviting a renewal and reinvention of the capacity to use the future to foster societal change rooted in African experiences and aspirations is getting beyond state-centric and elite-driven visions. Both elements – the need to diversify ways of using the future, and finding ways of fostering greater capacity – informed the design of the Johannesburg All Africa Futures Forum with a wide range of participants from different parts of Africa. The design of the All Africa Futures Forum started with an understanding that futures thinking is not new to the continent and that many of the efforts in the recent past were often modelled on dominant global approaches to thinking about the future. The designers of the Forum recognised that the challenge of getting beyond the conventional frameworks for imagining the future called for significant investment in developing African capabilities. Developing capabilities thus became the main aim of the Forum and the primary challenge for the design of the different activities at the Forum.

Using a co-creation approach to the design of the Forum the different organisers decided to privilege learning-by-doing as much as possible. This meant engaging Africans in processes where they could articulate and question a range of imaginary futures, including predictive, normative and novel. Forum participants would be invited to respect and find inspiration in their own history through carefully designed efforts to break out of the dominant anticipatory assumptions, like extrapolation-based conventional economic growth. The challenge was to find ways to take the knowledge creation at the Forum beyond simply invoking transformation to walking-the-talk. The Forum design took the need for creativity and inventing the attributes of transformation as the starting point. By design the Forum's learning-by-doing activities would engage participants' capacities in ways that not only nourish the richness of imagined futures but also enable less instrumental and arrogant approaches to human agency in a complex emerging world.

The objectives of the Transforming Africa's Future Forum were to:

- explore innovative foresight concepts, tools and planning methods that are transforming Africa's future;
- strengthen the anticipatory capabilities of African policy makers, practitioners and planners;
- allow the private, public and civil society sector to input, debate and interrogate the thinking, application and potentials for partnerships; and
- enable the establishment of an African network of foresight practitioners.

The Forum was designed to foster the discussion of these issues from a variety of angles and perspectives. A process for negotiating shared meanings was devised as a way to invite collective intelligence knowledge creation through which participants could build up a common yet diversified understanding of anticipation.

Structure

The Forum was convened through a multi-institutional arrangement that leveraged the significantly different perspectives on why and how to use the future to produce a creative design for the conference. Among the different perspectives were those who see:

- **futures study as a way to emancipate and empower Africa** – the concern from this perspective was about the agency of foresight and planning as a means to correct or reinvent Africa's future away from what were termed 'used' futures – imposed on the continent by colonial and neo-colonial elite influences;
- **the future as being a distraction from the now** – the argument being for realism and a recognition of the emergent, whereas a concern for the future might be perceived as a distancing abstraction;
- **the future itself as freedom** – a perspective about the future presenting a more open terrain not to be colonised by our assumptions and plans, but as evolving and empowering;
- and more.

As such, the programme for the Forum was structured so that participants could engage with different ways of 'using-the-future'. By working together participants could make explicit their varying initial positions on the future and how to transform Africa. This sharing and learning-by-doing together was deemed particularly important in light of the need to take advantage of diversity and willingness to learn as a way to spark the creative thinking about the urgent and decisive action to change Africa's trajectory. The Forum was crafted to take into account the anxiety and hope, strong motivating pressures for all participants, without falling into the trap of believing that there is only one 'right or wrong way'. Rather the approach taken sought to contextualise, critique and advance the discipline through authentic learning, meant to move beyond being satisfied with just hearing many different voices.

The Forum structure was designed to take participants on a 'collective intelligence knowledge creation' style learning voyage over three days, with each day targeting a specific level of inter-action and reflection.

> **Day 1 Conceptualisation**: The focus of questioning on Day 1 was on how African futures are being conceptualised, by whom, for whom, with what outcomes, and in whose interests.
>
> **Day 2 Methodologies**: Day 2 was designed to take advantage of the fact that there are various methodologies and methods used to think about the future. A series of activities enabled participants to engage with these different perspectives and discuss the choices and underlying reasons for applying these methodologies to imagining Africa's future.
>
> **Day 3 Planning**: Given a high level of demand for agency and change on the continent, the discussions on Day 3 targeted the question of what 'owning' African futures could mean (if not equated to 'colonising'), and what the implications might be for rethinking planning and governance across sectors.

The second day (Methodologies) in particular was designed to recognise different ways of thinking about the future, with three parallel sessions for capacity building employing various methodological approaches applied to a thematic area. One of these sessions was a full-fledged simulation of a Futures Literacy Lab-Novelty (FLL-N) carefully co-designed with members of the Forum organising committee. This simulation was aimed at equipping participants with a basic understanding of anticipatory systems thinking and the action-learning collective intelligence knowledge creation design for developing Futures Literacy. The FLL-N involved about a third of the Forum participants, some 30 people, who self-selected to participate in the Lab. The plenary facilitator was from UNESCO, and the three break-out group facilitators were from East, West and South Africa. The diversity and preparation of the facilitators was important to the success of the process. It enabled a rich, inclusive, and creative learning process among the participants, who came from diverse backgrounds – international organisations, ministries, universities, private firms, non-governmental organisations, etc.

Engagement

The Future Forum succeeded in its effort to enlarge the scope of participants' understanding of what it means to 'use-the-future' to include both closed and open anticipatory systems and processes. On Day 3, as the different threads were being drawn together, the conversation demonstrated a shared understanding of the fundamental anticipatory systems that span everything from a tree that sheds its leaves to humans that deploy a wide spectrum of conscious approaches to imagining tomorrow. As participants exchanged views about how Africans might change the way they 'use-the-future' it became clear that conscious imagining of the future serves many distinct purposes, from shaping perceptions and priorities in the present to creating the shared visions upon which hope depends. Participants grasped the importance of 'using-the-future' in a more rigorous, futures literate fashion, and the critical role of collective intelligence processes – able to draw on specific, locally rooted experiences and points-of-view.

Many of the discussions and speakers made reference to the conventional ways of depicting Africa's tremendous potential and the commonly expressed expectations that Africa would grow rapidly over the coming decades, following in the footsteps of the Asian Tigers, China and even India. There was also an acute awareness of the challenges faced by the continent, from the difficulties in the food and agriculture sector and extreme poverty (even in the most successful countries) to a lack of resilience of the social and governance fabric when hit by powerful disruptive forces like violence and epidemics. The scourge of human insecurity is still too important in rural life, often pushing people to live in very difficult conditions in the shantytowns within cities. Overall participants expressed frustration with the narrow models of the future being used to understand the Africa of today and tomorrow. There was a desire to find new ways of using-the-future and to imagine the future in new ways.

Important references were made to futures past, or the way the future of Africa had been imagined in the past. For instance, at the Berlin Conference in 1884 (Gates and Appiah, 2010), Africa was referred to as a 'geological scandal' that could not be left unattended, assuming that Africa was simply a place to be mined and exploited for its natural resources. Europeans imagined futures in which the existing powers of the time remain in hegemonic roles. Given these futures the tasks were for soldiers, merchants and missionaries to conquer the continent. The futures imagined by others and different ways of imagining the future were not granted much credence or authority, even if many other views and ways of thinking existed. After World War II, decolonisation began and a range of different anticipatory systems also started to develop, based largely on the then dominant planning paradigms of the Cold War era, from Soviet and Maoist five-year plans to World Bank and Manhattan Project-style critical path planning. However, as is evident from the images of the future and the methods that are still being used today, it is not easy to replace the dominant paradigms of industrialisation from either the East or the West.

Results

The Forum produced a number of key observations. For one, it was argued that African universities and think tanks potentially have a significant role to play in the development and diffusion of different approaches to anticipation. As some participants pointed out however, it is important to bear in mind that universities (in Africa or not) are largely dominated by ways of using the future that fail to encompass a diversity of anticipatory systems and processes. Additionally, much academic research is confined to the grand narratives of industrial societies. Diversifying thinking about the future should therefore not be restricted to universities and government departments steeped in academic orthodoxy. A broader, more bottom-up and heterodox approach was seen as necessary, one that touches villages and enterprises, and creates a new more futures literate context for researchers and policy makers when they 'use-the-future'.

A strong consensus emerged that the design of such capacity building investments needs to take into account the specifics and immense diversity of African culture and history of 'using-the-future'. Connecting innovative approaches to imagining the future to people's local traditions is fundamental for realising the potential of what is too often an undervalued resource and an essential ingredient to understanding the past, present and future in deep ways. Cultivating African Futures Literacy was seen as one mechanism for fostering identity precisely because it depends on a meaningful consciousness of heritage. This was considered of particular importance in light of how today's growing connectivity and interdependency can offer an enriched sense of identity, but also the disempowerment and insufficiency of links that do not provide enough meaning or autonomy.

Participants in the Forum noted that many young people are yearning to be creative and may feel less encumbered by existing ways of perceiving the world, but they can also demonstrate an ignorance of the origins and nature of the stories they tell. Here Africa's strong traditions of storytelling and artistic expression offer an important resource for generating the creativity and innovation needed to combine endogenous and global dialogue on using the future in new ways.

One of the strongest messages to emerge was that Africa is rich with change-makers. More and more people in Africa are creating change, taking the initiative in their communities, acting to identify and take advantage of the opportunities around them. In theory and practice, the African narrative is being transformed from a conventional story of growth through industrialisation and catch-up to a story of local economic and cultural empowerment. Participants in the Future Forum refused to be simply 'Afro-pessimist' or 'Afro-optimist', asking instead: "What does it mean to be African in the 21st century?"

The sense of urgency expressed by the scholars, practitioners and activists in the Forum was tempered with a cautionary call to calm down and be more considered in our eagerness and boldness to rush about trying to create a different future. One speaker reminded participants of an old African proverb: "The times are urgent; it is time to slow down".

Lessons and ways forward

The All Africa Futures Forum provided an important opportunity to consolidate some key insights arising from the Africa Future Forum series and pointed to a number of directions for next steps.

The overarching conclusion was two-fold: first, that more investment needs to be made in developing the capacity in Africa to use the future in ways that suit the needs of the continent; and second, that the way to do this is by conducting learning-by-doing processes that build capacity involving diverse populations. In effect, the main idea was that more Africa Future Forums should be organised, with a strong emphasis on action learning collective intelligence methodologies that 'use-the-future' to address issues of critical concern at a local level while generating rigorous research and actionable agendas.

The Forum's discussions provide the following insights for efforts to design next steps.

- When tackling the challenge of cultivating and connecting people's capacity to 'use-the-future' it is important to take into account that anticipation is a universal attribute of our universe and is embedded in all systems and processes in one way or another. Being aware that conscious human anticipation is just one sub-set of anticipatory systems and processes connects directly to many African perspectives. Renewal and innovation in how people 'use-the-future' could play a central role in changing what we see and do. Working throughout Africa to gain a better understanding of how to use the future has the potential to improve people's capacity to understand complex emergent reality and make choices with respect to that reality.
- The future cannot be a source of freedom without a critique of dominant narratives; the following quote by Gaston Berger was mentioned in this regard: "The purpose of looking at the future is to disturb the present" (Berger, 1958).
- Current approaches to using the future are too narrow, excluding both alternative imaginable futures and alternative ways of using the future. These approaches tend to treat uncertainty as the enemy, even though it is not only a permanent and unavoidable attribute of reality, but also the source of the novelty that underpins the capacity to be free.
- Decision-makers and planners in particular need to become more able to understand and use a wide range of anticipatory systems and processes. Being able to think in multiple temporal horizons and invent alternative scenarios is a minimum requirement. Being able to integrate complexity is equally critical, as well as recognising that the capacity to sense and make-sense of novelty calls for being able to 'use-the-future' in different ways.
- Scenarios or stories of imaginary futures should be understood as heuristic devices to help in policy dialogue and decision-making in both open and closed frameworks. At times, a scenario gets locked in, the assumptions underlying it accepted, at least for the time being, and then it serves as a target-based framework for prediction, choice, and risk assessment. But scenarios can also be open and disposable; sources of continuously changing non-predictive, non-normative descriptions of the imaginary future that assist in re-perceiving the present and making it easier to integrate unknown unknowns. This particular point raises a challenge to the orthodox

approaches of many decision-makers in most of the dominant institutions in the contemporary African context, creating an opportunity to take some of the approaches used by the Africa Future Forum in Johannesburg as a way to begin diversifying 'use-of-the-future' in Africa.
- Our capacity to imagine meaningful futures is limited, even if the future is fundamentally open and infinite in its potential variations. Yet, it is important to push the envelope of our thinking and find creative and disruptive models for imagining tomorrow that go beyond trend extrapolations and dominant paradigms.

The Forum offered a strong message: that getting better at 'using-the-future' can help to create synergies among actors from different backgrounds, and to capture emergence in ways that take advantage of novelty. The Forum showed that open and pluralist discussions that 'use-the-future' differently can serve to engage traditional and 'other' points-of-view in rethinking governance systems. Nurturing Futures Literacy renews and inspires the sources of hope within and across diverse communities. Such hope is essential for empowering people to find common interests and shared investments, in other words fostering the capacity for people to build their own meaningful and sustainable communities, which is exactly the aspiration for Africa's future today.

Note

1 With thanks to Jacques Plouin for his contributions to this text.

References

Berger, G. (1958) 'L'Attitude Prospective', *Prospective*, 1(May).
Gates, H. L. and Appiah, K. A. (eds) (2010) *Encyclopedia of Africa*. Oxford University Press.
SAMPNODE (2014) *All Africa Futures Forum: Transforming Africa's Future, African Futures Forum*. Available at: http://www.sampnode.org.za/events/africa-futures-forum (Accessed: 17 August 2017).
UNESCO (2014) *All Africa Futures Forum: Transforming Africa's Future*. Available at: http://en.unesco.org/events/all-africa-futures-forum-transforming-africa's-future (Accessed: 17 August 2017).

Case 8: Overcoming fragmentation in Ecuador: the *Manabí Será* initiative

Orazio Bellettini Cedeño and Adriana Arellano

Background

Grupo FARO is an Ecuadorian, non-partisan, independent, plural, and secular think-and-do tank. The overarching aim of Grupo FARO is to advance the development of Ecuador by addressing the problems of geographic, social, political and economic fragmentation. Grupo FARO works to create a shared understanding of the country's challenges. By strengthening the capacity of all segments of Ecuadorian society to use the future to diagnose problems, hopes and policies, Grupo FARO is cultivating a broader base for decision-making processes and enlarging people's understanding of different development models as well as the generation of shared responsibilities to face the country's challenges.

From its inception, Grupo FARO has sought to use collective intelligence methods to tackle directly social and political fragmentation that can inhibit innovation and change. Building a shared base for seeing and doing for individuals, organizations and communities is what fosters both the pluralism of actors and systems of mutual open accountability that are crucial for Ecuador's development.

In 2011, Grupo FARO organized *Ecuador Será*, (Ecuador will be), an initiative focused on prospective research aimed at identifying trends and strategies to transform Ecuador into a knowledge society in which creativity and innovation are the drivers of development. In 2012, Grupo FARO explored the topic of sustainability and the ways in which Ecuador could become a model of effective natural resource management. The initiative had the support of five allied organizations and ten financial supporters, reflecting the capacity of Grupo FARO's initiatives dealing with the future to promote multi-sectoral collaboration.

Despite its capacity to promote a dialogue among different sectors, *Ecuador Será* followed a top-down process meant to generate images of likely or probable futures. In addition, the event was not designed to generate action plans that connect visions of the future to concrete steps to change the present. From this perspective, there were several aspects of the process that Grupo FARO wanted to change when presented with the opportunity to experiment with the design principles being tested by UNESCO to promote an action-learning approach.

Grupo FARO decided to take the initiative to the local level and chose Manabí, a northern province on the coast of Ecuador, to promote a process that enabled citizens to create a shared vision of the future for this province. The initiative was called *Manabí Será* (Manabí will be) and its methodological design as a Futures Literacy Lab (FLL) was carried out at the UNESCO Foresight Unit in Paris with participation from professionals with a diversity of perspectives to assure a holistic approach.

The *Manabí Será* case study gathered evidence of the application of FLL design principles as a way of exploring anticipatory systems and processes in Manabí, cultivating Futures Literacy (FL) in Ecuador, and advancing citizen engagement with the challenges facing their communities.

Manabí Será *(Manabí will be)*: using the future to change the present at the local level

The province of Manabí is located in the northern part of the Ecuadorean coast. Manabí's economy is based heavily on natural resources and agriculture products that include cacao, bananas, cotton and seafood. Its cuisine is recognized as the most diverse and rich in Ecuador. In addition, its industrial sector is based on tuna, high quality tobacco, and *agua ardiente* (Spanish whisky) production.

Local products include Montecristi hats (also known as Panama hats) and furniture. Finally, tourism, as an economic resource for the Manabí province, has been growing in recent years since there are natural, cultural and landscape attractions that make it a favourite place for tourists.

Manabí's population is 1.3 million inhabitants, which makes it the third most populated Ecuadorian province. Manabí, with 22 counties (cantones) is the only province in Ecuador that has several important cities, which creates the possibility of a more diversified development model and multi-polar governance. Even though there is a shared pride of being Manabita, because different cantones have different historical roots and their own productive characteristics, it has been difficult to identify a shared development project that motivates Manabí's population and institutions to work for a common goal.

Grupo FARO believed that a conversation about the future could create a space to build the common ground that enables different sectors of society to meet and find spaces for collaboration and a more resilient development model for the province. With that aim, Grupo FARO implemented the *Manabí Será* initiative in alliance with UNESCO, four universities, civil society organizations and private companies.

Design specifics

There were several design differences that distinguish the *Ecuador Será* process from *Manabí Será*.

Selection principles

Unlike *Ecuador Será*, participants in *Manabí Será* were not selected primarily on the basis of being experts in a particular field. The selection process was designed to incorporate mechanisms to promote citizen participation and a broader cross-section of stakeholders. This choice was consistent with two FLL design principles: (1) that participants were selected on the basis of their tacit as well as explicit knowledge about the subject so that the collective intelligence process can tap into a wide range of information, and (2) the participants needed to both care about the subject and have roughly equal knowledge of the subject as a whole, even if each participant has their own specific experience.

Anticipatory systems principles

The design of the *Manabí Será* process stressed the importance of developing a greater awareness of anticipatory assumptions underlying people's imaginary futures and starting the learning process related to Futures Literacy. Unlike *Ecuador Será*, which focused on generating scenarios based on probable futures, the *Manabí Será* initiative used the discussion of probable futures to build an awareness of the importance of the models used to describe imaginary futures. Grupo FARO, working with UNESCO and the FLL community of practice, was able to design and implement *Manabí Será* in ways that targeted the use of the future for a range of objectives, in particular as a way to change the province's present.

FLL objectives

The *Manabí Será* initiative had the following objectives:

- promoting citizen engagement and knowledge sharing by thinking together about the future of Manabí;
- bringing together diverse actors to build a shared vision for the future of the province;
- contributing to the development of long-term policies for provincial development; and
- promoting futures literacy among citizens and key stakeholders in Manabí, as the capacity to understand and deploy anticipatory systems and processes for different aims and on the basis of appropriate tools.

FLL process

The *Manabí Será* initiative was implemented in three phases: Phase 1, in which the initiative was presented to citizens in public forums; Phase 2 in which Futures Laboratories gathered key actors in the province and produced three visions of future for the province; and Phase 3, when a shared vision was selected from the three options and then presented to authorities and citizens at a public event. This last phase continues as actors in the province are following through with discussions on how each sector can contribute to Manabí's future and operationalize its shared vision.

Phase 1: Collecting individual visions of the future

The first phase concentrated on disseminating the objectives of *Manabí Será*, raising awareness among citizens of the different uses of the future as well as collecting individual visions of the province's future.

To achieve these goals we conducted these efforts in citizen forums held in universities around the province. To accomplish this goal, we developed compelling and powerful narratives, hoping to break with participants' traditional ways of thinking about the future.

For this purpose, the following materials were developed.

- **A visual metaphor that clearly communicated the existence of plural futures**. The metaphor was made up of two images, an initial image of a room that looked outside, in which people could see through the window frame (the framing in our present) and a road leading away outside of the room (the future). The second image presented the landscape as if the room's wall and window had been torn apart, and now with a full view people could see that outside of the room there where two roads leading away (futures) and not only one road that was visible initially through the window. Additional materials are available at the *Manabí Será* website (Grupo FARO, 2017).

- **A case study of the distortion of future thinking presented in the paper** End of History Illusion (Quoidbach, Gilbert and Wilson, 2013). We used questions posed by the researchers which invited people to think how much they had changed in terms of friends, music tastes, interests, etc. in the past 20 years and then to imagine how much they would change in the future. This exercise helped us make the point of how easy it is for humans to reconstruct the past while it is challenging to construct futures and imagine scenarios of change.
- **An example of another territory in Latin America, the Antioquia Department in Colombia**. Antioquia suffered greatly from violence generated by the Medellín Cartel in the 1990s. People were filled with fear and lost their ability to dream about the future. Nonetheless, a group of leaders decided something needed to change so they worked to transform fear into hope by investing in education. They developed the vision *Antioquia la más educada*. With this vision uniting and inspiring the Department, people from all sectors of society worked together to identify potential projects that used science and technology to enable innovation throughout Antioquia. This enabled us to share with people from Manabí how a shared vision enabled different sectors to collaborate to turn the vision into a reality.

One of the challenges for the Manabí Será project was to prepare participants prior to the FLL face-to-face events to help them to embrace a more open and pluralistic approach to using the future. To set the scene, an on-line engagement process designed to harvest people's existing visions of Manabí's future was initiated. The intention was to offer an easy and enticing way for people to become sensitive to the fact that they are obliged to use their imaginations and that their expectations and vocabulary for using the future are caught up with probability. Grupo FARO worked closely with UNESCO's Futures Literacy team to design and implement a survey approach to revealing how the future is used (awareness, discovery and choice). A simple format was made available through the Manabí Será website (Grupo FARO, 2017) enabling online participation. Participants were asked the following questions.

1. What is good about being *Manabita*? This question aimed at connecting people with their emotions towards Manabí.
2. How does it look when you imagine Manabí in 2033? What makes it unique? These questions aimed at challenging people to use their imagination and propose a vision that goes beyond a projection of the present.
3. Provide a detailed description of Manabí in 2033. Here we hoped to invite participants to connect deeply with their imagined vision.
4. Complete the phrase (with a maximum of three words): Manabí will be . . . This final question aimed at condensing people's imagined futures of Manabí in a powerful vision statement, revealing the metaphors and myths that underpin these futures.

The first phase gathered more than 500 visions of citizens and, in an effort to engage and promote participation by young people, we included the presentation of children's visions for Manabí in pictures through collaborative work with local schools. This phase was useful to understand the difficulties that arise when citizens start thinking about the future. Although we sought to stimulate citizens' futures literacy, it was clear that this process could not get beyond the basic level of awareness (Miller, 2007). Most visions of the future proposed by citizens were based on a continuation of the past and present into the future. They focused on what they knew in terms of already prominent aspects of the province: tourism, nature, and its gastronomy.

As expected, when we designed this first phase, the development of futures literacy and of more imaginative futures was relatively limited. However, as hoped, this phase did bring a greater awareness of the importance of thinking about the future of the province and raised interest and support for the project among diverse actors. In fact, this phase generated financial support from private sector actors in the province.

Phase 2: Implementing three FLLs

These action-learning workshops followed the design principles for collective intelligence knowledge creation that use the future as developed by UNESCO as part of scoping anticipatory systems around the world. The FLLs were conducted in universities in Calceta, Bahía de Caráquez and Manta on 28, 29 and 30 April 2014. One hundred stakeholders from different sectors and counties in the province including political representatives, professors and high-level directors from local universities, journalists and media representatives, civil social organization members and private business entrepreneurs participated in the laboratories. Workshops were conducted by Lydia Garrido Luzardo, Orazio Bellettini Cedeño and Adriana Arellano.

The aim of the workshops was to guide participants through a learning-by-doing process that challenged the implicit and explicit anticipatory assumptions they use to think about the future. This, in turn, was meant to advance the participants' awareness of why and how they use the future, introducing them to thinking about the future in different ways, and generating inputs into the development of a shared vision of the future of Manabí. The goal of the exercise was not building a utopian vision of the future or coming up with predictions; our goal was to identify and question current assumptions about the future to be able to expand the understanding of the present and pose new questions.

In this phase, we attempted to spark some 'rigorous imagining' by inviting participants to leave behind probable and desirable futures in order to experiment with a discontinuous framework. Consistent with the FLL design principles we did not suggest that these alternative futures were likely to happen or were even desirable; the point of the exercise was to experience the power of anticipatory

174 FLL-N case studies

assumptions in shaping the futures we imagine and the potential to address the creative challenge of inventing paradigmatically different futures.

This was the steep part of the learning curve – the reframing phase. For this phase we used the framework shift to a Natural Knowledge Society (Bound, 2008).

Phase 3: Selecting a shared vision of the province

During this phase, we focused on questions that arose from rethinking the visions participants shared in Phase 1. Participants started to explore the implications for the present of alternative and even discontinuous scenarios of the future. The innovative ideas that emerged motivated the participants to realize the array and diversity of possibilities in the present. Some of the ideas discussed were:

- promoting Manabí as a territory of innovation;
- developing a set of interconnected ecological cities;
- Manabí as a province that promotes and uses renewable energy;
- consolidating Manabí as a province that pursues sustainable development;
- Manabí, a land that rescues the best of its traditions;
- a territory with education according to its reality, needs and potentialities;
- Manabí, a province working together; and
- a land whose cuisine is appreciated globally.

From the inputs that emerged during the FLLs and that were collected in the initial phase of Manabí Será, Grupo FARO developed three new visions for the province of Manabí.

MANABÍ, A LAND COMMITTED TO PROSPERITY THROUGH DIVERSITY

One of the greatest strengths of Manabí is that it is the only province in Ecuador that has several important cities and therefore the power, wealth and capabilities are spread over several poles of development. The challenge is to find a shared vision that take advantage of the different cultures, ecosystems and traditions that coexist in Manabí. The vision: a land committed to prosperity through diversity means that the citizens of Manabí are unified by a passion and commitment to achieving the prosperity of its people and to sharing it with those who find in Manabí a land of opportunity.

MANABÍ, INNOVATION INSPIRED BY IDENTITY

Manabitas are proud of their traditions, their history and their customs. These are their greatest strengths but also pose the challenge of getting trapped in past glories. The challenge is to use the past as a source of innovation and progress. The creativity of Manabí's pre-Columbian culture can be found in the objects that allowed them to connect with the spiritual world and as the cradle of Ecuador's liberal revolution that contributed to the construction of a modern society. Manabí's identity has in fact been built around the concept of change and renewal. This vision invites *Manabitas* to recognize that the province's identity is deeply rooted in championing transformation and innovation.

MANABÍ, INNOVATION INSPIRED BY NATURE

Places that combine abundant natural resources with low levels of industrialization are often associated with socio-economic under-development. Sometimes it is even argued that knowledge can only be generated in the industrialized societies. At the same time, there is a growing recognition of the importance of developing knowledge and technologies that allow for sustainable and innovative post-industrial ways of managing energy, food, water and housing. The abundance and diversity of resources in Manabí and its pride for its gastronomy, its fields and beaches, make it fertile grounds for a different development paradigm. For Manabí, the challenge is to learn how to use existing resources wisely and to promote the generation of new knowledge that allows the province to take advantage of its history. In this vision, *Manabitas* add knowledge to the province's richness, focusing on the talent of the community, the commitment of politicians and the entrepreneurial energy of its people.

Finally, the three visions outlined above were submitted to a vote by citizens of Manabí. With the support of 125 university students, votes were collected in public places in seven districts of the province. We received voting results from approximately 2,700 citizens. The results were unveiled at a concluding event in Portoviejo, the capital of the province. The vision both created and selected by the people of Manabí to inspire the province's present was: 'Manabí, innovation inspired by identity'. The design of this closing event of the *Manabí Será* project included a collective art-making process aimed at reinforcing how collaboration in the elaboration of a shared vision inspires collective action in the present.

Preliminary conclusions

The *Manabí Será* initiative was born from *Ecuador Será,* an initiative focused on the views of academic experts that attempted to predict the future. However, as we connected with the territory of Manabí, its challenges and opportunities, we grappled with the question: should the future or futures be imagined top-down or bottom-up, in predictive mode or in an exploratory creative framework? Our experience in *Manabí Será* offers a convincing case that richer images of the future can be developed if different aims and methods for using the future are combined. The design principles of Futures Literacy enabled us to conceive and implement a process that allowed stakeholders to enlarge their images of the future beyond expected futures. Being able to propose visions not constrained by efforts to ensure high levels of probability created space for conversations that made explicit and invented futures and provided a different way of looking at the present. Furthermore, tapping directly into people's visions in Phase 1 of the *Manabí*

176　FLL-N case studies

Será project and then soliciting their judgements in Phase 3 provided important local context for the visions. The outcomes were both more multi-dimensional and legitimate in terms of local knowledge and preferences.

As with any process of this kind there were several difficulties, particularly with respect to specifying and agreeing on visions for Manabí. The challenges included:

- framing the project with the title Manabí *will be...* (*Manabí Será...*) suggested to some people that Manabí *was not*, in the present; this challenged some sectors and actors to recognize and assume limitations in the present that were not always comfortable or accepted;
- capturing the diversity of interests and visions in a fragmented province presented a challenge; the FLL allowed us to sit at the same table as leaders from different sectors and cantones from Manabí and enabled them to express the diversity of visions of the future existing in the province, while recognizing common challenges and opportunities that can create a vision shared for all the people of Manabí; and
- developing a dynamic vision that incorporates continuous change and evolution was a challenge since people often fixated on static images.

In the end, inputs provided by citizens in Phase 1 and key stakeholders' ideas provided in Phase 3 gave the team the elements necessary to develop visions for the future of Manabí that incorporated diversity and permanent evolution. Moreover, the vision 'Manabí, innovation inspired by identity', has proven to be a compelling vision that is engaging different sectors and promoting concrete activities and initiatives for change.

Next steps: using Manabí's vision of the future to change the present

Since the final event of the *Manabí Será* initiative, Grupo FARO has continued efforts to promote the dialogue about ways in which each sector can contribute to implement the shared vision, in which innovation is born from the territory's identity. At present, and after a series of editorials in the local newspaper, interest has risen again and new ideas for next steps are being discussed and implemented and local authorities in Portoviejo, the capital of the province, are organizing a conference to discuss ways to promote innovation in the territory.

On 16 April 2016, an earthquake of 7.8 Mw magnitude hit Manabí. Almost 700 people died and more than 80,000 people were displaced. The Ecuadorean government has estimated infrastructure damage at USD 4,000 million, and first evaluations reveal that at least USD 3,500 million will be required to finish the first reconstruction phase. This disaster also affected the main productive sectors of Manabí, such as tourism, agriculture and aquaculture.

Despite these many challenges, tragedy can become an opportunity for the people of Manabí. This difficult moment may be a chance for *Manabitas* to collaborate for a common project that promotes a new mindset with refreshed ethics for local relations and strong institutions that encourage learning, creativity and innovation. This will allow not only infrastructure reconstruction, but also social fabric renovation and the creation of new opportunities. A group of young leaders from the province is using the vision developed in the *Manabí Será* initiative to promote innovation and opportunities for people and communities affected by the earthquake while rescuing local traditions through research, capacity development and seed funding.

The plan is to continue implementing actions that enable political, social and business leaders as well as ordinary citizens in Manabí to use what was generated at the FLLs to understand the present, creating new opportunities for people to act in ways that are consistent with their values and hopes. The use of the future in Manabí is mobilizing people in this province and inspiring the country to overcome fragmentation and work together. The challenge is to continuously re-imagine the future, not as a place we are going to, but one we are creating today.

References

Bound, K. (2008) *Brazil: The Natural Knowledge Economy*. London: Demos Press. doi: ISBN 978-1-90669-300-8.

Grupo FARO (2017) *Manabí Será*. Available at: http://www.manabisera.org/ (Accessed: 13 June 2017).

Miller, R. (2007) 'Futures Literacy: A Hybrid Strategic Scenario Method', *Futures*, 39(4), pp. 341–362.

Quoidbach, J., Gilbert, D. T. and Wilson, T. D. (2013) 'The End of History Illusion', *Science*, 339(6115), pp. 96–98.

Case 9: Young citizens for a sustainable planet

Matthew Giuseppe Marasco, Jennifer Rudkin, Geci Karuri-Sebina and a conclusion by Bayo Akomolafe

Introduction

Every two years since 1999 young people from around the world have gathered together at the UNESCO Youth Forum to share their hopes and fears, aspirations and advice for a better tomorrow. The Forum generates recommendations that are transmitted to UNESCO's highest decision-making body, the General Conference, which also meets every two years. The stated ambition of the UNESCO Youth Forum is to contribute in a constructive and significant way to the deliberations and decisions of the General Conference and UNESCO's mission in general. Pursuit of this goal plays a central role in the design of the Youth Forum, influencing all aspects, from who is invited to attend and the topics discussed to the structure of the agenda and the forms the messages take. Explicit factors, like the issues that have already been chosen as central for the General Conference and official policies like making 'youth' a priority, shape the design of each Forum.

Implicit factors also play a role, such as the assumption that the young people attending the Forum will conform to the agendas already set out by the organisers of the Forum, the General Conference and, often, the governments in power in the young person's home country. The inherent virtues of participation, democratic procedures and belonging to a particular age group form unquestioned, largely tacit foundations for everyone involved.

The 9th UNESCO Youth Forum (UNESCO, 2015a) was held in Paris, from 26 to 28 October 2015. The challenges of climate change and the post-2015 Sustainable Development Agenda were identified as the most salient topics for this version of the Youth Forum, as it was scheduled to take place one month after the United Nations Summit convened in New York to deliberate and adopt the post-2015 Development Agenda and one month before the United Nations Climate Change Conference (COP 21) in Paris. Subsequently the results of the deliberations at the 9th UNESCO Youth Forum were presented to the UNESCO General Conference (COP21), the Conference of Youth 2015 (COY 11), and the Commonwealth Youth Forum 2015 (The Commonwealth, 2015). At all these events the recommendations from the 9th Youth Forum were received and acknowledged. What is less clear is the extent to which the 9th Youth Forum recommendations played a role in these global political events, particularly in light of the fact that in most cases the agendas and resolutions had already been negotiated well in advance.

Many other questions about the content and effectiveness of UNESCO's Youth Forums preceded the design and implementation of the 9th version. Although this case study is not the place to examine the political rationales and effectiveness of this type of 20th-century institution, it is worth noting that part of the motivation to undertake a more innovative approach for the 9th Youth Forum was a general sense that the historical context had changed. In particular, there were concerns about the selection processes that determined who participated in the Forum and how the basic impact of the Forum on the world was conceived. To make a long story short, the challenge – at least for some of the designers and organisers of the Forum – was how to get beyond the conventional, conformist and largely tokenistic content of the topics, agenda, processes and outcomes, while at the same time safeguarding the obviously valuable experiential aspects of an event that brings together hundreds of strangers from all around the world to deliberate and learn. No one pretended that there was a magic solution or that there was some way to cut through the inertia of an international system, gummed up by the parochialism and tensions of national perspectives, to liberate the creativity and power of any group of people, let alone inexperienced young people largely selected or self-selected on the basis of their conformism and enthusiasm.

Given these factors, and many more, a decision was made to experiment with an innovative approach meant to leverage the learning potential of this type of global gathering and seek new ways for their deliberations and exuberance to have an impact on the world around them. Based on UNESCO's in-house capabilities to design Futures Literacy Laboratories (FLL) and the ongoing UNESCO Futures Literacy Project, there was an agreement to collaborate across two units of the

Social and Human Sciences Sector (SHS) to design and implement a FLL-Novelty exercise as a part of the 9th UNESCO Youth Forum. The FLL-N segment of the Forum agenda was tailored to introduce and engage some 500 young people from 159 Member States with an action-learning collective intelligence knowledge creation process that used the future to explore novelty. For one and a half days out of the Forum's three-day running time these young people plunged into a specially designed FLL-N, building on the standard design discussed in Chapter 4. This 9th Youth Forum FLL-N is by far the largest single experiment so far and called for extensive preparation, adaptation and improvisation.

Design considerations

In light of the very large scale of the event a series of preparatory initiatives were undertaken in order to respect the co-creation criteria for FLL-N and ensure sufficient real-time expertise to accompany the expected and desired improvisation as the process unfolded. A global team of experienced and futures literate facilitators was assembled. They collaborated in the design of the overall FLL-N and contributed to the development of an innovative social-networking process that used a cutting-edge internet platform, Timescape (2015). This social-networking tool was deployed a few weeks before the event and served to 'prime-the-pump' for the FLL-N processes and heuristics.

A couple of days prior to the Forum the international group of experienced FL designers and facilitators convened in Paris to rehearse each step of the FLL-N and prepare a training process to be run in advance for the eight plenary peer-facilitators and the 60 break-out group peer-facilitators. The eight plenary peer-facilitators were selected from participants in the Youth Forum who had already gained some initial experience with FL. The break-out group peer-facilitators were invited to volunteer through an on-line process using the social-networking tools set up for the Forum. The plenary facilitators were given an in-depth, experiential initiation into FL, through a compressed FLL-N process that tested the design for the Youth Forum. The volunteer peer-facilitator also got a chance to experience some FL-related action-learning and to work their way through the detailed scripts prepared to assist them in their task of animating break-out groups of approximately six to eight participants. In addition, some of the peer-facilitators volunteered to take on the role of rapporteurs with the responsibility of reporting the group discussions to the sub-plenary summary sessions and of sub-plenary sessions to the full plenary. The break-out groups were designated in advance, on the basis of the full participants list, and were composed so as to ensure the gender and geographic diversity that encourages rich and creative conversations.

As per the standard FLL-N design, participants were invited to move through the three action-learning phases, called here: Reveal, Reframe and Rethink. Quite a few participants had been primed for Phase 1 through their involvement with the Timescape platform that had invited them to 'take a voyage into the future' by submitting contributions on-line. This consisted of a series of requests that participants capture images of sustainability in 2040 within their own community

180   *FLL-N case studies*

and share them with the other participants across the world by publishing them on the interactive Timescape map. This step sensitised participants to their anticipatory assumptions and provided raw material for Phase 1 discussions of expectations and hopes. The general use of social networking platforms also established preliminary contact between organisers and participants as well as across the far-flung participants themselves. Timescape was also used throughout the workshop. Six volunteer 'Timescapers', trained prior to the start of the FLL-N, updated the input of all 60-plus working groups to the Timescape maps as each step in the process unfolded.

The three-day 9th UNESCO Youth Forum also included several traditional passive plenary sessions, networking opportunities, capacity building workshops and other extra-curricular activities over the course of the event. This case study focuses predominantly on Day One of the Youth Forum and provides some highlights of the FLL-N process, particularly the first two phases. Phase 1, Reveal, asked young people to explore their expectations and hopes for 2040. Phase 2, Reframe, focused on breaking away from the anticipatory assumptions of Phase 1. This second phase encouraged participants to look beyond the parameters set by the narrow confines of possible futures, inviting them to discover and invent their own imaginary worlds in the form of a temporary sculpture, crafted from 'leftover' office supplies. The following account provides a few selected windows on what happened during the FLL-N process.

Glimpses of what happened during the 9th UNESCO Youth Forum FLL-N

The Forum's catchphrase was 'Young Global Citizens for a Sustainable Planet'. While facilitators prompted participants to explore this theme through the lens of technology, culture, ecology and economics, they also encouraged them to consider how sustainability might be looked at through personal, inter-personal and emotional lenses. This allowed the participants to not only place themselves as a protagonist in the future, but also provided the opportunity to create a narrative about their presence in 2040. The overall group of some 500 was divided into six sub-plenaries covering the following themes: Rights, Freedoms and Responsibilities; Diversity and Identity; Learning, Personal Development and Sustainability; Knowledge, Awareness and Media; Local Practices, Biodiversity and Prevention of Natural Disasters; and Capture the Energy of Youth. These six topics were loosely adapted from a pre-event effort to discover the different interests of participants. Such analytically unstructured and semantically ambiguous data can still serve to identify key words and trendy slogans that can catalyse a Phase 1-type CIKC exercise that shift participants' anticipatory assumptions from tacit to explicit.

Concurrent conversations involving 500 young people across some 60 breakout groups created an opportunity to generate vast amounts of information very quickly. The peer-facilitators encouraged a focused yet agile exchange within their group in order to ensure that they could cover the different phases of the process within the time constraints of the Forum. There were no evident gender barriers or language limitations with multiple groups speaking in English or French. The summary offered below is only impressionistic, culled from one or two specific break-out group discussions and a few snippets from the sub-theme and then overall plenary sessions; a more detailed program is available (UNESCO, 2015b).

Phase 1: Reveal (hopes and expectations)

The following questions about the world in 2040 were asked to prompt group discussion:

- What does work look like?
- What is it like for wildlife and nature?
- What is the weather generally like?
- What is new and hopeful in your community?
- What is new and worrying in your community?

Participants were reminded that a prediction was about something likely to happen. In other words, something you would bet money on. This task initiated passionate conversations that examined contemporary moral, social and political issues. Exploring the imaginary futures of people living in Sub-Saharan Africa or China may look completely different from those in Sweden or Australia. Discussions revolved around issues like future voting rights – what age was appropriate or whether voting would be allowed at all. For some participants, the nature of democracy in the future was not self-evident, so they had difficulty choosing one likely future. Others were unsure about the future of education and unwilling to predict the price one might have to pay for tertiary qualifications. Some viewed the prospects for gender equality optimistically, contending that today's pay gap would become obsolete. They also projected that more women will lead countries and occupy a higher proportion of executive roles and girls from developing countries will have equal access to education in 2040.

Facilitators underscored that there are no right or wrong answers, but that participants should try to focus on what they really think is probable. Not all predicted futures were optimistic, some participants believed that in 2040 the world would be facing serious scarcity. Other participants argued for a more positive future in which today's efforts to tackle climate change, gender equality and the political turmoil will have paid off. As is typical of Phase 1, the discussion centred on today's prevalent problems, even if some of the expectations simply flipped them on their head. Of course, this primary phase did not call for innovation, but was rather created for participants to appreciate the way in which they use the future. The next task explored an alternative technique that provided participants with an opportunity to wear their heart on their sleeve by imagining their preferred future. For some participants, this was an extension of their predicted futures, simply projecting the achievement of the United Nation's Sustainable Development Goals. Participants expressed the hope for a future without hunger and poverty, a world without borders and with open access education for all. Other participants seized the opportunity to create much more distinctive or eccentric ideas. For instance, the following idea was shared in one of the break-out groups:

> *In 2040, armed drones will perpetually orbit the globe with cognitive capabilities of identifying and eradicating terrorists.*

This hope, that there will be a 'moral philosopher in the sky', was contentious but paved the way for others to be a bit more creative. A number of participants thought that this image of the future also has something in common with visions of open access education and an end to poverty. Still the visions of 2040 continued to resemble the problems today. For instance, troubles such as the threat of terrorism loomed large, even if it was hoped that in the future development of aviation technology and cognitive robotics would solve the problem. Some participants had difficulty imagining that today's dilemmas would look much different in 25 years. Still, in most groups the effort to grapple with 'utopian' narratives provided participants with an opportunity to realise that imagining the future, even hopeful ones, required making some pretty important assumptions. This in turn provoked a few participants to resist the game, arguing that imagining hoped-for futures was delusional or too luxurious to even consider. All of which contributes to the process of uncovering and challenging participants' assumptions about the future.

Phase 2: Reframe (discontinuity assumptions and a sculpture)

Phase 2 was a pared-down reframing exercise, since there was little time and insufficient shared framing across the full group to propose a specific detailed alternative paradigm for participants to play with. Instead for the 9th UNESCO Youth Forum the point of departure for reframing was the elimination or 'disappearance' of some key attributes of the expected and desired futures elaborated in Phase 1. Peer facilitators assisted their groups in adding or removing elements from their expectations and hopes. The following questions were used to prompt discussion:

- Is there an important part of your image or headline that you can remove?
- Is there something missing from the headline or image that you could add?
- How would your headline or image change if one of the big problems or big solutions that you included initially did not happen?
- What would the opposite headline or image look like?

This discussion provided a significant step forward to reimaging the future by making participants more aware of their assumptions and initiating the process of inventing new ones. Reframing, as usual, proved to be an arduous process and gave rise to very animated exchanges. Peer facilitators encouraged the identification of specific aspects of a reframed world in 2040 in each of the sub-theme fields – assisting the groups to focus on key terms and topics. Some groups imagined a future where carbon emissions are still on the rise or a world where there is no shortage of water as a way to challenge their assumptions and began to explore discontinuous futures. One participant shared the opposite of her hoped-for future: a vision of 2040 where climate change was still on the political agenda. Participants tended to agree with this position and believed that any future without global warming is very unrealistic. Therefore, the following reimagined headline was proposed:

In 2040, drones will perpetually orbit the globe with capabilities of identifying carbon emissions in urbanity.

Other participants asked: what implications would a world without terrorism imply? Does this mean that societies have eradicated fundamentalism or religion itself? How might our cities look if biodiversity was able to thrive in the cities that many of us call home? And what might a world look like without scarcity? Or without gender or social strata or nationalities? Some argued that the elimination of these central characteristics could in turn eliminate personal identity. Others said that it could create egalitarian societies that treat individuals as equals. These controversial headlines underscored the difference between the anticipatory assumptions that prevailed in the Phase 1 effort to think about predictions and preferences.

With these alternative headlines and images in mind, each group constructed a physical model that was meant to provide a symbolic representation of this reframed imaginary world. The challenge of this materialisation step is to use constrained and limited types of material to give shape to a 3D image of the group's imagined future. The difficulty lies in building a shared symbolic representation of the scenarios discussed by the group. The creation of a model of an imaginary future generates new insights and unpacks meaning. Building a 3D representation of a discontinuous future provided the opportunity for participants to first articulate their anticipatory assumptions to themselves and then to negotiate shared meanings while explaining their idea to the group. The groups thereby engaged in a collective process for defining the nature and significance of their imaginary future. Through this process they exposed the boundaries of their thinking, the box for their imaginations, and also started to challenge those limits.

Building a 3D representation of their imaginary future also entailed grappling with how to communicate what their model represented, further adding to the details and dimensions of a different 2040. With these 3D models participants had a chance to go beyond an individual assembling a lone vision to express a collective idea of tomorrow and the assumptions underlying these visions. Creating images of different futures opened up a space for a critical dialogue and the analysis of a different landscape from the perspective of different cultures. Each group gave their 3D prototype a title that represented their understanding of a transformed world order. At the end of the session each break-out group's sculpture was digitally photographed and then projected on screen to the full sub-plenary.

184   FLL-N case studies

Phase 3: Rethink (proposing an activity)

With the aim of anchoring the enthusiasm of participants to 'make a difference' in their own context and the local conditions for taking action this session targeted the expression of personal projects. Building on the discussions from the earlier phases participants were invited to work with their groups to identify micro and macro actions to be undertaken at a global, regional, national or individual level. Actions were then uploaded by the Timescape team on site to the online platform, Timescape Phase 3 (Timescape, 2015). This map records individual commitments, with a photograph of each participant and their location around the globe. The Youth Forum concluded with a final presentation where all working groups and facilitators came together to present the Youth Forum's global recommended actions (UNESCO Youth Forum, 2015c).

The experience of the participants in going through these stages was transformational, as has been the experience with the other FLL-N. The initial excitement about expressing predictions and hopes was quickly transformed into a new energy – initially challenging, but ultimately captivating – as participants started to think outside the box. In all the usually structured and traditional spaces at UNESCO there was an incongruous buzz of creativity, exploration, interaction and experimentation. The effectiveness of Phases 2 and 3, the reflective and creative presentation of the results by the designated leaders to the Forum plenary, and the evaluative comments from the participants showed how the process encouraged participants to reconsider what it means to 'use-the-future'. Their understanding of thinking about the future moved from the expectation that such activities are regimented, formal and elite plan-generating processes oriented to finding solutions, to searching to understand the assumptions behind the images of the future that shape what people see and do. Participants took a step towards becoming futures literate and becoming more appreciative and hopeful about the complexity of the world around them.

Living it: a personal perspective as concluding observation on the 9th UNESCO Youth Forum

Bayo Akomolafe, Expert Futures Literacy Facilitator, Nigeria.

As I negotiated my way through the aisles of seats in the spacious bunker-like hall, strolling past the intense stares of some young people – some of whom were dressed in smarter suits than the UNESCO officials that hovered around them, I recalled a fascinating quantum physics experiment called the dual slit experiment. I'll skip the intricate details. Perhaps it might suffice to know that the popular experiment is a mind-boggling endeavour with a cautionary moral-of-the-story ending: things do not have pre-set values or features, and only benefit those within relationships. As such, there are no 'things' outside of context, and the way we define or understand the phenomenon is part of the phenomenon. In the very process of measuring a 'thing', the thing comes to be – and not prior to that moment.

I looked around. 'Youth.' Five hundred restless bodies of every colour and hue. The typical expectation of a 'Youth Forum' is that if young people are gathered together, their voices will provide a creative burst of freshness in otherwise run-of-the-mill contexts where adults do all the talking. Nothing less than 'the future' itself is at stake. And these young people are supposed to conjure remedies to any and all of the inadvertently barbaric deviations that may be creeping maliciously into the vaunted trajectories charted by their parents. They are supposed to right the ship and deliver coordinates to the preferred future of global imagination. And what inspires confidence that they can pull off such a feat? Their youth.

Given the heavy investments we make in youthfulness, I silently wondered about the particular ways it was being performed. How it was being measured. My impression was that the impressive concrete walls, bright lights, flashy slogans, loud mics, prestige of UNESCO, and the surreptitious promise that those who did well enough would have the chance to shine before the important people, all conspired to create a particular iteration of 'youthfulness' that – I feared – served more to clone the prevalent assumptions about the future than contest them. In short, this 'youthfulness' was manufactured – and very much a part of a larger apparatus that included big money, big money shots, a fixed notion of the future, the transhumanist aspirations for techno-economic development and progress, and a bureaucratic funnel process that made sure only the 'right' things to say or conclude made it to the top. In spite of this Youth Forum's commendable resolve to address critical challenges by expanding the thinking pool, the whole setup was akin to asking 500 'youth' to write their own answers to mathematical equations for achieving the Sustainable Development Goals, while the correct 'approved' answers were behind the book the whole time.

Forget the unctuousness of the word itself – 'youth' (a more ambiguous or ambitious word has never been contrived: is youthfulness of the heart or of bones? Who gets to be part of the gang? At what point does youth stop being youth?); a more critical look at this 'youth priority' business suggests a labour paradigm of sorts, wherein a careful selection of deserving ones make the cut, and are enlisted to be the faces within structures adults have built and continue to maintain. Much like the emotion emojis on a Facebook post that silently manages feelings, many institutionalised platforms collectively predefine the range of expression and spectrum of responsivity, thereby training the next generation to think in the same ways as the previous one. What is left out, what is excluded from the youth apparatus, what doesn't make the cut is the disruptiveness, angst, spontaneity, disenchantedness and redeeming foolishness of being young. But it is exactly those qualities that are needed in these times when climate discourse is fixated on carbon reductionism, when poverty is seen through the keyhole of GDP, and when the Future is just another app or USB port away from the obsolete.

As a young black kid growing up in West Africa, I was already used to the antics of politicians who promised change and transformation, while lining their pockets with the sweat and toil of the downtrodden. I knew a certain cynicism and despair when I heard seasoned activists and operators of civil society platforms speak regretfully about the slow pace of development in Africa – painfully oblivious to the terrible costs of progress and the deep colonial imperatives it served. I had watched promising heroes turn into the enemies they once fought. Why would anyone trust that youth – conditioned, schooled and bred in the same contexts and institutions as their parents before them – had anything to offer but slightly different iterations of the same?

Acutely aware of this largely invisible framework of conformism, *I negotiated my way through the aisles of seats in the spacious bunker-like hall, strolling past the intense stares of some young people – some of whom were dressed in smarter suits than the UNESCO officials that hovered around them.* The initial stages of the FLL-N process were underway. In one group, in response to a prompt asking the participants to imagine some distant future, some of the delegates were speaking glowingly about a future where phones would be engrafted in bodies. Others later spoke about flying cars, green technologies, climate stability, and peace on earth.

I leaned in, and engaged one of the delegates: "Yes, this is all fine and dandy," I said. "But whose future is this? Whose future do you see when you close your eyes and claim to imagine a different world? Whose future are you unwittingly perpetuating?" The young man stared back at me, perhaps wondering what other future there was to salvage except the one – *the one Future* – that contained self-driven cars, neon-lit neighbourhoods and a universal humanism convenient to commercial interests.

But my intervention was perhaps hasty and needless in another important way: the FLL-N process was already designed to ask those very questions; to query the particular ways participants 'use-the-future'; to bring to light the hidden contours and Trojan elements that were already part of our many imagination projects; to meet the sticky assumptions that keep us tethered to the same habits of thought/ action that maintain the status quo; and, to trouble these patterns well enough that a deeper appreciation for complexity and multi-agential emergence might occur.

In a sense, the FLL-N process was a way of saying 'Map, meet Terrain'. A cathartic release into the wilds where human agency itself becomes part of a larger tapestry of becomings. An unburdening of the Future of the weight of its singular responsibility to deliver. An unshackling of anticipation from its matrix of sameness, so that many other futures can be performed.

And then, low and behold, I started to hear people speaking of their own lives and their own struggles to climb the hill or plunge into the pool of their imaginations. Confounding expectations the conversations started to dismantle convention. Something disruptive, irreverent and ambiguous was afoot. Participants in the FLL-N at the 9th UNESCO Youth Forum were misbehaving, they were losing their certainties. They seemed to be accepting the invitation to take their diversity as a creative asset rather than an obstacle to be dissolved in the pablum of reductionist universal slogans squeezed onto the pin-head of the ideal wealthy society. My worry that collective intelligence would serve as a solvent that washes away distinctions was, on the contrary, like a dye that highlights the boundaries of the otherwise indistinguishable organisms on a microscope's slide. Was there a way to punch some holes in the premises that congealed the visions of the future into confirmations of yesterday's agendas?

Perhaps nothing was more satisfying than watching a collective grimace slowly spoil the creaseless certainty and conformism that was present in the room hours earlier. A deep alchemy was at work in recuperating a sense of wonder. And with wonder comes the clarity of confusion. Of inquiry. Of experiment and risk-taking. Of consultation and new alliances. Of recovered meanings and unexplored terrain.

Halfway through the multi-tiered FLL-N process, I made friends with one of the participants, who told me she was now beginning to question her previous attitudes about education and schooling. She wanted to investigate further. She wanted to know how to ask the half-questions that were tugging at her sleeves. As such, she said, she no longer thought that the major culminating event – where she was to make a presentation – was that important. Harvesting a set of recommendations to fire off at the high and mighty did not seem as alluring as when she flew into Paris. Now, starting to see her own context, home and history, through the lens of different and open futures, she wondered. She wondered.

And in that moment, *that moment of justice*, I recognised a different quality of youthfulness that we probably might do well to pay attention to; that might recommend slowing down in times of urgency; that might insist on dancing where the data might call for a studious stoicism; that might open up new places of power and multiple futures: irreverence.

References

COY11 (2015) *Conference of Youth.* Available at: http://coy11.org/en/ (Accessed: 16 August 2017).

The Commonwealth (2015) *Commonwealth Youth Forum.* Available at: http://thecommonwealth.org/media/event/commonwealth-youth-forum-cyf (Accessed: 16 August 2017).

Timescape (2015) *Timescape.* Available at: https://www.timescape.io/unesco-9yf-1 (Accessed: 16 August 2017).

UNESCO (2015a) *9th UNESCO Youth Forum.* Available at: http://en.unesco.org/9th-unesco-youth-forum (Accessed: 16 August 2017).

UNESCO (2015b) *UNESCO Youth Forum Program.* Available at: http://en.unesco.org/9th-unesco-youth-forum/program (Accessed: 16 August 2017).

UNESCO (2015c) *UNESCO Youth Forum: Recommendations, UNESCO Youth Forum.* Available at: http://en.unesco.org/9th-unesco-youth-forum/recommendations (Accessed: 13 June 2017).

Case 10: Future-proofing an entire nation: the case of Tanzania

Aidan Eyakuze and Edmund Matotay

Introduction

This chapter showcases the Tanzania Dialogues Initiative as an example of a creative approach to 'using-the-future' to engage an entire country in the process of contemplating and creating its own future. Expanding the range of participants

188   FLL-N case studies

beyond experts, researchers, policymakers and government officials to include ordinary citizens in social dialogue about the country's future is a hallmark of the initiative's social innovation. This chapter describes the use of Futures Literacy tools to structure nine conversations with 387 thought-leaders across Tanzania, with the objective of developing strategic scenarios to influence the national discourse before the April 2015 referendum on the country's revised Constitution and the October 2015 general election.

Tanzania has delivered impressive economic growth performance in the last decade, averaging between 6 per cent and 7 per cent per year between 2000 and 2014. While the poverty incidence has fallen from 39 per cent in 1990 to 33 per cent in 2007 and further to 28 per cent in 2012, population growth has expanded the absolute number of Tanzanians living below the poverty line from 10 million in 1990 to over 12.6 million in 2012. The share of malnourished children has risen (National Bureau of Statistics – NBS/Tanzania, & ICF Macro, 2011). Additionally, despite its taking a very large share of the public purse, education continues to deliver poor learning outcomes at the foundational primary school level (Uwezo, 2014). Tanzania has failed to achieve robust and sustainable pro-poor and pro-jobs growth. The need to prioritise the latter outcomes is increasingly urgent.

Signs of intensifying social tensions are becoming apparent. Religious tolerance, long a hallmark that differentiated Tanzania from other countries in the region, is evaporating as clerics and religious leaders are murdered and places of worship are desecrated. The past decade has also seen an intensified re-evaluation of the union between Tanganyika and Zanzibar. The majority of grievances expressed by Zanzibaris are not new, but the expression of dissatisfaction with the status quo has become more aggressive and is questioning a political marriage that was once thought to be sacrosanct.

Tanzania is at a transitional moment. The general elections in 2015 ushered in a change of top leadership and a new administration. It was the country's most contested election since 1995, and it tested the maturity of the country's political, economic and social discourse, and its national institutions. The outcomes of that election continue to play out.

Imagining the future of Tanzania

The Society for International Development (SID) is an international network of individuals and organisations founded in 1957 to promote social justice and foster democratic participation in the development process. Through locally driven programmes and activities, SID strengthens collective empowerment, facilitates dialogue and knowledge-sharing on people-centred development strategies, and promotes policy change towards inclusiveness, equity and sustainability. SID has over 30 chapters and 3,000 members in more than 50 countries.

SID's Tanzania Dialogues Initiative curated an informed, future-oriented dialogue among Tanzanians. The immediate goal was to shape the country's narrative from the contemporary discussion about a new Constitution, to the discourse around the 2015 General Election and the design of a new policy agenda in 2016 and beyond.

Methodological approach

This chapter summarises the outcomes of combining three methods used to describe and explain the contemporary state of the country and explore possible future trajectories through commissioned research, assess the national perspective on the future through a nationally representative mobile phone survey, and initiate a future oriented national discourse through nine sub-national one-day Futures Literacy Laboratories (FLL). It describes SID's early experience of implementing the Futures Literacy methodology and, by sharing some of the emerging 'stories' provides an early assessment of its efficacy in inspiring a forward-looking conversation within the communities with whom SID has engaged between July and September 2014. It also briefly explores the possibility that the consolidated outcome, in the form of scenarios from the nine sub-national conversations, could catalyse a broader national discussion about the possible future trajectories that may face Tanzania.

Every five years Tanzanians participate in a general election that allows for a possible change of President and administration. October 2015 yielded the fourth such change. The period preceding the election provided an opportune moment to engage Tanzanians in a structured and future-informed reflection about the choice that they will make on a very specific date, and that will significantly shape their future. Ahead of the October 2015 polls, a number of forward-facing questions were ripe for exploration:

- Will the election campaigning be informed by issues rather than by personalities?
- Will the political discourse focus on immediate issues or the long-term prospects for Tanzania?
- Are campaigning politicians aware of the deep uncertainty facing the country?
- Might they temper their promises to their voters?
- On what basis will Tanzanians make their choices on voting day?

Regional Futures Literacy Laboratories

In order to explore those questions, and many other emerging ones, we carried out nine regional Futures Literacy Laboratories (FLL) across the following regions of Tanzania: Dar es Salaam, Arusha, Pemba (Zanzibar), Unguja (Zanzibar), Mbeya, Kigoma, Mtwara, Dodoma and Mwanza. Working with Tanzania's leading civil society grant-making organisation, the Foundation for Civil Society, we attracted a total of 387 citizens. They came from a diverse set of backgrounds, occupations, experience, expertise and physical ability and included academics and teachers, farmers, religious leaders, journalists, police officers, representatives from women groups, farmers, youths, people with special needs (blind, deaf, and albino) and in one instance a District Commissioner (one of the senior positions in local public administration).

Phase 1: Revealing awareness

Our Phase 1 activities aimed to achieve three things. The first was to provide a package of facts and analysis – a *Picture of Now* – that was logically sound, insightful in terms of offering clear explanations and mentally portable or memorable. We wanted to ensure that conversations about the future of Tanzania started from a common understanding or awareness of the state of the country in a holistic way and why it was that way (underlying drivers). This *Picture of Now* was developed from the highlights of the think pieces and insights from some additional socio-economic and political research. The following main challenging messages of the *Picture of Now* were identified.

- **Rapid structural economic change is marginalising the majority**. As Tanzania's economy grows rapidly, the share of agriculture is shrinking and being replaced by services faster than the rate at which citizens can re-tool themselves in order to earn a living using higher intellectual skills rather than physical capabilities.
- **High and rising malnutrition is sapping the country's strength**. The country's rate of malnutrition, measured as the number of children aged 0–5 years who are stunted, shows a worsening trend between 2004 (38 per cent) and 2010 (42 per cent) with an improvement to a still significant 34 per cent in 2016 (Ministry of Health Community Development Gender Elderly and Children (MoHCDGEC) [Tanzania] *et al.*, 2016). The effect is to seriously impede these children's cognitive abilities and constrain their, and the country's, future earnings.
- **Poor quality schools are producing an unskilled and unprepared generation**. The poor quality of state-run primary schooling manifested by lack of sanitation and teacher absenteeism reinforces the children's nutritional disadvantages and traps them in low productivity economic activities and incomes.
- **Tanzania's gas resources may underperform in terms of boosting the economy**. Despite the discovery of major gas reserves in Tanzania, the uncertainty that is engulfing global energy markets due to anaemic growth in rich countries, and growing alarm over climate change suggest that the possibility of major cuts in carbon emissions (United Nations News Service, 2014), could deny Tanzania some highly anticipated, salutary windfall gas revenues.

These four key challenging messages were outlined at the outset of every engagement, to create a sense of urgency and inspire immediate engagement with the process and content.

The second goal was to reveal people's expectations about the future in a bid to make them appreciate the temporal or chronological elements of change. We did this through role playing. Discussion participants were asked to imagine themselves as news reporters in mid-2035. Working in groups of 10–15 people, their task was to create news headlines – and the opening sentence of an article, or radio/TV broadcast – that expressed the major stories in the economic, political and social life of a future Tanzania.

The third goal was to complement the shared analytical awareness with an emotional and/or visceral awareness by revealing participants' hopes and fears about the future. We wanted to help articulate explicitly the subconscious basis for some of the choices that have been and would likely continue to be made by individuals and communities about the future. We quickly discovered that attempting to separate expectations/predictions about the future from their hopes and fears about it were futile and ultimately unnecessary. This specific exercise was also done through the creation of imaginative newspaper headlines from a future Tanzania in 2035.

Phase 2: Reframing and discovery

Tanzania's economy is deeply dependent on the global economy. It relies on external markets for its exports of agricultural commodities (cotton, cashews, tea, coffee) and mineral commodities such as gold. In 2013, the $1.4 billion earnings from tourism overtook gold export receipts due to an increase in visitor arrivals, while gold prices continued to be weak. In 2013, Tanzania attracted $1.9 billion in foreign direct investment, the largest volume in East Africa. Commitments in donor aid and loans have retreated from 21 per cent of the country's budget in 2013 to 15 per cent in 2014. In 2014, donors committed $558 million in aid to support Tanzania's budget (Ng'wanakilala, 2014). However, due to concerns about fraud and corruption, donors withheld these funds, leading to a serious strain in public finances and exposing Tanzania's vulnerability.

This context provided an almost ideal opportunity to engage Tanzanians in a rigorous imagining exercise. Participants were invited to 'think the unthinkable' (*kufikiri yasiyofikirika* in the Kiswahili language) by contemplating a future with no inflows of foreign funds. The aim was to encourage participants to confront the deeply embedded assumption, developed over decades of experience, that donors would continue to bridge any and all funding gaps in Tanzania's budget. Evidence was provided to make it clear that there is a real possibility of funding drying up. It was not difficult to provide a scenario in which Tanzania's traditional bilateral donors – seven European countries, the European Commission, Canada and Japan – experience such a severe and sustained economic stagnation that aid funds are cut. There were indicators of this scenario in October 2014, when Sweden's newly elected government suspended all new disbursements to East Africa pending a review of its aid strategy. Denmark has also suspended all new development assistance commitments to the East African Community as it considers reallocating funds to humanitarian crises in Syria and West Africa. It was relatively easy to outline a roadmap to possible future autarky for Tanzania as foreign investment dries up, commodity markets collapse and tourism receipts shrink.

The simple questions put to participants were, "How will Tanzania cope? Is it a fragile or resilient country?"

Phase 3: Rethinking choices

As mentioned above, in 2015 Tanzanians were to make two of the most important decisions in the country's post-independence era. On 30 April 2015, the country was expected to hold a referendum on a revised constitution. If passed, the new constitution would have come into force ahead of general elections due in October 2015. In the end, the referendum was called off. However, the incumbent president, Jakaya Kikwete, had served two terms and could not run again, meaning that Tanzanians were to elect a new head of state and administration.

This context informed our synthesis and consolidation of the outputs of the Awareness and Discovery phases of the Futures Literacy engagement into a set of strategic scenarios in which choice emerges. Their essential character is outlined in the next section on results.

AWARENESS

The major outcome of the Futures Literacy approach was to reveal participants' expectations, predictions, hopes and fears about Tanzania's future. Across the country, some common themes emerged.

On the optimistic side, these themes included: a shared desire that Tanzania become a middle-income country by 2025, in line with the current Vision 2025; the union between Tanganyika and Zanzibar would last although there was also a strong desire for Zanzibar to regain the seat it forfeited at the United Nations in 1964; and a hope that the East African Community would be a strong socioeconomic bloc, with a female East African Commission President from Zanzibar. Interestingly, it was expected, or hoped, that citizens would become much more assertive in holding government to account, with an activist parliament impeaching a non-performing head of state.

Pessimism about the future was informed by: a sense that Tanzania was experiencing a period of immiserising growth – commendable macroeconomic growth performance that left increasing numbers of people in the darkness of poverty; an unskilled generation facing exclusion, marginalisation and destitution as the country's natural resource wealth is squandered; national values of peace, unity and respect eroding further and a union in danger of rupturing.

DISCOVERY

The rigorous imagining of a state of autarky for Tanzania was, unsurprisingly, a significant challenge for participants. This suggested that it was a relevant and significant thought experiment for collective reflection at group and national level. Contemporary events such as the withholding of almost $500 million in budget support by donors lent further credence to the idea.

This exercise led to the discovery of arguably the fundamental question for Tanzanians to contemplate for the future. Faced with the distinct possibility of an autarkic shock, are Tanzanians collectively resilient enough to bounce back from the major economic, social and political stress that they face? Or are there some structural fissures that leave the country vulnerable to irreparable damage in its social fabric?

Choice – Ujamaa 2.0 or Freeconomy?

The narrative of the scenarios started from the *Picture of Now* in which rapid structural economic change is radically altering the livelihood foundation for citizens, who are ill-equipped to respond due to high levels of malnutrition and poor quality learning. Game-changing gas revenues are not guaranteed. In the near future, a Tanzania heavily reliant on foreign financial inflows experiences a severe shock in the form of a prolonged cash crunch as aid disappears, shrinking foreign direct investment evaporates, along with tourist receipts and commodity export revenues. Tanzanians are faced with a choice between two alternatives, namely *Ujamaa 2.0* and *Freeconomy* (Figure 5.10.1).

Ujamaa 2.0 sees the revival of the communalist ideology of 1969–85. The new *Ujamaa* emerges from fundamental agreement between citizens and government to share the pain of austerity and adjustment in an equitable way. Such broad consensus emboldens government to undertake a deep and far-reaching wealth redistribution programme. Overwhelmed by popular support for *Ujamaa*, business has no choice but to acquiesce. Shared pain fosters an unprecedented level of unity and common purpose among citizens. As the state's management capability is strengthened and legitimised, shrinking domestic resources are invested in social services. However, Tanzania's social resilience is accompanied by severe economic fragility and it is not clear how long *Ujamaa 2.0* can last.

The alternative, *Freeconomy*, unleashes and supports individual initiative and commercial energy in ways that expand the national economy, in part through deeper regional integration. A successful appeal by the administration to citizens' sense of enterprise and instinct for individual self-reliance forges a broad

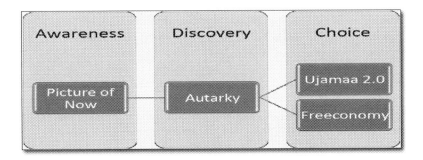

Figure 5.10.1 Emergence of choice scenarios

consensus for light regulation and a focus on aggressively reducing the costs of doing business in the country and across East Africa. As trade and business regulations are radically reformed, available financial resources are invested in priority infrastructure upgrades across the country. Business, big and small, expands to take advantage of the unprecedented openness, although trading dominates economic activity. Income and profits are increasingly concentrated among those who had assets and capital prior to the global economic shock. Most struggle to cope with the widening dominance of economic activity and growing evidence of state capture by a small commercial elite. Tanzania's economy proves itself resilient, but at the cost of social tension and fragility.

Discussion and implications

One of the major motivations for the Tanzania Dialogues Initiative was to catalyse an issue-based discourse in the country as citizens were scheduled to make two important choices in 2015: on the constitution in April; and a new administration in October. A previous national public interest scenarios initiative on Tanzania was published in 2004. Dubbed *Tutafika: Imagining Our Future*, it was the outcome of an intense exercise in introspection and foresight but it involved a small group of about 40 Tanzanians and took two years from inception to conclusion (Society for International Development, 2004). This initiative took place in less than half that time, and involved almost 400 people in a structured conversation about what the potential futures facing the country might mean for collective decisions today.

We published the strategic scenario stories as an insert in Tanzania's highest circulation Kiswahili daily newspaper in December 2014 and went on a dissemination tour in the nine regions that participated in the Futures Literacy Laboratories. Our aim was to popularise even further the use of foresight to inform the two major collective decisions that Tanzanians were due to make in 2015. While it is difficult to evaluate the extent to which the Futures Literacy methodology was effective in raising a general public awareness of Tanzania's prospective future in a way that could usefully influence contemporary decision-making, two observations are worth noting.

First, Futures Literacy is an efficient and effective way of allowing diverse groups to use the future to surface their assumptions, to examine the present and to rehearse the range of alternative decisions that could be made to shape an emergent future. The sequential logic of awareness (fact and analysis), discovery (rigorous imagining) and choice (using the stories) is both powerful and deeply operational.

Second, done well, the Futures Literacy approach can confer confidence and legitimacy on the futures outputs in the form of alternative stories, and build a significant coalition of allies and supporters who can promote the process, the products (descriptions of the present, the plausibility of the autarkic shock, the alternative futures and the choices that are incumbent upon the citizens to make) and maintain a national discourse on its own future.

References

Ministry of Health Community Development Gender Elderly and Children (MoHCDGEC) [Tanzania Mainland], Ministry of Health (MoH) [Zanzibar], National Bureau of Statistics (NBS), Office of the Chief Government Statistician (OCGS), and ICF (2016). *Tanzania Demographic and Health Survey and Malaria Indicator Survey (TDH-MIS) 2015–16*. Dar es Salaam, Tanzania and Rockville, Maryland, USA: The DHS Program.

National Bureau of Statistics – NBS/Tanzania, & I C F Macro (2011). *Tanzania Demographic and Health Survey 2010*. Dar es Salaam, Tanzania: NBS/Tanzania and ICF Macro. Available at: https://www.dhsprogram.com/publications/publication-FR243-DHS-Final-Reports.cfm (Accessed: 22 January 2018).

Ng'wanakilala, F. (2014). 'Donors Delay Some Aid to Tanzania Over Graft Claims', Reuters, 11 October 2014. Available at: https://www.reuters.com/article/us-tanzania-donors/donors-delay-some-aid-to-tanzania-over-graft-claims-idUSKN0I00E720141011 (Accessed: 30 January 2018).

Society for International Development (2004). *Tutafika: Imagining Our Future Tanzania*. Dar-es-Salaam, Tanzania: Society for International Development.

United Nations News Service (2014). 'Leaders Must Act' Urges Ban, as New UN Report Warns Climate Change May Soon Be 'Irreversible'. Available at: http://www.un.org/apps/news/story.asp?NewsID=49232&Kw1=climate+change+&Kw2=&Kw3=#.WnA4G0x2t9A (Accessed: 30 January 2018).

Uwezo (2014). *Are Our Children Learning? Literacy and Numeracy Across East Africa*. Nairobi, Kenya: UWEZO. Available at: http://www.uwezo.net/publications/reports/ (Accessed: 22 January 2018).

Case 11: Africa Horizon 2035

Sandra Coulibaly Leroy, Ngarkidané Djidingar and Nicolas Simard

Introduction

On 21 May 2015, the Organisation de la Francophonie (OIF) organised its first UNESCO Management of Social Transformation (MOST) Futures Literacy Lab-Novelty (FLL-N). This event was organised by the Foresight section of the Veille-analyse et Prospective Department inside the Directorate of Programming and Strategic Development (DPDS) and in partnership with the Observatory of French Language of the OIF. This was the first implementation of the OIF's new collaborative approach to co-constructing the way the future is used. The entire activity, including design and all facilitation, was conducted in French. The aim of this exercise was to:

- reinforce the thinking skills of the OIF's staff and its stakeholders;
- improve horizontal partnerships and transversality practices between administrative units;

- develop distinctive competencies in terms of futures thinking and strategic monitoring within the OIF to help program staff initiate exploratory and more open reflection on the future; and
- create new partnerships in terms of foresight and strategic monitoring.

This event is part of an active collaboration between UNESCO and OIF in the field of Anticipation and Foresight framed by the longstanding Memorandum of Understanding signed by the two organisations in 1976. This specific FLL-N also follows on from a first OIF foresight dialogue held in April 2015, where Riel Miller introduced the conceptual and methodological framework of Futures Literacy.

Issues

Anticipation lets us understand how foresight processes, whether implicit or explicit, affect the choices we make in our daily lives. This exercise practised in groups and debated in plenary sessions, helps people to 'use-the-future' in order to elaborate collective strategies and possible interventions to improve the quality of decisions that have to be made today.

For this first OIF-UNESCO FLL-N, the DPDS selected the topic 'Africa Horizon 2035'. This topic was relevant for both institutions because most programmes of the OIF's four-year plan focus on Africa. This is in large part because of the expected demographics of the French language, as analysed by the Observatory of the French Language (Wolff, 2014).

In keeping with the standard FLL-N design the focus here was on revealing people's anticipatory assumptions. The action learning methodology was seen as a way to reveal the patterns/models and cognitive biases deployed/generated by thinking about the future of Africa. The process was meant to encourage discussion of alternative assumptions and strategies relevant to the OIF.

Such reflection is of interest to leaders of multilateral institutions such as the OIF as it contends with a wide range of complex challenges. On the one hand, current crises of values or identities, socio-economic and development models are strong cues attesting to ongoing fundamental changes. On the other hand, there is a growing pressure to reduce doubts and make appropriate choices, particularly as part of structural and organisational change.

Unfortunately, these two imperatives are often contradictory. The first calls for innovation and experimentation to adapt to a world that is radically changing. The second invites flight to apparent safety by relying on strategies that have worked in the past.

The FLL-N design was adapted by the OIF to encourage:

- asking new and precise questions on the future, locally relevant and of common interest shared by all OIF's boards, about the Africa of tomorrow;
- raising the scope and the nature of the communities of practice that 'use-the-future' in specific places/groups and the tools they deploy to think about the future, including OIF staff; and
- the development of the participants' capacity to use futures literacy in a post-workshop analysis in terms of change/reinforcement of capacities.

Proceedings

Two days before the lab, a training session was organised for the break-out group facilitators to acquaint them with the various FLL techniques. Thirty-nine participants from the OIF, UNESCO, the students of the association *Sciences-Po for Africa* and the Director of the think-tank *Thinking Africa* were involved in this event.

The methodology used in this lab is based on a simple action learning and collective intelligence knowledge creation model: collaborative and participative work, interactive dialogue, and plenary sessions for sharing group work. Standard to FLL-N there were three phases:

- **Phase 1**: reveal by inviting participants to expose their values/aspirations and hopes, on one hand, and on the other hand, their expectations/predictions;
- **Phase 2**: reframe by exploring discontinuous futures based on an alternative set of anticipatory assumptions that invite participants to imagine a societal context fundamentally different from current paradigms; and
- **Phase 3**: initiate the exploration of new strategic questions that arise from the review of the assumptions that influence participants' understanding of the present, query the specific images of the future that render certain aspects of the present more or less visible, more or less central to decision-makers.

Participants were divided into five diverse groups of six to eight participants, covering different fields of operation, functional roles and hierarchical levels within the OIF.

Phase 1: Revealing projections and hopes

Participants were reminded that they had been invited to take part in the FLL-N as individuals, to feel free to express their own points of view, and to remember that there were no right or wrong answers. The groups were asked to formulate their predictions for Africa in 2035. Most participants justified their expectations using what they called 'facts' or statistical projections that reflected a range of perspectives, often rooted in institutional or media points-of-view. Then the facilitators encouraged the group to extend the reach of the discussion to cover hoped-for futures reflecting the values of each person.

By undertaking these exercises participants started to discern the difference between the imaginary futures that they predict or expect and those that they desire or hope for. They started to differentiate those anticipatory assumptions that are about jobs, governments, nations, industries, banks, climate change, demography, etc., and those that are more open to change.

Summaries of the discussions in the different groups were presented in the final plenary session by the rapporteurs from each group, who had been designated by their peers. These reports incorporated both agreements and disagreements, consensus and conflict within the groups. The summaries covered a wide range of issues – the following are a few of the highlights:

- the place of education and gender issues;
- the need for common security and the place of Africa in global governance;
- the development of infrastructures that would enable a better flow/fluidity of trade between countries in sub-regions and across the continent;
- monetary issues/financial aspects related to the continent's autonomy/independence/self-sufficiency on a sub-regional basis and in local economic communities;
- regional integration as opposed to continental integration, and the current surge of nationalism, identity and religious issues, terrorism, migration; and
- adaptation strategies to deal with climate change.

The FLL-N allowed participants to identify a range of anticipatory assumptions that generated a scenario in which Africa is attractive and creative in 2035. Participants articulated their shared values at the OIF, including the importance of civil service, a faith in change and in the impact of staff members' work. In their effort to distinguish the foreseeable/predictive from the desired/preferred futures the participants produced five sets of observations/scenarios.

AN 'IDEAL' AFRICA: AN ATTRACTIVE AFRICA

- An Africa and Africans who attract investments and reverse a migratory flow;
- Governments that make a difference;
- A politically stable Africa, where a supranational structure such as the African Union plays its full role as regulator and integrator of Africa; implementation of new and effective public policies that cover civil servants and, in particular, the large number of young people.

A 'CONSIDERED' AFRICA: A BUBBLING/BURGEONING AFRICA

- A politically unstable Africa, ripped and fragmented;
- Rise of uncontrolled economies but with more individual liberties/freedom;
- Rise of creation/creativity with an energy liberalisation;
- Identity affirmation within creativity.

A 'LEAD/ER/ING' AFRICA: AN EDGY/DARING AFRICA

- Investment in youth training;
- Development of a quality training allowing civil servants to propose policies that encourage the exploitation of human capital and raw materials;
- Even more globalised, which leads to a loss of Africa's cultural identity.

A 'DIVERSE' AFRICA: AN AFRICA THAT ORGANISES AND STRUCTURES ITSELF

- Diverse dynamics (economic, demographic, political) within Africa;
- Emergence of regional blocks with, on the one side, western, eastern and southern countries, and on the other side, northern and central states (emergence of federal states);

- Establishment of a megalopolis because of cash flow growth;
- Confirmation/statement of a cultural identity that can create extreme social tensions;
- Restructuring of the African Union;
- An Africa subject to current challenges (climate change, emerging/growing civilian society, terrorist threats).

AN AFRICA OF 'CONTRASTS': A FRAGMENTED AND DIVIDED AFRICA

- Rise of political instability;
- Rise of the gap between rich and poor countries, as well as within each country;
- A new economy oriented to China and the Gulf states;
- Development of technology innovation sectors;
- A continent vulnerable to climate change.

This summary process captured the diversity of perspectives on the future. These can be classified in terms of interchangeability, synergy and emergence as well as breakdown, but all point to significant change.

Phase 2: Reframe

In the second session participants were asked to reframe their imaginary futures and express these alternative worlds in material form by creating sculptures. Participants were provided with a framework for reframing called 'The African Knowledge Society'. This model was an adaptation of the Learning Intensive Society parameters (Miller, 2001), used in other FLL-N, that deconstruct the industrial paradigm and Western models of growth and development. Participants were invited to 'rigorously imagine' an alternative world and invent their lives within that scenario.

Kits composed of various arts and craft materials such as ropes, balls, magazine photos, etc. were given to each group to build a model representing their imaginary futures.

The aim of this practical exercise was (1) to build a 'future reality' materialised as a 3D object, that mirrored collective reflection and was centred on a new societal context in terms of institutions such as schools, banks, police, companies, jobs, parks, etc., and (2) for participants to question the way that things function and what contributes to 'inventing' new social systems. Five sculptures were produced by the break-out groups.

AFRICAN RELOCATION

The first group rethought development models at the local level, inspired by African innovations, including initiatives in participatory governance/democracy (e.g. Somaliland), that take into consideration the need to create an environment conducive to the use of renewable energy.

200   FLL-N case studies

Subscribing to a logic of sustainable development and thinking of an ecosystem distant from global economic exchange/trade this scenario expressed a middle ground between local isolation and global integration.

The group imagined the creation of communities that established collective areas conducive to learning where the transmission of knowledge and values happened through alternative pedagogical methods. Schools were at once a place to share and produce knowledge using traditional mediators such as the DadaRabe of Madagascar or griot, a west African preacher, singer, poet and storyteller. In this scenario, there was a renewal of such traditional functions, voluntary and community based approaches including female intermediaries such as Mamarabes knowledge transmitters.

CREATING NEW WORLDS

Another group was inspired by the prospect of creating new organisational paradigms to connect individuals with both modern and traditional societies. This scenario placed a strong emphasis on the senses and underscored the role of structures and norms like ownership (appropriation and utilisation of collective goods, locations), identities (representation through individual choices, new codes for attributing meaning, rewards for different and diverse cultural mixes), governance (communities tied together through values, the use of numeric data) and territories (borders are abolished through nomadism).

Pushing their imaginations this group invented a world where complex emergent relationships modulated/deconstructed systems/models by constantly re-establishing and mobilising shared values within and between communities. These dynamic transversal relationships established the conditions to escape from the old state bureaucracies and develop governance beyond old forms of administrative management. In this context 'traditional' values of solidarity that protected individuals/communities were combined with 'a universality where diversity is valued!'

AFRICAN FORESIGHT AND CONQUEST

This group's future took on the image of Africa as a tree, solidly rooted in time and attached to endogenous values but with hospitable, open arms as it welcomes modernity and others. The group was willing to renew a tradition by inspiring itself through the practices of Fang, an ethnic group living in Gabon, where when children are born, they take a bath with a spear. The group replaced the spear by a pen. The child does not only need to be a soldier, and with a pen, he or she is preparing to confront the upcoming challenges of the modern world.

On the right-hand side of this group's sculpture was a seal that symbolised the normality of the innovative dispute resolution methods. Inspired and adapted from traditional values such as dialogue and consultation, African approaches prevailed in a world in which dialogue rendered the use of weapons obsolete. This group's imaginary future is also feminine because women have as many rights as men. Africa is economically integrated, in part through technological progress that will permit Africans to conquer the moon, space and to push back the limits of the known world.

THINKING OF AFRICA IN 2035: STEPPING OUTSIDE THE FRAMEWORK

This group stepped outside the dominant frameworks by imagining the disappearance of borders between African countries, replaced by a vibrant and fluid civil society. They described a world where money has disappeared because wealth has become more holistic and human rather than narrowly 'economic'. In this scenario, there is an equitable (re)distribution of goods and knowledge. The greater internalisation of universal values overcomes the particularism characteristic of international relations in the early 21st century, enabling Africa to take a place in the world.

In this scenario time is re-appropriated through a focus on wellbeing. This is what it means to 'be African', taking control of your own life and time. People and their relationships are functionally tied to wellbeing (like rhizomes). All these elements are irrigated/fostered by what constitutes the force and attractiveness of Africa: the creativity (the green rope). This power, which is not a closed circuit, connects with other geographic locations (Europe, America, Asia). Another part of the sculpture uses balls to symbolise a society that can enrich itself with new elements that express the aspirations of 'being African'. This scenario is composed of the following elements:

- debates, that remind us of the African 'agora' tree, like an African version of the Italian piazza, that facilitates interaction through measured and shared decision-making;
- the last cup: a word play reminding us of a festive spirit;
- environmental preoccupations;
- creativity as a motor of African society;
- knowledge acquisition through experience or the transformation of the educational system;
- a society that lives by its values;
- the abundance of biodiversity and the awareness of human dignity; and
- the freedom of conscience and beliefs.

THE IDEAL AFRICA OF TOMORROW INCARNATED IN A BOTTLE

How do we imagine the ideal Africa (and its social life in general) in future decades?

- through an organisation, a social life around biological rhythms, symbolised in the sculpture by confetti that circulates freely in the water;
- 24-hour days in which activities follow the rhythms of natural cycles of the organism (5–7h; 15–20h). This rhythm has an impact on the social organisation. The exchange of goods and services is demand driven and no longer

constrained by the fixed 9 to 5 type schedules imposed by society. Human beings are synchronised with natural rhythms and, at the same time, society becomes more efficient;
- reinforced proximity to the surrounding nature (symbolised by the colour green underneath the bottle that represents the natural basis of society):
    o by encouraging the use of local products;
    o organic agriculture; and
    o sustainable development
- through social relationships (the different elastics that surround the bottle). These connections are operationalised by the mechanisms that induce sympathy and understanding amongst people (music, religion, taste, etc.) and the fluidity of social networks. People are no longer scared of meeting new people, since they recognise each other through these circles;
- through an 'other' governance: there is no nationality; relationships are established through individuals as part of communities.

However, the equilibrium of this system is fragile. There is always a risk that the society could fall back to a rhythmic society, where people and nature are no longer centred, connected and in balance. Once again, it is the economic interests that bring rhythm to life, all this with a constant urgency of time.

Phase 3: New questions

The concluding plenary session provided an opportunity to consider how the anticipatory assumptions that emerged in the previous two phases revealed different aspects of the challenges and potential of the present. By asking what is the future and how do we engage in anticipation the participants in the FLL-N started the process of becoming futures literate. The discussions in plenary confirmed that by deploying collective intelligence participants were able to explore previously unknown ideas, pushing the boundaries of their thinking by inventing frameworks that generate new meanings and emergent possibilities. By privileging holistic and systemic approaches, the FLL-N revealed and clarified assumptions regarding existing systems and invited creative efforts to define and explore innovative frameworks, new strategies and programmes. The design of the FLL-N enabled participants to 'use-the-future' to interrogate their narratives and cognitive capacities, to question and re-examine fears and hopes.

Implications for the OIF at an organisational level

Running the FLL-N provided input into efforts to rethink the way that OIF builds its strategic vision. The plenary discussion at the end and reflection after the conclusion of the lab pointed to the following conclusions regarding the FLL-N as a tool for assisting with strategic thinking.

- **Economic**: the cost of actually running such a lab is relatively low since the on-site activity requires only a modest physical space and minimal working materials (Post-it notes, flip-charts, etc.). However, compared to some workshops or traditional topic oriented gatherings the FLL-N design requires much more investment in the collaborative joint-design, up-stream training of facilitators, preparation and selection of participants, and the involvement of expert facilitators able to improvise in real-time as the process unfolds.
- **Strategic learning**: this FLL-N provided a learning process that is playful and gradual for developing participants' Futures Literacy skills and is flexible enough so that different participants can develop different levels of futures literacy capacity.
- **Strategic innovation**: this FLL-N encouraged innovation and introduced new concepts and dynamics to the organisation. By using the future in a structured and theoretically informed manner the FLL-N can engage participants in a coherent process that deploys their collective intelligence to effectively and efficiently create new knowledge and learning.

Evaluation

Entry and exit surveys were used to evaluate the level of knowledge and the perceptions of the participants before and after this FLL-N.

Futures Literacy and the need for capacity reinforcement

More than 70 per cent of participants of this FLL-N were staff members of the IOF. In addition to these staff members, there were participants from UNESCO, the Association Science PO for Africa and from the Thinking Africa institute. These participants held at least a Bachelor's degree (licence) and had an interest in the field of anticipation and questions on the future in general. This level of training was taken into account in the customisation of the FLL-N and given the selection of heuristics and sequencing of topics played an important role in bringing participants to engage with unfamiliar methods and potentially intimidating topics.

Before the FLL, 47 per cent of participants estimated that they did not hold any expertise in terms of methodological approaches for thinking about the future and 53 per cent identified themselves as beginners. After the training sessions, 76 per cent self-proclaimed themselves beginners and 24 per cent felt as though they still did not have much expertise in the subject matter. In both cases, surveys revealed that no participants considered themselves as experts or had considerable experience in this field.

Importance of prospective/future

In the pre-survey, most participants (41 per cent) responded that thinking about the future helps to determine the best choices. However, the remaining participants indicated that information about the future would be unlikely to help address the challenges of our time (30 per cent), or even assist with the invention of new possibilities (29 per cent). At the end of this FLL-N, 53 per cent of participants leaned towards 'using-the-future' in ways that would enhance their capacity to invent new possibilities.

These results show us the evolution of people's thinking about specific futures and about how to 'use-the-future' – moving from an initial position before the FLL-N that focused on continuity and research into the past, in order to seek solutions to current and future problems, to starting to see that different futures can be imagined by 'letting go' of existing paradigms and inventing new possibilities. They felt more comfortable with uncertainty because they detected ways of going further in discovering and inventing the possible. Within an institutional environment, such as intergovernmental organisations constrained by constant planning, the challenges of this approach are significant, but necessary and possible to address, as demonstrated by such FLL-N exercises that invite deconstruction/reconstruction.

Ninety-four per cent of participants stated that as a result of their participation in this FLL-N their understanding of anticipation had evolved. For the majority, this FLL-N had not only helped them to rethink how they approached uncertainty and the future but also exposed them to a new strategic tool that they would like to continue to develop and deploy.

Follow-up

This was the OIF's first FLL-N; since then the OIF has been involved with five more FLL-N organised in collaboration with UNESCO and other partners on the following themes:

- October 2015: at UNESCO Headquarters: 9th World Youth Forum or the World in 2030;
- December 2015: at the Institute for Research and Strategic Studies of Morocco: The Future of the Arab World: Imagining the Future of Water and Cities in North Africa;
- March 2016: at the Tunisian Institute for Strategic Studies: Foresight and Social Transformation;
- July 2016: at UNESCO Headquarters: The Future of Human Mobility and Identity: Horizon 2050; and
- July 2017: at Mohamed V University of Rabat: The future of sciences in Africa.

References

Miller, R. (2001) '21st Century Transitions: Opportunities, Risks and Strategies for Governments and Schools', in *What Schools for the Future?* Paris: OECD, pp. 147–155.

Wolff, A. (2014) *The French Language in the 2014 World*. Paris: Observatory of the French Language.

Case 12: Rethinking non-formal education for sustainable futures in Asia-Pacific

Ace Victor Franco Aceron

Introduction

The focus of the Futures Literacy Laboratory-Novelty (FLL-N) held in Bangkok, Thailand on 2–5 September 2015 was on how non-formal education can be instrumental in contributing to sustainability. At a general level the FLL-N was designed to explore the relationship between learning and sustainable development. The outcomes of the process can be summarised under three headings: thinking about forever; a process of learning; and a dynamic balance (UNESCO, 2010).

The participants

The theme of this FLL-N, 'Rethinking Education through Imagining Futures Scenarios', attracted applications from all over the Asia-Pacific region. The selection of participants by UNESCO Bangkok's Education Research and Foresight Team was restricted to practitioners with at least five years of experience in non-formal education. As such, selected participants were those who had leadership roles and a proven track-record working in community-based learning centres, technical and vocational education institutes, as well as NGOs and universities with mandates in non-formal education. Two other important selection criteria were used: the ability to articulate ideas in English and an indication that the participant would be able to apply what they learned to his/her community context.

Forty participants in all joined the FLL, 20 of whom were selected from an online application process and the other 20 were invited participants from UNESCO offices in Bangkok and Paris, UNESCO partners and affiliates, and Chulalongkorn University, the host university of the FLL. The 40 participants were highly diverse, including both junior and senior professionals, aged between 25 and 70 years, and coming from Australia, Bangladesh, Cambodia, France, Germany, India, Japan, Kazakhstan, Malaysia, Nepal, Pakistan, the Philippines, Thailand, Tuvalu and Vietnam. In the FLL-N, participants were divided into five diverse groups, balanced in terms of nationality, gender, age and field of work. Each group had an expert facilitator, familiar with FLL processes and techniques, who assisted conversations through the three phases: Phase 1: Imagining 2040; Phase 2: Describing the Future Differently; and Phase 3: New Questions and Perspectives about the Future (UNESCO, 2015b).

"Thinking about forever"

UNESCO's teacher education programme on teaching and learning about sustainable futures defines thinking about forever as a commitment to the common good, "by thinking differently, considering things previously forgotten, broadening our perspectives, clarifying what we value, connecting with our neighbours, and providing hope for future generations" (UNESCO, 2010). During the lead-up to the FLL-N and during the first phase of the Lab, participants shared their specific ways of articulating their commitments to these goals. The design of this FLL-N included an online preparatory component. Two weeks before the FLL-N in Bangkok all the participants were invited to engage with UNESCO's NESPAP Open Platform. This was a virtual space designed to enable the sharing and exchange of resources, experiences and expertise for all interested in education from across the Asia-Pacific region and beyond (UNESCO, 2017). The invitation to start expressing views about the future online was a way for participants to get acquainted with each other and with the issues as they took part in conversations about topics which ranged from presenting one's professional background to sharing one-word statements on the future of education. These initial exchanges were useful in determining similarities and differences in the group's anticipatory assumptions and helped with the design and implementation of the FLL-N in Bangkok.

The face-to-face part of the FLL-N spanned three days and was accompanied by a team making a video (UNESCO, 2015a) and a team of experienced FL facilitators. The basic learning-by-doing structure followed the three-phase approach: Phase 1: tacit to explicit regarding expectations and hopes; Phase 2: a locally customised reframing exercise; and Phase 3: new questions. The design included the novelty-reframing component meant to test the diversity of participants' anticipatory systems and took advantage of a strong team of break-out group facilitators able to adapt specific tools to context. The workshop report (UNESCO, 2015b) provides a highly detailed, step-by-step, group-by-group report of the FLL-N, including photos and a full agenda.

Phase 1: Imagining 2040

In the first phase, participants were asked to imagine the world in the year 2040 by considering two different future scenarios: the probable future and the preferred future. When comparing participants' ideas on these two futures, striking similarities can be observed. All of them saw a world that is increasingly interconnected and globalised. In this context, the most consistent view about the two futures was the blurring boundary between formal and non-formal education. This referred to the assumptions that teaching and learning can take place anywhere, anytime, and that many forms of technological advancements in education – from the preponderance of using mobile and internet-based learning to highly advanced concepts of artificial intelligence, genetically modified learning and robot instructors – could narrow the capacity gaps between learners and teachers. The dynamics of learning is also constant in both futures as it moves from a highly structured, teacher-centred system to a more flexible, student-centred one where learning is seen as flexible and self-directed.

Plotting the imagined probable and preferred futures presented solutions and problems to potential issues in education, where for instance, an expected information overload and increase in knowledge products meant having greater access to them in the preferred world. While it was expected that neoliberal influence in education will continue to thrive, visions of a preferred future also saw the coexistence of profit and social responsibility.

Aside from the shared and complementary features of the probable and preferred futures, there were contrasting features of each future. Imagining education in 2040 was easier when it was free from reality-checking. For one group, when they thought of an ideal world for education, they simply listed their aspirations and described situations they hoped would come true. Hence, the expected future presented more problems and concerns such as the dominance of Western thinking, financial constraints, slow education reforms, overpopulation, redundant development goals, etc. There was a difference between what is feasible and what is desirable, and what seemed feasible were the events that can be confirmed by the realities of the present.

Phase 2: Describing the future differently

Transitioning the discussion in Phase 2, the lead facilitator introduced the groups to an alternative frame that they could debate and discuss, a catalyst for their imaginations. For instance, this alternative frame invited them to question the relationship between school systems and learning. Motivated by the distinctive and challenging features of this alternative future, participants began the process of moving beyond the anticipatory assumptions underlying their probable and preferred tomorrows. This FLL-N design called for the use of a specific tool to encourage the group to use their collective intelligence to articulate a reframed future – they were asked to build three-dimensional sculptures – symbolic representations of non-formal learning in a radically different context.

A box of art supplies and stationery were given to each group. Using these materials, they created group exhibits by patching, assembling and decorating a shared object that collectively represented their ideas. One group, for example, made a 3D collage with three sections: probable, preferred and alternative futures. In each section, a CD disc representing the world was placed on top of a cup. The CDs were connected by a piece of thread, which represented the connectedness of the three future worlds. Images cut out from magazines that depicted various ideas and themes for each future scenario were added to the collage (for photos and detailed accounts see UNESCO, 2015b).

However, not all groups created a static object like a sculpture. Participants were given the liberty to be innovative and find the best ways to represent and present their imagined alternative futures. One group decided to illustrate their alternative future through a performance in which all the group members played roles. To characterise the connected and inclusive learning community that they had envisioned, the group surrounded themselves with straws that were put together and strung them around other members of the group. Each member also wore a crown with a symbol of a vocation to show that every vocation was valued in this future. A phrase that describes learning in this future was also written on each crown, while objects that represented robots were created and placed on a table meant to be a field to illustrate that robots work and humans learn in this future.

Phase 3: New questions and perspectives about the future

Though the exhibits generated in Phase 2 made thoughts about sustainable learning futures more detailed and evocative, the process of rethinking how to 'use-the-future' did not culminate here. Phase 3 opened up further opportunities for review and reflection of the participants' anticipatory assumptions and the implications. By looking back at the past activities, Phase 3 was about generating new ideas, questions and policy options that might enable community-based learning and non-formal education to make a more powerful contribution to meeting the global challenges of today. The questions focused on the 'how-to' aspects.

Coming from the non-formal education sector, there were two questions common to all groups. The first question was about how to integrate formal, informal and non-formal learning approaches. This question considered the context of a changing educational landscape, where future technological advancements and the availability of learning resources allow teaching to happen whenever and wherever. The second question was about preparedness. For most participants it felt 'natural' at this stage in the process to wonder how communities and individuals might become more aware of both different futures and what is involved in thinking about the future. In addition, the group discussions gravitated towards value-based topics, questioning their previous ideas on how to humanise education, widen space for participation, provide more opportunities for learning, nurture talents and skills, and promote a culture of peace. By contrasting the futures they imagined in Phase 1 with those they imagined in Phase 2 participants started to see their present circumstances differently and began to explore alternative possibilities for now and tomorrow.

Observations on the design and implementation of the Bangkok FLL-N learning process

FLL are action-learning processes that introduce participants to FL and to rethinking the nature and role of the future in decision-making. The Bangkok FLL-N was tailored to invite experienced non-formal education practitioners to play with the future and explore different ways of seeing and doing. Enabling this kind of collective intelligence knowledge creation processes calls for a range of approaches, in the joint design process leading up to the event, during the Lab and afterwards to analyse the results. Numerous choices were made along the way, including the decision to initiate online discussions prior to the event, the selection of the group sculpture and/or role-playing option for Phase 2 and, as discussed briefly below, the introduction of the 'layered analysis' heuristic that originates with the work of Sohail Inayatullah on the method of Causal Layered Analysis (Inayatullah, 1998). The power of CLA in this context is not so much with the causal dimensions of the future but rather with the richness that emerges when participants deepen their descriptions of the imaginary futures they have invented together by using the CLA filters: litany, systems, worldview and myth.

Layered analysis

In each phase of the process Causal Layered Analysis (CLA) offered an analytical framework that assisted participants to add detail and understand the multi-dimensional nature of the pictures they were painting of imaginary tomorrows. First they discuss *litany*, or which aspects of the future they imagine can be captured by everyday phrases or the headlines of a newspaper. Participants identify those aspects of the future that are considered – in the future – to be obvious and commonplace. Next is the *systemic perspective*, where participants explain how the economy and political processes work in the imaginary future. Third is the protagonist or actor's *worldview* that fills in the picture from the point-of-view of the teacher or parent or politician or business person, etc. The last layer is the *myth/metaphor* that encapsulates the overarching message or 'flavour' of the future being described by the participants in this particular phase. Myths are associated with emotive and historical characteristics, like when people call Paris the 'city of lights' or New York the 'city that never sleeps'.

In keeping with the standard design for FLL-N the facilitators emphasised that the goal was to imagine snapshots of the future, not movies. Participants were asked to paint a picture of a specific point in time, in this case 2040, without worrying about how or why the future turned out this way. In Phase 1 the facilitators invited participants to close their eyes and imagine the future world. As they opened their eyes, the participants were then asked to recall images that came to mind as they were imagining the future. These images or ideas were used to fill up a table with the four layers of the CLA.

In both the probable and preferred futures, the ideas under litany (also called headline) were readily generated as this layer refers to commonplace aspects of the future. Forms of globalisation and technological advancement, and their impact and implications for education, were the most obvious outcomes that filled participants' observations of tomorrow. Next participants were asked to describe the systems – the perceptions of economic and political functioning in 2040. Working on these descriptions led participants to examine underlying structures and connections of an increasingly networked world and a much more open environment for learning. They described a wide range of systemic elements such as government policies, rule of law, business practices, climate change, education reforms, and behaviour change, among others (UNESCO, 2015b).

The next step went deeper by exploring the perspectives or ideologies of specific actors that embody or dominate their perceptions of phenomena in 2040. In imagining the probable future, the participants evoked worldviews that spoke to democratic, capitalist and neoliberal perspectives. Though the same belief systems were carried over in imagining the preferred future, it is worth noting that in this future, ideas of cooperation, interconnectedness and sustainable development surfaced in many group responses. This may be the case because, as mentioned in the previous section, thinking about an ideal future is not constrained by reality checks and is inspired by the patterns of present discourse. In general and as expected, the probable future was problem-oriented, a projection of today's concerns, while the aspirational and optimistic although liberated from some of the constraints, stayed within the same currently topical concerns.

Lastly, in the final layer participants used myths/metaphors as a powerful way to summarise the descriptions offered in the three preceding layers. Overall the groups' one-liner summaries of expected futures were somewhat grim, even if the promises of technology and the massive need for learning tended to counter the worries about climate change and inequality. Desired futures elicited metaphors that were, in a general way, anchored in the networking and openness that are part of the promise of the Internet and globalisation.

Layered Analysis was also used in Phase 2 to assist the groups to reflect and describe reframed futures. As per the standard FLL-N design the focus in Phase 2 is not on probable or desirable futures to describe futures based on distinctive, alternative anticipatory assumptions. They engaged actively in thinking 'outside-the-box' and initiating re-examinations of their existing anticipatory assumptions for imagining the future. In this round of Layered Analysis participants were challenged to be creative, inventing new visions of the future based on different anticipatory assumptions. While they echoed the same ideas such as 'education innovation' and 'learning for all', there were new insights picking up on the potential for more significant change and imagining radically different ways of learning. This highlighted the role of broader learning systems with different structures of organisational power to address diversity and expand the 'ownership' of learning.

Compared to Phase 1, the efforts to think about reframed futures stretched the imagination of participants. One group for example named their alternative future as an 'infinite flying magical playground'. This idea was no longer labelled under myth/metaphor but in the litany layer – where what we readily see is a fun place, where all learners soar high, and enjoy free and infinite access to resources and opportunities to learn.

The results of Phases 1–2 then became cognitive maps which guided the groups to list new questions and perspectives about the future of non-formal education in Asia-Pacific.

Other methods and styles of facilitation

In the plenary sessions the main facilitator was able to draw together the range and distinctiveness of the different anticipatory assumptions articulated through the group exercises. The highly experienced group facilitators, each with their own style and specific tools, were able to draw out a variety of perspectives, giving meaning to both shared and distinctive points-of-view, contexts and knowledge. The capacity of the facilitators to adapt to specific group dynamics meant that the process took full advantage of the knowledge creation potential of collective intelligence. The use of the Layered Analysis tool throughout the process also helped to further deepen descriptions of future. As participants became more familiar with the Layered Analysis they were able to go even deeper and wider as they explored imaginary worlds.

Besides CLA, facilitators made use of other techniques to support the thinking process of their groups. For instance in Phase 2, one group opted for a flexible analytical framework, brainstorming independently of the facilitator. Participants decided to pick colours that best represented their idea of a reframed future. Many participants said that their idea of a reframed future was best symbolised by a 'rainbow of colours', no single colour can describe it. Next participants adopted a storytelling heuristic, starting their account of the future with the phrase: "Once upon a time in the future . . .". For this group this was the approach that worked, allowing them to think deeper and connect their ideas to a picture of an alternative future.

Similarly, another group made use of colour coding to organise their inputs from Phase 1. They called it a spiral rainbow, which was diagrammed in layers of colour-coded circles. Each colour represented the factors and attributes that relate to an individual learner. In this illustration, a line was drawn to signify the importance of dialogue and communal interaction. The use of colours also aided this group in making their exhibit and to describe the story behind its design and structure.

In Phase 3, a unique approach was used by one of the groups to help them categorise the questions they had developed. Through the INSPECT (Innovation, Natural, Social, Political, Economic/Environmental, Cultural, Technological) model, the group was able to synthesise and explain their questions to the plenary session.

Evaluating the learning process

In the post-workshop evaluation survey, 20 out of 29 respondents said that the FLL changed the way they think about education and learning; four said that it did not, while five remarked that they had gained new ideas and deep insights but were not absolutely sure about whether the workshop did change their perspective on education and learning. Respondents whose way of thinking changed added that they appreciated the new ideas, the broadening of their perspectives and the enhancement of their understanding of how thinking about the future could be related to their field of work. Based on the comments of the nine respondents whose ways of thinking about education and learning did not change, they did learn something but this only validated their current views (UNESCO, 2015b).

For many of the participants, particularly those who gained new perspectives and posed new questions, the FLL-N contributed directly to the development of innovative action proposals related to non-formal education.

A dynamic balance

The participants in the FLL-N were all leaders in the field of community-based learning and non-formal education. They came to the process already having visions of what a sustainable future might be like. At the end of the workshop, these visions, which were changed, developed or affirmed in the three-phase exercises, had deep regard for a dynamic balance between cultural differences and the emerging global ethic of "interrelatedness and sanctity of life" (UNESCO, 2010). This dynamic balance was central in the learning process, and especially in the design of action agendas. The diversity in each group and their differing perspectives were opportunities for them to create universally appealing and highly workable projects. This could be observed in two complementary features of the project design.

First, the type of projects, as listed in Table 5.12.1, found strength in diversity and the idea of connecting units with different functions to work together toward a similar end. In Group 1, the feasibility of realising the virtual playground and virtual companion depended significantly on the cooperation of different stakeholders who could assist with its experimentation and implementation phases. Groups 2–5 proposed a learning hub or a network from which learning could be facilitated, and could provide space for knowledge exchange and the promotion of values. Group 3's Spiral Rainbow project, for example, envisioned that unity between suppliers and receivers of formal, informal and non-formal education programmes could only take place once a common ground – a space for dialogue – is established. This coincided with a more concrete plan proposed by project *Nantuapan* on creating hubs all over the Asia Pacific region that will provide intergenerational and transformative learning. An interesting aspect of this project is its name of local origin, indicating a unity in function amidst diversity in language and culture.

Second, the projects considered the principle that education for sustainable futures is founded on local actions in communities and their potential to extend outwards, through efforts based on shared understandings and changed outlooks. This is most visible in the design of Group 2's project, where collecting and disseminating ordinary stories about different ways of learning can educate adults on peace, compassion and sustainability. This could later extend to more families through learning hubs where reflection and learning between families take place. Similarly, the 'People's Lab' of Group 5 aims to connect community-based learning centres to different industries (for example, factories, universities, hospitals, media, etc.) to pool knowledge and information for the education and training of a community. The project invests in scalability, meaning it is expected to widen its reach – the more local, regional and national industries or stakeholders it connects with, the greater the educational value it will bring to many members of the community.

Next steps – building a community of practice

The experiences from this FLL-N, be it "Thinking about Forever", facilitating an action-oriented learning process, or seeking a dynamic balance as the governing

Table 5.12.1 Action agendas developed by the five groups

Group project	Description
Group 1: Virtual Companion and Virtual Playground	This project was inspired by the group's alternative future based on the idea that learning would be an 'infinite flying magical playground' where all children would be able to explore unlimited knowledge in a constantly available virtual playground. They would also have access to a virtual companion that would serve as a tutor/mentor, but not replace teachers or parents. The project will start with a research paper co-authored by the group members and will later seek support from governments, communities, institutions and companies for its the experimentation and implementation phases.
Group 2: Collection and dissemination of stories about different ways of learning	The project will collect and disseminate stories to convince adults to recognise and value different ways of learning, especially to promote peace, compassion and sustainability. In partnership with community learning centres, the project will provide learning support and resources for those who are inspired by the stories and create family learning hubs where reflection and learning between families take place.
Group 3: Rainbow Spiral Project	This project was based on the idea that dialogue and information exchange among communities is important in inspiring and empowering individuals to act and break the imaginary line between suppliers and receivers of formal, informal and non-formal education programmes. It is also necessary to create a space and promote dialogue between different groups such as youth, children and elders.
Group 4: *Nantuapan*	The project *Nantuapan*, named after a local word from the Murut ethnic group in Borneo which means "The Meeting", aims to create learning hubs all over the Asia Pacific region that will fuse formal, non-formal and informal learning systems. Through capacity building workshops and institutional partnerships, these hubs will provide intergenerational and transformative learning to create the group's vision of an ideal society. It will be built on the value of empowerment and initially target children and youth in the community.
Group 5: People's Lab	The "People's Lab" could take the form of a virtual learning space or a hub of learning, which would closely connect a CLC with the important sectors in society, and pool knowledge and information for the training and education of the community. The Lab could also function as a safe space for dialogue on social issues (e.g. women's rights), not necessarily through a fixed meeting venue, but through other concerned institutions actively connected to this multi-sectoral network.

principle for learning that contributes to sustainable futures, all contributed to the development of a nascent community of practice. In a follow-up survey conducted by Social and Human Sciences Sector, UNESCO Bangkok in April

2016, it was learned that although none of the action agendas have been fully implemented, advancing the capacity to 'use-the-future' remained of interest to 21 respondents, with 20 actually having pursued activities which directly and/or indirectly made use of their enhanced understanding of futures thinking as a result of the FLL-N.

About half of the respondents look to UNESCO to provide them with more opportunities to deepen their understanding of Futures Literacy and help build communities of practice. Prospects for further collaboration in this regard appear promising given that 70 per cent of them were able to engage their own communities in futures work. To develop and sustain a community of practice, the participants have stressed the importance of two methods: first is the creation of an association or centre dedicated to helping develop capacity around 'using-the-future'; and second is the organisation of special meetings to bring together practitioners and experts to share case studies and recent developments in research related to 'using-the-future'. This is closely followed by their choice of conducting dedicated training sessions before and/or after another FLL-N that they hope UNESCO will organise.

Another finding of the survey, one that relates closely to the discussion of Dynamic Balance, is that Futures Literacy needs to be deeply rooted in local communities. One way of doing this would be to conduct FLL-N workshops in the local native language and tailor the heuristics to the specific needs and expectations of the community. Because FLL-N workshops are designed to 'consider people's ability to think, imagine, analyse and articulate' it would be a good idea, according to one of the participants, to run these workshops at a local level. Indeed, the survey shows that around 60 per cent of the participants who work at the national level and some 24 per cent who work at the local level believe that building local communities of practice is highly feasible. These participants could open venues of interaction and help facilitate the integration of these communities at the regional and global level.

Conclusion

Revisiting themes of education for sustainable futures in describing the activities and outcomes of the Bangkok FLL-N demonstrates the interdisciplinary role of futures thinking. This case study supports the view that enhancing participants' understanding of anticipation not only contributes to thinking about the future per se, but also plays a role in changing their framing of the present. Furthermore they grasped the potential that Futures Literacy might have for creating conditions conducive to learning and sustainable development. Participants displayed a different understanding of the unknown and unknowable. The Rethinking Education through Imagining Future Scenarios with Non-Formal Education Practitioners FLL-N was a conscious effort to actually 'use-the-future' in new ways.

References

Inayatullah, S. (1998) 'Causal Layered Analysis: Poststructuralism as Method', *Futures*, 30(8), pp. 815–829.

UNESCO (2010) *Towards a Sustainable Future, Teaching and Learning for a Sustainable Future: A Multimedia Teacher Education Programme*. Available at: http://www.unesco.org/education/tlsf/mods/theme_gs/mod0a.html?panel=2#top (Accessed: 25 June 2016).

UNESCO (2015a) *Rethinking Education through Imagining Future Scenarios*. Available at: https://www.youtube.com/watch?v=PKFUXsZQbuk&feature=youtu.be (Accessed: 20 July 2017).

UNESCO (2015b) *Rethinking Education through Imagining Future Scenarios with Non-Formal Education Practitioners: A Workshop Report*. Bangkok. Available at: http://www.unescobkk.org/fileadmin/user_upload/epr/Foresight_Workshop/Foresight_Workshop_Revised_Report_Dec21.pdf (Accessed: 25 June 2015).

UNESCO (2017) *NESPAP Open Platform: National Education Systems and Policies in Asia-Pacific*. Available at: http://bangkok.unesco.org/content/national-education-systems-and-policies-asia-pacific-nespap-open-platform (Accessed: 2 January 2018).

Case 13: Water and urban renewal in North Africa

Nisreen Lahham

Background

The Futures Studies Forum for Africa and the Middle East (FSF) is a non-profit organisation that brings together the Middle East and North Africa (MENA) regions with Sub Saharan Africa (SSA) by conducting futures studies, sharing knowledge, and exchanging experiences in relation to all aspects of development.

To fulfil the above mission, FSF focuses its research and networking efforts on North Africa as the common region between Sub Saharan Africa and the Middle East.[1] Believing in the role futures studies can play in transforming Africa's future, FSF aims to strengthen the capacity of all segments of North African society to use the future to help inform perceptions, alternatives and choices, to assist in understanding potential developments and to articulate and work towards desired futures.

FSF – a Futures Literacy Lab champion

The adoption by FSF of an action-learning approach to 'using-the-future' for Africa was not the only motivation for seeking to collaborate with UNESCO. Developing foresight capacities in the MENA region – one of the core objectives of FSF – also led to the decision to work with UNESCO's innovative anticipatory systems and process approach, and take on the role of a local Futures Literacy Lab (FLL) champion.

216 FLL-N case studies

In May 2015 FSF held its first 'One Africa Roundtable' in Amman, Jordan. The meeting aimed to facilitate knowledge and experience-sharing between experts and futurists from MENA and Sub Saharan Africa. The meeting discussed areas for cooperation between the two regions, based on the findings of two Bulletins (Futures Studies Forum for Africa and the Middle East 2015b, 2015c). In addition, it discussed the state and role of futures studies in transforming Africa's future.

At this meeting, UNESCO presented the design principles of the general purpose FLL, and FSF decided to apply this innovative approach in its next meeting that aimed to explore the findings of the next two bulletins.

In December 2015, the second 'One Africa Roundtable' meeting was held in Rabat, Morocco, jointly with the Royal Institute for Strategic Studies (IRES) in cooperation with the Foresight Unit at UNESCO and funded by the Rockefeller Foundation.

The main objectives of this meeting were:

- rethinking the systemic challenges and opportunities for sustainable approaches to water management and urban renewal in North Africa, through engaging participants with the content of the two monitoring bulletins produced by FSF: *Managing Water Scarcity in North Africa* (Futures Studies Forum for Africa and the Middle East, 2015b) and *Future of North Africa's Slums* (Futures Studies Forum for Africa and the Middle East, 2015a);
- facilitating knowledge and experience-sharing between experts and futurists from MENA and SSA;
- identifying cooperation areas between MENA region and SSA, based on thinking about the future as it relates to both water and urban slums in Africa;
- exploring the potential for joint projects among participating organisations such as FSF, IRES, UNESCO; and
- building the capacity to 'use-the-future' (Futures Literacy) through greater familiarity with diverse anticipatory systems and processes.

In order to achieve these objectives, the event was organised as a UNESCO MOST Futures Literacy School taking the standard Futures Literacy Laboratory-Novelty design as the starting point for co-creating the process and its implementation.

The FLL-N engaged the collective intelligence of participants through discussions and brainstorming, with a strong emphasis on learning-by-doing. FSF believed that a conversation about the future could create a space to build the common ground that enables different stakeholders from the MENA and SSA regions to meet and find areas for collaboration and a more sustainable development model for water management and urban renewal.

Workshop participants were selected on the basis of their knowledge of the subjects as a whole, and their geographic representation covering North Africa, SSA and the Middle East. The workshop had 25 participants from Morocco, Egypt, Senegal, Cote d'Ivoire, Cape Verde, Mali, Sudan, Tunisia, Ghana, South Africa, Canada, the UAE and Jordan. They represented a broad cross-section of stakeholders including policy makers, leaders from the business community, civil society, academic institutions and universities, and representatives from national and international organisations.

Futures Literacy Lab-Novelty – the three phases

The design of the FLL-N targeted the development of greater awareness of the anticipatory assumptions underlying the futures that people imagine and starting the learning process related to Futures Literacy. FSF collaborated with UNESCO and facilitators drawn from the community of practice emerging around the Futures Literacy Laboratories to design and implement this FLL-N.

The FLL-N opened with a discussion of the objectives of the workshop as a way to invite a diverse group of participants to start building a shared discourse around their different ways of thinking about the future. This was followed by the standard three phases of the FLL-N action-learning process. Participants were divided into four groups, with an experienced facilitator to moderate each group. These groups worked through three FLL phases with plenary feedback and discussion after each phase.

Phase 1: Reveal expectations and normative visions

Phase 1 focused on revealing anticipatory assumptions by asking participants to discuss their expectations and hopes for water and slums. This exercise helped to turn tacit knowledge into explicit knowledge. The participants were asked to describe the attributes of water, in all its dimensions, and low-income neighbourhoods in 2045. Expectations in this part were supposed to be 'realistic'. Then the participants were asked: What would you consider to be a desirable state for water and slums in 2045? This part was about hopes and participants were urged to be imaginative in describing the values underpinning what is 'good' in 2045.

Each group was then asked to present its results to a plenary session. During presentations participants were invited to be open and trusting, because the purpose was to provide an open space to express fears, hopes and expectations as an important phase of a learning process. Some of the ideas on the expectations and hopes for water and slums are shown in Table 5.13.1.

At the end of the presentations participants provided their general comments and ideas on the results of the exercise.

Phase 2: Rigorous imagination and reframing

In this phase an attempt was made to spark some 'rigorous imagining' by inviting participants to leave behind probable and desirable futures in order to experiment with a discontinuous framework.

Consistent with the FLL-N design principles it was not suggested that this alternative future was likely to happen or was even desirable. The point of the exercise was to experience the power of anticipatory assumptions in shaping the futures we imagine and the potential to address the creative challenge of inventing paradigmatically different futures. This was the steep part of the learning curve – the reframing phase.

218 FLL-N case studies

Table 5.13.1 Expectations and hopes for water and slums

	Expectations	*Hopes*
Water	Migration from water-scarce areas to water-rich areas.	A green revolution in Africa.
	Drought will increase and will disturb demographics and cause conflicts.	Setting up a global structure for free of charge access to water.
	Transporting water from rich water areas to poor water areas.	Technological progress to address water issues.
	Technological advancement and large scale renewable energy will be used.	Reusing waste water in agriculture.
Slums	Slums would become autonomous and uncontrollable by authorities.	More smart cities.
	Slum dwellers will be able to employ technologies to better organise themselves making slums more autonomous.	Reversed migration flows and circular flows.
	Private sector will lead housing market.	End of macro civilisation of management of large cities.
		Development of cities, transforming informal settlements into productive segments of society.

For this purpose, Riel Miller introduced an adapted version of the Learning Intensive Society (LIS) scenario (Miller, 2006) as a catalyst or playground for Phase 2 discussions. He stressed that the idea is to play with the assumptions we use to imagine the future. The LIS is a world where formal/informal has been transcended and the relationship to resources is endogenous to quality of life. As per the standard FLL-N design the primary task in this phase was to use the analytical model of the LIS to challenge participants to invent different social, economic, political, organisational, behavioural, etc. contexts. The goal being to describe in as much operational and 'day-in-the-life' detail what it is like to live in this Learning Intensive Society of 2045. Participants were asked to deepen their picture of the LIS using a four-layer Causal Layered Analysis (Inayatullah, 1998) framework:

1 Headlines – what do people talk about at the café?
2 Systems – what are the words for the economic or social system?
3 Point of view – how do different stakeholders describe the world around them?
4 Myth/Metaphor – what is the overarching nature/purpose/character of the society?

The final question helps participants to articulate their imagined futures through a powerful vision statement, revealing the metaphors and myths that underpin those futures. On this basis the groups were then asked to build 3D models or sculptures that would provide a symbolic representation of 2045 built upon the LIS anticipatory work. They were asked to provide a detailed description of water and slums in 2045. Participants were invited to connect deeply with their imagined vision.

This exercise represents an important step in building Futures Literacy as a capacity. It helped to make the point that it often seems easy to reconstruct the past but challenging to construct futures and imagine scenarios of change. Participants come to see the role of their anticipatory assumptions in what people see and do. Using the LIS as a model for thinking about water and slums in 2045, the groups were able to begin working with a different set of framework conditions – social, economic and cultural. They were able to illustrate – as a snapshot – how water management and slums looked given an alternative set of boundaries and conditions. The scenarios created by the four groups are described below.

GROUP 1 SCENARIO

Global nomadism in combination with local neighbourhoods and communities, where the local identity is important but what will change is the prime marker of those identities. Glocalisation will be dominant. With the disappearance of the Weberian state there will be more localised power leaders at the community level. Leaders could have symbolic power due to knowledge or religion or any other factor but will differ from one community to the other. The leader will be close to the identity marker.

The economic framework will be one in which knowledge will be gained on a non-institutional basis (de-institutionalising knowledge) with radical implications for all other economic and social systems. The economic system will no longer be based on demand and supply but on community 'do it yourself' systems, a model that will change patterns of production. This alters what happens with food and water and dwellings.

Dwellings under this scenario are either transient or temporal with the possibility of moving homes around the globe, or moving to host homes, or to printable biodegradable houses. The city is a 'plug-in' city. Nutrition is very different with either a return to hunting food or taking food tablets/injections or other modes not yet imaginable.

GROUP 2 SCENARIO

Emergence of United States of Africa, leading to an African identity fostering autonomy and common policies. The Sahara perceived as an ocean will turn into a link between SSA and North Africa. Africans will set up several learning communities acting in a smart manner with an African agenda. Technology will be intensively used to gain better command of water resources and agricultural development. This promotes a diversity of agricultural value chains. People talk about cities, not slums. Concepts involved: identity, a common Saharan space, a Pan African learning network through the use of technology,

GROUP 3 SCENARIO

AfriMer(e) (AfriWater) where water shapes the future of Africa. The use of water determines all activities, with optimal use of available technology. An African Water Council engages in water resources research, with the sea as a central element. In the second scenario *AfriTerra (AfriLand)*, the society is the opposite of that of AfriMer, with a maximum exploitation of land, with mobility of African populations, suppression of borders, successful monetary integration leading to Africa becoming a global power. People are very well endowed with knowledge, generated by an indigenous model of knowledge creation and use that rests on an Afro-Maghreb identity – this also serves as a melting pot for the East and West.

GROUP 4 SCENARIO

Chinese company opens sun capsule factory in Angola: IRES (Royal Institute of Strategic Studies of Morocco) innovation celebrated. The myth or metaphor is 'Atom the Head of Gods, God of the Poor'. This is a sun economy in a corporate and hyper globalised world, where the human worker is focused on innovation and robots undertake manual work. Families are small and individualistic, with increasing reliance on robots. Women rule; they occupy positions of power and leadership, with leadership expressed mostly at the community level, through a return to elected community heads.

Phase 3: Using the future

The third phase focused on the questions that arose from the contrast between the reframed scenarios participants developed in Phase 2 and the futures described in Phase 1. During this phase, participants started to explore the implications for the present of alternative and even discontinuous scenarios of the future. The innovative ideas that emerged motivated the participants to realise the array and diversity of possibilities in the present.

The aim of the process was to get people to ask new questions, not to come up with a blueprint for the future. Riel Miller discussed how to think about change and continuity, by asking questions such as:

- How can we change the way we think of change? We can think of change within the system, and think of change outside the system, and understanding better how to set the menu then choose the components from the menu.
- How do we know what we do not know? What we see and do in the present depends heavily on what we imagine in the future.

- How can we use the future to discover the present? To grasp novelty, emergence, and systemic boundaries.
- How can we detect human anticipatory information? FLL-Ns can serve as microscopes of the 21st century.

Conclusions: the journey is more important than the destination

The goal of foresight exercises is usually to set an agenda or develop a plan. Foresight sets a goal and planning tries to implement the steps needed to get there. Often enough there is a sense that the ends justify the means. In this exercise, the means are the ends, since discovery through learning-by-doing is the point. Learning how to think 'outside-the-box' involves knowing what the box is and how to construct it and many others. Thinking about the future as an extrapolation of what has happened in the past is still one way of setting out a menu of choices. But reframing and Futures Literacy, developing a capacity to change the way we 'use-the-future', enables people to invent new items to choose from the menu of action or even to throw away that menu.

Most of today's foresight initiatives explore the possibility of different futures in order to consider the opportunities to shape the future, working with the assumption that today's decisions form and create the societies of tomorrow. FLL-N can expand the terrain of opportunities by enlarging what is imagined beyond what is currently considered probable or desirable. In this way the FLL-N process is useful for policy development meant to address different societal challenges, and also to raise awareness and create consensus around innovative ways to enlarge the opportunities and appreciate the nature of new developments. It contributes actively to improving anticipatory intelligence and an increased awareness of knowledge resources and strategic orientations for the actors who participated in the FLL-N.

The anticipatory assumptions of the participants changed during the FLL-N. The inputs provided by participants in the second phase provided new elements necessary to ask new questions and to develop new insights in the third stage. Participants expressed their ability to use the future in a more self-aware fashion and mentioned that they understood that the future can be used in different ways.

There were several challenges in designing and implementing this FLL-N. Some of the challenges arose because of the specific characteristics of the participants in this FLL-N and the topics selected for the process. FSF collaborated with UNESCO and the facilitators to assess what would be the best language, terminology and heuristics for inviting the participants to think about how the future is used, how to embrace a more open and pluralistic approach to 'using-the-future', how to use their imaginations creatively, and to understand that their expectations and vocabulary for using the future are caught up with probability. The experiences of this FLL-N showed that participants' visions of the future are largely based on a continuation of the past and present into the future and that it is hard to escape this way of thinking. They tended to focus on what they know in terms of already prominent aspects of issues around water and slums. Moreover, specifying and agreeing on the scenarios was a challenge, since it requires capturing the diversity of participants' interests and backgrounds.

The challenge is to continue implementing future tools such as FLL, to continue using the future to understand the present, creating new opportunities for Africans to act in ways that are consistent with their values and hopes. This tool can inspire experts from SSA and MENA region to work together to continuously re-imagine the future, not as a place where we are going to be but as a place where we are living today.

The results of this FLL-N were presented to the Council of Futures Studies and Risk Management at the Academy of Scientific Research and Technology on 19 March 2017, at the first conference of this Council, which aimed to disseminate Futures Studies methodologies to other scientific councils.

Note

1 In 2015 the Rockefeller Foundation supported the Futures Studies Forum for Africa and the Middle East to produce four quarterly bulletins scanning future possibilities in North Africa, as well as to conduct two meetings titled *One Africa* to exchange knowledge and experiences.

References

Futures Studies Forum for Africa and the Middle East (2015a) *Future of North Africa's Slums: 'Slums of Hope' or 'Slums of Despair'*. Available at: http://www.foresightfordevelopment.org/fsf/ (Accessed: 1 October 2017).

Futures Studies Forum for Africa and the Middle East (2015b) *Managing Water Scarcity in North Africa: Trends and Future Prospects*. Available at: http://www.foresightfordevelopment.org/fsf/ (Accessed: 1 October 2017).

Futures Studies Forum for Africa and the Middle East (2015c) *Securing Wheat Availability: What Prospects for North Africa*. Available at: http://www.foresightfordevelopment.org/fsf/ (Accessed: 1 October 2017).

Futures Studies Forum for Africa and the Middle East (2015d) *The Future of Millennials in North Africa*. Available at: http://www.foresightfordevelopment.org/fsf/ (Accessed: 1 October 2017).

Inayatullah, S. (1998) 'Causal Layered Analysis: Poststructuralism as Method', *Futures*, 30(8), pp. 815–829.

Miller, R. (2006) 'Equity in a Twenty-first Century Learning Intensive Society: Is Schooling Part of the Solution?', *Foresight*, 8(4), pp. 13–22.

Case 14: Youth leadership and the use of the future

Ace Victor Franco Aceron and Shermon Cruz

Youth programmes often offer avenues for young people to channel their vigour and, in certain cases, learn to appreciate the nature of their aspirations for the future. One approach to designing such programmes is to attempt to create an empowering environment that helps young people to explore social innovation and imagine what it might be like to be agents of change. This was the challenge taken up by the MVP Future Thought Leaders Summit, an annual youth event, in honour of Philippine businessman and philanthropist Manuel V. Pangilinan (MVP). The group organising the event, the First Pacific Leadership Academy, turned to UNESCO Bangkok to work with them in designing parts of the Summit. This joint effort was inspired by the widening space for youth action in the Philippines and aimed to reach out to passionate young leaders from different provinces in the country. The overriding goal was to provide participants in the process with the opportunity to enhance their knowledge; practise their leadership skills; and collaborate with equally enthusiastic individuals in seminar-workshops and team-building activities.

The Summit organisers decided to introduce thinking about the future as one of the means to achieve their goals. This provided an opening for a collaborative implementation of UNESCO's Futures Literacy Laboratory-Novelty (FLL-N) that aligned directly with the overarching objective of equipping young leaders with the exemplary practices of thought leadership (Kouzes and Posner, 2014). The purpose of this case study is to discuss this specifically customised FLL-N design and present the process, results and achievement. This brief summary concludes with the recommendation to continue similar efforts that use the future to effectively and efficiently leverage the vitality of young people in ways that advance their desire to learn (UNESCO Bangkok, 2016).

Participating young leaders

Over 100 senior high school students who had demonstrated leadership excellence in their schools were chosen to participate in the Summit. These included not only academic achievers but also student leaders in arts, sports and journalism. Coming from eight Philippine provinces including Bataan, Batangas, Bicol, Cagayan de Oro, Caloocan, Pangansinan, Rizal and Tarlac, the participants were proud representatives of their communities. They were eager to share the experiences of their community. They displayed a strong desire to contribute to their communities using what they learned at the Summit.

The diversity of participants and enthusiasm of the youth were instrumental in meeting the Summit's overall objective to equip young leaders with the exemplary practices of thought leadership. The background of the participants also played a key role in the design and implementation of the FLL-N. The richness of diverse perspectives, interests and experiences allowed for a more active exchange of ideas. This was ensured by conducting a pre-workshop survey a day before the FLL-N which helped determine the background of participants and their prior knowledge of why and how they 'use-the-future'.

A total of 46 male and 52 female respondents, between 13 and 18 years old, took the survey. Sixty per cent of them consider themselves to be leaders who are 'creative entrepreneurs', meaning leaders who create their own 'greatness', while 40 per cent see themselves as 'reactive adapters', those who believe that greatness is thrust upon leaders. The survey also found that most participants envision their future jobs as being doctors, lawyers, broadcasters and engineers.

Putting the FLL design to work

The FLL-N was designed to broaden the perspective of the participating youth on how to imagine future scenarios, find alternative solutions and create impact in their own communities. This included exercises on harnessing the power of imagination, creativity, goal-setting and teamwork. Specifically, the lab designers crafted a process involving the three standard phases of FLL, which were complemented with introductory lectures and plenary discussions. As usual the design of the FLL-N followed a collaborative process that tailored each phase to the experiences and expectations of the participants, as well as the organisers of the Summit and the local socio-political conjuncture. As a result, the heuristics for each phase were chosen with the aim of connecting with a school age group, filled with hopes for leadership, in a context that reflected Philippine culture, values and current events. The process was carefully customised in ways that it was hoped would be effective at moving expectations and hopes from tacit to explicit in Phase 1, inducing a reframing experience of leadership in Phase 2, and generating new questions in Phase 3.

Given these considerations the FLL-N design was customised as follows: Phase 1 was divided into two parts. In the first part participants played The Thing from the Future, an imagination game that challenges players to collaboratively and competitively describe objects from a range of probable and hoped-for futures. This was followed by a second Phase 1 activity that enabled the participants to be more explicit about their preconceived notions of leadership using the Futures Triangle process (Inayatullah, 2008). Phases 2 and 3 were brought together in an exercise that called for reframing and rethinking assumptions about leadership by materialising their ideas in a group sculpture depicting a day in the life of a leader in a different future. Overall the process followed the action-learning curve approach of the standard FLL-N design, but with considerably more time devoted to the Phase 1 goal of making anticipatory assumptions explicit because it was believed that such an exercise for this particular group required indirect and playful techniques. As a result, Phases 2 and 3 needed to be compressed so the selected design integrates the reframing and questioning by setting up a collective deconstruction/reconstruction process, using 3D sculptures, around the participants' conceptualisation of leadership.

Phase 1, Step 1: Playing with assumptions

Phase 1 was a fun starter for the FLL-N as it introduced the Situation Lab's The Thing from the Future (Situation Lab, 2017). The game engaged participants with their anticipatory assumptions by coming up with the most entertaining and thought-provoking descriptions of hypothetical objects from different near-, medium-, and long-term futures.

In this phase, 10 groups were given a deck of 108 cards, together with a supply of note pads and pens for each player. The card deck is divided into four 'suits', just like in a deck of playing cards; the four suits are: Arc, Terrain, Object, and Mood (see Table 5.14.1). These four suits served as the parameters or constraints for imagining a thing from the future. The rules for playing the game were adapted to the context of the Summit. At each of the 10 tables, participants were divided into teams of two, with triads for tables with an odd number of participants. Each team (five per table) had to compete with other pairs at their table by generating the most disruptive and thought-provoking object. In a span of 10 minutes per round, the teams had to write or draw their imagined object on a notepad and explain it to their table, after which all players at the table were given time to decide on which team's object won the round, based on the given criteria. The winning team then received coloured stickers to mark their victory in a particular round, and the team with the most coloured stickers at the end were deemed winners of the game.

At the end of the game, the groups were asked to review all their objects and nominate one object that they believed to be the best of all. They could nominate one from their list of winning objects, or any of the imagined objects that they believe could compete with the other groups. Their nominations were then to be judged by a panel composed of members of the event secretariat.

The selection process for the nominations used the same criteria of disruptive thinking or thought provoking 'things'. The panel found it difficult to narrow down the finalists so they took the following steps. First, they eliminated objects which already exist or have appeared in science fiction. Second, the objects were reviewed based on how effectively they were generated according to the four types of cards. Third, the presentation skills of the participants in the plenary session had a bearing since this showed how well students were able to articulate and promote their visions.

Table 5.14.1 Four types of cards in The Thing from the Future (see Chapter 6)

ARC CARDS

ARC cards broadly describe different kinds of possible futures. These cards contain two kinds of information. The main (top) text of each Arc card specifies one of four generic images of alternative futures for players to imagine: Grow, Collapse, Discipline, or Transform.

- **Grow** is a kind of future in which everything and everyone keeps climbing: population, production, consumption. . .
- **Collapse** is a kind of future in which life as we know it has fallen – or is falling – apart.
- **Discipline** is a kind of future in which things are carefully managed by concerted coordination, perhaps top-down or perhaps collaboratively.
- **Transform** is a kind of future in which a profound historical transition has occurred, whether spiritual or technological in nature.

TERRAIN CARDS	OBJECT CARDS	MOOD CARDS
Terrain cards describe contexts, places, and topic areas. Two terrains appear on each card in order to provide richer possibilities for the deck.	Object cards describe the basic form of the thing from the future.	Mood cards describe emotions that the thing from the future might evoke in an observer from the present.

In the card game, the creative and problem-solving aspect of futures thinking was evident. It could be observed that when students think about the future collectively, critical and creative thinking skills are at work. In nominating their best objects for instance, sharing imaginative insights with the group sparked criticism and invited debate. Teamwork was important. Thinking as a team allowed them to learn to accept opposing views and find ways to compromise. In doing so, they had to be both creative and strategic in choosing a winning object.

For these young people, the future – whether growing, collapsing or transforming – will continue to present challenges that require creative and practical solutions. The facilitators observed that the assumptions about the future revealed by playing the card game were infused with a sense of fear and insecurity. For the students, all the objects from the future must be functional and needs-based. Although the participants were given explicit prompts by the Mood and Terrain cards, their underlying anticipatory assumptions were very powerful, pushing them to find objects that address preconceived problems in the future such as the spread of disease, lack of space, loss of morality, and less family time. These reflected a future that they extrapolated on the basis of what they know about the present and the past. Anticipatory assumptions were made more explicit but, as expected from Phase 1, there was little exploration of more creative non-linear futures.

Phase 1, Step 2: Mapping leadership

Phase 1, Step 2 of the FLL-N began with asking the participants to define exemplary leadership based on their understanding of the term in the present. The session found that their typical understanding of the term pertained to a leader who is a role model, a good follower and a communicator. They often described an exemplary leader as someone with the qualities of being generous, responsible, willing, friendly, passionate, caring and inspiring.

After having consolidated their group's ideas, the participants were introduced to the Futures Triangle – an organising device or method to help them map and deepen their understanding of exemplary leadership. The Triangle was instrumental in Phase 2 because it invited participants to reframe exemplary leadership. The participants' ideas, images and stories about a plausible future of leadership were organised and created under the three dimensions of the Futures Triangle. First is the push of the present. This categorises trends and drivers that push us toward a particular future. Second is the pull of the future or the compelling images of future that draw us closer to it. And third is the weight of the future, which relates to barriers to change or simply the factors that hold us back and get in our way.

In this process, there were often lengthy discussions about ideas that the participants found difficult to categorise into push or pull or weight of history. Some could even belong to more than one category. For example, the leadership quality of 'obsession with achievement' may push or pull us to the envisioned future, and at the same time it could hold us back.

Based on this Triangle, the most common image of an exemplary leader was a passionate servant-leader who acts as a role model and driver of change. This leader was described as a person who could communicate effectively in order to inspire and command others to follow. This quality of leadership was seen as a pull of the future. What pushes a future society to achieve this kind of leadership was the presence of family and good relationships. A leader has to be equipped with the right education and leadership values, for example, selflessness, responsibility, respect. Most students believed that greed, incompetence, low self-esteem and false limiting beliefs were the weight of history or the major hurdles to achieving their envisioned future of leadership.

Guided by their facilitators, the last step of this activity was for participants to use the ideas under each dimension to create the plausible future of exemplary leadership. The word 'leadership' was put inside the triangle to represent the future which they had to develop through their collective ideas.

Hybrid Phase 2/3: Using reframing to materialise new contexts and conceptions of leadership

Having identified the elements that make up leadership on the basis of their Futures Triangle, along with a list of assumptions about exemplary leadership, the participants were asked to reflect on any disruptive assumptions about the future from the very first activity – starting from the winning objects – and how those aspects of the imaginary future might influence the nature of leadership in 2040 or 2050. Using all the data and information they produced, the primary goal of this hybrid Phase 2/3 was to help participants reframe their ideas by identifying one or two new aspects of leadership in the future. While some groups started from scratch, most of them came up with new aspects of leadership by using the results of the Futures Triangle, which provided them with a basis for critical thinking about what it means to be a leader.

In the last activity the hybrid Phase 2/3 directed participants to create a sculpture that would concretise their visions and ideas about daily life in a future they had reframed by distancing themselves from what they had discerned in Phase 1. Through the sculptures, the participants were able to integrate many of the new ideas and perspectives generated across all the different activities they engaged in throughout the Summit. The sculptures expressed the group's ideas because the participants were guided by design principles that called on them to create the sculpture in an open and collaborative fashion. Some groups were more effective than others at incorporating their deconstructed or reframed descriptions of leadership in the future into their sculpture. Others built their sculptures using the more radical ideas that had been generated by playing The Thing from the Future in Step 1 of Phase 1.

Most of the sculptures provided tangible manifestations of the participants' altered perceptions of what it might mean to be a leader in the future. Building and then describing the sculptures also allowed the participating Filipino youth to make visible the centrality of family, ethics, moral precepts, spirituality and strength of character. An 'awakened conscience' could also be further attributed to their sculptures as all these reflected leadership qualities of being sensitive, caring, inclusive, magnanimous, reflective, decisive and courageous.

Evaluating the FLL-N

According to the FLL-N post-evaluation survey, 98 out of the 102 respondents replied "yes" when asked if their understanding of leadership changed as a result of the workshop, and 97 of them affirmed that the FLL-N sessions changed their expectations of leadership. The survey also asked about what actions the participants are going to take after the workshop. All of them responded with enthusiasm and broadly stated their will to serve their communities and make a difference. Specific actions such as organising a leadership workshop were mentioned by students who are officers in their school organisations. They plan to introduce futures thinking in their club activities.

The students' understanding of the future also expanded. This could be observed in statements like "I want to be a futurist leader" which implies their recognition of knowing how to use the future (Futures Literacy) as a quality of a leader, not just a term which refers to what might happen. However, when asked if there is one ideal future, 60 per cent of the participants said yes. This underscores how difficult it is to achieve one of the main goals of Futures Literacy: to enhance the capacity to invent and consider a range of imaginary futures as a way to both diversify planning and better appreciate complex emergence in the present. The students' belief or yearning for one ideal future merits further exploration and could be used as an indicator for the success of different designs of the Futures Literacy Learning process.

Conclusion

Foresight and anticipation as a tool for leadership development were new to the participating student leaders. The freshness of the approach may have inspired enthusiasm and great interest from the participants, as can be concluded from their active performance and positive feedback. But it also stimulated the accompanying school coordinators to learn more about Futures Literacy and consider how they might 'use-the-future' in new ways in classroom teaching and education. Volunteer facilitators from the academy likewise found value in FLL-N, and felt that they could improve on the logistics and commit to a more in-depth train-the-trainer session for subsequent FLLs. Suggestions included preparing guidelines on how to determine if the objectives of each phase are achieved, and training on "effective facilitation through the art of questioning".

A major achievement of the Summit was its effort to include young leaders from cities outside Metro Manila, especially those who are less exposed to new ideas and forms of international collaboration. This custom designed FLL-N had a direct impact on the participants by enlarging their understanding of why and how to 'use-the-future' and illustrating the value of action-learning. From the early co-design phase through implementation, the FLL-N proved its relevance to changing perceptions and actions.

References

Inayatullah, S. (2008) 'Six Pillars: Futures Thinking for Transforming', *Foresight*, 10(1), pp. 4–21.

Kouzes, J. M. and Posner, B. Z. (2014) *The Student Leadership Challenge: Five Practices for Becoming an Exemplary Leader*. 2nd edn. San Francisco, CA: Jossey-Bass.

Situation Lab (2017) The Thing From the Future: Singularity University Edition. Available at: http://situationlab.org/projects/futurething (Accessed: 14 August 2017).

UNESCO Bangkok (2016) *Pioneering Futures Literacy with Filipino Youth*. Available at: www.unescobkk.org/ru/news/article/pioneering-futures-literacy-with-filipino-youth/ (Accessed: 1 July 2017).

Part III
Parallel and convergent developments

6 Gaming Futures Literacy

The Thing from the Future

Stuart Candy

Amid pervasive uncertainty and accelerating change, one of our great challenges, and opportunities, is to make high quality engagement with the yet-to-be more widespread.

Futures Literacy (Miller, 2007) is lacking from most people's experience, even in core social institutions where we might hope to find it well established, such as education, politics, and the media. So the foresight field finds itself with much room for improving public uptake towards the fulfilment of what I consider to be its most important promise: the development of a distributed, society-wide capacity for anticipation.

Richard Slaughter has described such a collective capacity as 'foresight culture' or 'social foresight' (Slaughter, 1996, 2002), echoing Alvin Toffler's outline of 'social futurism' and 'anticipatory democracy' a generation earlier (Toffler, 1970), and amplifying an argument made decades before that by none other than H. G. Wells, calling for professors, and indeed a profession, of foresight: "All these new things, these new inventions and new powers, come crowding along; every one is fraught with consequences, and yet it is only after something has hit us hard that we set about dealing with it" (Wells, 1989, pp. 3–4).

The stakes could hardly be higher. Without adequate means to visualise and apprehend the large-scale and long-term systems where the spectres of peak oil, climate change, and economic collapse reside, the civilisation-scale, existential risks humanity has to face are mounting, underimagined and under-addressed (Dator, 2009b; Candy, 2010, p. 70).

On the other hand, as Riel Miller observes (p. 9) in introducing this volume, "changing the way the future is used holds out a promise of changing the future".

To echo Stewart Brand (1999, p. 2), how then may we take strategic foresight from difficult and rare to automatic and common?

This question confronts a tension between introducing ways of thought and perception that are unfamiliar – and that can therefore be quite challenging at first – and the hope of increasing popular accessibility.

The good news is that our repertoire of uses of the future, the set of available ways to map and manifest possible paths or waypoints ahead, is far from exhausted. Exciting vistas have recently opened up with foresight's 'experiential

234 *Stuart Candy*

turn' towards fuller exploration of design, media and games (Candy, 2010; Li, 2013; Haldenby and Candy, 2014; Selin, 2015; Candy and Dunagan, 2017). Such exploration may help us reconfigure the playing field – or reshuffle the deck – to make it easier to engage people in the relatively novel modes of thought that increasing Futures Literacy entails.

This chapter presents a case study of an experiential futures card game called The Thing from the Future (Candy and Watson, 2014; Situation Lab, 2015b), reflecting on it as a method for popularising and demystifying futures, and explaining the design mechanisms that make it tick. While undoubtedly a limited tool (like all tools), its potential significance as part of a wave of efforts to spread Futures Literacy which are actually enjoyable to use may give heart to those in search of new ways towards distributed anticipation and social foresight.

Let us briefly situate the project in relation to currents in games and futures

Surveying a rapidly changing field, game designer and educator Traci Fullerton observes: "There has been an explosion in new platforms of play and an emergence of exciting new markets and genres of games. . . Game design is everywhere" (Fullerton, 2008, p. xv). Increasingly ubiquitous, it seems, and in some quarters increasingly aspirational. Games scholar Mary Flanagan wonders:

> What if some games, and the more general concept of 'play' not only provide outlets for entertainment but also function as means for creative expression, as instruments for conceptual thinking, or as tools to help examine or work through social issues?
>
> (Flanagan, 2009, p. 1)

Meanwhile designer and futurist Jane McGonigal asks: "What if we decided to use everything we know about game design to fix what's wrong with reality?" (McGonigal, 2011, p. 7). Not merely rhetorical questions, these represent far-reaching agendas for research and creation, as well as key entryways into a rich, fast developing bibliography – and ludography – that takes games seriously as a way to accomplish real change.

And, just as games are venturing into serious territory, the at times over-whelmingly serious practice of futures has been learning to be more playful. Games have of course long been used for foresight-related purposes, in the context of military strategy for example: at the U.S. Naval War College, war games have been played since 1866 (Bell, 2017, p. 287). The past decade or so however, has seen a surge of experimentation in participatory games, using the web's recently possible 'massively multiplayer' gameplay environment. Some key projects in the futures domain have included *World*

Without Oil: "the first massively scaled effort to engage ordinary individuals in creating an immersive forecast of the future" (McGonigal, 2011, p. 303), *Superstruct* (McGonigal, 2011, p. 317), the U.S. federal CDC-funded 'emergent reality game' *Coral Cross* (Pescovitz, 2009) and the *Foresight Engine* (Dunagan, 2012).

This game design strand represents one important part of a broader pattern.

I began working in and writing regularly about the intersections of futures with design and media in 2006, eventually completing a doctoral dissertation on the topic (Candy, 2010). Through a combination of theory and extensive collaborative practice, 'experiential futures' emerged as an overarching frame to denote "the gamut of approaches involving the design of situations and stuff from the future to catalyse insight and change" (Candy, 2015), a literally vast design space of foresight activity encompassing

> all manner of other things that one might create in order to manifest, evoke and make available thoughts, feelings and insights about the whole gamut of possible futures ... Tangible, immersive, interactive, live, and playable modes are all in scope.
> (Candy and Dunagan, 2017)

Here we will comprehensively survey neither the fast-moving arena of games designed for futures purposes, nor the wider territory of experiential futures, but we can explore one particular project which happens to exemplify both currents, and which points up their potential for contributing to advancement of Futures Literacy and, beyond that, social foresight. Our focus will be on how the game provides a structure of participation (Jeremijenko, 2002) for helping people imagine, probe, and therefore navigate change more effectively.

The Thing from the Future is a foresight tool and imagination exercise in the form of a deck of cards. Part scenario generator, part design method, and part party game it invites players to collaborate and compete in describing, telling stories about, and sketching or physically prototyping artefacts that could exist in alternative futures. Co-designed by the author, a futurist and design professor at Carnegie Mellon University, with Jeff Watson, a games professor at the University of Southern California's School of Cinematic Arts, the first edition was published in early 2014 by a research unit we jointly run, Situation Lab.

To date it has been played by thousands of people around the world, in settings ranging from the United Nations Development Programme's annual strategy gathering in New York to Nesta's Futurefest in London; academic programmes from Stanford d.School to MIT Media Lab and the National University of Singapore; and countless conferences, workshops and loungerooms. It has been an Official Selection of the international games festival IndieCade, and winner of a Most Significant Futures Work award from the Association of Professional Futurists. It has received international media coverage and been translated

236 Stuart Candy

into other languages; a Portuguese/English edition produced for the Museum of Tomorrow in Rio de Janeiro, and a French/English edition for delegates at UNESCO's Youth Forum in Paris. For a perspective on where The Thing from the Future fits into the design community's recently flourishing interest in speculative and futures-oriented practice, see Lupton (2017, pp. 50–51).

Gameplay is simple. In a small group, usually three to five people, players co-create a prompt and are each challenged to describe an artefact from the future which meets the parameters. Any prompt offers the necessary constraints for one to describe a specific cultural fragment from a possible future. In competitive mode, it is the 'best' response (which could mean the funniest, or most thought-provoking, disturbing, resonant, etc.), as determined by those at the table, that wins the round.

In the original design, the deck of cards contains four suits or categories of card to kindle and guide imaginations. *Arc* is the applicable time horizon and type of future, building on Jim Dator's four generic futures (sometimes also called archetypes) framework (Dator, 2009a). *Terrain* is the context for the object, either a physical location or a domain of human activity. The *Object* is the category of hypothetical 'future thing' for which players will generate a description (not always a physical artefact), ranging from Device, to Headline, to Monument. Finally, *Mood* says how it feels to interact with that thing, lending an 'interior' inflection to the other three more 'external' elements.[1]

A creative prompt comprises any set of four cards, one from each suit (ATOM). For example see Figure 6.1.

This combination challenges us to describe an artefact from just a few years into the future; a *beverage* relating somehow to a *zoo*, that evokes a *continued growth trajectory* in the wider society, and that imparts a sense of *disgust*. In response one player proposed a product called ZooShooters, a hypothetical product from animal rights activist group PETA. This drink, when imbibed, gives one the experience of the suffering of a caged animal.

For another example see Figure 6.2. And a sort of vignette in response: "With mobile devices increasingly distracting from religious leaders' sermons, to enter

Figure 6.1 An example prompt (no. 1) from The Thing from the Future's original four-card design: Arc, Terrain, Object, and Mood (first edition, revised 2015). Image courtesy of Situation Lab

Figure 6.2 An example prompt (no. 2) from The Thing from the Future's original four-card design. Image courtesy of Situation Lab

a place of faith one must wear a mask that prevents interaction with mobile electronic devices, allowing only polarised light from the speaker's podium."[2]

There's often a humorous or eccentric quality to players' creations, which is due in part to the playful tone which the medium of the card game invites, but which also seems typical of a randomising combinatorial structure (see also Weidinger, 2014). The design question becomes: how to make a structure more reliably generative of useful outcomes? For recent thinking in this area see Compton (2016).

A later iteration of the design, first released in August 2017 at the Singularity Summit in San Francisco, uses a simplified structure with just three suits: *Future, Thing* and *Theme* (Candy and Watson, 2017; 2018). Also included is a 'phrasal template' on the cards themselves, to make clear to players at a glance how to sequence, understand and synthesise the three elements. This design element emerged from Situation Lab projects developed between the original and revised editions of The Thing from the Future: Rilao (Watson, 2015) and Futureschool (Stein, Watson and Candy, 2015).

Some example prompts from the three-suit deck design can be seen in Figures 6.3–6.5:[3]

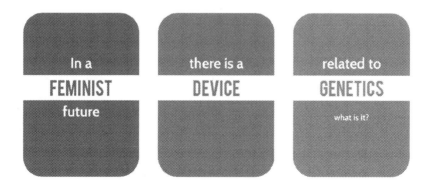

Figure 6.3 An example prompt (no. 1) from The Thing from the Future's simplified three-card design: Future, Thing, and Theme (Singularity University edition, 2017). Image courtesy of Situation Lab

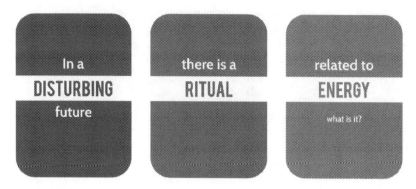

Figure 6.4 An example prompt (no. 2) from The Thing from the Future's three-card design. Image courtesy of Situation Lab

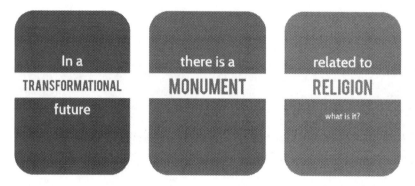

Figure 6.5 An example prompt (no. 3) from The Thing from the Future's three-card design. Image courtesy of Situation Lab

While recognisably the same game, it should be readily apparent how these design changes (the reduced cognitive load of three elements instead of five,[4] one idea per card instead of two, and the syntactic 'connective tissue' of the phrasal template) make it more playable.

Watson has described The Thing from the Future as a "combinatorial creative prompting system" (personal communication; see also Watson, 2012 for discussion of a "card-based procedural creative prompting system" devised to help aspiring filmmakers create more diverse student films). Indeed, its possibilities are practically inexhaustible: the several dozen options in each of the suits multiply out to yield close to 40,000 unique permutations in the redux edition (and over 3.7 million in the more complex, multivariate earlier version), any of which could in principle give rise to innumerable artefact ideas.

Duly scaffolded into thinking and feeling out a particular corner of this rich possibility space, players often generate thoughts genuinely new to them. The Indian cultural commentator and sometime futurist Ashis Nandy has proposed that the futures field is "basically a game of dissenting visions" (Nandy, 1996); The Thing from the Future is at its core literally that. If Dator's 'Second law of the future' – any useful statement about the future should at first appear to be ridiculous (Dator, 1995) – is true, then the cards demonstrate high potential for yielding useful ideas. A corresponding downside is of course that playful thinking is not always valued, especially in more conservative organisational settings.

Still, a game format or framing can be helpful in and of itself for the futurist facilitator seeking to trigger a hypothetical, exploratory mindset, affording players not only permission to think along heterodox lines, but offering the specific materials of imagination with which to do so. The cultural norm associated with card games of literally 'playing the hand you are dealt', rather than rejecting the terms of the hypothetical – a common problem when working with future scenarios in more prosaic formats – also may help players grant permission *to themselves* to range into previously uncharted imaginative territory.[5]

There is flexibility in the game's uses – from group icebreaker to imagination gym, tool for structured exploration of a design space[6] or, more ambitiously, ideation engine for tangible outcomes. Several design jams have been held by Situation Lab, where players turned their game-enabled artefact ideas into popup design fiction shows (see The Extrapolation Factory, 2014 and Situation Lab, 2017 for more details).[7]

This process of artefact-idea generation could be thought of as a sort of 'reverse archaeology'. Whereas from a found artefact, an archaeologist infers the world that produced it, here one creatively devises a specific artefact based on a skeletal description of 'the world' (Candy, 2013). Just as history leaves behind innumerable traces – in attics, museums, and other treasure troves – and these can speak volumes about what has happened in the past, the card deck is intended to help players to imagine evidence from the countless scenarios that *could* happen.

The game's 'artefact from the future' premise dates back at least as far as *Wired* magazine's long-running back-page feature *Found* (Wired, 2002–2013), but also finds counterparts in work by Jason Tester and colleagues (Institute for the Future, 2017); in Dunagan and Candy's 'guerrilla futures' collaboration, *FoundFutures* (Candy and Dunagan, 2007); and not least, in the rapid, recent spread of popular futures-inflected design practices such as design fiction (Bleecker, 2009; Sterling, 2009, 2013) and speculative design (DiSalvo and Lukens, 2009; Auger, 2012; Dunne and Raby, 2013).

Naturally there are also numerous antecedents, ancient and modern, to the generative card deck, ranging from tarot and playing cards to a parade of more recent creations with similar procreative intent, including IDEO's Method Cards (IDEO, 2003), ArtCenter College of Design's Mobility VIP (Walker *et al.*, 2008) and Near Future Laboratory's Design Fiction Kit (Near Future Laboratory, 2014).

Still, what The Thing from the Future tackles is something that has previously tended to be a specialist activity of futurists and designers – taking relatively abstract ideas about future narratives and distilling concrete ideas for future artefacts – and it makes that task easier.[8]

The typology or structure underpinning each prompt splits the attributes of a future thing into three complementary levels of abstraction, which offers players disparate elements to synthesise: the macro (type of scenario; *Future*, formerly Arc), meso (geographic or thematic area of interest; *Theme*; formerly Terrain), and micro (the unit of cultural output, and focal point of the description you create; *Thing*; formerly Object). The original design (Candy and Watson, 2014) used a separate card to bring an interior state (Mood) into play, while the three-card second edition (Candy and Watson, 2017; 2018) seeks to integrate these key emotional cues into the Future suit. Either way, this emotional spin on the prompt integrates a dimension often neglected in the cognition-heavy thought experimentation that is standard in foresight practice. In this sense, as pointed out in a recent overview of experiential futures, this move lets us *enact* some of the vital interior-exterior bridging work suggested by Integral Futures literature, rather than mainly talking about how valuable it would be to do so (Candy and Dunagan, 2017).

Each round of gameplay asks the player to scale a sort of 'ladder of abstraction' (Hayakawa, 1947) – a notion we have elsewhere used to develop a design tool for experiential futures projects called the Experiential Futures Ladder (Candy and Dunagan, 2017). While formal scenarios can take an enormous amount of time and effort to prepare, here is a rapid descent from abstract, high-level descriptors of possible future worlds – whether Grow or Discipline (original); Feminist or Disturbing (second edition) – to numerous ground-level ideas for artefacts that evoke this larger narrative premise.[9]

This power to generate coherent prompts in large numbers, 'automatically' as it were, and also the key to helping players pull off responses, lies in the relationship between the suits. There is a built-in typological complementarity such that all members of each card category are logically compatible with all the others. A pioneering project in this combinatorial cards-for-future-imagining design space, Mobility VIP, has eleven categories per prompt; see Walker *et al.* (2008).[10] Put another way, The Thing from the Future provides an approach to exploring a combinatorial possibility space that is structurally similar to morphological analysis (Ritchey, 2009) – one of the richest approaches to scenario generation, but perhaps also, in its usual form, most intimidating, and therefore not often used.

Happily, a player need not know or worry about such details at all in order to play The Thing from the Future, much as one need not understand precisely how an internal combustion engine works in order to drive a car safely to any number of destinations. The playful interface of a card game renders a certain complexity as simple and approachable, which is a large part of why it works. What The Thing from the Future offers as a futures method might be said to consist in the way its design and storytelling engine operates mostly unseen 'under the hood', with the effect that without great effort, players can engage in a quite sophisticated form of integrative, imaginative thinking, embedding abstract future-narrative notions in particular concepts for future things, all while actually enjoying themselves.

None of this is to suggest that the game replaces proper scenario generation processes, but it might be a way to make some of the distinctive modes of thinking involved less intimidating and therefore more common.

What 'distinctive modes of thinking' do I have in mind? It seems to me to be, for starters, a matter of *thinking divergently* (in terms of multiple alternatives) as well as *concretely* (as opposed to vaguely or abstractly) about possible futures. We could call these dimensions respectively diversity (or breadth) and depth (Candy, 2010, p. 17). We might also hypothesise that the game makes the future psychologically less remote to players (see Candy, 2010, p. 83). It renders not only the particular ideas that one generates while playing, but in a sense the whole futures possibility space, and the endless array of situations and stuff that make it up, available to be explored, thought and felt, by anyone so inclined.

To highlight the flexibility of the method encoded in this simple deck of cards is not to imply some kind of universal applicability: the selection, adaptation, and skilled deployment of appropriate foresight tools in context looks set to remain among the futurist's dark arts for a while yet. But with this addition the toolkit expands, becoming incrementally more flexible, participatory and diversified. It has shown a way to tie the high-level abstractions of scenario types (Arc/Future) to the specifics that those futures might disclose, leaving but a short step to countless design fictions and other experiential futures creations. And bringing futures closer, mediating people's relationship to them so they become more playfully open and less opaque, seems a useful step on the road to more widespread foresight literacy.

Experience so far shows that it does not take long for players and facilitators to understand how the game's suits work, from which point it is straightforward to augment or adjust the contents, leading exploration into specific sub-territories in the future's vast cone of possibilities. When using the original edition in workshops we would sometimes provide blank Terrain or Object cards to let players customise the constraints to workshop themes. The new edition, we hope enabled by its more self-explanatory structure, includes several blanks of each category in every deck. Ultimately a grasp of the underlying structure amounts to an infinitely extensible, customisable, layered way of using the imagination, with or without cards in hand.

Let us be clear that this systematic use of limitations or guidelines to elicit imaginative engagement with possibility is not new. Arguably it is a core to any kind of useful foresight or anticipatory thought. The Dutch sociologist Fred Polak, pioneer of the concept of "images of the future", observed:

> The domain of the future, however, is without boundaries. Yet it is only by drawing boundaries in the thought-realm that man can produce a problem that can be grasped and worked with, and it is only by redrawing the boundaries of the unknown that man can increase his knowledge. No problem so persistently defies our skill at drawing boundaries as the problem of the future, and no problem presses quite so hard on our intellectual horizons.
>
> (Polak, 1973, p. 4)

From this perspective any story or scenario about a future, and indeed, the next level of abstraction up, any technique for scenario generation (and there are dozens; see for example Bishop, Hines and Collins, 2007), can be thought of as simply a different way of 'drawing boundaries in the thought-realm' in order to make futures psychologically tractable.

In a sense, what The Thing from the Future attempts is to make a kind of generative 'source code' for boundary-drawing in futures available to more people. Each prompt is a different set of "enabling constraints" (Hayles, 2001), and the limits that confine and challenge the imagination in each round of gameplay present a pathway disclosing potentially brand-new vistas unimaginable until one ventures along it.

As the game's co-designer has observed, "Limitations don't just inspire creative solutions to problems: rather, they are necessary to them" (Watson, 2012, p. 54). To recognise the importance of limitations on creativity and imagination, and deliberately crafted prompts for them, helps move our inquiry forward. This chapter began with the question of how to take strategic foresight from being rare and difficult to being easier and more common. It seems this is one way: to invite gameplay with the boundaries and parameters (assumptions, causal chains, narrative premises, themes, etc.) that frame particular conceptions of times to come.

As a recent overview and case study of experiential futures suggested:

> [P]erhaps *the* central challenge for the next generation of foresight practitioners will have less to do with generating and broadcasting ideas about the future, than it will have to do with *designing circumstances or situations in which the collective intelligence and imagination of a community can come forth*. To design and stage an experience of the future is one class of activity. To attend to the design of processes whereby such experiences are designed – making structures of participation – is another.
> (Candy and Dunagan, 2017, emphasis in original)

This peek at the inner workings of a futures card game highlights the potential of continuing to develop structures of participation for manifesting futures in story, materiality, and performance (see Situation Lab, 2015a),[11] in turn to enrich our collective vocabulary of anticipation (see Meadows, 2009).[12]

This project is necessarily a work in progress. Designing playful systems is – or should be – iterative, so they improve over time as lessons are learned via encounters with different player populations (Situation Lab, 2017). And wherever it might go from here, the larger possibility to which it points, the promotion of distributed anticipation or social foresight, continues to inspire and beckon.

It has been observed that humans' native, everyday foresight capacity serves as the basis, duly ramified and amplified, for the professional and pedagogical activity of futurists (Slaughter, 1996; Hayward, 2003). The development of a social capacity for foresight is perhaps the ultimate promise of a futures practice that does not hoard or guard its insights and tools as the preserve of a class of experts, but one that closes the circle by handing user-friendly tools back to a wider population. I suggest that experiential futures generally, and games especially, can help make good on this democratic promise.

A little further along that path, now, we are beginning to make out a not too distant future in which futures thinking enjoys far greater currency and impact, by becoming not only more accessible – but also more fun.

Notes

1. The introduction of the Mood card in the first edition of the game owes some inspiration to the Systems Mythology Toolkit created by Dylan Hendricks from the Institute for the Future (IFTF).
2. These examples both come from gameplay with a class in 'Science Fiction-Inspired Prototyping' at MIT Media Lab. My thanks to Dan Novy and Joost Bonsen, and to their students.
3. In this later version, two most concrete elements of the original four-card prompt have been retained; the artefact or Thing, and a context for it or Theme (corresponding to the original edition's Object and Terrain suits). However, the Arc and Mood cards have been unified under a single macro-category, the Future suit, describing the kind of world or scenario in which a player's imagination is invited to roam. In the later edition, instead of focusing on a small set of four primary Arcs that all describe an external shift in the state of the system (Grow, Collapse, Discipline, Transform), the Future card provides a larger container for possibilities with various inflections; towards externally observable conditions (including variations on the generic futures; Exponential, Slow, Regimented, Transformational, Spiritual), or more specific external states (Digital, Postnational, Handmade), or aesthetic conditions (Steampunk, Poetic, Grotesque) or feelings (Dark, Funny, Thrilling) more closely resembling the role of the Mood card.
4. Arc cards also included a time horizon, which represents a fifth piece of information for players to incorporate – on top of the generic future type, plus the other three cards. Reducing cognitive load for players was one of the design aims of The Thing from the Future second edition.
5. Thanks to Riel Miller for sharing this insight.
6. For example, holding a certain parameter steady, say a particular Theme/Terrain, while pivoting other variables around it to challenge and reframe how that domain could evolve.
7. One design jam that we ran with the game as an ideation engine resulted in a collection of street vendor merchandise from the future, produced on campus at New York University, then put on sale at the corner of Canal St and Broadway in Manhattan. Another generated an exhibition about future live music performances, created by Stanford d.School students and mounted at the Tech Museum of Innovation in San Jose. Another yielded a series of short films from the future, created by young filmmakers at Hot Docs International Documentary Film Festival in Toronto. Note that generating ideas for physical things is by no means the only way to use the deck. In the very first edition, the Object suit had focused on small-scale, tangible items, such as Wallet, Postcard, and Toy, reflecting the game's origins as an ideation engine for the first Futurematic design jam, where participants filled a vending machine with future artefacts produced in a single day. Subsequent revisions have incorporated more diverse cultural outputs in the Object/Thing category, including intangible, performative or larger-scale fragments such as Headline, Festival, and Building.
8. Having been involved in these hybrid design/futures practices for some years before design fiction (and then speculative design, a more recently popular term) caught on, one hope that I have for this game is that it may help accelerate the process of people getting over the flimsy novelty value of artworks, exhibits and various other 'things from the future', so that these practices can proceed sooner to higher-value questions around discerning what makes particular ideas and works of this kind more or less effective, interesting and worthwhile.
9. This is not to suggest that every single combination yielded by the deck is as valuable or evocative as any other. The question I find interesting goes to the results yielded by players as a result of design choices made at the structure level: some are more consistently or fruitfully generative than others. The importance of typological complementarity across

the suits (a design dimension that appears often to be overlooked) was highlighted after several creators let us know about having made their own combinatorial card sets inspired by The Thing from the Future. When categories jostle at the same level of abstraction (e.g. at a meso-level, 'user', 'location', 'theme') they seem apt to lead to more eccentric or simply confusingly contradictory prompts. Of course, there is a certain potential creative generativity in almost any prompt. As co-designer Jeff Watson has pointed out in personal communication during our design process, even reading names out of the phone book is mildly generative.

10 There are challenges of working with such complexity; a mix of cognitive load on players and typological complementarity among suits in the deck, I would think. So even one of the lead examples of excellent, ingenious responses in the project Gallery de-emphasises (greys out) three of the eleven. Similarly, in the original version of The Thing from the Future, players would regularly forget about one or other of the prompt elements, which was part of the reason we simplified the second edition. A deeper investigation of 'generativity', looking more closely at design choices in the structure (e.g. number and framing of categories or 'suits') and content (e.g. cards included in each category), and what kinds of results these yield from players encountering them, awaits another time.

11 In 2015, Situation Lab created a specifically performance-oriented adaptation of The Thing from the Future for arts/activist group US Department of Arts and Culture, populating the Object/Thing suit with a set of future scenes or interaction types (instead of artefacts), such as Interview, Reunion, and Announcement.

12 Environmental scientist Donella Meadows, lead author of the seminal *Limits to Growth* report to the Club of Rome, once proposed a hierarchical list of 'places to intervene in a system', which we might use to pose two key questions relating to the generativity and potency of a framework for foresight literacy (whether in game form or not): where does it intervene, and how does it orient and enable participants within the system?

References

Auger, J. (2012) *Why Robot? Speculative Design, the Domestication of Technology and the Considered Future*. London: Royal College of Art.

Bell, W. (2017) *Foundations of Futures Studies: History, Purposes and Knowledge* (Volume 1: Human science for a new era). London: Routledge.

Bishop, P., Hines, A. and Collins, T. (2007) 'The Current State of Scenario Development: An Overview of Techniques', *Foresight* 9(1), pp. 5–25.

Bleecker, J. (2009) *Design Fiction: A Short Essay on Design, Science, Fact and Fiction, Near Future Laboratory*. Los Angeles: Near Future Laboratory. Available at: http://www.nearfuturelaboratory.com/2009/03/17/design-fiction-a-short-essay-on-design-science-fact-and-fiction/.

Brand, S. (1999) *The Clock of the Long Now: Time and Responsibility*. Basic Books: New York.

Candy, S. (2010) *The Futures of Everyday Life*. University of Hawaii at Manoa.

Candy, S. (2013) 'Time Machine/Reverse Archaeology', in Briggs, C. (ed.) *72 Assignments, The Foundation Course in Art and Design Today*. Paris: PCA Press, pp. 28–30.

Candy, S. (2015) *La Chose du Futur à Paris, The Sceptical Futuryst*. Available at: https://futuryst.blogspot.com/2015/11/la-chose-du-futur-paris.html (Accessed: 22 March 2017).

Candy, S. and Dunagan, J. (2007) *FoundFutures*. Honolulu: Hawaii Research Centre for Futures Studies.

Candy, S. and Dunagan, J. (2017) 'Designing an Experiential Scenario: The People Who Vanished', *Futures*, 86, pp. 136–153. Available at: https://www.scribd.com/document/134636809/FoundFutures.

Candy, S. and Watson, J. (2014) The Thing from the Future (Card game). Toronto: Situation Lab. Available at: http://situationlab.org/project/the-thing-from-the-future/ (Accessed: 30 August 2017).

Candy, S. and Watson, J. (2017) The Thing from the Future: Singularity University Edition (Card game). Toronto: Situation Lab.

Candy, S. and Watson, J. (2018) The Thing from the Future: Second Edition (Card game). Pittsburgh: Situation Lab.

Compton, K. (2016) *So You Want to Build a Generator. . ., Kate Compton Blog*. Available at: http://galaxykate0.tumblr.com/post/139774965871/so-you-want-to-build-a-generator (Accessed: 26 September 2017).

Dator, J. (1995) *What Futures Studies Is, and Is Not*. Honolulu: Hawaii Research Centre for Futures Studies.

Dator, J. (2009a) 'Alternative Futures at the Manoa School', *Journal of Futures Studies*, 14(2), pp. 1–18.

Dator, J. (2009b) 'The Unholy Trinity, Plus One', *Journal of Futures Studies*, 13(3), pp. 33–48.

DiSalvo, C. and Lukens, J. (2009) 'Towards a Critical Technological Fluency: The Confluence of Speculative Design and Community Technology Programs', in *Digital Arts and Culture 2009*.

Dunagan, J. (2012) 'Massively Multiplayer Futuring: IFTF's Foresight Engine', *Journal of Futures Studies*, 17(1), pp. 141–150.

Dunne, A. and Raby, F. (2013) *Speculative Everything: Design, Fiction, and Social Dreaming*. Cambridge, MA: MIT Press.

Flanagan, M. (2009) *Critical Play: Radical Game Design*. Cambridge, MA: Massachusetts Institute of Technology.

Fullerton, T. (2008) *Game Design Workshop: A Playcentric Approach to Creating Innovative Games*. 3rd edn, *Technology*. Boca Raton: CRC Press/Taylor & Francis.

Haldenby, T. and Candy, S. (2014) 'The Age Of Imagination: A History of Experiential Futures 2006–2031'. Paper prepared for *Alternate Endings: Using Fiction to Explore Design Futures*, ACM CHI Conference on Human Factors in Computing Systems, Toronto. Available at: https://www.researchgate.net/publication/305386609_The_Age_Of_Imagination_A_History_of_Experiential_Futures_2006-2031 (Accessed: 23 January 2018).

Hayakawa, S. I. (1947) *Language in Action: A Guide to Accurate Thinking, Reading and Writing*. New York: Harcourt Brace and Company.

Hayles, N. K. (2001) 'Desiring Agency: Limiting Metaphors and Enabling Constraints in Dawkins and Deleuze/Guattari', *SubStance*, 30(1), pp. 144–159.

Hayward, P. (2003) *Foresight in Everyday Life*. Melbourne: Australian Foresight Institute.

IDEO (2003) *Method Cards*. Available at: http://www.ideo.com/work/method-cards (Accessed: 14 August 2017).

Institute for the Future (2017) *Artifacts from the Future*. Available at: http://www.iftf.org/what-we-do/foresight-tools/artifacts-from-the-future/ (Accessed: 14 August 2017).

Jeremijenko, N. (2002) *What's New in New Media?, Mute*. Available at: http://www.metamute.org/editorial/articles/whats-new-new-media (Accessed: 30 August 2017).

Li, Z. (2013) 'A Canticle for Mary Sue: What Transmedia Aesthetics Might Do for Futures Communication', *Journal of Futures Studies*, 17(3), pp. 137–140.

Lupton, E. (2017) *Design Is Storytelling*. New York: Cooper Hewitt.

McGonigal, J. (2011) *Reality Is Broken: Why Games Make Us Better and How They Can Change the World*. London: Penguin.

Meadows, D. (2009) 'Places to Intervene in a System (In Increasing Order of Effectiveness)', *Whole Earth*, 91, pp. 78–84.

Miller, R. (2007) 'Futures Literacy: A Hybrid Strategic Scenario Method', *Futures*, 39(4), pp. 341–362.

Nandy, A. (1996) 'Bearing Witness to the Future', *Futures*, 28(6), pp. 636–639.

Near Future Laboratory (2014) *Design Fiction Product Design Work Kit*. Available at: https://shop.nearfuturelaboratory.com/products/design-fiction-product-design-work-kit (Accessed: 14 August 2017).

Pescovitz, D. (2009) *Coral Cross: ARG About Pandemic Flu, Boing Boing*. Available at: https://boingboing.net/2009/05/21/coral-cross-arg-abou.html (Accessed: 14 August 2017).

Polak, F. (1973) *The Image of the Future*. Translated and abridged by E. Boulding. San Francisco: Elsevier.

Ritchey, T. (2009) 'Morphological Analysis', in Glenn, J. and Gordon, T. (eds) *Futures Research Methodology Version 3.0 (CD-ROM)*. 3rd edn. Washington, D.C.: The Millennium Project.

Selin, C. (2015) 'Merging Art and Design in Foresight: Making Sense of Emerge', *Futures*, 70, pp. 24–35.

Situation Lab (2015a) *#DareToImagine*. Available at: http://situationlab.org/daretoimagine/ (Accessed: 15 August 2017).

Situation Lab (2015b) *#FutureThing Print-and-Play Edition*. Available at: http://situationlab.org/futurething-print-and-play-edition/ (Accessed: 15 August 2017).

Situation Lab (2017) *Gameplay Variations for The Thing from the Future*. Available at: http://situationlab.org/gameplay-variations-for-the-thing-from-the-future (Accessed: 30 August 2017).

Slaughter, R. A. (1996) 'Futures Studies: From Individual to Social Capacity', *Futures*, 28(8), pp. 751–762.

Slaughter, R. A. (2002) 'Future Shock Re-Assessed', *Futures Bulletin*, 27(2), pp. 4–7.

Stein, J., Watson, J. and Candy, S. (2015) Futureschool (Card game). Los Angeles: Situation Lab.

Sterling, B. (2009) 'Design Fiction', *ACM Interactions*, 16(3), pp. 20–24.

Sterling, B. (2013) *Patently Untrue: Fleshy Defibrillators and Synchronised Baseball Are Changing the Future, Wired UK*. Available at: http://www.wired.co.uk/article/patently-untrue (Accessed: 15 August 2017).

The Extrapolation Factory (2014) *Futurematic*. Available at: http://www.extrapolationfactory.com/futurematic (Accessed: 26 September 2017).

Toffler, A. (1970) *Future Shock*. New York: Random House.

Walker, L., Wardle G., Ogden, A. and Muyres, D. (2008) *Mobility Vision Integration Project*. Pasadena Art Center College of Design. Available at: http://www.mobilityvip.com/ (Accessed: 15 August 2017).

Watson, J. (2012) *Reality Ends Here: Environmental Game Design and Participatory Spectacle*. Los Angeles: University of Southern California.

Watson, J. (2015) *Rilao Remote Viewing Protocol*. Los Angeles: Situation Lab. Available at: http://situationlab.org/project/rilao-remote-viewing-protocol/ (Accessed: 14 August 2017).

Weidinger, N. (2014) *Artifact Engine*. Palo Alto: Institute for the Future. Available at: http://www.iftf.org/future-now/article-detail/artifact-engine (Accessed: 15 August 2017).

Wells, H. G. (1989) 'Wanted – Professors of Foresight!', in *Studying the Future*. Melbourne: Australian Bicentennial Authority/Commission for the Future, pp. 3–4.

Wired 2002–2013 *Found: Artifacts from the Future*. Available at: https://futuryst.blogspot.com.au/search/label/Found gallery (Accessed: 22 March 2017).

7 An extended Futures Literacy process

Design lessons from measuring wellbeing

Stefan Bergheim

This chapter provides another example of the kind of tools or heuristics that can be deployed in designing and implementing Futures Literacy Labs and other collective intelligence knowledge creation processes. In late 2013 a two-year collective intelligence knowledge creation process began in Frankfurt am Main, Germany, under the title 'Schöne Aussichten – Forum für Frankfurt' (*Positive Futures – Forum for Frankfurt*). The process used four core elements: dialogue, visions, indicators and actions. Indicators were published in mid-2015 (Bergheim, 2015). It was an experiment influenced by the global wellbeing movement and with plenty of room for the emergence of new insights and actions. The future was integrated explicitly in this knowledge creation process by asking about changes that citizens would like to see in the future and by formulating visions for the year 2030.

One of the salient conclusions from this process is that appropriately modified versions can be used in rich and poor countries at the public or private, local, regional or national levels or for smaller sub-topics or constituencies. The outcomes from the process extend well beyond the pinning down of visions and indicators as tools for planning.

The global wellbeing movement

Collective intelligence knowledge creation processes can be used to improve the wellbeing of societies. There are some linkages to the global movement on measuring and fostering the wellbeing of societies, which has been developing since the early 2000s. Initially, this was highly expert-driven, but more and more elements of collective intelligence knowledge creation processes are being added to this movement. *Positive Futures* provides a bridge between compatible approaches and paradigms: first, by using wellbeing and the future together and second, by combining expert knowledge and participatory approaches. The expectation was that this would allow the creation of new and useful results.

In the wellbeing sphere, the Organization for Economic Cooperation and Development (OECD) took a lead and organized several World Forums on Statistics, Knowledge and Policy. It recognized that standard indicators such as Gross Domestic Product do not provide a complete picture of wellbeing

(Bergheim, 2006). In 2011 the OECD changed its official claim to 'Better policies for better lives' and published the first 'Better Life Index', one of the most widely used indicator systems (OECD, no date).

Meanwhile, many national projects enhanced the capacity to understand and improve wellbeing. The Australian Bureau of Statistics was one of the frontrunners, publishing the first edition of its *Measures of Australia's Progress* in 2002 (Australian Bureau of Statistics, 2002). In Canada, an academic-led process started in 2004 and developed the Canadian Index of Wellbeing (University of Waterloo, 2016). In France, President Sarkozy established a high-level commission on the Measurement of Economic Performance and Social Progress in 2008, which published its report in late 2009 (Stiglitz, Sen and Fitoussi, 2009). Bhutan developed its Gross National Happiness Index with the help of western academics starting in 2010 (Centre for Bhutan Studies and GNH, 2017). In Germany, several wellbeing measures were constructed, such as the Progress Index (Bergheim, 2010) published by the Center for Societal Progress.

Initially, these projects were driven mostly by statisticians or advocacy organizations with sometimes strong worldviews and had almost no participatory elements. However, questions came up regarding the representativeness, legitimacy and impact of these efforts, so attention turned to ways of involving the public and political decision makers. The idea behind this move towards collective intelligence knowledge creation was to provide a stronger anchoring of visions and indicators, but also to include the potential to create new knowledge and insights (Hall and Rickard, 2013).

Successful participatory wellbeing processes are most advanced at the local and regional levels and in Anglo-Saxon countries. Examples include *Vital Signs* (Vancouver Foundation, 2016), Scotland's *Humankind Index* (Walker et al., 2012) and the now discontinued projects, Jacksonville Indicators and Tasmania Together. They all include elements of dialogue, visions, indicators and actions. They use the future explicitly and are models for the Frankfurt process.

The first attempt to do something similar at the national level was the UK's national wellbeing dialogue, which began in late 2010 (Evans, 2011). Widespread participation was used to create an admirable set of indicators. However, national policymakers did not use the insights as much as was initially hoped for.

Following proposals from the author of this chapter and using insights from the processes just mentioned, the German federal government began its own national wellbeing dialogue in early 2015. Indicators were published in late 2016 (The Federal Government, 2016). The hope is that this structured process will strengthen society's capacity to address cross-cutting issues, that new emerging topics will be identified and that more resources will be directed towards what Germans find important and where the indicators suggest there is a particular need for action.

So, what is wellbeing? It describes the general subjective and objective condition of an individual or a group. Measurement is usually multidimensional. The OECD's Better Life Index includes 24 indicators from 11 topics covering housing, income, jobs, community, education, environment, civic engagement, health, life satisfaction, safety and work-life balance. Other projects at the national and local level mentioned above cover similar topics.

Positive Futures – Forum for Frankfurt: general setup

From the experience of successful local wellbeing processes in other countries and using insights from the change management literature (e.g. Kahane 2012) *Positive Futures – Forum for Frankfurt* was developed. The process was led and coordinated by the non-profit think tank Center for Societal Progress. There was no mandate or funding from the city administration. The process was implemented by a team of volunteers with different experiences ranging from process design, networking, analysis and web-design all the way to writing. The shared task and purpose was to discover and implement new ways to improve the future of their hometown. The design of the process included four core elements (Bergheim, 2015) as shown in Figure 7.1 and described below.

Element 1 – Dialogue: An open dialogue on wellbeing with as many citizens from highly diverse backgrounds as possible was the starting point in *Positive Futures*. The team visited people in their neighbourhoods and held larger events. By asking open questions, listening and asking deeper, the hope was to reach three goals: (1) detect societal patterns including those that are not so visible in current media reports; (2) anchor the whole process within society; and (3) build legitimacy for the outcomes of the later stages.

Element 2 – Visions: The richness of hundreds of answers to our questions (outlined below) was structured into 10 topics. The team created short visions as easy-to-understand summaries of what people said about the Frankfurt in which they would like to live in the year 2030. The hope was that ambitious but realistic shared visions would generate energy to make them real. The visions were formulated in a very general way, knowing that indicators would not be able to cover their full breadth. A first draft of the visions was reviewed and revised at an event with 100 participants.

Element 3 – Indicators: Wellbeing indicators are necessary to compare the preferred future situation with today's reality and identify priorities for action. Identifying the five best indicators for each of the 10 topics was a time-consuming effort, but produced valuable results such as the share of youth binge-drinking or neighbourly help. It was clear from the outset however, that not everyone likes to use indicators. Some people distrust all data, especially if (mis)used as policy objectives. Others have difficulties understanding and interpreting them. As a result, some people moved straight to actions, which was always a possibility as the process in Figure 7.1 illustrates.

Element 4 – Actions: Clear priorities for action emerged during the process where it became clear that living together peacefully and respectfully is the overarching

250 *Stefan Bergheim*

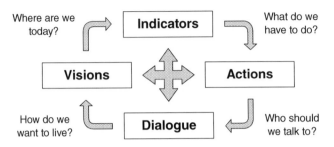

Figure 7.1 Four elements of a quality of life process
Source: Center for Societal Progress, Frankfurt

concern of citizens in Frankfurt. This was later confirmed by the indicators on trust, integration, safety etc. The energy within the team therefore turned to projects that improve the quality of living together: neighbour parties, living room travels[1] and repair cafes. As a small non-profit NGO, our own actions necessarily had to be inexpensive. The hope was that other, better funded organizations and the local government would set their own priorities for actions in the future more in line with the visions and the indicators. There are now some signs of this in the areas of littering in public spaces and traffic noise – both areas that were flagged as priorities by the indicator system.

The design of the process with four core elements was expected to generate at least four valuable outcomes that could serve as enablers of societal change.

1   **Empowerment of individuals**: the capacity of people to think about the future and act accordingly was strengthened in the process. This happened during the dialogue phase, when individuals felt encouraged or motivated to act in order to improve one of the issues they thought was important for their quality of life. Since we were not a resource-rich institution, they could not ask us for help beyond giving some advice. In addition, the actions that emerged also have elements of empowerment, again partly because of financial restrictions. We encouraged people to connect with their neighbours; we facilitated intercultural exchange during the 'living room travels' and we supported them in setting up repair cafes.
2   **Enable new relationships**: during the process, we offered multiple occasions for people from different backgrounds to meet and connect. This ranged from two large events, where participants self-selected into thematic groups, to small events, where leaders from different organizations connected. Several new relationships led to new, co-created projects outside the core team or sometimes even outside the core intention of *Positive Futures*.
3   **Uncover relevant insights**: the events, the visions and the indicators all brought new insights to almost everyone involved. People may have been familiar with some aspects or indicators, but were surprised by others and by the connections across the 10 content topics. For example, links emerged

between drug abuse among youth and the pressure they experience at school and at home.
4   **Update the societal narrative**: the dominant societal narrative in Frankfurt has been that more growth of inhabitants, income and activity is always better. During the process, it became clear that many of the current 700,000 inhabitants suffer from this growth because of increasing anonymity, human disconnection and because of bottlenecks in the traffic infrastructure, in schools and most visibly in housing.

The sponsors of this experiment in collective intelligence knowledge creation were satisfied by the content and connections that emerged. However, no formal evaluation of the process has been conducted and only a small fraction of the 700,000 citizens of Frankfurt has been reached.

Eight design decisions in Positive Futures

Within the general setup of dialogue, visions, indicators and actions, many more design decisions had to be taken. Eight examples highlight our choices as well as other possibilities and their probable consequences. Each example finishes with an attempt at generalizing the implications for collective intelligence knowledge creation processes.

1   **Institutional setup**: for several reasons, we chose to host the process with the small non-profit NGO Center for Societal Progress and to run it as a volunteer project. The main advantage was the Center's competencies with respect to such a process and its neutrality on content. Funding for such a cross-cutting process was not available in 2013 and no other private or governmental organization was ready to act as a host and/or fund the process. Additionally, starting a new organization was seen as too time consuming. After an attempt with a steering group did not lead to sufficient activity, the Director of the Center for Societal Progress (author of this chapter) contacted a number of action-oriented team members and took the lead in the process. The general insight is that an ideal institutional setup for such a collective intelligence process is difficult to find. Compromises have to be made regarding openness on content, the power to attract participation, funding and team size.
2   **Language and illustration**: from the beginning, we aimed for an easy-to-understand language and were aware that illustrations and pictures were crucial to reach a large number of people in Frankfurt. However, at the same time we had to show that the process was a professional and serious activity. Ideally, a spectrum of audience-specific approaches should have been used, ranging from videos and games, postcards and flyers all the way to thick and text-heavy publications. Given limits of time and money, we opted for a single compromise solution.
3   **Questions and content**: from the international wellbeing processes mentioned above it was clear that the Frankfurt process needed to be open

regarding content, and that team members should not impose their own values and priorities on that content. This general principle led some to leave the team or to take on roles that were more in line with their own values. Consistent with the openness on content, four open questions were selected, moving from the personal to the societal level and from the present to the future: What's important to you personally in your life? What constitutes a high quality of life in Frankfurt? What hurts you in the heart, when you think about Frankfurt? Frankfurt in 15 years: which changes would you like to see? Any collective intelligence process is likely to face these issues on questions and on openness.

4. **People involved**: within the core team a broad spectrum of competencies was needed, including trained facilitators, design experts, networkers and data experts. For the dialogues, we made a conscious effort to reach out to the seldom heard voices and visited youth clubs, a home for the elderly, immigrant communities, long-term unemployed, single parents etc. The aim was to achieve a high diversity of backgrounds and perspectives – going well beyond the largely white and university-trained core team – without requiring a statistically accurate representative sample. To get there, we had to tap into the networks of the core team and explored personal and business contacts for different groups. Two groups rejected our approaches, apparently because they thought the project was too supportive of the current systems of governance. Our large events twice drew 100 people with a strong bias towards middle-aged white academics. We also spoke bilaterally about the process with many key decision makers in Frankfurt across the 10 topics, who would not usually participate in bigger events. These people included representatives from the main political parties, the administration, as well as individuals with large networks or special expertise. Our attempts for online interaction did not generate much response. The general insight is that a very large number of people should be involved in such a broad collective intelligence process through a variety of different approaches. Organizing this is time consuming.

5. **Marketing and visibility**: from the start, it was clear that it would be difficult to generate visibility for such a new process which is so open on content and run by a small team of volunteers. Experts from the fields of marketing and communications found it difficult to formulate a clear message that they thought would resonate with the media. Bilateral media-contacts generated positive feedback but little concrete results. The general insight is that such an open collective intelligence process is – at least in Germany and run by a small NGO – not easily marketable. But more visibility clearly would have been helpful both in the initial dialogue phase and in the marketing of the results and the action projects. Maybe this would have attracted more participants and more volunteers into the process, with the hope of making a bigger difference to quality of life in Frankfurt. Also, change takes time and persistence: two significant press reports about the process came out in 2016, well after the indicators were published.

6 **Design of the visions**: based partly on earlier research on successful visioning processes (Bergheim, 2013), we decided that the visions should be for the city of Frankfurt (as opposed to the region or one city district), for the year 2030 (well beyond one electoral period), short (it turned out that even the short text was too long), positive (generating a motivating feel-good factor) and posing a real challenge to society without turning into a utopia. While writing the visions, we struggled, for example, with the issue of combining a clear general direction with enough freedom for each individual. For example, we did not write that people in 2030 would eat 'healthily', but rather 'consciously'.

7 **Choice of indicators**: clear selection criteria for the indicators were developed during the process and in light of other research (Trewin and Hall, 2010). Ideally, the indicators had to be compatible with the visions, outcome-oriented, have a clear preferred direction of change, be modifiable by human activities, understandable by the public, cover the breadth of the visions, be available in real time and ideally as time series. In practice, many compromises were necessary and we even opted for place-holders in case of relevant and feasible indicators, for which no numbers were yet available for Frankfurt. Supporting collective intelligence knowledge creation with indicators appears to be helpful, but one needs to be aware of the limitations. Although there is a common core of indicators in many wellbeing projects, there always will be specific local topics as well as specific local weights and urgencies on comparable topics.

8 **Emergence of actions**: actions emerged during the whole process. Some came up already during the dialogues, others during research and conversations on the material generated during the dialogues. For example, a dialogue participant told us of her neighbourhood festivity and the motivations behind it. This resonated strongly with what we had heard in other dialogues, so we supported her in spreading the idea. Another example includes a team-member researching activities that can promote the quality of living together. She discovered the 'living room travels' in another city. At our second large event, we found volunteers who then brought these travels to Frankfurt. During the overall process, we developed criteria for actions that would be supported by the team of Positive Futures: they would have to be compatible with the visions, ideally help improve at least one indicator and should be possible to implement across Frankfurt.

Mostly because of scarce resources of time and money, but also in the interest of limiting the size of the overall process, other design options were not discussed during the process. Some more reframing might have been useful to enhance collective knowledge creation. In particular, we stayed with one vision for each topic, knowing that this was a limiting decision. We could have run a scenario workshop to open up the thinking even more. This could have created valuable insights to make the visions more robust and to include indicators relevant in the non-preferred futures.

Seven challenges for Positive Futures

While the overall process of 'dialogue – visions – indicators – actions' proved to be valuable and created many new insights, some general restrictions and challenges for collective intelligence knowledge creation processes became visible.

- Some people see no need and no legitimacy for a citizen-led process to discuss societal priorities in the current form of representative democracy. However, we see quality of life processes as a much-needed addition to representative democracy to give room for new and specific insights generated from the interaction of different individuals. They also promote citizens' self-empowerment.
- There was also an urge to opt for simpler processes and for more narrow issues. We appreciate this urge, but also think that complex modern societies exhibit many attributes and interlinkages, which are not appreciated and explored enough.
- Others wanted to jump straight to action. This was widespread in the process and easy to understand. However, we see the search process to generate visions and indicators as providing a potentially wider and more solid basis for the choice of actions, given scarce resources of time and money.
- During the large events, participants showed different levels of abstraction. While some wanted to discuss more philosophical issues of society, others wanted to learn what they could do themselves the next day to improve the situation of Frankfurt.
- There was also the well-known impulse to turn to experts for answers. Indeed, expert knowledge was helpful in the process at many stages. But it has to be closely linked to what citizens see as important and to their own role as change agents. And it is well-known that experts are not necessarily the best source for help in complex systems. Rather, participants' capacity to understand their complex environment has to be enhanced as well as their ability to act in it.
- The organizational silos and hierarchies with their roles and expectations limit the potential for individuals to engage in such an open process. We nevertheless see the need and the potential for dialogue and for capacity building. This is a way to improve people's ability to use the future in order to act in the present.
- Many actors have their own projects, which they want to or have to push in this process. We appreciate the efforts of all these actors, but also allow the possibility that some projects turn out to be less helpful than others in a quality of life process – independent of the strength of the voices behind them. Furthermore, we wanted to provide room for experimentation and for the emergence of new projects.

Summary

Despite several challenges and limitations, this two-year collective intelligence knowledge creation process was worth the effort. Using the future was particularly effective at helping to create shared meaning, new insights and new relationships that can enhance wellbeing. Visions provide a positive picture of the future. Indicators help improve the basis for making decisions regarding scarce resources of time and money. Action projects are helping to move Frankfurt in the desired direction. This four-step process is more time consuming and more costly than traditional methods of desk research or panel discussions. However, the benefits outlined above outweigh those costs. We hope that the insights and background provided here and in our manual (Bergheim, 2015) encourage others to share their own insights on similar processes and provide an impulse for newly emerging processes at the corporate, local, regional or national levels.

Note

1 In German this is called *Weltreise durch Wohnzimmer*. A person who is not born in Germany (the 'travel guide') opens their living room for about two hours for a group of up to 10 people (the 'travellers') and tells them something about his/her country of origin. This way travellers learn about different cultures without having to travel to distant places.

References

Australian Bureau of Statistics (2002) *Measuring Australia's Progress*. Canberra: Commonwealth of Australia.
Bergheim, S. (2006) *Measures of Well-Being*. Frankfurt: Deutsche Bank Research. Available at: http://fortschrittszentrum.de/dokumente/Bergheim_2006-Measures_of_well-being.pdf (Accessed: 23 Jan 2018).
Bergheim, S. (2010) *The Progress Index*. Frankfurt: Center for Societal Progress.
Bergheim, S. (2013) 'Die Kraft gesellschaftlicher Visionen'. [The power of societal visions]. Frankfurt: Zentrum für gesellschaftlichen Fortschritt. Available online at: http://fortschrittszentrum.de/dokumente/2013-08_SA_Synthese.pdf (Accessed: 23 Jan 2018).
Bergheim, S. (2015) *Quality of Life Processes – A Manual*. Frankfurt: Center for Societal Progress.
Centre for Bhutan Studies and GNH (2017) *Gross National Happiness*. Available at: http://www.grossnationalhappiness.com/category/survey-report/ (Accessed: 2 October 2017).
Evans, J. (2011) *Findings from the National Well-being Debate*. London: Office of National Statistics, UK.
Hall, J. and Rickard, L. (2013) *People, Progress, Participation. How Initiatives Measuring Social Progress Yield Benefits Beyond Better Metrics*. Gutersloh: Bertelsmann Stiftung.
Kahane, A. (2012) *Transformative Scenario Planning; Working Together to Change the Future*. San Francisco, CA: Berrett-Koehler Publishers.
OECD (no date) *OECD Better Life Index*. Available at: http://www.oecdbetterlifeindex.org/#/11111111111 (Accessed: 2 October 2017).
Stiglitz, J. E., Sen, A. and Fitoussi, J.-P. (2009) *Report by the Commission on the Measurement of Economic Performance and Social Progress*. Paris: Government of the French Republic.
The Federal Government (2016) *Bericht der Bundesregierung zur Lebensqualität in Deutschland*. Frankfurt: The Federal Government.

Trewin, D. and Hall, J. (2010) *Developing Societal Progress Indicators: A Practical Guide*. Paris: OECD Publishing.

University of Waterloo (2016) *How are Canadians Really Doing? The 2016 CIW National Report*. Waterloo: University of Waterloo.

Vancouver Foundation (2016) *Vital Signs*. Available at: vancouverfoundationvitalsigns.ca/.

Walker, P., Mihaelson, J., Strauss, K. and Trebeck, K. (2012) *Oxfam Humankind Index for Scotland – Background, Methodology, Consultation and Report*. Oxford: Oxfam GB.

8 Gender and the future
Reframing and empowerment

Ivana Milojević

Introduction: asking questions

Is gender a significant factor impacting anticipation? Is it a factor that should be taken into account within the discipline, theory and practice of anticipation? And if yes, how could this factor be used within the practice of *using the future* or when *doing* foresight and anticipation?

Some 15 years ago, Goldstein (2001, p. 57) conducted thorough research within the field of peace studies and concluded that not only does gender continue to be "invisible in political science and history as well as within peace theorising", but also that those who pay attention to the issue of gender are nearly all women. Furthermore, "all gender references concern women; men still do not have gender" (2001, p. 35). So instead of immediately making an argument in terms of the invisibility or visibility of gender within the fields of futures studies/ foresight or the discipline of anticipation perhaps readers may wish to conduct their own research, asking: (1) is gender commonly addressed within these fields/ disciplines?; (2) if so, what is the gender of those asking/talking/writing about gender-related questions?; and, (3) do gender references concern mostly women or men as well? Finally, and most importantly, do these discourses go beyond the *women and men dichotomy*, and are they in line with 21st-century changes in both global gender regimes as well as in our contemporary understanding of gender itself?

Doing future, doing gender

It is commonly acknowledged that the future does not yet exist; however, upon closer examination, we can see that the future has already been colonised. It is filled with our expectations, hopes and dreams, or alternatively, fears and nightmares. Subsequently, these ideas and images of the future shape our decisions and actions in the present moment. We believe certain futures to be more or less likely, and adjust our thinking or behaving accordingly. By all rational accounts, the future is not predetermined and cannot thus be known or predicted. Yet it is neither an empty space nor an impotent element; rather, it is an active principle in the present. We simply cannot act without using the notion of the future or futures in some way. It is our repertoire of future imaginings that sets direction, gives meaning and makes sense of our very existence. Moreover, not everything is possible or plausible in the future, though many things are. This is because the future is influenced partly by, on the one hand, history, social structures and the current reality, and, on the other hand, by chance, innovation and human choice. The future does not yet exist, and by its very definition it never will, and yet the concept is at the very core of our human functioning and identity. We feel superior to the other species that cannot so well plan and anticipate; we take pride in being able to engage in strategy and design, and to implement early interventions to avert disasters. Other species, we believe, can mostly react and/or adapt to the changing conditions which they did not themselves create. While our species is notorious for also waiting for habitual responses to hit a dead end before we change, we take solace knowing that there is at the very least a possibility of transforming before it is too late, and well in time to produce more beneficial outcomes for most of us.

Contrary to this, it is commonly acknowledged that *men* and *women* do exist; however, upon closer examination we can see that these categories are mostly invented. In certain historical periods and places men wore make up and skirts, and some still do. Women waged wars and ran states, and some continue to do so. Even in hyper-masculine cultural spaces, men sometimes cry, because 'nature' or physiology has provided them with a tear duct. And even in hyper-feminine cultural spaces, women sometimes abandon their children, in spite of the 'natural' maternal instinct allegedly given to all who give birth. These facts, however, have not stopped our societies from imagining what the only 'right', possible or normative/desired activity or appearance is for those assigned 'women' or 'men' labels. From our very births, we are prescribed future pathways which, more commonly than not, limit our life experiences and possibilities. Based on our 'prescribed' gender, we are then told about our own limits, duties, future roles and responsibilities, and indeed, how to engage with the future itself.

In the realm of the symbolic, for example, the two standard and in our globalised world, universally accepted symbols denoting female ♀ and male ♂ tell a very different story of two genders in relation to *doing* futures. From many secret symbols that celebrated the power of women and female principles, the symbol of Venus, representing love and sexuality, was chosen for women. Its differentiation from the male symbol and its essence is in the cross below, the cross which, especially if surrounded with the circle, has traditionally been the symbol for the Earth. The men's symbol, the sign of Mars – god of war – has its essence in the arrow: a symbol often viewed as a phallic symbol and as a weapon of war. In the male symbol, the arrow is pointed upright, which is how we commonly draw trends and movements towards the future. Such symbolism implies on the one hand, that the role of women is that of conservers, deeply rooted in the ground, with their essence in the body. Men, on the other hand, are expected to be the ones who transcend their mind, and to be in charge of the future. They are 'the chosen ones' who bring about social, technological and political changes, anticipate where power will move next and preach radically new prophecies.

From sociological, ethnographic and anthropological research, we also learn that historically, and specifically within patriarchal societies, women have been commonly viewed as unchanging essence independent of time, place and social context, relegated to the private sphere of family. In that same context, men were prescribed the role of 'culture agents', the heroic envoys who created civilisation and the public sphere, as well as superiority, hierarchy and dominance. In this context, the 'realistic' future is seen to be the one that maintains this dichotomy and superiority.

It is thus often techno-maniacal and/or dystopian colonisations of the future that are seen as realistic, far-reaching and even logical. When the women's liberation movement threw a challenge to such imaginings and started creating a view of the future based on an alternative reading of gender and gender relationships, they were, and still often are, labelled unrealistic, naïve and utopian. To this day, such thinking is applied to all 'feminine' futures – defined as those diametrically opposite to the 'realistic' futures described above – irrespective of whether these alternative renderings are proposed by women or men. In other words, partnership approaches intended to create more gentle or SHE (sane, humane, and ecological) societies (Eisler, 2001; Boulding, 1976; Robertson, 1980) continue to be marginalised. Instead, HE (hyper-expansionist) or BAU (business as usual) futures, which are sometimes associated with catastrophic or collapse scenarios, continue to be assumed and even expected by global mainstream and dominant discourses about the future.

There is a profusion of evidence to support this interpretation: from the multitude of catastrophic and violent events reported in the news to the dystopic mainstream science fiction futures imaginings – in both cases, and by implication, the future remains bleak. The future continues to be gendered in a very specific and rather conservative way. For example, the three most pressing challenges of our time and for our collective future – ecological, economic and violence related – are also a consequence of previous patriarchal gender arrangements. In the field of gender studies in general, and ecofeminism in particular, research has long established that the nature–culture differentiation in patriarchal societies has been imagined along gender lines. First, women were seen as somehow 'closer' to nature. Second, as women were devalued so was the natural world deemed inferior to human civilisation. Similarly, the assigned role for men was to control, dominate and subdue nature, women included. Cultures and civilisations that had a different approach to the human–nature connection were made invisible and marginalised, and/or colonised.

A similar dichotomy was applied to the sphere of economy – based on measuring 'productive' vs. 'unproductive' work, the first being paid work in the formal economy, even if it meant employment in life destroying industries (e.g. weapons manufacturing, sale and use). Caring work within the *love economy* (i.e. raising of children and managing households) upon which the formal economy rests, was discounted, taken for granted and underappreciated. Recent changes in gender relationships have only slightly dented these structural arrangements. Women have entered the sphere of 'productive' work while simultaneously, and usually, remaining the main workers within the love economy. The incentive for men entering the latter economy is low, given that irrespective of whether it is done by men or women, this type of work structurally remains free from financial rewards and continues to be invisible to mainstream economics. Lastly, perpetual warfare, militarisation and violent conflict have been gendered in a similar way. The distinction between life-giver-maintainer (i.e. parent) and life-taker (i.e. soldier) has been mostly along female/male lines. The 'doing of gender' remains one among several key variables, if not the key variable, in the 'doing of war/peace'.

On the other hand, where a minimum of gender-role differentiation is imagined or practised, it is usually accompanied by a minimum of overall dominance patterns taking place. It is thus this new vision, a different vision based on different values and a change in power relationships, including a change in the social construction of gender identities – grounded "no longer in dominance and submission but in harmonised acceptance of differences" – which has one of the highest potentials of bringing about "harmony and future of life and hope, instead of wars [nature destruction, severe economic exploitation] and nuclear holocaust" (Accad, 2000, p. 1987). So if we are to address these three most pressing challenges of our time – ecological, economic and violence related – all closely linked to how we 'colonise' and anticipate the future – we also need to address the gendered imaginings behind them.

Developing futures and gendered literacy

These previous examples notwithstanding, the world as well as our common understanding of gender and gender relationships has been changing. First, there is a change in how we see or understand the notion of gender itself. Developments in feminist and gender theories (Butler, 1990) have focused on the performativity of gender; that is, on gender as something that we do rather than who we are. Gender in gender studies is understood as distinct from one's biological sex, the former term denoting social practices by which specific gendered orders are established and maintained and the latter denoting male/female physiology and biology. Women and men are, in social theory, no longer seen as existing ontologically, objectively, sui generis, a priori, generically and ahistorically. Rather, this binary division has been replaced by a multitude of visible genders which are seen as existing epistemologically, culturally and psychologically and via a daily practice of reaffirming socially constructed gender roles, identities and discourses. This is critically important because an understanding of gender as a social construction also means that dominant constructions could be deconstructed, reconstructed and alternatives enhanced and developed. Through the creation and re-creation of our gender identities and behaviours we construct both ourselves as well as our societies and the present-future world(s). Here lies the liberatory potential for our futures, a promise and a hope of a transformation towards better worlds.

However, these theoretical developments are not yet accepted as a shared understanding of gender within mainstream gender discourses in wider society. That is, "many people [continue to] imagine masculinity, femininity and

Gender and the future   261

gender relations only in terms of their own local gender system" (Connell, 2009, p. ix). They therefore simultaneously "miss the vast diversity of gender patterns across cultures and down history" (Connell, 2009, p. ix). This is why one's own local gender system still often appears natural, ahistorical, universal or even 'God given'.

Globalisation and new information technologies are currently both forcing us out of such locally grounded myopias as well as reinforcing them. On one hand, we now collectively know more, including knowing more about the alternative social and gender arrangements through time and space. On the other, the 'Filter Bubble' phenomenon (Pariser, 2011) enhances our confirmation biases and specific communal preconceptions and thus limits our awareness and choices. These two contradictory occurrences are expected to continue and become even stronger in the future. We will most likely know more overall in the future and will be able to find desired information very quickly, but the knowing will be bounded by the doing of what feels emotionally comfortable and safe.

Parallel to the evolution and stagnation of our gendered understandings, the actual role of genders in contemporary societies is likewise evolving under pressure from cultural, economic, religious and socio-political factors. It is well recognised that different cultures engage with the future differently. Gender, as part of the cultural landscape, also influences how that engagement takes place. Changes in the global economy, for example, are disrupting the myth of provider vs. home maker and the actual ways different genders engage with current economic conditions. Family wages are all but gone and jobs requiring manual strength are being increasingly replaced by automation of work. Jobs in the service and caring industries are on the rise in most places, simultaneously changing the gendered composition of local and migrant workers. New digital technologies also allow for a multitude of gendered expressions – where physical identity can be masked, seen as only one of possible selves – inherently increasing the fluidity of doing gender. As was the case with understandings of gender discussed in the previous paragraph, here too there are contradictory forces at play. On one hand, 'the real' as well as the 'digital' world demands recognition of what has always been human experience – that of multiple and fluid gender diversities. On the other hand, there are various forms of backlash and 'back to the past' efforts which are pushing in a diametrically opposite direction. There are, of course, arguments why such push back is preferential, better for most (i.e. for 'families' – here read nuclear or traditional patriarchal families), even 'natural'. However, more gender equitable worldviews have always allowed for the expression of multiple gender diversities but supressed, even severely penalised by death, within more totalitarian and fundamentalist systems of thought and societies. If we are to create a better world in the future, it is the former rather than the latter that needs to be enhanced.

To add to the uncertainty and fragility of creating better futures we can see that three main scenarios of arranging gender regimes (Milojević, 1998) are all currently happening simultaneously (Table 8.1). There are places which continue to insist on strict male/female polarity, those that promote unisex androgyny and then more open and flexible mindsets comfortable with multiple gender diversities. The first scenario of male/female polarity is the most widespread, still the 'common sense' approach to gendered understanding. In line with its essence, this approach insists that not only women and men see the future differently, but that it is men's seeing that is of more value. The second scenario is pushed by, for example, liberal feminist or communist ideologies of the past, and though fading, is finding some sort of resurrection in our digital era of postgenderism and transhumanist imaginings. In a nutshell, the unisex androgyny scenario asserts that we all see the future irrespective of gender; that is, that gender is not or should not be a variable. This scenario is sometimes extenuated by either technological or spiritual imaginings of genderless techno and/or spiritual beings. These imaginings portray the future beyond gender; the future where this category either does not exist at all or is completely irrelevant.

Lastly, the third scenario assumes different views of the future by different, multiple genders, based on their interaction with history, present environment and both natural and cultural influences. It also assigns them an equal value and asserts the importance of learning from all these multiple gendered perspectives. The proponents of the third scenario, including myself, argue that achieving gender equity and celebrating multiple gender diversities is the very basis and crucial ingredient for the creation of a transformed and better world. In other words, as long as gendered fluidity is repressed and penalised, and as long as our future imaginings are based on one-dimensional gender identities where 'men are men' and 'women are women', our future presents will remain stifled and limiting. Therefore, the process of transforming futures and of anticipating differently is not and cannot be separated from the process in which we engage collectively in more positive and flexible gender-based understandings and arrangements.

Using the future differently

While the previous discussion may sound abstract and overly theoretical to some readers, the application of these new understandings can be quite simple and straightforward.

Table 8.1 Three gendered scenarios for the future

Scenarios	Gender arrangements	Value	Social arrangements
Traditional	Two genders. Strict male/female polarity.	Men and masculinity more valuable.	Hierarchical, oppressive to the marginalised.
Androgyny	One gender or genderless.	Equal but under the male norm.	Pressure to conform to the norm.
Multiple gender plurality	Multiple genders. Gender diversity, multiplicity.	Equal valuing of all genders.	Equalitarian, democratic, open societies, fluid.

One concrete application is an education project that focused on an alternative cognitive frame to the one based on dichotomous and hierarchical arrangements described previously in the chapter. This alternative cognitive frame envisions a present/future society marked by gender equality, simultaneously challenging all other social hierarchies and focusing on the centrality of human relatedness, valuing peace, justice and life.

As a starting point, the project engaged with traditional stories studied in schools in Serbia and beyond, and while recognising the aesthetic and cultural values of the stories, it challenged various gendered and cultural dichotomies. These include: (1) representation of young women as victims, passive, sleeping beauties who wait for the prince to wake them up and save them (Cinderella, Red Riding Hood, Snow White, Beauty and the Beast, Little Mermaid); (2) representation of older women as evil and dangerous (evil witches, fairies, queens, step-mothers) especially for young women whom they are trying to destroy; (3) representation of men as warriors; and (4) stories directly or indirectly advocating violence against women and creating prejudice against marginalised groups (the story Magical Language, the poem Building of Skadar). Gender-based, racial and national stereotypes are preserved in a number of these traditional European and Serbian stories. Selfishness, cruelty, spitefulness and manipulations are often common characteristics of 'the heroes' and the methods they use to achieve their personal goals. Revenge instead of reconciliation, forgiveness and dialogue is also a common theme. Often other nations are presented as enemies and not as collaborators and potential friends. These stories – chosen for deconstruction within the project – are all part of what has been termed "destructive storytelling" (Senehi, 2010) expressed in folklore, stories, songs, national epics, proverbs and fairy tales, including in various futures imaginings. Destructive storytelling portrays humans as "bad, cruel, violent and selfish", stories are commonly "full of cruelty, trickery and violence" (Eisler, 2001), including violence against women, children and those who are deemed "different" (Eisler, 2001). Such storytelling is part of the "dominator" mindset (Eisler, 2000), the same mindset pushing towards HE or BAU futures – and which has been challenged from the margins for decades by those of all genders wishing to enhance SHE futures and to establish SHE presents.

Intervention into the previously described discourse was also done via a medium of storytelling that retold these traditional, widely known stories. Storytelling was chosen because it has been shown to be a powerful, flexible, accessible and inexpensive method when working with youth – including being "a more indirect and respectful rather than prescriptive and didactic method" (Senehi, 2010) of communicating new ideas. By providing alternative descriptions of societies and gendered arrangements among the protagonists, the stories worked indirectly on developing both futures and gender awareness and literacy. For many children and even some adults, it was the first time they were exposed to the notion that "the other world is possible", if only as a seed, an image and an idea. The retold stories were based on the principles of "constructive storytelling", described as "inclusive, [which] fosters shared power and mutual recognition, creates opportunities for openness, dialogue, and insight, brings issues to consciousness, can be a means of resistance . . . and an important means for establishing a culture of peace and justice" (Senehi, 2010).

The retold stories reflected values of a democratic, pluralistic and inclusive culture, as well as partnership/gentle/SHE futures for both genders as well as society as a whole. Further, they provided an implicit critique of less desirable, and directly and indirectly violent, ways of behaving and communicating based on traditional dichotomous and hierarchical worldview. They provided an explicit description of more desired ways of behaving and communicating and educated about viable and preferable alternatives based on diversity and inclusion. They also promoted a dialogue and critical literacy, including critical futures literacy, among children – specifically asking questions in terms of how to make informed choices between alternative ways of behaving and communicating with others; and how to make best choices about multiple alternative futures.

Active participation of youth was critical in the final process of creating new stories in which they themselves became the creators of plots and meanings. In this process they engaged with the age-old question of the interaction between social structure and human agency and the role of power in making of knowledge. Practical strategies for further stimulating dialogical approaches and critical literacy when working with students included design of specific embodied activities, arts-based undertakings and games for children. To give a brief idea of the cognitive input and the narratives employed the following summaries of some retold stories is provided in Figure 8.1.

In summary, the retold stories tell of different possible future pathways that expand our gendered life experiences and possibilities. Gendered limits were questioned and future roles and responsibilities, including how to engage with the future itself, were given more flexibility and fluidity. The alternatives created did not stop with the first phase of retelling as later engagement saw teachers, parents, students and whole schools create their own narratives for radically transformed and empowered futures. The students, now authors of new stories themselves, composed texts that commonly went beyond traditional dichotomies and hierarchies and which were then presented to the whole school community (Milojević and Izgarjan, 2014). At the end of the project, the multitude of stories for different presents and improved futures came into being. Follow-up analysis showed that not only was the mindset of those involved expanded, and their gender/future literacy enhanced, there were also changes in actual behaviour and a number of actionable steps taken in the direction of creating more positive presents/future.

Conclusion: gender, future and new avenues to empowerment

The development of a better, more inclusive, equitable, ecologically sustainable and peaceful world throughout the 21st century is directly premised on the re-making of traditional and patriarchal gender identities. We cannot create new, better futures, without creating new, better gender identities and arrangements. We cannot anticipate differently if old cultural templates still limit our

Gender and the future 265

Figure 8.1 Examples of retold story narratives

imaginings based on narrowly prescribed gender categories. This is because old identities based on dichotomous hierarchies have been complicit in creating hierarchies of domination; of devaluing human life and nature. Revaluing nature, peace and sharing and the love economy goes hand in hand with the revaluing of previously suppressed genders and their contribution to the world. The closing of various gender gaps and work on equality for all genders is therefore paramount if we are to make more informed choices for our future, including more informed choices about our own gender-based identities and behaviours.

On the one hand, there are some indications that current global developments will indeed lead to more inclusive and equitable futures. The globalisation of human, women's and LGBTQ rights discourses, the rise in ecological awareness, flattened networks via social media and digital technologies, increases in peer to peer global communication and the influence of postmodern as well as feminist theories will continue to push towards such futures. On the other hand, economic and ecological collapse, increases in social conservatism and fundamentalism, various forms of backlash against socially progressive movements and ideas will continue to act as both our 'weight of history' and a detrimental pull towards inequitable futures.

As is always the case, any future is premised on actions by humans at present, and dependent on their beliefs about which particular visions of the future are preferable for themselves and the groups to which they belong. Actions by various individuals, groups, communities and societies will remain diverse, conflicting and pulling towards different futures both equitable and inequitable. Hope remains that individuals and groups working towards equitable futures in general and equitable gender futures in particular will prevail eventually, bringing about a better world benefiting most.

For this to happen, enhancing futures and gendered literacy and the awareness of how we *do futures and gender* is the first step in that direction.

References

Cited in the text

Accad, E. (2000) 'Violence and Peace: Overview', in Kramarae, C. and Spender, D. (eds) *Routledge International Encyclopedia of Women: Global Women's Issues and Knowledge*. London: Routledge, pp. 1986–1991.

Boulding, E. (1976) *The Underside of History: A View of Women through Time*. Boulder, CO: Westview Press.

Butler, J. (1990) *Gender Trouble: Feminism and the Subversion of Identity*. New York: Routledge.

Connell, R. (2009) *Gender (Polity Short Introductions)*. Cambridge: Polity.

Eisler, R. (2001) *Tomorrow's Children: A Blueprint for Partnership Education in the 21st Century*. Boulder, CO: Westview Press.

Goldstein, J. S. (2001) *War and Gender: How Gender Shapes the War System and Vice Versa*. Cambridge: Cambridge University Press.

Milojević, I. (1998) 'Learning from Feminist Futures', in *1998 World Yearbook for Education*. London: Kogan Page, pp. 83–95.

Milojević, I. and Izgarjan, A. (2014) 'Creating Alternative Futures through Storytelling: A Case Study from Serbia', *Futures*, 57(1), pp. 51–61.

Pariser, E. (2011) *The Filter Bubble: What the Internet Is Hiding from You*. New York: Penguin Press.

Robertson, J. (1980) *The Sane Alternative: A Choice of Futures*. St Paul, Minnesota: River Basin Publishing.

Senehi, J. (2010) 'Storytelling and Peace', in Young, J. B. (ed.) *The Oxford International Encyclopedia of Peace*. Oxford: Oxford University Press.

Gender and the future 267

Previous publications by the author informing this chapter

Milojević, I. (1999) 'Feminising Futures Studies', in Z. Sardar (Ed.), *Rescuing All Our Futures*. Twickenham, England: Adamantine Press, pp. 61–72.

Milojević, I. (2008) 'Developing Futures Literacy', in S. Inayatullah, M. Bussey and I. Milojević, (Eds.), *Alternative Futures of Education: Pedagogies for Emergent Worlds*. Rotterdam: Sense Publishers, pp. 305–314.

Milojević, I. (2011) 'Gender Issues', *World Affairs*, 15(4), pp. 68–75.

Milojević, I. (2012) 'Why the Creation of a Better World Is Premised on Achieving Gender Equity and on Celebrating Multiple Gender Diversities', *Journal of Futures Studies*, 16(4), pp. 51–66.

Milojević, I. (2013) *Breathing In Violence, Out Peace*. Brisbane: University of Queensland Press.

Glossary

AA Anticipatory Assumptions – the elements that make up the different frames that people use when consciously imagining the future

Kinds of AA:

AfF Anticipation-for-the-future. (AA1 to AA4) 'Using-the-future' to prepare or plan for the future, typically on the basis of closed or semi-closed anticipatory systems, probabilistic and normative. See Chapter 1

- AA1: Closed/AfF and General-Scalable: 'Forecasting'. Totalising deterministic imagination. *Doing. Colonisation of tomorrow. Insurance for tomorrow.*
- AA2: Closed/AfF and Specific-Unique: 'Destiny'. *Doing. Atrophy of the imagination. Fatalism.*
- AA3: Semi-closed/AfF and General-Scalable: 'Creative Reform'. *Deterministic creative imagination. Doing. Slogan: 'Make a Difference'.*
- AA4: Semi-closed/AfF and Specific-Unique: 'Self-improvement'. *Introspective adaptive imagination. Doing. Slogan: 'Consciousness raising'.*

AfE Anticipation-for-emergence. (AA5 and AA6) 'Using-the-future' to understand the present on the basis of non-deterministic anticipatory systems, semi-open AA, non-probabilistic, non-normative. See Chapter 1

- AA5: Semi-open/AfE and General-Scalable: 'Strategic Thinking'. *Combines doing and not-doing imagination related to general-scalable repetition.*
- AA6: Semi-open/AfE and Specific-Unique: 'Wisdom–Tao–Being'. *Combines doing and not-doing imagination related to specific-unique difference as being.*

Action-Learning A wide range of learning-by-doing methodologies for exploring and developing capabilities across a wide range of fields/topics

APF Association of Professional Futurists

ASP Anticipatory systems and processes. Describing anticipation involves describing ASP

AS/AST Anticipatory systems/Anticipatory Systems Theory. Originating from the work of Robert Rosen, also see Roberto Poli and Aloisius Louie, anticipatory systems are viewed as part of all living organisms and serve as the

Glossary 269

conceptual starting point for exploring different kinds of future as anticipation. See Introduction, Chapter 1, Chapter 2

CDES Centre for the Law and Economics of Sport

CGEE Centre for Strategic Studies and Management, Brazil

CIKC Collective Intelligence Knowledge Creation processes involve groups generating knowledge together, often through some form of learning-by-doing process that enables people to sense and make-sense of phenomena together

CLA Causal Layered Analysis is a method for thinking about the future invented by Sohail Inayatullah

Conscious Anticipation Is distinguished from non-conscious anticipation that occurs in living organisms but without them being 'aware' of it

COP 21 United Nations Climate Change Conference 2015

CoP Community of Practice: Is a term for a group or network of people who do things together on the basis of shared norms and practices

COST European Cooperation in Science and Technology

DoA Discipline of Anticipation: The term for the underlying theory of the future as anticipation

DPDS Directorate of Programming and Strategic Development

EU European Union

FL Futures Literacy. Is a human capability that consists of the ability to use anticipation for different ends, in different ways and in different contexts. People become more futures literate as they gain a better understanding of the diversity of anticipatory assumptions

FLF Futures Literacy Framework. A set of categories along two axes, ontological and epistemological, that describe different AA that make up different aspects of FL. The FLF also covers non-conscious anticipation, which is not part of FL

FLL Futures Literacy Laboratories. FLL are actually a design meta-framework for implementing different specific FLL that address different sets of AA. At the most general level FLL consist of CIKC processes that explicitly integrate anticipatory systems and processes (ASP) into the design. Thus FLL=CIKC + ASP. An example of applying the FLL design meta-framework is the Futures Literacy Laboratories- Novelty (FLL-N)

FLL-N Futures Literacy Laboratories-Novelty. Is an FLL process designed to cover all six AA, from AA1 to AA6

FMM Foresight Maturity Model

FS Futures Studies

FSF Futures Studies Forum for Africa and the Middle East, http://www.foresightfordevelopment.org/fsf/

FuMee The Futures Meeting Network, http://www.fumee.org/

GS General-Scalable. Is a category for describing the world using common denominators or universals. GS is a category in the Futures Literacy Framework (FLF) used to describe different sets of AA that make up FL as a capability

ICF MACRO ICF Macro Inc.

INSPECT Innovation, Natural, Social, Political, Economic/Environmental, Cultural, Technological

IOF International Organization of Francophones

Glossary

IRES Royal Institute of Strategic Studies, Morocco
JPI Joint Programming Initiative on Cultural Heritage, European Commission
KCP Knowledge Creation Process. Any general process for creating knowledge, used in this book as the general epistemological category in the FLF
KnowLab Knowledge Laboratory, a CIKC process
LIS Learning Intensive Society
LSE Local Scoping Exercise. Terminology deployed at the outset of the UNESCO FL Project
MENA Middle East and North Africa
MESGO Executive Master in European Sport Governance, http://www.mesgo.org/
MoHCDGEC Ministry of Health Community Development Gender Elderly and Children of Tanzania
MOST Management of Social Transformation, is a UNESCO programme
MSTI The Brazilian Ministry of Science, Technology and Innovation
NA North-Africa
NBS The Tanzanian National Bureau of Statistics
NESPAP National Education Systems and Policies in Asia Pacific
NGO Non-Governmental Organization
NIS The Brazilian National Innovation System
OECD Organization for Economic Cooperation for Development
R&D Research & Development
RED ORMET Red de Observatorios Regionales de Mercado de Trabaio
SENA The Colombian National Apprenticeship Service
SHS Social and Human Sciences Sector, UNESCO
SID Society for International Development
SIVA Industrial Development Corporation of Norway
SRA Strategic Research Agenda
STI Science, Technology and Innovation
SU Specificity-Unique
UEFA Union of European Football Associations
UNDP United Nations Development Program
UNESCO United Nations Educational, Scientific, and Cultural Organization
UNIDO United Nations Industrial Development Organization
WFSF World Futures Studies Federation

Index

Note: Page numbers in *italics* denote figures.

abstraction 104
accountability 55
action learning 17, 34, 36–37, 38, 39–40, 42–43, 69
Africa Horizon 2035 195–204
Agenda 2030 9
age progression 15–16
Akomolafe, B. 184–187
All Africa Futures Forum 161–168
alternative cognitive frame 263–264
anticipation: future expressed through 19–20; impact of 2
anticipation-for-emergence (AfE) 20, 22–23, 26–27, 33, 54, 67, 105
anticipation-for-the-future (AfF) 20–23, 26, 32–33, 39, 41, 54, 67, 105
anticipatory assumptions (AA): clusters of 23, *24*, 31–34; description of 24; exploration of 4–5, 15; FLL and 70, 97–99; FLL-N and 5–8, 95–96, 100; FS and 41–44; gathering evidence of 35–36; in Sierra Leone case study 16, 17
Anticipatory Capability Profile (ACP) 62
anticipatory democracy 233
Anticipatory Governance theory 135
anticipatory systems (AS): AA and 5–6; description of 72; FLF and 25; research on 18; theory of 1–2, 17, 53; types of 20, 27
anti-planning paradigm 58
Archetypal Core 71, 75, 83–84
Archetypal Memory 83
Arellano, A. 173
ArtCenter College of Design 239
Art of Conjecture (De Jouvenel) 51
aspirations round 102

assessment 57–58
Athena scenario 114–115

Bateson, G. 19, 25
BAU futures 259, 263
being 33–34
'Being versus begins' distinction 20
Bell, W. 51
Bellettini Cedeño, O. 173
Bennett, J.W. 53
Berger, G. 167
Better Life Index 248–249
Bishop, P.C. 62
Brazil 119–130
Brazilian National Innovation System (NIS) 119

Candy, S. 239
capability component 62–63
categories, social systems and 75–76
category theory 70, 71, 72–74, 75–76, 87
Causal Layered Analysis (CLA) process 103, 128–129, 135, 149, 156, 208–211, 218
Center for Societal Progress 249, 251
Center for the Law and Economics of Sport (CDES) 154
Centre for Strategic Studies and Management (CGEE) 119, 120, 129–130
choice scenarios *193*
closed system anticipation 25, 32, 59, 74
co-creation 117–118
Cognitive Development, Theory of 18
colimit 76
collective intelligence knowledge creation (CIKC): choice of 96; FLL and 69–76, 98–99; FL-MES and 82–87; introduction to 66–69; MES and 69–82;

272 Index

project design and 17, 37–38, 39–41, 100–101, 107–108; wellbeing and 247
collective learning approach 34
Colombia 131–139, 172
comparison and contrast exercise 105–106
Complexification-Decomplexification Process (CDP) 81–83, 85, 86
complexity 37, 60–61, 62, 66–67, 79–80
complexity theory 17, 18, 22, 71
complicated problems 60–61
composition law 76
concretization 104
confirmation bias 261
contingency 59–60
Coral Cross 235
co-regulators 76, 81, 82
creative reform 32
cultural diversity 115
cultural heritage research case study 110–118

Dator, J. 236, 239
decision making 119
degeneracy 80
De Jouvenel, B. 51
Delphi method 59, 109
depth 56, 241
design fiction 239
Design Fiction Kit 239
destiny 32
Dewey, J. 6, 97–98, *97*
disciplinarity 43, 54–58
Discipline of Anticipation (DoA) 3, 25, 51–63, 74
diversity 241
'Dream Commitment' (Drømmeløftet) 145–146
drivers meta-analysis 109
Dunagan, J. 239
dynamical systems 74

ecofeminism 259
economy, gender and 259–260
Ecuador 168–177
Edelman, G.M. 80
education, non-formal 205–215
Ehresmann, A.C. 68
Eilenberg, S. 75
Emergence Theorem 82, 84
empowerment 117–118
End of History Illusion 172
epistemological side of FLF 23, 28–31
ergodic anticipation 84–87
ergodic assumption 21

evolutive systems 78–79, *79*, 80–81, 87
Executive Master in European Sport Governance (MESGO) 154–155
experiential futures 234, 235
Experiential Futures Ladder 240

Faber, E.M.H. 53–54, 135
fatal error 30
'Filter Bubble' phenomenon 261
First Pacific Leadership Academy 223
'first scientific revolution' 70
Flanagan, M. 234
FL Archetypal Pattern 83–84
FLL-Innovation Norway (FLL-IN) 142–143
focus 57
forecasting 32, 55–56, 62
foresight 55, 56, 59, 61–62, 221, 233
Foresight Engine 235
Foresight Maturity Model (FMM) 61–62, 62t
Foundations of Future Studies (Bell) 51
FoundFutures 239
framing 62
Freeconomy 193–194
Fuerth, L.S. 53–54, 135
Fullerton, T. 234
functional organization 72
future: definition of 19; types of 20–21
Future of Futures, The (Curry) 51
Future of Science in Society workshop 118–130
FuturesIreland initiative 34
Futures Literacy (FL): AS and 2; AA and 4, 6; description of 15; DoA and 58–60; findings on 7–9; FS and 41–44; mapping 17–23; overview of chapters related to 9–10
Futures Literacy Framework (FLF): applying 34–44; description of 3–4, 23–34, *24*; mapping *40*; overview of chapters related to 9–10; project design and 6, 8; summary of use of 44–45
Futures Literacy Laboratories (FLL): AA and 5, 6–7, 8; designing 34–41; FLF and 15; general structure of 97–99; map of *3*; mapping *40*; MES and 68–76; overview of chapters related to 9–10; in practice 86–87, *87*
Futures Literacy Laboratories-Novelty (FLL-N): description of 5–7; designing 34–41; findings on 8; FLL and 95; overview of chapter related to 10; phases of 102–107; in practice 97–99; in Sierra Leone 15–17; start-up phase

of 100–101; *see also individual case studies*
Futures Literacy – Memory Evolutive Systems (FL-MES) 82–87
Futures Meeting (FuMee) 51
Futures Studies (FS) 15, 18, 31, 41–44, 51
Futures Studies Forum for Africa and the Middle East (FSF) 215–222
Futures Triangle 149, 226–227
Futures Wheel 149

Gally, J.A. 80
games/gaming 233–243
Garrido Luzardo, L. 134, 173
gender 257–266
General-Scalable (GS) 29, 32–33, 37
globalisation 261
global wellbeing movement 247–255
Goldstein, J.S. 257
governance 18
'growing-up' frame 15–16, 147–154
Grupo FARO 168–177
'guerrilla futures' collaboration 239

Handbook of Anticipation (ed. Poli) 51
HE futures 259, 263
Heidegger, M. 20
Hines, A. 62
historical context 55
human agency/behaviour 18, 21
hybrid strategic scenario method 34

identity 56
IDEO 239
imagination 25
'Imagining Africa's Futures' project 97
'impredicative' anticipatory systems 69, 71–75
Inayatullah, S. 51, 103, 208
Industrial Development Corporation of Norway (SIVA) 140
Innovation Norway 139–147
Integral Futures literature 240
International Anticipation Conference 51

Joint Programming Initiative (JPI) 108, 117

Kamara, K. 148, 154
Kan, D. 76
Kayanja, R. 151, 152, 154
key theories 57
Kikwete, J. 192
knowing the future 52–54

knowledge, valuing 117–119
knowledge creation/management 18
knowledge creation processes (KCP): AS and 20–21, 23; AA and 24–25; FLF and 28–31; FLL and 97; project design and 37–38, 40; sub-categories of 69
knowledge laboratory (knowlab) 4
Konneh, Mr 153–154
Korean foresight 34
Koroma, Mr 153–154

labor markets 131–139
landscape 81–82, 84
learning, cycle of 97–98, *97*
learning curve 98, *98*, 102, 107
Learning Intensive Society (LIS) scenario 105, 113–114, 123–125, 135–136, 199, 218–219
legitimacy 56–57
long-term thinking 103
love economy 259–260

MacLane, S. 75
macro-landscape (ML) 82–83, 84, 85
male/female polarity 261–262, 262*t*
Manabi Será initiative 168–177
management 18
McGonigal, J. 234
Meadows, D. 60–61
memory 81
memory components 77
Memory Evolutive Systems (MES): applied to social system 76–82; FLL and 68–76; FL-MES 82–87
meta-cognitive process 106
metalogue 19, 25
Method Cards 239
Miller, R. 51, 109, 134, 141, 143, 155, 218, 233
Mobility VIP 239, 240
modelling 73, *73*
multi-faceted components 80
multiple gender plurality 262, 262*t*
multiplicity principle 80
MVP Future Thought Leaders Summit 223–229

Nadin, M. 53
Nandy, A. 239
Natural Knowledge Society 174
Near Future Laboratory 239
non-ergodic anticipation 84–87
North Africa 215–221
Norway 139–147

274   Index

Nosarzewski, K. 134, 135
novelty 52–53, 59–60, 61, 67, 74, 95, 95–108, 101

observation and measurement tools 77
OECD International Futures Programme 34
OECD Schooling for Tomorrow project 34
ontological side of FLF 23, 25–28
optimization 59–60
Organisation de la Francophonie (OIF) 195–204
Organization for Economic Cooperation and Development (OECD) 34, 247–248

Pangilinan, M.V. 223
peer-evaluation 57
performativity of gender 260
Piaget, J. 18
Polak, F. 241
Poli, R. 19–20, 51, 53
policy learning 139–147
Popper, K. 38, 257–226
Positive Futures – Forum for Frankfurt 247, 249–255
prediction round 102
predictive scenario building 59
preservation 109
Profile component 63
propagation delay 78
public traces 57
purpose level 26

quality of life process *250*

Rashevsky, N. 72
rational knowledge 83
records 83
reframing 39–40, 104–105, 113–114
Regional Labor Observatories (Red de Observatorios Regionales de Mercado de Trabajo, RED ORMET) 131, 137, 138
relational biology 72
relative ontological expansion 108
repetition 33
resilience 53
resistance 128
resource allocation 31, 117–119
Rhisiart, M. 109
Rockefeller Foundation 216
Rosen, R. 20, 53, 72–73
Royal Institute for Strategic Studies (IRES) 216

scanning 62
science, future of 118–130
S-curve approach 98–99, *98*
self-improvement 32–33
semi-closed/semi-open systems anticipation 25–26, 32–35
SHE futures 259, 263–264
Sierra Leone 15–17, 147–154
simulations 53–54, 59
Singularity Summit 237
Slaughter, R. 233
social foresight 233
social futurism 233
social network 75
social systems: categories and 75–76; MES and 76–82; structural and dynamic organization of 77–78
Society for International Development (SID) 188–189
Specific-Unique (SU) 29–30, 32–34, 37
speculative design 239
sports 154–161
statistics 29
storytelling 29, 148–149, 152–153, 211, 263–264, *265*
Strategic Research Agenda (SRA) 108, 117–118
strategic thinking 33
Superstruct 235
sustainability 140–141, 177–187
system level 25

Tanzania 187–195
Tanzania Dialogues Initiative 187–195
Tao 33–34
Tester, J. 239
Thing from the Future, The 224–226, 233–243, *236*, *237*, *238*
Thom, R. 81
Thomas, M. 109
Timescape 179–180, 184
Toffler, A. 233
Traaseth, A.K. 145–146
transitions 78, 80–81
transitivity condition 78, 79
trend extrapolation 59

Ujamaa 2.0 193
UNESCO Foresight Unit 120
unisex androgyny scenario 261–262, 262*t*
urban renewal 215–221
Using the Future for Local Labor Markets 131–139

values, importance of 117–118
Vanbremeersch, J.-P. 68

water 215–221
Watson, J. 235, 238
wellbeing, measuring 247–255
Wells, H.G. 233

Wilenius, M. 51
wisdom 33–34
Wittgenstein, L. 2
World Science Forum 120
World Without Oil 234–235

youth leadership 221–229

Taylor & Francis eBooks

www.taylorfrancis.com

A single destination for eBooks from Taylor & Francis with increased functionality and an improved user experience to meet the needs of our customers.

90,000+ eBooks of award-winning academic content in Humanities, Social Science, Science, Technology, Engineering, and Medical written by a global network of editors and authors.

TAYLOR & FRANCIS EBOOKS OFFERS:

- A streamlined experience for our library customers
- A single point of discovery for all of our eBook content
- Improved search and discovery of content at both book and chapter level

REQUEST A FREE TRIAL
support@taylorfrancis.com